When in Doubt,
Fire the Skipper

ALSO BY GARY WEBSTER

.721: A History of the 1954 Cleveland Indians
(McFarland, 2013)

*Tris Speaker and the 1920 Indians:
Tragedy to Glory* (McFarland, 2012)

When in Doubt, Fire the Skipper

Midseason Managerial Changes in Major League Baseball

GARY WEBSTER

McFarland & Company, Inc., Publishers
Jefferson, North Carolina

Photographs are from Library of Congress unless credited otherwise.

LIBRARY OF CONGRESS CATALOGUING-IN-PUBLICATION DATA

Webster, Gary, 1956–
When in doubt, fire the skipper : midseason managerial changes in major league baseball / Gary Webster.
         p.   cm.
Includes bibliographical references and index.

ISBN 978-0-7864-7892-7 (softcover : acid free paper) ∞
ISBN 978-1-4766-1594-3 (ebook)

1. Baseball—Management. 2. Baseball managers. I. Title.
GV875.7.W45 2014   796.357'64—dc23   2014016278

BRITISH LIBRARY CATALOGUING DATA ARE AVAILABLE

© 2014 Gary Webster. All rights reserved

No part of this book may be reproduced or transmitted in any form or by any means, electronic or mechanical, including photocopying or recording, or by any information storage and retrieval system, without permission in writing from the publisher.

On the cover: New York Yankees owner George Steinbrenner, left, and manager Billy Martin, during spring training in Fort Lauderdale, Florida, on March 1, 1983 (Associated Press/Ray Howard)

Printed in the United States of America

McFarland & Company, Inc., Publishers
Box 611, Jefferson, North Carolina 28640
www.mcfarlandpub.com

Table of Contents

Preface
1

Midseason Managerial Changes, 1902–2013
5

Afterword
256

Notes
259

Bibliography
265

Index
267

Preface

At 9:45 in the morning on July 30, 1971, Vernon Stouffer, the beleaguered owner of the moribund Cleveland Indians, and the team's equally beleaguered president, Gabe Paul, met with the media to announce the team's latest move in its quest to achieve a .500 record, which was all Tribe fans were asking for in those days. After standing at 28–29 on June 13, following a stretch of 20 victories in 30 games, the Indians had fallen apart, winning just 14 while losing 32 and plunging into the cellar of the American League's Eastern Division. That plunge cost veteran manager Alvin Dark his job.

After praising Dark for doing a great job assembling the young ball club that currently sat in last place in its division, with a 42–61 record, Paul cut to the chase: "Sometimes, a team does better when a change is made or you don't make it. Winning games is what counts. We just weren't winning. We hope this helps us start winning."

"We are looking for ways to produce a good team," Stouffer added. "This is why we decided a change of managers was needed right now." The 1971 Indians were not a good team, nor did they suddenly become one under Johnny Lipon, elevated from third-base coach to serve as interim manager for the rest of the season. After winning 41 percent of their games for Dark, they won just 30 percent of the games (18–41) managed by Lipon. Dark wasn't the problem, and his dismissal didn't help the Indians start winning.

When in doubt, fire the manager. It's a remedy for an ailing ball club that is as old as baseball itself. The majority of the time, a managerial change accomplishes what the change in Cleveland accomplished in 1971: nothing. If anything, the situation gets worse. A change in leadership creates the illusion that the front office has done *something* to try to turn the season around, but in most cases, the new manager fails to improve the club's showing since most managers can't make silk purses from sow's ears or spin straw into gold. Lousy players make lousy teams, and Lipon couldn't do any more with the Indians' lousy players than Dark did. Lacking Dark's vast managerial experience, he did less.

There are, of course, exceptions. Managerial changes aren't always merely cosmetic. Such was the case with the 1982 Milwaukee Brewers, who were treading water under manager Bob (Buck) Rodgers at 23–24 when management decided to make a change. Batting coach Harvey Kuenn replaced Rodgers and the Brewers were soon atop the American League East, winning 72, losing 43, holding off Earl Weaver's Baltimore Orioles to clinch the division title on the season's final day, then eliminating the California Angels in the American League Championship Series and stretching the St. Louis Cardinals to seven games in the World Series before losing. Had management displayed a bit more patience with Rodgers, would the club that became known as Harvey's Wallbangers have eventually realized their potential and become Buck's Bashers? Or does management deserve kudos for recognizing (before it was too late) that the Brewers just weren't responding to Rodgers and making a change? Who knows?

How about the 2003 Florida Marlins, who were a less-than-mediocre 16–22 for Jeff Torborg when management decided to shake things up by hiring elderly veteran Jack McKeon? The 73-year-old McKeon led the Marlins to the National League wild card and a four-game victory over the San Francisco Giants in the Division Series. That was followed by the improbable, come-from-behind, seven-game win over the Chicago Cubs in the league championship series that Cubs fans are still trying to get over, and a six-game conquest of the New York Yankees in the World Series. Would the Marlins have righted the ship and done the same for Torborg, or did management somehow know McKeon, who was old enough to be the grandfather of every one of his players, was the right manager for an underachieving ball club?

Again, who knows?

During baseball's so-called modern era, beginning in 1901, there have been hundreds of in-season managerial changes. Many had no effect whatsoever, some altered a team's trajectory slightly, and a few worked miracles, as in Milwaukee and Miami. This book will provide details for most of the in-season managerial changes made over the past 111 years, with a focus on the conditions that led to the managers' replacement and their teams' response (as gauged by won-lost record, primarily) to the new leader. How many switches led to improved play? How many had no effect or, worse, backfired, accelerating rather than slowing a team's slide? What led to Manager Smith's being replaced by Manager Jones and not the likelier candidate, Manager Brown? Manager Smith was replaced by manager Jones. The team won X number of games for Smith and X number for Jones. The ball club's plight dictated that something had to be done, to appease angry fans if nothing else, and you can't fire the players. But the decisions that go into these moves can reveal much about the expectations and priorities of the front office.

It was necessary to define just what constituted an "in-season" managerial change. For purposes of this study, the manager who started a team's season must have managed at least 10 games, and the manager who finished a team's season must have managed at least 10 games. In other words, the outgoing manager must have had at least a minimal opportunity to put his imprint on the team before being fired, and the incoming manager must have had the same opportunity after being hired. Thus, a number of in-season managerial "shifts," made just a handful of games into a season, or with just a handful of games left, aren't examined here.

Also omitted are the medical leaves of absence taken by Napoleon Lajoie with the Cleveland Naps in 1905, John McGraw with the New York Giants in 1924 and 1927, Johnny Evers with the Chicago White Sox in 1924, Dave Bancroft with the Boston Braves in 1924 (which must have been a bad year for managers), Connie Mack with (of course) the A's in 1937 and 1939, Mickey Cochrane with the Detroit Tigers in 1936 and 1937, George (Birdie) Tebbetts with Cleveland in 1964, Chuck Dressen with Detroit in 1965, or George Bamberger with Milwaukee in 1980. In none of those instances was the manager being replaced, but rather substituted for until his health allowed him to resume his duties.

The handful of instances in which a manager was forced to retire because of medical conditions that proved fatal are likewise excluded: Miller Huggins with the Yankees in 1929, Fred Hutchinson with Cincinnati in 1964, Chuck Dressen and Bob Swift with Detroit in 1966, and Dick Howser with Kansas City in 1986. As with the leaves of absence, these changes had nothing to do with the performance of the clubs involved. They therefore fall outside of the scope of this book.

Finally, I ignore Chicago Cubs owner Phil Wrigley's grand experiment, the "College of Coaches." From 1961 until June of 1962, Wrigley's team functioned (more accurately, *malfunctioned*) without a manager. Wrigley instituted a rotating system of "head coaches" that failed to improve the team. Wrigley didn't officially abandon the experiment until appointing Bob Kennedy as the Cubs' "permanent head coach" for the 1963 season, still steadfastly refusing to use the term "manager."

With those ground rules established, let's examine 286 in-season changes of managers made during baseball's modern era and measure the impact of each one.

MIDSEASON MANAGERIAL CHANGES, 1902–2013

1902

New York Giants
Horace Fogel to Heinie Smith

Horace Fogel hadn't managed in the major leagues for 15 years when he was hired by New York Giants owner Andrew Freedman to replace George Davis, who'd led the team to a seventh-place finish, 37 games behind pennant-winning Pittsburgh, in 1901. Fogel took over a team with only one obvious asset: a right-handed pitcher named Christy Mathewson. Mathewson won 20 games for a team which posted just 52 victories the previous season, but Fogel decided he was better suited to play first base. Fortunately for the Giants, their new manager quickly abandoned the wrong-headed experiment. Mathewson's victory total (achieved under three different managers) would fall to 14 in 1902, but he'd lead the NL in shutouts with eight.

Freedman, who was possibly the least-liked man in baseball not only by his players but his fellow owners as well, was sick of the sport and was selling the Giants to Indianapolis businessman John Brush while Fogel was leading the club to a lackluster 18–23 record. The slow start earned him a pink slip, and he never managed in the major leagues again. Fogel's record with Indianapolis (which he managed for 70 games in 1887) and the Giants was 38–72. He was replaced by second baseman Heinie Smith on an interim basis while Freedman negotiated not only with Brush, but with the man he really wanted in charge of his team, Baltimore Orioles player/manager John McGraw.

Fogel wouldn't manage in the major leagues again, but he'd return to baseball as owner of the Philadelphia Phillies in 1909. He'd be banned from the sport in 1912 for alleging National League umpires favored the Giants and purposely made calls against the Phillies.

Cincinnati Reds
"Bid" McPhee to Joe Kelley

John (Bid) McPhee *was* baseball in Cincinnati.

McPhee made his major league debut at second base with Cincinnati in 1882, when the team was a charter member of the newly-formed American Association, which had been created to give some competition to the then seven-year-old National League. McPhee was still with the Reds when they rejoined the NL in 1890. Playing without a glove until 1896 (or '97, depending on the source of the information), McPhee retired after the 1899 campaign. Cincinnati was the only team he ever played for.

Thus, it was only natural that, when the Reds needed a manager to replace Bob Allen after a seventh-place finish in 1900, they turned to McPhee. He didn't enjoy the same success as a manager he'd enjoyed as a player. Cincinnati staggered home in last place in 1901 with a record of 52–87, and wasn't doing much better in 1902, struggling in seventh place with 27 wins and 37 losses. McPhee heard rumors that he was about to be replaced and beat management to the punch, resigning on July 11, following a 6–3 victory over the Boston Beaneaters. Former major league manager Frank Bancroft, who had managed the Providence Grays to the 1884 National League pennant, was then the Reds' business manager, and came down from the front office to guide Cincinnati for 16 games, winning nine and losing seven, while the club obtained the replacement it really wanted.

In Baltimore, John McGraw was ripping the second-year American League Orioles apart to get revenge on league president Ban Johnson. Among the Orioles whose releases McGraw was able to secure was outfielder Joe Kelley, one of McGraw's teammates with the pennant-winning Orioles of the National League in the 1890s. Once freed of his commitment to the American League, Kelley signed with Cincinnati and took over for Bancroft as manager ... in addition to playing the outfield and batting .321 for his new team. Kelley's Reds won 34 games and lost 26, finishing fourth with a record of 70–70, 33½ games behind pennant-winning Pittsburgh. Overall, the Reds were 43–33 after McPhee resigned. His season and a half with the Reds represented the sum total of his major league managerial career. His career record was 79–124.

New York Giants
Heinie Smith to John McGraw

Call this one "the mother of all in-season managerial changes."

The New York Giants started the 1902 season playing poorly for their new manager, Horace Fogel. They played far worse for the man who replaced Fogel after 41 games, second baseman Heinie Smith. While the Giants were losing 27 of the 32 games Smith managed, owner Andrew Freedman was planning to sell the club after it had given him nothing but aggravation. In order to make it attractive to potential buyers, most notably John Brush, the owner of the Cincinnati Reds who was looking to move into a much larger, higher-profile market, Freedman needed to make a big splash.

After a season and a half as player/manager of the Baltimore Orioles of Ban Johnson's new American League, John McGraw was looking for the exit. Although Johnson was originally ecstatic when a player of McGraw's stature agreed to jump from the National League to the American, it should've been obvious to both men that theirs was a marriage made in Hades. Johnson wanted "clean baseball" to be a large part of the allure of his new league. McGraw had been baseball's foremost practitioner of trickery, deceit and deception as the third baseman for the battling, brawling Orioles of the 1890s. Johnson planned to back his umpires to the hilt in disputes with players and managers. Intimidation and abuse of the umpires was dealt with severely by the league president. To McGraw, baiting the umpires in an effort to gain even the slightest advantage for himself or his team was standard operating procedure.

The two men clashed immediately and repeatedly. McGraw spent almost as much time in the Union Park stands serving suspensions handed down by Johnson as he did in uniform. By the middle of the 1902 season, McGraw had had enough. He used the fact that the cash-strapped owners of the Orioles owed him $7,000 to negotiate the releases (in lieu of cash payment) of several Baltimore players, including himself. Johnson had to step in and assume control of the Orioles before McGraw completely gutted the club. The owners of the other seven American League franchises loaned Johnson the dregs from their rosters to allow the Orioles to play out their schedule. Johnson was, however, glad to be rid of McGraw, who negotiated a deal with Freedman to take over the Giants.

JOHN MCGRAW: Possibly the greatest manager of them all. McGraw took over a laughingstock of a ball club in New York in July of 1902 and won pennants in 1904 and 1905.

The agreement made McGraw the Giants' field manager, paid him $11,000, and gave him full authority to run the club from the dugout. McGraw would make all player personnel decisions. He assumed control of an eighth-place team with a record of 23–53 on July 19 and spent the rest of the season evaluating the talent on hand. He didn't like what he saw, aside from a gem of a pitcher named Christy Mathewson. The experiment with Mathewson at first base was over. McGraw said the idea of converting Mathewson to first base was insane, and the man who concocted it should've been locked up. McGraw never was the type to mince words.

New York's players were reported to be nervous about their new manager's arrival, and deservedly so. McGraw promptly released nine of the 23 players on the Giants' roster, requiring Freedman to eat some $14,000 in salaries. Despite promises not to raid the Orioles' roster because of his respect and love for the city of Baltimore and its fans, who'd treated him so royally over the years, McGraw brought four ex–Orioles with him, the most prominent being pitcher "Iron Man" Joe McGinnity.

New York's players may have been apprehensive about the new era that was dawning, but Giants fans were excited. After playing before minuscule crowds since the 1902 season began, nearly 16,000 patrons swarmed the Polo Grounds to watch the Giants' first game under their new boss. Although New York lost to the Phillies, 4–3, the players hustled for McGraw as they hadn't hustled all season. Newspapers reported a palpable feeling of enthusiasm, hope and promise among the players and the fans.

Four days later, the Giants beat the Dodgers, 4–1, for their first victory under McGraw. The next day, Mathewson blanked Brooklyn, 2–0, and a beautiful if odd relationship was born. It was assumed that the rough, crude McGraw and the genteel, college-educated Mathewson would mix like oil and water. Exactly the opposite turned out to be the case. McGraw idolized Mathewson, and Matty, a fierce competitor despite his outwardly calm demeanor, liked and respected his manager. The two men formed a mutual admiration society as they dragged the franchise out of the muck of defeat and molded it into a champion.

McGraw didn't spend a lot of time on the Giants' bench during the final stages of the 1902 season. He hit the road to scout talent the Giants might acquire in the off-season, either by purchase or by trade. New York won 25 and lost 38 after McGraw arrived, finishing in last place with a record of 48–88, a mind-boggling 53½ games behind Pittsburgh.

Freedman eventually sold the Giants to Brush. Brush was happy to abide by the agreement Freedman had made with McGraw. The Giants were McGraw's team to run as he saw fit. The changes McGraw made transformed the cellar-dwellers into a second-place club in 1903 and National League champions in 1904. McGraw would manage the Giants until 1932, winning 10 pennants and three World Series titles. McGraw made the Giants into baseball's flagship franchise. No other in-season change in managers has had such an enormous, or lasting, impact.

Baltimore Orioles
John McGraw to Wilbert Robinson

Wilbert Robinson had the thankless, and hopeless, task of managing the burning wreckage his friend John McGraw left behind in Baltimore.

When McGraw defected to New York, taking four of Baltimore's key players with him (and securing the release of a fifth player, Joe Kelley, who signed with Cincinnati), Robinson chose to stay behind and was appointed manager for the remainder of the 1902 season. Minus such stalwarts as Dan McGann, Kelley, "Iron Man" Joe McGinnity, and McGraw himself, Robinson managed to coax 24 victories (against 57 losses) from the roster Ban Johnson pieced together to keep the franchise from folding in mid-season. The Orioles finished last with a record of 50–88.

Robinson's career as a manager had gotten off to a rocky start, but he'd get another chance. He'd soon join his old friend McGraw as a coach on the Giants' staff, and after a

WILBERT ROBINSON: Two Hall of Famers who took over teams in mid-season. Robinson (left) replaced John McGraw in Baltimore in July of 1902, then joined him with the Giants before signing with Brooklyn in 1914. Tris Speaker (right) succeeded Lee Fohl as manager of the Indians in July of 1919 and led the team to its first pennant in 1920. Robinson and Speaker are pictured here exchanging greetings before the first game of the 1920 World Series.

bitter falling-out between the two led to Robinson's being fired by McGraw in 1913, he'd take the job managing the Giants' arch-rivals, the Brooklyn Dodgers, in 1914. He'd manage the Dodgers until 1931, winning two pennants but losing the World Series in both 1916 and 1920.

1904

Washington Senators
Malachi Kittridge to "Patsy" Donovan

There may have been worse jobs than managing Washington's American League baseball team during the first decade of the 20th century, but not many.

Washington had been a laughingstock during its two seasons in the American Association (1886 and 1891) and its two terms in the National League (1887–89, 1892–99). Ban Johnson wanted the city in his new league, but with his focus on making sure the American

League teams in Chicago, Boston, St. Louis and Philadelphia could more than hold their own against their National League competition, Washington, which had its home city all to itself, didn't get much attention.

The Senators finished sixth under Jimmy Manning in 1901, sixth under Tom Loftus in 1902, and sixth under Loftus again in 1903. Manning had never managed before, and never managed again. Loftus, a veteran who had guided teams in the Union Association, the American Association, and the National League before arriving in Washington, also never managed again.

Washington decided to try a player/manager in 1904, possibly in order to save a salary since the residents of the nation's capital hadn't beaten down the doors to the ballpark to watch their team in action. The Senators played before just under 129,000 spectators at home in 1903, the only American League club to attract fewer than 212,000 fans. Veteran catcher Malachi Kittridge, whose career began with the Chicago Colts of the National League in 1890, was given the task of trying to elevate the Senators into the first division ... or, at the very least, out of sixth place. Kittridge had joined the Senators the previous season, having jumped from the Boston Beaneaters of the National League. He had logged 60 games as an American Leaguer when he was placed in charge of the Senators.

Kittridge needed 14 games to rack up his first victory as a major league manager. Washington's 9–4 conquest of the New York Highlanders snapped a 13-game season-opening losing streak and was the only game they'd win for Kittridge. After three more defeats, Kittridge was replaced by Senators outfielder Patrick (Patsy) Donovan. With only 17 games in the books, 16 of them defeats, Washington was already 12½ games out of first place. Kittridge's winning percentage of .059 is the worst in big league history for a manager with more than 10 games on his ledger.

Donovan wasn't likely to be overwhelmed by the job of managing such a horrible team, as Kittridge may have been. Donovan had managed Pittsburgh in 1897 and '99, and came to Washington fresh off a three-year stint as manager of the St. Louis Cardinals. The Senators were 37–97 for Donovan, finishing a wretched eighth with 38 wins and 113 losses ... the worst record an American League club had compiled to date, and the worst record any AL team would compile until Connie Mack's 1916 Philadelphia Athletics lost a horrid 117 games. The Senators trailed the pennant-winning Pilgrims by 55½ games, and the seventh-place Detroit Tigers by 23½.

The shell-shocked Kittridge never managed again

PATSY DONOVAN: Managed the Cardinals, Senators, Dodgers and Red Sox in an undistinguished career. Took over for Malachi Kittridge after Washington lost 16 of its first 17 games in 1904.

but played two more seasons, retiring in 1906. Donovan's reputation as a manager wasn't damaged by his eighth-place finishes with St. Louis in 1903 or Washington in 1904. He'd manage Brooklyn in 1906 and '07, and the Red Sox in 1910 and 1911, with a career record of 684–879.

Chicago White Sox
"Nixey" Callahan to Fielder Jones

In the early days of the American League, Ban Johnson got what he wanted.

In 1903, as a result of the peace agreement between his league and the National, Johnson got the New York franchise he knew the AL needed to be considered truly "big time." In order to compete with the established Giants and Superbas, who were soon to be known as the Dodgers, Johnson's New York team had to be a winner immediately. Winning started at the top, so Johnson searched for the best available manager to call the shots for the infant Highlanders. Connie Mack wasn't about to leave Philadelphia, and Boston fans would've rioted in the streets had Johnson asked Pilgrims owner Henry Killilea to release third baseman/manager Jimmy Collins. Johnson also had no desire to weaken either of those clubs.

JIMMY "NIXEY" CALLAHAN: Succeeded Clark Griffith as White Sox manager in 1903, and was replaced by Fielder Jones in June of 1904. Callahan managed the Pirates in 1916 and was replaced by Hugo Bezdek in July of 1917.

So, he turned to his friend Charles Comiskey, whose White Sox won the league's first pennant but slipped to fourth place in 1902. Comiskey released his manager, Clark Griffith, for the good of the American League, replacing him with Jimmy (Nixey) Callahan, his veteran third baseman, in 1903.

Callahan's major league career began with Philadelphia in 1894. He saw action with the Chicago Colts from 1897 through 1900, and jumped to the American League's White Stockings in 1901.

While Griffith skippered the Highlanders to a 72–62 record and fourth-place finish, Callahan's White Sox, despite Callahan's .292 batting average in 118 contests, skidded to seventh, winning 60 and losing 77. With Frank Selee's Cubs on the rise across town, and the league office located in Chicago, Johnson, as much as he wanted to win the battle for New York, didn't want the White Sox to become second-class citizens in the nation's second largest city.

Callahan appeared to have the White Sox moving in the right direction in 1904 (while Griffith's Highlanders were battling Collins's Pilgrims for the pennant), but that didn't stop Comiskey from dismissing him as manager on June 5, with the team in fourth place, its record 23–18. Callahan, who had moved from third base to left field, was replaced by the man who stood next to him. Centerfielder Fielder Jones, possibly the most aptly named baseball player of all time, took the reins and the White Sox took off, winning 66 and losing 47 the rest of the way. Chicago finished third, six games in back of Boston.

The White Sox responded well to Jones's leadership, finishing second to Mack's Athletics in 1905 (but winning just as many games, 92, as the league champions, who played four fewer contests) and winning the title in 1906 despite a .230 team batting average, weak even by dead ball-era standards. Jones's "Hitless Wonders" then stunned the Cubs, winners of a staggering 116 games (the White Sox won 93) in a six-game World Series. The White Sox finished third in 1907 and 1908, losing the '08 pennant by just a game and a half to the Detroit Tigers. Jones retired after that near-miss.

Comiskey called on Callahan to manage the White Sox again in 1912. He retired as a player in 1913 but kept the Chicago managerial job through 1914.

Detroit Tigers
Ed Barrow to Bobby Lowe

The American League's fourth season was a difficult one for managers. Managing the Senators proved to be more than Malachi Kittridge could handle after just 17 games. Nixey Callahan was demoted from player/manager to player in Chicago after 41 games. And Ed Barrow lasted only half a season with the Detroit Tigers.

Barrow became Detroit's third manager in as many seasons in 1903. George Stallings had departed after bringing the Tigers in third in 1901, with a record of 74–61. Frank Dwyer succeeded Stallings and Detroit dropped to seventh, winning 52 and losing 83. Dwyer surrendered the reins to Barrow, who lifted the Tigers into fifth place (65–71) in his first year on the job. Barrow's 1904 club was wallowing in seventh place, ahead only of the nearly comatose Senators, when management decided to make a change. In fact, it was a late July weekend in Washington that sealed Barrow's fate. When the best the Tigers could muster was a single win during a four-game series in the nation's capital (one game ended in a scoreless tie), Washington's 15th and 16th victories of the season convinced Barrow that it was time to step aside. His decision was aided by a season-long feud with the team's secretary/treasurer, Frank Navin. The Tigers had won 32 games and lost 46 when Barrow was replaced by outfielder Bobby Lowe, whose contract had been purchased from Pittsburgh on the last day of April.

Lowe's career dated back to 1890, when he'd broken in with Boston of the National League. Lowe's chief claim to fame was being the first major league player to swat four home runs in one game, which he accomplished during an 1894 campaign that saw him lead the NL with 613 at-bats and accumulate 17 homers. His career was on the decline when he joined the Tigers. He batted just .208 in 140 games for Detroit in 1904.

What ailed the Tigers under Barrow continued to ail them under Lowe. Detroit won 30 and lost 44 for its new manager, finishing seventh with a record of 62–90. The Tigers escaped the cellar only by the grace of the Senators. Things would start looking up for Detroit in 1905, particularly after a young outfielder named Ty Cobb reported to the club in August. The Tigers would grab three straight pennants beginning in 1907.

Barrow would manage again in the major leagues. Lowe wouldn't. Lowe retired after playing just 17 games for Detroit's 1907 pennant winners. Barrow would serve as a minor league manager, team executive, and president of the International League before taking the reins of the 1918 Boston Red Sox and leading them to a world championship.

1905

St. Louis Cardinals
"Kid" Nichols to Jimmy Burke

It's difficult to believe today that the St. Louis Cardinals were once one of the National League's weakest franchises.

The fans loyally supported a doormat from 1892 through 1900, but strong attendance didn't stop owners Frank and Matthew Robison from needing a $48,000 loan to keep the club solvent as it prepared for competition from the American League's St. Louis Brown Stockings, beginning in 1902. It was a battle the Brown Stockings were winning in 1904, when Patsy Donovan was replaced after three seasons as Cardinals manager by former pitcher Charles (Kid) Nichols. By going the player/manager route, the Robisons were able to save a salary.

Nichols played 12 seasons in the National League, all of them with Boston, before retiring after the 1901 campaign with 329 wins, including seven seasons of 30 victories or better. The Robisons convinced him to return to baseball both as a pitcher and a manager. Despite the presence of a pair of 21-game winners in Nichols and Jack Taylor, the best the Cardinals could manage in 1904 was a 75–79 record and fifth-place finish. In 1905, after just 14 games, Nichols was replaced with St. Louis in seventh place, having won five and lost nine. Nichols turned the managerial job over to a coach, Jimmy Burke, but hung around long enough to pitch in seven games for St. Louis, winning one and losing five. Burke didn't call on Nichols often, and the future Hall of Fame pitcher was sold to the Phillies for the waiver price on July 16. Nichols perked up in Philadelphia, winning 10 and losing six the rest of the way before retiring for keeps. Nichols' 361 victories were tops in National League history when he hung up his spikes. He didn't manage again and posted a career record of 80–88.

Burke inched the Cardinals up one notch in the standings, to sixth place. But his 34–56 record didn't impress the Robison brothers. Another change in managers would be made later in the season.

Chicago Cubs
Frank Selee to Frank Chance

Illness prevented Frank Selee from finishing what he started in Chicago.

After winning four pennants in the rough-and-tumble 1890s as manager of the Boston Beaneaters, Selee was dismissed when the club tumbled to fifth place in 1901. He was quickly hired by the Chicago National League team, which was coming to be known as the Cubs, and faced stiff competition from the White Stockings of the infant American League. Selee's ability to spot talent hadn't deserted him, and the Cubs improved steadily thanks to the players he acquired. The Cubs finished fifth in 1902, third in '03, and second in '04. One obstacle stood between Selee and another pennant: John McGraw's mighty New York Giants. The Cubs finished a distant 13 games behind the Giants in 1904 and weren't gaining any ground on McGraw in 1905 when Selee was forced to step aside, at least temporarily, due to tuberculosis. He turned the club over to his first baseman, Frank Chance, with Chicago in fourth place at 37–28, nine games behind the Giants.

Chicago played .625 ball for its new manager (55–33) but the Giants' lead was too much to overcome. The Cubs moved up to third for Chance, finishing the year at 92–61, 13 games off the pace. He'd lead the Cubs to four pennants and a pair of World Series victories over the next five seasons.

Selee's Boston and Chicago teams won four pennants and 1,284 games while losing just 861. When he died at age 50 in 1909, the Cubs team he built and handed over to Chance was the reigning World Series champion.

St. Louis Cardinals
Jimmy Burke to M. Stanley Robison

Any true baseball fan feels, at least from time to time, that he or she can manage his or her favorite team better than the bonehead standing in the dugout flashing the signals to the third base coach. Aside from the day in 1952 that St. Louis Browns owner Bill Veeck provided a small crowd at Sportsman's Park with cards (bunt, steal, intentional walk, etc.) giving instructions to manager Zack Taylor as a promotional gimmick (it worked, as the Browns won the game), no fan has ever had a chance to prove he can manage his favorite team better than the manager can.

Owners probably often feel the same way, but few act on it. In 1929, Judge Emil Fuchs appointed himself manager of his Boston Braves, although there's plenty of debate as to how much managing Fuchs actually did. In 1977, in the midst of a long losing streak, Atlanta Braves owner Ted Turner demoted manager Dave Bristol and called the shots from the dugout himself. Commissioner Bowie Kuhn put a stop to Turner's managerial ambitions after one game, a 2–1 loss to Pittsburgh, and owners are now prohibited from managing their teams.

There was no commissioner to put a stop to Matthew Stanley Robison, the co-owner, along with his brother Frank, of the St. Louis Cardinals, from taking over for manager Jimmy Burke in August of 1905. Burke won 34 and lost 56 after replacing Kid Nichols on May 4. Three months later, with the Cardinals 33½ games out of first place, Robison assumed the managerial reins himself and led the team to a 5–4 victory over the Dodgers at Robison Field on August 10. The Dodgers and Boston Beaneaters were the only teams that would finish behind the Cardinals in 1905.

Robison managed the Cardinals for nearly one-third of the season, winning 19 and losing 31. St. Louis finished sixth with a record of 58–96.

Burke would manage again, but not until 1918, when he was hired by the Browns. Robison would return to the front office in 1906 and leave the managing to John McCloskey, whose efforts produced six fewer victories than the combined 1905 total of Nichols, Burke and Robison.

1906

Boston Pilgrims
Jimmy Collins to "Chick" Stahl

How the mighty had fallen.

Just two seasons earlier, the Boston American League club and its player/manager, Jimmy Collins, stood atop the professional baseball world, winners of consecutive pennants and the 1903 World Series. Boston wasn't a factor in the pennant race of 1905, falling to fourth place, and crashed and burned in 1906. Collins remained a hero in Boston, but that didn't stop Pilgrims owner John I. Taylor from suspending him twice during the season, the suspensions leading to his dismissal as manager on August 26, with the club in last place, 34 games behind the front-running White Sox, with a record of 35–79. Taylor's choice to replace Collins, who was limited by injuries to just 37 games in 1906, was center-

CHARLES (CHICK) STAHL: Stahl took over for Jimmy Collins during the 1906 season and stunned the Red Sox and the baseball community by taking his own life in spring training of 1907.

fielder Charles "Chick" Stahl. Stahl had no previous managerial experience and guided the Pilgrims to 14 victories and 26 losses the rest of the way. Boston finished in the American League basement with a record of 49–105, 45½ games behind Chicago.

The job of managing the Pilgrims proved to be too much for Stahl. He was found dead in his hotel room in West Baden, Indiana, on March 28, 1907, as the team barnstormed its way north from spring training. A suicide note Stahl left behind said simply, "Boys, I just couldn't help it, it drove me to it." Historians have been trying to identify what Stahl meant by "it" ever since. It has been reported that he was despondent over having been ordered by Taylor to dismiss his close friend Collins from the club.

1907

Boston Red Sox
Bob Unglaub to "Deacon" Jim McGuire

Chick Stahl's stunning suicide in late March of 1907 understandably left the Boston Red Sox in tatters emotionally. Pragmatically, it left the team without both a manager and

CY YOUNG: Red Sox owner John Taylor turned to Young in desperation after manager Chick Stahl committed suicide in March of 1907. Young had his fill of managing after only six games and turned the Red Sox over to coach George Huff. Boston would have four managers in 1907.

a centerfielder. The centerfield job went to Denny Sullivan, whose major league experience consisted of three games with the Washington Senators in 1905. Sullivan played in 144 games for the Red Sox, batting .245 with a home run and 26 runs batted in.

To fill the void in the dugout, owner John I. Taylor, not surprisingly, turned to the Red Sox' ace pitcher and elder statesman, Denton T. "Cy" Young. Young quit after six games (3–3) and turned the team over to coach George Huff, who lasted just eight games (2–6). First baseman Bob Unglaub succeeded Huff and called the shots for 29 games, from May 1 through June 8. Unglaub led the Red Sox to a 9–20 record before Taylor settled on "Deacon" Jim McGuire as the team's permanent manager. McGuire, whose baseball career began in 1884, inherited a last-place team with a 14–29 record. The Red Sox were 15½ games out of first and wouldn't get any closer.

McGuire's previous managerial experience consisted of 68 games with Washington's National League club in 1898, winning 21 and losing 47. The Red Sox were 45–61 for McGuire, finishing seventh with a mark of 59–90. McGuire was retained for 1908.

1908

New York Highlanders (Yankees)
Clark Griffith to "Kid" Elberfeld

The 1908 baseball season, the most exciting in the sport's history, showed just how far New York's American League team had to go to catch New York's National League team.

After losing the 1904 pennant on the season's final day, and finishing three games behind the champion White Sox in 1906, the Highlanders were floundering. The team finished fifth, 21 games out of first, in 1907 and was struggling again in '08 when manager Clark Griffith called it quits. After occupying first place as late as June 1, the Highlanders had slipped to fifth with 24 wins and 32 losses. Griffith resigned on June 24.

"Yes, I have resigned," Griffith said in a statement released to the newspapers.

CLARK GRIFFITH: Griffith led Chicago to the first American League pennant in 1901 and brought the Highlanders in second twice. He also managed Cincinnati and Washington and owned the Senators until his death in 1955.

KID ELBERFELD: Elberfeld succeeded Clark Griffith as manager of the Highlanders in 1908 and won just 27 games while losing 71. He returned to his shortstop duties the next season and never managed again.

> I called Mr. Farrell on the telephone this morning and told him of my determination. I have been desirous of resigning for some time. I met Mr. Farrell today and told him I had a very high regard for him, and for that reason I wished to resign as manager and make way for someone who may be more successful than I have been.
> There is no soreness between Mr. Farrell and myself and we part the best of friends. Mr. Farrell told me he did not wish me to leave, but I insisted, and so the matter ended. I had become disgusted and felt that some other person should take the helm. Mr. Farrell did not tell me who that person would be. I had hard luck with the team last year, and this year things are again going wrong. Players have been out of the game and my pitchers have not rounded into form as they should, and I felt that it was time for me to get out.[1]

For the remainder of the season, co-owner Frank Farrell appointed shortstop Norman (Kid) Elberfeld manager. Farrell may have selected Elberfeld in order for him to earn his salary since he spent all but 19 games on the bench, recovering from a serious leg injury. Under the feisty Elberfeld's leadership, the Highlanders promptly collapsed, winning just 27 games while losing 71. At season's end, they occupied the American League's cellar with a record of 51–103. The Giants, meanwhile, were busy battling the Chicago Cubs and Pittsburgh Pirates in the most exciting and controversial pennant race in major league history. It was the season of the famous "Merkle boner" game at the Polo Grounds in late September between the Giants and Cubs. The replay of that game, in early October, was won by the Cubs, clinching their third straight pennant. The breathtaking race lured 910,000 fans to the Polo Grounds. The Highlanders were watched by just 305,000 spectators at Hilltop Park. The American League was losing the battle for New York.

Griffith was finished with the Highlanders, but not with managing. He called the shots from the Cincinnati Reds dugout from 1909 through 1911, and managed the Washington Senators from 1912 through 1920 before spending the rest of his long and illustrious career as the Senators' owner. He'd retire as a manager with a career record of 1,491–1,367 and one pennant. Elberfeld was back at shortstop for the Highlanders in 1909 and didn't manage in the major leagues again.

Boston Red Sox
"Deacon" Jim McGuire to Fred Lake

Jim McGuire wasn't going to stay where he wasn't wanted.

Rumors had been swirling that Red Sox owner John I. Taylor was displeased with the performance of his team and his manager. McGuire got tired of the constant speculation about his future and, after the season's 115th game, paid a visit to his boss.

FRED LAKE: Lake had only minimal minor league managing experience when he replaced Jim McGuire as manager of the Red Sox in August of 1908. His Red Sox won 88 games in 1909, but his Doves (Braves) lost 100 in 1910.

"This thing has been coming on for some time," McGuire said.

I heard yesterday that a change was intended, and accordingly I waited upon Mr. Taylor at the office of the club this morning and asked if there was any truth to the rumor I was to go. Mr. Taylor told me my work had not been satisfactory and accordingly I placed my resignation at his disposal and I retired in favor of Mr. Lake.

Our relations have been exceedingly pleasant and our differences have been confined to his idea of my handling of the club. So far as I am concerned, I think I have done very well indeed and I have nothing to reproach myself for. We had a little slump of late, but it came after the club had landed ten games out of seventeen on a western trip, the best showing of any club on a trip this season.

I got along finely with the players, and my relations with them were of the most harmonious, and to a man they expressed their sincere regret that I was to leave the club. I still think the Boston club is one of the best in the country.[2]

The Red Sox had won 53 games and lost 62 when Taylor dismissed McGuire. The Deacon hung around to watch his successor, Fred Lake, manage his first game, taking in the action from a seat in Boston's Huntington Avenue Grounds as the Red Sox defeated the St. Louis Browns, 3–1. Lake, a Boston scout, had only minor league managerial experience, having piloted the Lynn and Lowell, Massachusetts, teams of the New England League. The Red Sox showed improvement under Lake, winning 22 and losing 17 over the remainder of the 1908 season. Boston was in sixth place when McGuire was fired, and moved up one notch to finish fifth with a 75-79 mark. Lake's Red Sox finished third in 1909 with an 88–63 record. McGuire was apparently correct about the Red Sox being one of the best teams in the country, and Taylor was apparently right about McGuire not being able to get the club to play up to its ability. Lake then took his managerial skills next door (the two Boston ballparks were, literally, adjacent to each other, separated only by a railroad yard) and managed the Doves to an eighth-place finish in 1910 with a record of 53–100. Those two-and-a-fraction seasons in Boston represented Lake's entire major league managerial career. His overall record was 163–180.

McGuire would get a chance to redeem himself the following year when there was a managerial opening in Cleveland.

1909

Boston Doves (Braves)
Harry Smith to Frank Bowerman

Light-hitting catcher Harry Smith, a native of Yorkshire, England, spent parts of seven seasons as a back-up catcher in the major leagues, breaking in with the Philadelphia Athletics in 1901 and joining the Pittsburgh Pirates the following year. Smith saw action in as many as 61 games in a campaign (1903, with the pennant-winning Pirates) and as few as one (twice, 1905 and '06, again with the Pirates). Smith found himself with the Boston Doves in 1908 and, based on what he showed management in 41 games, was named the Doves' manager for 1909. Although Smith was born on Halloween, even that distinction didn't prepare him for the horror show he'd be presiding over.

The 1909 Doves featured a pair of shortstops, Jack Coffey (the regular) and Bill Dahlen, who committed 69 errors between them. Bill Sweeney's 43 errors were high among National League third basemen, and right fielder Beals Becker managed to flub 18 chances, also the worst in the league. Centerfielder Ginger Beaumont, a former batting champion with the Pirates, led the Doves with a .263 average. Al Mattern allowed more hits (322) and walks (108) than any other NL pitcher, but still managed to post a 2.85 earned run average and win 16 games (while losing 20). Mattern didn't lead the league in losses, however. His teammate, George Ferguson, earned that dubious distinction with 23 defeats in 28 decisions. Manager Smith didn't contribute much on the field, batting .179 and driving in four runs in 41 games.

Smith couldn't have been expected to do much with the talent he was given, and he didn't. The Doves had a record of 23–54 when Smith was stripped of the title of manager, with those duties being turned over to Frank Bowerman, like Smith a catcher and also like Smith, unable to win games with the 1909 Doves. Bowerman's record was almost identical to Smith's: 22 wins and 54 losses, leaving the Doves with a final tally of 45–108, good for last place, a gargantuan 65½ games behind the league champion Pirates.

Neither Smith nor Bowerman ever managed in the major leagues again. The Doves hired Fred Lake, who'd brought the neighboring Red Sox home third in 1909 with 88 victories, to right the ship in 1910. Lake's Doves lost 100 games and he was gone at the end of the season.

Cleveland Naps (Indians)
Napoleon "Larry" Lajoie to "Deacon" Jim McGuire

A common practice in the early days of baseball was to elevate one's star player to the dual role of player/manager. It was a logical move since the star player was often also the team captain and, in some cases, actually ran the club on the field anyway. When Bill Armour resigned in frustration effective at the end of the 1904 season, owner Charley Somers gave the reins to second baseman Napoleon (Larry) Lajoie, the American League's first superstar. The team was already named for Lajoie, and he was its unquestioned leader, not to mention its captain, so it was only fitting that he be placed officially in charge.

The Naps played well for Lajoie and might have won the 1905 pennant had Lajoie not been limited to 65 games, thanks to blood poisoning sustained after a spike wound absorbed the dye from the second baseman's sock. Cleveland finished third, five games behind the "Hitless Wonder" Chicago White Sox in 1906, despite outscoring the champions by 93 runs. The 1908 Naps were involved in a three-way struggle with the White Sox and Detroit Tigers, finishing a mere half game behind. Detroit's record of 90–63 bested the Naps' mark of 90–64. The Tigers had an August game in Washington rained out, and there was no league rule at the time requiring that postponed games be made up if they had a bearing on the pennant race.

The ever-so-close call left Lajoie, the fans, and management convinced that the Naps were poised to win their first pennant in 1909. Instead, the team struggled all season, and Lajoie resigned on August 17, after a double-header sweep of the St. Louis Browns at Cleveland's League Park improved the Naps' record to 57–54. He agreed to stay on until Somers could find a replacement, and Cleveland lost the three games it played under its suddenly lame-duck skipper while Somers conducted a search.

In his letter of resignation, Lajoie told Somers, "I feel that my obligations to you, to the public and to the players compel me to take this action at the present time. You have given me liberal support for the past five years and I feel that if anyone can accomplish more with the club than I have been able to do, you deserve to have an opportunity to take advantage of same."[1]

Naps team president John Kilfoyl, who would soon step aside himself, noted how Lajoie had been on the receiving end of harsh fan derision as the disappointing season progressed. "I do not blame Larry much for wanting to unload the responsibility of the management in the face of all the abuse which has been heaped upon him during the past month. But I am mighty sorry, just the same, that he has determined to step out under fire."[2] Kilfoyl made it clear the Naps had no intention of cutting their ties with Lajoie, the player. Lajoie remained the face, and the name, of the Cleveland team through 1914.

Somers hired "Deacon" Jim McGuire, a scout who had served as a coach for the Naps during spring training and thus had a familiarity with the team's players, to succeed Lajoie. Somers wasn't fazed by McGuire's dismissal as Red Sox manager the previous season.

"I expect the co-operation of the players," McGuire said on his arrival in Cleveland.

> The boys have been playing in hard luck, but I feel sure they can produce better results than they have of late. Larry has worked hard to bring a pennant to Cleveland, but he has been handicapped by injuries to some of his most valuable players. I think we have picked up some valuable men for next year and I predict the club will finish higher up in the race. Cleveland is a good baseball town, and we will all try to pull together to give the fans of this city the kind of baseball club they want.[3]

Lajoie was happy to relinquish the manager's job to McGuire: "Jim McGuire should make a good manager for the club. I wish him success and will try my hardest to help him turn out a winner. I can do no more." Lajoie looked forward to being a mere ballplayer again: "I am glad I am through. Someone else can do the worrying from now on. I am done as manager and will try now to make up on some of the sleep I have been losing the last few years."[4] Lajoie's career record was 377–309 with one second place finish.

The players McGuire had expected cooperation from threw in the towel after Lajoie resigned, winning just 14 and losing 25 for their new manager, for a final season record of 71–82. The Naps finished sixth, 27½ games behind the pennant-winning Tigers. It was a far cry from what had been expected when the season began.

1910

New York Highlanders
George Stallings to Hal Chase

Who knows how different the history of the New York Yankees might have been had co-owner Frank Farrell not made a fateful miscalculation in 1910?

Following the disastrous 1908 campaign, the franchise still technically named the Highlanders hired George Stallings as manager, replacing Kid Elberfeld. Stallings, who managed the Detroit Tigers to a third-place finish in the American League's first season of 1901 and then enjoyed success in the minors, improved the Highlanders' record to 74–77 in 1909 and had the club in second place the next year when he lost a power struggle with first baseman Hal Chase, one of baseball's shadiest characters.

Stallings claimed Chase was a malingerer who didn't give 100 percent effort when he was healthy enough to play. Chase denied the accusation. By late September, the confrontation between the two men reached a boiling point. Farrell had grown weary of Stallings's constant complaints about the Highlanders' star player and summoned his manager to New York while the club was playing in Chicago. Stallings welcomed the summons.

"I want to find out who is running the New York American League team, Chase or myself," said Stallings. "If Mr. Farrell decides in favor of the first baseman, I will quit at once. If he decides in favor of my regime, Chase will have to step down and out. There cannot be two bosses, especially when one is double-crossing the other. Chase has refused to obey orders and has tried to disrupt the team. Mr. Farrell must give me a square answer to the question: who is running your team, Chase or I?"[1]

GEORGE STALLINGS: The first manager of Detroit's American League club, Stallings was ousted as manager of the Highlanders in a dispute with first baseman Hal Chase in September of 1910. He earned a place in history by rallying the 1914 Braves from last place in early July to the pennant and a sweep of the dynastic Athletics in the World Series.

HAL CHASE: One of baseball's most notorious characters, Chase won a power struggle with George Stallings and took over the New York Highlanders with 14 games left in the 1910 season. He led the team to a .500 finish in his only full season as manager.

"I will demand that he prove that Hal Chase is 'laying down' and refusing to give his best services," Farrell fired back. "Stallings must show me a whole lot of things. When we meet, ours is going to be a talk straight from the shoulder. If Chase is guilty of Stallings's charges, there is no place on the New York American League team for him or any other team, in my judgment. If Mr. Stallings fails to prove his charges against Chase, it is up to me to deal with Stallings as I see fit, as Chase is too great a ballplayer to have his reputation blackened by such charges."[2]

After meeting with Stallings in his New York office, Farrell went to Cleveland, the next stop on the Highlanders' road trip, to watch the team play and personally investigate Stallings's accusations, which Chase denied. "His charges are lies. I have always given my employers the best I could. I am able to do no more," the first baseman claimed.[3] The Yankees split the two-game series at League Park, winning 2–1 and losing 7–2 on September 22 and 23.

What Farrell saw from Chase in Cleveland convinced him that his first baseman was giving the Highlanders his best effort, and Stallings was out. Among those pleased with the turn of events was American League president Ban Johnson: "Stallings has utterly failed in his accusations against Chase. He tried to besmirch the character of a sterling ballplayer and has utterly failed to injure his character. Anyone who knows Hal Chase knows he is not guilty of the charges brought by Stallings."[4]

Chase was made manager upon Stallings's dismissal, and the Highlanders won 10 of their final 14 games to finish second with a record of 88–63, 14½ games behind the eventual World Series champion Athletics. They wouldn't fare as well under Chase's leadership in 1911, limping home in sixth with a record of 76–76. Chase the manager wrote Chase the first baseman's name in the lineup 133 times and was rewarded with a .315 average, three home runs and 62 runs batted in. The slickest-fielding first baseman in the game committed 36 errors, more than any other first baseman in the league.

Chase's tenure as Highlanders manager was brief. He surrendered the job to Harry Wolverton in 1912 and concentrated on playing first base. Despite his reputation as fielder par excellence, Chase again led all American League first basemen in errors with 27, and his .979 fielding average was the league's worst at his position.

Stallings took the reins of the Boston Braves in 1913 and led the team to major league baseball's most improbable World Series championship the following year. The 1914 Braves were in last place on July 4 before catching fire, winning the pennant, and sweeping the supposedly invincible Athletics, winners of four pennants in five years, in four straight games. It will never be known how different the Highlanders/Yankees' fortunes might have been had Farrell decided to keep Stallings and sack Chase, rather than the other way around.

1911

Cleveland Naps
"Deacon" Jim McGuire to George Stovall

In Boston, Red Sox owner John Taylor had been dissatisfied with the way "Deacon" Jim McGuire had managed his team. In Cleveland, McGuire was dissatisfied with the way he managed Charley Somers's team.

Perhaps it should have been regarded as an omen that McGuire took command of a team that had played .500 baseball for previous manager Napoleon Lajoie and led it to a 14–25 record over the final six weeks of the 1909 season. The 1909 Naps had been expected to challenge for the American League pennant. Not nearly as much was expected from the 1910 Naps, and they lived up to their modest expectation, finishing a poor fifth, 32 games behind the pennant-winning Athletics. The only bright spot was Lajoie's return to form as a batter after shedding the nerve-wracking responsibilities of managing. Lajoie battled Ty Cobb for the AL batting championship down to the season's final day, losing the title by one-tenth of a point.

JIM MCGUIRE: McGuire's playing career dated back to 1884. He was replaced by Fred Lake in Boston in August of 1908 and George Stovall in Cleveland in May of 1911 after posting losing records with both teams. Lake and Stovall turned their teams into winners.

When the Naps failed to show the improvement McGuire anticipated early in 1911, stumbling out of the starting block and losing 11 of their first 17 games, McGuire threw in the towel. With an overall record of 91–117 during his stint in Cleveland, McGuire tendered his resignation to Somers, who accepted it. Somers asked McGuire to return to the scouting position he'd abandoned to take the managerial job, and within a week McGuire was back on the road, looking for the talent that might make Cleveland's next manager more successful than McGuire had been. He joined the Detroit Tigers in 1912, but never managed in the major leagues again. His lifetime record as a dugout strategist was 210–287.

As speculation swirled pertaining to Somers's choice to replace McGuire, the owner selected first baseman George Stovall to take the reins on an interim basis. The choice proved wise as the club immediately showed a spark it lacked under McGuire, and Stovall's appointment lasted for the rest of the season. The Naps won 74 and lost 62 for Stovall, finishing third with a record of 80–73. Stovall, the players and the fans logically assumed he'd earned another crack at managing the Naps in 1912, but they were mistaken. From the moment McGuire stepped down, Somers had his eye on a particular candidate to manage his club. That candidate was on the roster of another American League team, however, and unavailable until the end of the 1911 season. Stovall's success didn't dissuade Somers from his belief that Harry Davis, first baseman of the world champion Philadelphia Athletics, should be the next manager of the Naps.

1912

St. Louis Browns
Bobby Wallace to George Stovall

It deteriorated so quickly in St. Louis.

American League president Ban Johnson wanted a team in St. Louis because it was the fifth largest city in the United States in 1902, and he wanted a team that would lure fans away from the National League's entrenched Cardinals. Johnson loaded the 1902 Brown Stockings with enough talent to finish second with a 78–58 record for manager Jimmy McAleer. The Browns wouldn't finish second again for 20 years and soon found themselves staring up at the rest of their brethren from the depths of the AL.

McAleer left St. Louis after the 1909 season, replaced by Jack O'Connor. O'Connor was fired after a 107-loss campaign and succeeded by veteran shortstop Roderick (Bobby) Wallace in 1911. Wallace duplicated O'Connor's feat of losing 107 games and brought the club home in last place, an appalling 56½ games behind Philadelphia.

When the Browns stumbled out of the starting gate in 1912, posting a 12–27 record through the end of May, Wallace was replaced by first baseman George Stovall, who'd been acquired from Cleveland during spring training in exchange for pitcher Tom (Lefty) George. The previous year, Stovall had taken over the Cleveland managing job after the resignation of Jim McGuire, with the team five games below the .500 mark, and steered it into third place. Any hope Browns management had that Stovall could perform the same kind of Lazarus act in St. Louis was quickly dashed. Although Stovall tinkered with his lineup, he got the same results Wallace and O'Connor had gotten. Stovall's Browns won 41 and lost 74 for an overall mark of 53–101 and a third straight last-place finish.

Unlike in Cleveland, where Stovall was dropped as manager despite a winning record, he was retained as St. Louis's manager, despite a losing record, for 1913. He didn't make it through the season.

Cleveland Naps
Harry Davis to Joe Birmingham

Harry Davis never stood a chance.

Davis, Connie Mack's first baseman on three pennant-winning Athletics teams (1902, '05 and '10) and Mack's right-hand man in the dugout, had been wise enough to spurn dead-end offers to manage the woeful St. Louis Browns. While the Athletics were winning another flag in 1911, Mack was working on a deal with Charley Somers to allow Davis, whose bat was slowing down and whose range in the field was diminishing at age 38, to replace George Stovall as Naps manager in 1912. Within hours after Philadelphia had completed its six-game World Series victory over the New York Giants on October 27, Davis was on a westbound train, ready to sign a contract and assume his new position.

Mack had nothing but praise for his departing lieutenant: "I don't often like to take a chance and predict what a man will do, but when the Naplanders got Harry they took the best man I have seen in a long time. He cannot walk right into a town and make it a winner, no one can do that, but he can put them in the first division in a year; in two years he can have them up fighting for the flag; in three years, well, I hate to think of the trouble I will have with his team along about that time."[1] Putting the Naps in the first division in 1912 would've amounted to treading water, since the club had finished third under the dismissed Stovall.

"I regard the Naps as a good ball club—a very good ball club. Lots of good material there which I hope to bring out," said Davis. As to his managerial philosophy, Davis said, "I don't believe in the player knowing everything a manager knows, and I don't believe in the rooter knowing what the player knows. Connie Mack has always run his team on such a basis. Connie has never tipped his hand completely, even to his players. Often, we wondered why he did this or that and we had to wait until the play went through before we discovered why. Again, if the public is tipped off to all the inside stuff, what chance have you got to win?"[2]

JOE BIRMINGHAM: Went from benchwarmer to manager in Cleveland in September of 1912. The team experienced its first cellar finish under Birmingham in 1914, and he was fired in May of 1915.

Unfortunately for Davis, despite his impeccable pedigree, having learned baseball at the foot of the master, he had little chance to win in Cleveland, because he inherited a team of angry ball players. The Naps were angry because they liked Stovall and had played hard and reasonably well for him. Cleveland's .544 winning percentage under Stovall had been the second-best in the American League, bettered only by the Athletics. But Somers had decided as soon as he accepted Jim McGuire's resignation 17 games into the 1911 season that Davis would be the Naps' manager in 1912, and nothing Stovall could've accomplished, short of winning the pennant, was going to change the owner's mind. Somers tried to ease the pressure on Davis by trading Stovall to the Browns for pitcher Tom (Lefty) George in the spring. Somers wanted his former manager gone so Davis wouldn't find himself looking over his shoulder at the man he replaced. The trade only added to the aggravation Somers's unhappy players already felt. First, they'd lost Stovall as their manager. Then, they lost him as a teammate.

"Disgruntled players, who didn't want to see the popular George Stovall leave the Naps, were ready to undermine anybody who replaced him," wrote historian Norman L. Macht. "The discipline that characterized the Athletics was absent among the Naps, and Davis's efforts to impose discipline drew more resentment than co-operation."[3] Still, the Naps hung close to the break-even mark until a disastrous eastern road trip in late August, during which the club lost 14 of 16 games.

The last straw, however, came after the Naps returned home to face Stovall's Browns. Stovall was still popular in Cleveland and got a thunderous ovation from 7,684 fans as he walked across the diamond before a game St. Louis won, 6–3, on September 1. Davis realized he had the support of neither his players nor the club's fans and submitted his resignation to Somers on September 2. Somers accepted it.

Davis took the high road before returning to his hometown of Philadelphia, where Mack was happy to welcome him back. Davis said in a prepared statement:

> I thought the best interests of the Cleveland club would be served by my resignation. That is why I gave up my position as manager of the Naps. Luck broke badly for me. Things did not go as well as I had expected. I did intend to wait until the season was over, but on second thought believed it would be fairer to Mr. Somers to let him try someone else out now, or give him a chance to get in touch with a manager who will do better than I did. I have no complaint to make. The players gave me their best, while the newspapers and fans have used me right.[4]

Somers promoted 28-year-old outfielder Joe Birmingham to succeed Davis. Birmingham marveled at how he'd gone from a benchwarmer to player/manager in a three-week span. "It has been my ambition ... to become a big league manager. Whether I am ready to fill such a job now remains to be seen. I shall devote my best energies to winning games for Cleveland and believe the fellows will co-operate with me," said the new manager.[5] Birmingham came highly recommended by his ex-teammate and manager, Stovall.

"I think Joe will make good. I had a long talk with him today and gave him the benefit of what I know about the job. I am not experienced myself, but at that I believe I gave Joe a few good pointers. Joe knows baseball. The boys all like him. I don't see why he shouldn't succeed," said the Browns' boss.[6]

Somers, stung by his mistake in letting Stovall go, made it clear that Birmingham wasn't Cleveland's "interim" manager:

> Joe is manager. He is in full charge to sign or release, to run the team as he sees fit, being clothed with the authority to exert the proper discipline. I believe we can secure just as good results as Stovall did a year ago. The other players believe in him. He knows their faults and their

HARRY DAVIS: Davis came highly endorsed by his former manager, Connie Mack, but couldn't make an impact in less than a full season in Cleveland in 1912. Davis's players were angry that he'd replaced the popular George Stovall and he was soon back with the Athletics.

good qualities and should do better than a stranger who would have to be with them for months or a season to get really acquainted. I feel so confident that Joe will make good that I am going to dismiss the matter and not think of anyone else.[7]

Birmingham inherited a team with a 54–71 record, a team that, in the opinion of Mack, had "laid down" on Davis in an effort to get him fired or force him to quit. Though the players denied the accusation, the 21–7 record they compiled under Birmingham the rest of the season would seem to support it. The Naps would be contenders in 1913, battling the Athletics into September before fading and finishing third.

Davis never managed again.

1913

Boston Red Sox
Jake Stahl to Bill Carrigan

Managers who win world championships don't often find themselves unemployed midway through the next season, but Jake Stahl did.

Paced by pitcher "Smoky" Joe Wood's phenomenal season (34–5, 1.91 ERA) Stahl's Red Sox set an American League record with 105 victories while winning the 1912 pennant, then took a thrilling eight-game World Series (one game ending in a tie) from the New York Giants to claim the world's championship in their first year in Fenway Park.

By mid–July of 1913, the defending champions were running in place with a 39–41 record, and an impatient club president Jimmy McAleer decided a change of managers would provide his lethargic team with a badly needed spark. On July 16, while the Red Sox were in Chicago, McAleer informed Stahl that he'd been replaced by the team's catcher, Bill (Rough) Carrigan. The decision drew immediate fire from the highest echelons of the American League.

"There was no reason for relieving Stahl of the management of the Boston team at this time, and he was entitled to

JAKE STAHL: After a pair of mediocre seasons as manager in Washington, Stahl's 1912 Red Sox set an American League record with 105 victories and beat the Giants in a classic World Series. When Boston floundered through the first half of the 1913 campaign, Stahl was fired.

BILL CARRIGAN: Carrigan (right, with Phillies manager Pat Moran in 1915) took over for Jake Stahl midway through the 1913 season and led the Red Sox to world's championships in 1915 and 1916.

every consideration the Boston club and the American League could give him," fumed league president Ban Johnson.

> Stahl won the world's championship for the American League last fall [defeating Johnson's sworn enemy, John McGraw, had earned Stahl a lot of points with the league president], yet in spite of that fact, he was released by Mr. McAleer and right in his home city, Chicago.

Stahl cannot be held accountable for the poor showing of the Red Sox this season. [Larry] Gardner, [Steve] Yerkes, [Heinie] Wagner, [Duffy] Lewis, and Wood have all been out of the game on account of injuries, and Stahl himself was unable to play on account of an injury to his foot. I feel that the American League may be sharply criticized for Mr. McAleer's hasty and ill-advised action, and if I had been in Chicago yesterday [where Johnson's office was located], Stahl would not have been let out in such a fashion.

If it were absolutely necessary to put someone else in charge of the Red Sox, it could have been done at the close of the season. As it is, Stahl has been humiliated in his home city and the American League has been placed in the unenviable position of dropping in mid-season a manager who won the world's championship last fall. Stahl was an honorable and competent manager and was highly esteemed in our league.[1]

Stahl's firing is the only managerial dismissal in modern major league history to draw such a stinging rebuke from a league president.

McAleer wasn't about to take the rap for replacing Stahl in the middle of the season:

> Mr. Johnson has been misinformed regarding the facts in the case. He takes me to task for not keeping Stahl until the end of the year, when as a matter of fact I offered to let Jake serve out his term. I told him I would let him go at the end of the season as I said I wanted a playing manager, but he said he preferred to be released at once, providing I would pay him in full for the season, which I agreed to do. Stahl suggested the arrangement and I fail to see wherein I have treated him badly.

BYRON BANCROFT (BAN) JOHNSON: Johnson was the founder and first president of the American League. He was involved in everything including the hiring of managers and personally selected Jimmy McAleer for the St. Louis Browns and Clark Griffith for the New York Highlanders. He applauded the ouster of George Stallings by the Highlanders and criticized the firing of Jake Stahl by the Red Sox.

As for the Red Sox' new manager, McAleer said Carrigan would keep the job "as long as he makes good."[2]

Stahl saw the situation differently than his ex-boss:

> I didn't resign from the Red Sox. I was fired. I gave the Red Sox the best of baseball that was in me. I was with them heart and soul. That club was the only one which I was ever really interested in. I am through with baseball. If I intended to stay in baseball, I would not permit the incidents of the past forty-eight hours to go by unnoticed. I should insist that I be placed right with the people, although I am free to confess that with my hosts of friends in this city I do not believe that any "setting right" is necessary.[3]

Stahl stayed true to his vow never to return to baseball. He took a job as a banker in Chicago, and although it was rumored in 1916 that he'd be part of a group that planned to buy the Cleveland Indians, nothing came of it. Carrigan couldn't propel the Red Sox back into the 1913 pennant race, but the club showed signs of life, winning 40 and losing 30 for its new manager. That was good enough for McAleer to keep Carrigan in the dugout, and the Red Sox would be rewarded with pennants and World Series victories in 1915 and 1916.

JIMMY MCALEER: McAleer was the first manager of the American League's Cleveland and St. Louis clubs. He was president of the Red Sox when they won the 1912 World Series, and fired manager Jake Stahl halfway through the 1913 season.

Acquiring a pitcher named Babe Ruth from the Baltimore Orioles of the International League in 1914 didn't hurt.

St. Louis Browns
George Stovall to Branch Rickey

Unlike the dismissal of Jake Stahl, George Stovall's firing as manager of the Browns sparked no outrage in the American League office ... or in St. Louis. Stovall had been able to light a fire under his charges while managing in Cleveland in 1911, but he couldn't do anything with the players he had to work with in St. Louis. Stovall had run afoul of Browns owner Bob Hedges, who accused his manager of not developing the young talent Hedges was providing. In a refrain that had been heard before and would be heard again, Hedges also felt that the Browns were better than a seventh-place club. And seventh place is where Stovall's team found itself, with 50 victories and 84 losses, when Hedges dismissed his manager on September 6.

Hedges replaced Stovall with Jimmy Austin, the Browns' third baseman. Austin was just a stopgap manager. After winning two games and losing six, Austin gave way to Branch Rickey, who posted a 5–6 record over the season's final 11 games, giving Stovall's replacements a record of 7–12 and the Browns an overall mark of 57–96. They finished last, 39 games behind the pennant-winning Athletics.

Stovall would land on his feet, managing the Kansas City team of the "outlaw" Federal League in 1914 and '15. In Stovall's five seasons as a major league manager, his clubs won 313 and lost 376. Austin would stay with the Browns and serve as interim manager twice more, for 16 games in 1918 and 51 games in 1923. Rickey would manage the Browns through the 1915 season.

1914

New York Yankees
Frank Chance to Roger Peckinpaugh

The "Peerless Leader" was coming to New York.

It's hard to imagine the New York Yankees being irrelevant, but that was the problem faced by Frank Farrell and Bill Devery following the 1912 season. Farrell had foolishly sacked a capable manager in George Stallings and placed his team in the hands of the nefarious Hal Chase late in 1910. Harry Wolverton, who succeeded Chase, proved to be a disaster as a manager, and the Yankees finished last in 1912 while John McGraw's Giants were winning another National League pennant. The Dodgers weren't doing much better than the Yankees on the field, but were opening a new ballpark in

FRANK CHANCE: The "Peerless Leader" didn't enjoy the same success with the Yankees that he had with the Cubs. Chance managed New York in 1913 through early September of 1914. He also managed the Red Sox in 1923.

1913. Farrell and Devery needed to do something to excite the people who still cared about their team.

In Chicago, Frank Chance and Cubs owner Charles Murphy had a difference of opinion as to Chance's value to the team. After winning four pennants and a pair of World Series titles from 1906 to 1910, the Cubs had slipped to third place in 1911 and '12. When it came time to discuss Chance's contract for 1913, he wanted more than the notoriously stingy Murphy was willing to pay. Not, however, more than Farrell and Devery were offering.

"I can say that I always wanted to work for the American League, and have always considered New York the best town to work in," said Chance. "I shall give my players a fair and equal opportunity, and the good people of New York may count to the full upon my giving them the best I have in me." Amid considerable fanfare, Chance signed a three-year deal to manage the Yankees for an astonishing $25,000 per year. For their investment, Farrell and Devery fully expected Chance to produce the same results in New York that he'd produced in Chicago. Unfortunately for Chance, the Yankees lacked the Cubs' talent. Equally unfortunate for Chance, his best player in New York was Chase. Chance and Chase were destined to clash, and the first confrontation came early.

In an era in which "fixed" games were neither commonplace nor without precedent, Chance had only to watch Chase in action briefly to become convinced that his first baseman was throwing games. Chance, who knew a little bit about playing first base himself, told reporters that ground balls and throws from teammates that were getting past Chase should've been fielded with ease, but Chase had perfected a method of making such chances look difficult to disguise his dishonesty. Faced with a choice between the most popular player in the Yankees' brief history, or his manager, with a history of winning and a fat contract, Farrell reluctantly shipped Chase to the White Sox in exchange for a pair of nondescript journeymen, Babe Borton and Rollie Zeider, in June. Chase would be banished from organized baseball in 1919.

Chase wasn't Chance's only problem. He inherited a miserable team that lost its first 17 home games and failed to win a game at the Polo Grounds until June 7. At year's end, the Yankees had improved one notch to seventh place, with a record of 57–94. In spite of their aversion to winning games at home, the Yankees' attendance increased by 115,000 over 1912. These, however, weren't the kind of results Farrell and Devery expected for their $75,000 investment.

Things didn't improve appreciably in 1914. The Yankees continued to flounder, and Chance continued to moan about the lack of talent on his team. Chance's bellyaching so infuriated Devery that the two men nearly came to blows in the New York clubhouse.

Soon afterward, Chance submitted his resignation. Farrell accepted it. The Yankees were in seventh place with a record of 60–74. Farrell agreed to pay Chance for the rest of the 1914 season, which had just 20 games remaining, but refused to pay off his ex-manager for 1915, the final year of his contract. Farrell reminded Chance that it was Chance's decision to walk away from the job, saying: "I know you do not want to take money you did not earn."

Farrell accepted Chance's recommendation that New York's 23-year-old shortstop, Roger Peckinpaugh, replace him as manager. Peckinpaugh accepted Chance's suggestion that he hold out for more money before taking the job. He got a $500 raise and guided the Yankees to a 10–10 record over the season's final 20 games. The Yankees finished tied for sixth with Chicago at 70–84. Peckinpaugh returned to playing shortstop full time in 1915.

Chance's 117–168 record as Yankee manager didn't tarnish his reputation as a great leader. Neither did one miserable season as Red Sox skipper in 1923. Chance's career record as manager shows 946 wins, 648 losses, four National League pennants and two world championships. Those numbers put him in the Hall of Fame.

Peckinpaugh would return to managing in 1928.

1915

Cleveland Indians
Joe Birmingham to Lee Fohl

Despite their insistence that they hadn't "laid down" on Harry Davis in 1912, the fact is the same bunch of Cleveland Naps who won 54 and lost 71 for Davis posted a 21–7 record for Davis's successor, Joe Birmingham, over the final month of the season. They then made a strong run at the pennant in 1913, chasing the Philadelphia Athletics, which Davis had rejoined as a coach, until Labor Day before fading and finishing third with a record of 86–66. Birmingham's managerial career had gotten off to a promising start.

The roof caved in on Birmingham and the Naps in 1914. Second baseman Napoleon Lajoie, the club's star player since 1902, was 40 years old ... and despised Birmingham. Lajoie's .258 batting average was 80 points below his lifetime mark, and he was released at season's end. Pitcher Cy Falkenberg, a 23-game winner in 1913, jumped to the Federal League. Fred Blanding, a 15-game winner in 1913, won just three games. For the first time in its history, Cleveland finished last, losing 102 games. Making matters worse, owner Charley Somers, who had spent lavishly to help Ban Johnson get the American League off the ground in the early years of the century, had squandered his personal fortune on bad investments. The Cleveland franchise was a mess.

The renamed Indians (Naps was no longer appropriate with Lajoie gone) opened the 1915 season with a 12–16 record ... a much better percentage than the .333 they'd posted the year before. Still, Somers wasn't satisfied and fired Birmingham on May 21. Somers elevated coach Lee Fohl to manager and promised to get more involved in the club's day-to-day operation. "Fohl will manage the team for the present, and I will look after more myself than I have in the past," said Somers. "Two heads may be better than one, and one reason why Birmingham was not successful was that he had no board of strategy to aid him. I have not given the appointment of a manager a thought. I merely deposed Birmingham. That is all."[1]

Somers answered critics who didn't think he should have fired Birmingham without selecting a permanent replacement and doubted whether Somers was qualified to exercise more control over his team:

> I own the club, and its success means much to me, probably more than to any other man in Cleveland. That being so, why should I not take an interest in its management and offer a word of advice now and then, when I thought such advice was needed? Sometimes things have come

up which required that I have the final word, but I will say that manager Birmingham has agreed with me in the release of every player we have disposed of.

I relieved Birmingham of the management because I believed the team would not be successful at the head. I do not care to go into the details, but I believe I had good reasons for taking the action that I did. I would like to have a manager who can go along and run the club without my interference, but until I do I shall protect my interests.[2]

Somers admitted that he'd ordered Birmingham to shift outfielder "Shoeless" Joe Jackson to first base and third baseman Terry Turner to second, as the Indians searched for Lajoie's successor. Somers's financial problems would, later that season, lead to the trade of Jackson to the White Sox in one of the worst deals in Indians history.

Birmingham was disappointed that he wouldn't get the chance to rebuild the Indians:

I was greatly surprised when Mr. Somers told me ... he was through with me as manager. The club has been up against it because of poor pitching, but now that our pitchers were coming through I wanted the chance to show I could make it a winner. I think this team is one that can come through. Every man on it was pulling for me, and I think we would have been successful. Personally, I do not blame myself for the failure of the club to be higher in the race. Considering the fact it has had but one pitcher until very recently, I think the club's present position is all that could be expected.[3]

Fohl couldn't accomplish much with the club Birmingham thought was "one that can come through," compiling a 45–79 record and finishing seventh only because Connie Mack's Athletics, just two seasons removed from winning their fourth pennant in five years, lost a staggering 109 games. The Indians lost only 95.

Birmingham didn't manage in the major leagues again. His Cleveland teams won 170 and lost 191 with one third-place finish.

1916

Cincinnati Reds
"Buck" Herzog to Christy Mathewson

After winning 369 games and pitching 4,707 innings for the New York Giants since 1900, Christy Mathewson's mighty right arm had given out.

Mathewson wanted to manage a major league team, but he wasn't going to displace his friend and mentor, John McGraw, as boss of the only team he'd ever played for. McGraw wasn't quite halfway through his 30-year tenure as Giants manager as the 1916 season opened. He had five more pennants and two more World Series to win, but he'd do it without Mathewson. McGraw idolized Mathewson and was determined to make Matty's dream of managing a reality.

By July 20, Mathewson had pitched in just 12 games for the Giants, winning three and losing four. With the Giants still in contention for the National League pennant, McGraw tried to bolster his lineup by reacquiring one of his former players, infielder Charles (Buck) Herzog. Herzog had played on McGraw's 1912 and '13 pennant winners before being traded to the Reds, whom he served as player/manager in 1914 and '15. The Reds, with Herzog still at the helm, were going nowhere in 1916 and gladly shipped Herzog back to the Polo Grounds, along with catcher Wade (Red) Killefer, in exchange for outfielder Edd Roush, infielder "Deacon" Bill McKechnie, and Mathewson ... on the condition Mathewson replaced Herzog as Cincinnati's manager. McGraw added a second condition that almost nixed the deal, insisting that the Reds send Mathewson back to the Giants in two seasons if McGraw requested his return. The deal didn't go through until McGraw backed off that demand.

Cincinnati was in last place when Mathewson arrived, having won 34 and lost 49 for Herzog. The Reds actually played worse for Mathewson, going 25–43, but managed to inch up a notch to seventh place. Mathewson pitched once for his new team. In a highly publicized match-up of former ace pitchers (and future Hall of Famers), neither of whom displayed anything remotely resembling their old form, Mathewson defeated Mordecai (Three-Finger) Brown of the Cubs, 10–8.

Left: BUCK HERZOG: The Cincinnati Reds were managed by a pair of ex–New York Giants in the 1910s. Herzog was Cincinnati's player-manager from 1914 until July of 1916, when he was traded back to the Giants in exchange for Christy Mathewson, who replaced him in the Reds' dugout. *Right:* CHRISTY MATHEWSON: John McGraw traded Mathewson to the Reds in 1916 on the condition he'd be named manager. Mathewson's Reds finished fourth in 1917 and were in fourth place in 1918 when he enlisted in the military during World War I.

Mathewson's Reds improved to fourth (78–76) in 1917, and stood in third place (61–57) in August of 1918 when Matty joined the armed services and was sent to Europe. In the waning days of World War I, Mathewson sustained a gas attack, the after-effects of which were believed to have led to the tuberculosis that took the great pitcher's life in 1925, at the age of 45.

The Reds team Mathewson left behind in August of 1918 was on the rise. Heinie Groh managed the Reds to wins in seven of their last ten games in 1918, the season having been ordered shortened by the War Department, which had decreed that all able-bodied men (such as Mathewson) were to enlist in the armed forces or find jobs in war-related industries. Mathewson was in no condition physically to resume his duties with the Reds after returning from Europe, and Pat Moran managed the 1919 Reds to their first National League pennant and World Series title.

Mathewson finished his baseball career as an executive with the Boston Braves. His record as Reds manager was 164–176.

1917

Pittsburgh Pirates
"Nixey" Callahan to Hugo Bezdek

It's never easy to follow a legend. Jimmy (Nixey) Callahan learned that lesson firsthand.

Callahan brought five seasons of experience obtained with the White Sox to Pittsburgh in 1916 when he was hired to replace Fred Clarke as manager of the Pirates. Clarke's Pittsburgh teams had finished in the National League's first division 12 times in 16 seasons, winning four pennants and one World Series. He'd be a tough act to follow, and his immediate successor, Callahan, failed miserably to fill Clarke's shoes. Callahan was no stranger to replacing a popular and prominent manager, having taken over for Clark Griffith in 1903, after Griffith had been tabbed to manage the American League's new team in New York.

HUGO BEZDEK: Managed Pittsburgh from July of 1917 through the 1919 season. The only man to manage a major league baseball team and coach an NFL team (Cleveland Rams, 1937–38).

The Pirates had begun to decline during Clarke's last two years in charge, and the slide continued after Callahan was hired. Pittsburgh came in sixth with a 65–89 record in 1916, and showed no signs of improvement in 1917. According to the Associated Press, there was "general dissatisfaction" among the fans, players, and management with Callahan's performance. The team had won just 20 of 60 games, and owner Barney Dreyfuss informed Callahan that his services were no longer needed on June 30.

Any thoughts Dreyfuss may have had of turning the team over to Honus Wagner, its former star shortstop who was in the final season of his Hall of Fame career, were quickly dashed when Wagner made it clear he wanted no part of the job. He agreed to pilot the team until Dreyfuss could find a successor, and rumored candidates included infielder "Laughing" Larry Doyle, who had played for John McGraw and was then with the Cubs; former Yankees manager Harry Wolverton; and Jack Hendricks, manager of the Indianapolis team of the American Association.

Dreyfuss chose Hugo Bezdek, a Pirates scout, to relieve Wagner of the burden of managing the team. The decision may have been made in haste. Wagner forced Dreyfuss's hand, announcing on the Fourth of July, after the team had lost four of five games under his direction, that he wouldn't serve one more day. Bezdek made his mark in athletics as a football player, having been a star fullback at the University of Chicago under the legendary coach Amos Alonzo Stagg. He also played baseball in college. His full-time job was supervisor of physical education at the University of Oregon, which included the positions of head football and basketball coach, making him one of the more unlikely men ever chosen to pilot a major league baseball team.

The Pirates did no better under Bezdek during the three remaining months of the 1917 season than they had under Callahan, winning 30 and losing 59 for a cellar finish and a record of 51–103. Dreyfuss nevertheless retained Bezdek for two more years.

Bezdek is the only man to serve as both manager of a major league baseball team and head coach of an NFL team. Bezdek's Cleveland Rams were 1–9 in 1937 and 0–4 in 1938 before he was fired.

Callahan reported to Forbes Field dutifully for several days after being fired, because he'd been relieved of his managerial duties but not released from his contract, and thus considered himself still an employee of the Pirates, even though Dreyfuss had nothing for him to do. He never managed in the big leagues again. His White Sox and Pirates teams won 394 games and lost 458.

HONUS WAGNER: Considered by some to have been the game's greatest player, Wagner wanted no part of managing. He reluctantly agreed to pilot the Pirates after Nixey Callahan was fired in 1917, then quit after five games.

1918

St. Louis Browns
Fielder Jones to Jimmy Burke

Fielder Jones had had enough.

Jones (and Fielder was his real name, not a nickname) had carved his niche in baseball history in 1906. After taking the reins of the Chicago White Sox from Nixey Callahan 41 games into the 1904 season, Jones won 66 and lost 47 the rest of the way for a third-place finish. The White Sox improved to second in 1905, and in 1906, despite an anemic .230 team batting average, Chicago's pitching paced it to a late season, league-record 19-game winning streak that vaulted the club into first place. The White Sox finished three games ahead of the New York Highlanders. Averaging just 3.8 runs per game, the White Sox became known as the "Hitless Wonders." Jones's team then somehow defeated the National League champion Chicago Cubs, whose 116 victories are still the major league single-season record, as is their .763 winning percentage, in a six-game World Series.

After third-place finishes in 1907 and '08, Jones retired. His name was linked to every managerial position that opened over the next several years, but Jones made it clear that he wouldn't put on another uniform unless he was part-owner of the club he was managing. That proved to be a deal-breaker until 1914, when Jones bought a piece of the St. Louis Terriers of the "outlaw" Federal League, owned by Phil Ball. Jones joined the Terriers too late in the season to help the team avoid a seventh-place finish, but brought the club home second in 1915. When the Federal League ceased operation after just two years of trying to

FIELDER JONES: Jones replaced Nixey Callahan as manager of the White Sox in June of 1904 and guided the "Hitless Wonders" to the 1906 World Series title. He later managed the Browns and retired during the 1918 season because he didn't need the money.

establish itself as a third major league, Ball was permitted to buy the St. Louis Browns and brought Jones with him to replace Branch Rickey as manager. The Browns finished a respectable fifth (79–75) in 1916, but skidded to seventh in 1917 with a 57–97 record. Forty-six games into the 1918 campaign, the Browns were in fifth place with 22 wins and 24 losses, and Jones retired for good on June 13.

"There is nothing connected with the business management of the club which influenced me to quit," Jones explained. "My relations with Mr. Ball, president of the club, have been most pleasant, but I feel I am unequal to the strain attendant on the management of a major league club when I do not have to depend on baseball for a livelihood."[1] Jones had lumber interests in Oregon which had skyrocketed in value thanks to the United States' need for war materiel, notably the boom in shipbuilding. He didn't need Ball's money, and he didn't need the aggravation of managing a perpetual tail-end ball club. Jones retired with a career record of 683–582.

Ball turned the Browns over to Jimmy Austin for the second time in five years. Austin won seven and lost nine while Ball decided his next manager was already on his coaching staff. Ball promoted Jimmy Burke, who hadn't managed in the major leagues since 1905, when he'd replaced Cardinals boss Kid Nichols 14 games into the season. Burke's Cardinals won just 34 of the 90 games he managed, and he was eventually relieved of his duties and replaced by the owner, M. Stanley Robison.

Burke posted a 29–31 record with the Browns over the last two months of the 1918 season. Under three managers, the club finished fifth with a 58–64 ledger. Burke managed the Browns for two more years, coming in fifth in 1919 and fourth in 1920. It was his last managing job. His Cardinal and Browns teams won 206 and lost 236.

1919

Philadelphia Phillies
Jack Coombs to Gavvy Cravath

The 1918 Philadelphia Phillies, three years removed from their first pennant, weren't a particularly good team. The Phillies finished fifth for manager Pat Moran with a record of 55–68, and owner William F. Baker didn't put up much of a fight when Moran, who'd guided the team to the 1915 pennant, accepted an offer to manage the Cincinnati Reds in 1919.

Baker hired a former Philadelphia hero

JACK COOMBS: One of many star players who either couldn't handle managing or proved not to be very good at it. Coombs managed the Phillies for just 62 games (44 of them losses) before resigning in 1919.

GAVVY CRAVATH: Baseball's modern career home run leader when he retired, Cravath succeeded Jack Coombs as Phillies manager in 1919, winning fewer than 100 games in his 1½ seasons on the job.

to replace Moran. "Colby" Jack Coombs, so nicknamed because he'd pitched for Colby College, had anchored the Philadelphia Athletics' pitching staffs that won pennants and World Series titles for Connie Mack in 1910 and '11 and finished third in 1912. Coombs posted sterling records of 31–9 and 28–12 during the pennant seasons, and won 21 more while losing 10 in 1912. Coombs's earned run average of 1.30, astonishingly, didn't lead the American League in 1910, but his 13 shutouts did. He beat the Chicago Cubs three times in the World Series, and added a fourth World Series triumph over the New York Giants in 1911.

Injuries limited Coombs to just four total appearances in 1913 and '14, and Mack parted ways with his former star hurler. Coombs signed with the Brooklyn Dodgers and won 43 games from 1915 through 1918. Brooklyn's only victory over the Boston Red Sox in the 1915 World Series was credited to Coombs, giving him a lifetime mark of 5–0 in the Fall Classic. Baker, however, didn't envision Coombs as a playing manager.

Hiring a manager direct from the playing ranks is risky, and Baker's gamble didn't pay off … not that Coombs had a plethora of talent to work with. Coombs's lack of managerial experience, despite having played for two of the best in Mack and Brooklyn's Wilbert Robinson, was evident. Coombs wasn't accustomed to losing and couldn't cope with it. With his Phillies in last place, mired in a 12-game losing streak, their record a gruesome 18–44, Coombs resigned on June 8. At least, his departure was announced by the Phillies as a resignation.

Two days later, however, the Associated Press reported that Baker had fined three Phillies players, catcher Forrest (Hick) Cady and pitchers Frank Woodward and Gene Packard, for their conduct in "protesting [the Phillies] change in managers." Baker claimed the three players, wearing street clothes, had gone into the bleachers at Baker Bowl, the team's home park, and "harangued the bleacherites against the action of president Baker in changing managers." This casts doubt on whether Coombs actually resigned, or was dismissed by Baker. Packard was fined $200, Woodward was docked $100, and Cady was both fined and released.

Baker chose his slugging right fielder, Clifford (Gavvy) Cravath, to take over for Coombs. Cravath the player did his best to assist Cravath the manager, batting a lusty .341 with a league-leading 12 home runs, but Cravath the manager could only win 29 games while losing 46. The Phillies, embarking on an extended period of historic futility, finished eighth with a record of 47–90.

Cravath managed Philadelphia to another cellar finish in 1920 (62–91) while playing in 46 games. He retired, as both a player and manager, at the end of the season.

Coombs never managed again, either.

Cleveland Indians
Lee Fohl to Tris Speaker

The rebuilding process undertaken by James (Sunny Jim) Dunn when he bought the Cleveland Indians in the winter of 1916 was progressing. Dunn had brashly promised a pennant within three years, and while his timetable had proven faulty, the Indians contended for pennants in both 1917 and '18, finishing third and second, respectively. The cornerstone of Dunn's rebuilding of the Tribe was future Hall of Fame centerfielder Tris Speaker. Speaker had been obtained from the Boston Red Sox, just weeks after Dunn had purchased the Indians, for the record sum of $55,000 plus two players ... neither of whom figured in Dunn and manager Lee Fohl's future plans. Speaker made himself at home immediately in Cleveland, winning the 1916 American League batting

LEE FOHL: Fohl managed Cleveland from May of 1915 until July of 1919, and piloted the Browns to 93 victories in 1923 ... but the Yankees won 94. Fohl was fired the next season.

championship (.386) and establishing himself as Fohl's right-hand man and assistant manager, in fact if not in title.

Speaker became Cleveland's manager on July 18. The second-place Indians had blown a 7–3 lead in the ninth inning and lost to the Red Sox at League Park. Babe Ruth's grand slam powered Boston to an 8–7 victory, its first over the Indians in 10 contests. Fohl and Speaker had disagreed over which relief pitcher to summon with the bases loaded, two out, and Ruth at the plate. Fohl's choice, left-hander Fred (Fritz) Coumbe, threw the slow curve that Ruth slammed far over League Park's 40-foot-high right field wall, costing the Indians a game. Fohl resigned immediately afterward.

Dunn didn't try to talk his manager out of a decision obviously made in the heat of emotion. Dunn found Speaker in the clubhouse and asked him to take over the team. Speaker agreed, on condition the request came directly from Fohl. Speaker didn't want Fohl to think he'd gone to Dunn behind the manager's back to ask for the job, or to suggest that Dunn make a change. Fohl assured Speaker he had resigned and that he wanted his assistant manager to replace him. Speaker agreed.

Speaker said the Indians were a good team that would win a lot of games and he didn't anticipate making many changes. He did make one move, however. He sent Coumbe to the minor leagues. Coumbe never pitched in the majors again.

The Indians did win a lot of games for Speaker. Their 40–21 record for their new manager left them in second place with a record of 84–55, 3½ games behind the pennant-winning White Sox. In 1920, under Speaker, who hit a thunderous .388, the Indians overcame a mountain of adversity to win the team's first pennant and World Series.

Speaker managed the Indians through the 1926 season. They finished second in 1921 and again in 1926, trailing the Yankees both years. Speaker would never again manage in the big leagues. His Indians won 617 and lost 520, with one pennant and world's championship.

1921

Philadelphia Phillies
"Wild" Bill Donovan to "Kaiser" Wilhelm

After the 1920 season, Gavvy Cravath took his 119 career home runs, the modern major league record, and his 91–137 record as manager of the Philadelphia Phillies, into retirement. Phillies owner William F. Baker entrusted the job of lifting his team out of the National League's basement, which it had occupied for the past two seasons, to former pitcher "Wild" Bill Donovan. Donovan was expected to improve a ball club that had undergone a significant facelift during the off-season.

Donovan won 186 games in a career that stretched from 1898, when he broke in with Washington of the National League, through 1918, when he pitched in two games for Detroit, winning one. Shortly after purchasing the New York Yankees in 1915, Colonels Jacob Ruppert and Tillinghast Huston made Donovan their first manager. He was released after guiding the Yankees to fifth-, fourth-, and sixth-place finishes. He returned to the playing ranks briefly in 1918 and then was tabbed by Baker to take control of the Phillies in 1921.

Baker expected results from a major shuffling of personnel during the off-season. The Phillies featured six new starting position players, including first baseman Ed Konetchy, who had played the same position the previous year for the pennant-winning Dodgers. Only outfielders Cy Williams and Irish Meusel kept their positions from the previous season, by virtue of having combined for 29 home runs (Williams led the NL with 15, Meusel was runner-up with 14.)

The pitching staff also had a new look. Future Hall of Famer Eppa Rixey, who led the league in losses in 1920 with 22, was traded to Cincinnati for pitcher Jimmy Ring, who wasn't much of an improvement. Ring would lose 19 games for the Phillies. Rixey, reunited with his former manager, Pat Moran, won 25 games for the Reds. Ring's Philadelphia teammate, George Smith, would lead the NL in losses with 20.

Donovan's tenure in Philadelphia was brief. Slightly more than halfway through the season, with the Phillies once again in eighth place, their record 25–62, Donovan was relieved of his duties and replaced by former major league pitcher Irvin (Kaiser) Wilhelm. Wilhelm's undistinguished career on the mound from 1903 through 1915 produced 57 victories and 108 defeats. Wilhelm would pitch in four games with no decisions after taking the managerial job with the Phillies.

WILD BILL DONOVAN: Managed the Yankees for three seasons pre–Babe Ruth, then spent half a year with the Phillies in 1921.

The Associated Press reported on August 3 that Donovan hadn't been fired, but temporarily reassigned to scouting duties, according to Baker. The owner claimed that Donovan had signed a highly prized (but unidentified) pitching prospect and was otherwise "doing his part to build up the team for next year."[1] Baker said he didn't know when Donovan would resume his managerial duties, since Wilhelm had won five of his first eight games, and the team was riding a three-game winning streak ... impressive by the Phillies' modest standards. Baker said he didn't think it wise "to disturb conditions at present."[2]

Donovan never returned to the Philadelphia dugout, and Wilhelm's run of success didn't last. He did, however, post a better record than Donovan, winning 26 and losing 41. The Phillies finished last for the third straight year with a record of 51–103.

Donovan's career as a manager was over, and Wilhelm's was short-lived. The Kaiser moved the Phillies up a notch to seventh (57–96) in 1922, but didn't return in 1923. He never managed again. Donovan's managerial record was 245–301. Wilhelm's was 83–137.

Chicago Cubs
Johnny Evers to "Reindeer Bill" Killefer

Never let it be said that William Veeck, the elder, was the type to kick a man when he was down.

Veeck, one of the few newspapermen given the chance to put his money where his mouth was by being afforded the chance to run a major league baseball team, expected big things from the 1921 Cubs. With a pitching staff anchored by Grover Cleveland Alexander, and managed by former Cubs second baseman Johnny (The Crab) Evers, Veeck anticipated the Cubs would challenge the Giants, Reds, and defending champion Dodgers for National League supremacy.

It was Evers's second tour of duty as Cubs manager. He was chosen to succeed his teammate, Frank Chance, when Chance and Cubs owner Charles Murphy couldn't agree on a contract and Chance made the ill-fated decision to sign with the Yankees. Evers led the 1913 Cubs to a third-place finish with a record of 88–65, and was then traded to the Boston Braves. Veeck was hoping for a repeat performance, or better, of the 1913 season when he re-enlisted Evers for 1921. He didn't get it.

With the exception of Alexander, Veeck hadn't given Evers much of a pitching staff, and Alexander suffered through an off-year, winning only 15 games while losing 13. No other Cub pitcher posted a winning record. It was too much of an obstacle for Evers to overcome. With the Cubs struggling in sixth place with a 41–55 record, Veeck, after meeting with the team's executive committee on August 2, decided to change managers. However, after selecting Cubs catcher "Reindeer Bill" Killefer to take Evers's place, Veeck learned that Evers was ill and in no condition to discuss his impending firing, in the words of a letter released to the newspapers. He was also in no condition to manage the team when it hosted the Braves in a double-header the next day. It was then decided that Killefer would be announced as the team's acting manager until Evers recovered sufficiently to be told that he was out of a job. That moment arrived shortly before noon on August 4, and Evers was fired with considerable regret, according to the same letter.

The 1921 Cubs simply didn't have the pitching to make any noise in the National League, and Killefer couldn't do much more with them than Evers did. On the field, Killefer played in 45 games and batted .323. In the dugout, Killefer's Cubs won 23 and lost 34 for an overall record of 64–89. They finished ahead of only the Phillies.

Killefer retired at season's end, after 13 years as a player, to concentrate on managing. He stayed at the helm of the Cubs until 1925. Killefer's teams finished fifth in 1922, fourth in 1923, and fifth again in 1924, winning 80, 83 and

JOHNNY EVERS: The middleman in the famous Tinker to Evers to Chance double play combination, Evers managed the Cubs in 1913 and again for 96 games in 1921. He moved across town to manage the White Sox in 1924.

81 games, respectively. Evers played in one game for the White Sox in 1922, then managed the team to an eighth-place finish in 1924. It was the end of his career as a manager. The Crab's Cubs and White Sox compiled a record of 180–192.

1922

Pittsburgh Pirates
George Gibson to "Deacon" Bill McKechnie

Hugo Bezdek had done a commendable job managing the Pirates in 1918 and '19. Bezdek, a football player by trade who'd been plucked from Pittsburgh's scouting ranks to succeed Nixey Callahan midway through the 1917 season, guided the Pirates to fourth-place finishes during his two full seasons as manager, winning 136 games and losing 128 (for a career record of 166–187). For the 1920 season, Pirates owner Barney Dreyfuss decided to put a baseball man back in charge of his team and selected former catcher George Gibson. Gibson had worn a Pittsburgh uniform from 1905 through 1916 and caught 150 games for the 1909 world champion Pirates. Gibson finished his career with the New York Giants, retiring after seeing action in only four games in 1918.

Gibson's first Pirate team ran the club's string of fourth-place finishes to three in a row, winning 79 and losing 75. The 1921 Pirates improved to second place. Led by a pitching staff that included the National League's leading winner, Wilbur Cooper (22–14), and allowed just 595 runs, by far the fewest in the major leagues, Pittsburgh posted a 90–63 record and finished four games behind John McGraw's Giants. Gibson's team got off to a strong start in 1922 and trailed the Giants by two games, with a record of 27–19, on June 12. The Pirates then slumped, losing 14 of their next 19, to fall 10 games off the pace.

The 14th defeat was a 6–0 loss to St. Louis at Forbes Field on June 30, dropping Pittsburgh a game under the .500 mark at 32–33. Bill Sherdel's five-hit blanking of the Pirates was Gibson's final game as manager. While the players prepared to shower in the clubhouse, Gibson made a brief statement announcing his resignation. According to the Associated Press, Gibson gave his players no reason for his decision to step aside; however, "a report had it that he has been dissatisfied with the poor showing of the team in the last two weeks and that he felt he should give some other man a chance at the helm."[1]

That other man would be "Deacon" Bill McKechnie, Gibson's assistant manager. Less than an hour after Gibson quit, McKechnie was chosen to replace him. McKechnie wasn't lacking in managerial experience, having piloted the Newark team of the short-lived Federal League for part of the 1915 season, winning 54 and losing 45. Whether the stretch that drove Gibson to resign was just the kind of slump that every team experiences over the course of a six-month season, or whether McKechnie's leadership lit a fire under the Pirates, the team snapped out of its doldrums almost immediately. McKechnie lifted Pittsburgh from fifth place to a third-place tie with St. Louis, guiding the team to a 53–36 record to finish the season at 85–69, eight games behind the Giants.

It was the beginning of a long and successful managerial career for McKechnie. His 1923 and '24 Pirates finished third. His 1925 Pirates captured the franchise's first pennant

GEORGE GIBSON: Gibson managed the Pirates twice, with a brief stint as interim manager of the Cubs thrown in. Gibson's Pittsburgh clubs finished second in 1921, 1932 and 1933.

since 1909 and overcame a 3–1 World Series deficit to defeat the Washington Senators and bring a world championship to Pittsburgh. And the Deacon was just warming up.

Gibson would manage the Cubs briefly in 1925, then return to the Pittsburgh dugout in 1932.

1923

St. Louis Browns
Lee Fohl to Jimmy Austin

Jimmy Burke may have been sorry he hired Lee Fohl.

Fohl, the former manager of the Cleveland Indians, had been hired as a coach midway through the 1920 season and replaced Burke as manager at season's end. Fohl guided the Browns to a third-place finish in 1921 (81–73), and then led the team to never-before-achieved heights in 1922.

With the defending champion Yankees dealing with the early season suspension of Babe Ruth, the Browns fought the New Yorkers until the season's final day, winning 93 games and fashioning a .604 winning percentage. Both would stand as high-water marks for the franchise until it moved to Baltimore in 1954. Despite George Sisler's sizzling .420 batting average and Ken Williams's 39 home runs and 155 RBI (all league-leading figures) and 24 victories from Urban Shocker, the Browns came up a game short in their bid for their first pennant. The Brown Stockings were expected to do just a little bit better in 1923.

Sisler, however, missed the entire season with vision problems. Williams's home run total declined to 29, and his RBI fell to 91. Shocker's victory total dropped marginally, from 24 to 20. The Yankees were running away with the pennant, and the Browns, who'd come so close the year before, were floundering. Owner Phil Ball did what most owners would under the circumstances. On August 6, he fired Fohl.

Ball dismissed his manager, who had the Browns in third place with a 52–49 record, "for the good of the game and the morale of the players."[1] How Fohl's managing was damaging the game wasn't elaborated upon. Ball was reportedly angry that Fohl hadn't joined his players in protesting the ejection of pitcher Dave Danforth from a game in Philadelphia for discoloring a ball a week before Fohl's dismissal. The incident recalled the words of Henry Edwards, baseball writer for the *Cleveland Plain Dealer*, when Fohl resigned as Indians manager in July of 1919. Analyzing the change in leadership, Edwards wrote that while Fohl couldn't be accused of "not trying," he was of the "phlegmatic type" and not as aggressive as his replacement, Tris Speaker. Fohl proved not to be aggressive enough to suit Ball as his team fell out of contention.

Rumor had it that Ball would turn the team over to Sisler, its future Hall of Fame first baseman, but Sisler declined, citing the health problem that kept him on the bench all season. If he couldn't see well enough to play, he couldn't see well enough to manage. Ball turned once again to the ever-loyal Jimmy Austin, who assumed the reins on an interim basis for the third time since 1913. Austin managed the Browns for the rest of the year, winning 22 and losing 29. In three tours of duty as St. Louis's temporary manager, Austin's teams won 31 and lost 44.

Another rumor claimed Fohl would pilot the Boston Red Sox in 1924, and that rumor proved to be correct. Three years at the helm of the pathetic Red Sox dragged Fohl's career managerial record well below the .500 mark. He spent the 1924, '25 and '26 seasons managing the wreckage left behind by former owner Harry Frazee to seventh-, eighth- and eighth-place finishes, losing 299 games. Fohl finished his career as a major league manager with 713 victories and 792 losses. He finished second once with the Indians and once with the Browns.

1925

St. Louis Cardinals
Branch Rickey to Rogers Hornsby

Four years after being dismissed as manager of the St. Louis Browns in 1915, Branch Rickey found himself back in a St. Louis dugout. This dugout, however, was in Robison Field, the rickety home of the St. Louis Cardinals, a franchise that had been around since 1892 but was short on cash, short on victories and short on stature within the community.

The Cardinals improved steadily under the innovative Rickey, finishing seventh in 1919, fifth in 1920, and third in 1921. While the Browns were battling the Yankees for the American League pennant in 1922, finishing just one game out of first place, Rickey brought the Cardinals home third again, tied with Pittsburgh with a record of 85–69. St. Louis was eight games behind the pennant-winning Giants but just one game behind second-place Cincinnati. Rickey's Cardinals dropped to fifth in 1924 with a 79–75 record and skidded to sixth the next year, winning 65 and losing 89. When they started the 1925 season with a 13–25 mark, owner Sam Breadon booted Rickey upstairs and replaced him in the dugout with his star second baseman, Rogers Hornsby.

BRANCH RICKEY: Rickey was an innovative manager with both St. Louis clubs, but couldn't turn either one into a contender. He made his greatest mark on baseball as a front office executive.

Hornsby was baseball's greatest right-handed hitter. He also had one of the game's prickliest personalities and eventually wore out his welcome everywhere he played. He was just the tonic the Cardinals needed, however. St. Louis won 64 and lost 51 for its new player/manager, jumping from last place to fourth and finishing the season on the plus side of the .500 mark at 77–76.

The Cardinals continued to play well for Hornsby in 1926, winning the franchise's first pennant, and the city's first since 1888. Their 89–65 record and .578 winning percentage were the worst-ever for a National League champion, however, and they weren't expected to provide much competition for the mighty Yankees in the World Series. But Hornsby's charges stunned New York in seven games, winning games six and seven in front of startled crowds at Yankee Stadium. In December of 1926, having rubbed Breadon the wrong way once too often, Hornsby was swapped to the Giants in exchange for Frankie Frisch and pitcher Jimmy Ring. Hornsby would spend part of the 1927 season managing the Giants while John McGraw was on one of the occasional leaves-of-absence he took for various reasons during the 1920s.

Rickey's major league managerial record was 597–664. He'd make his greatest contribution to baseball as a front office executive.

Chicago Cubs
Bill Killefer to "Rabbit" Maranville to George Gibson

"Reindeer" Bill Killefer had compiled a respectable record of 300–293 as Cubs manager when club officials, specifically club president William Veeck, decided in July of 1925 not to renew his contract for 1926. Once Veeck decided to dismiss Killefer, there seemed to be no reason to allow him to finish the season, and he was reassigned to scouting duties on July 6. Veeck's choice to succeed Killefer was Walter (Rabbit) Maranville, the Cubs' shortstop.

The reason given to the public for Killefer's dismissal was the desire of Cubs management to follow the lead of the Washington Senators, Boston Braves and St. Louis Cardinals and put their teams in the hands of playing managers. Bucky Harris, the 27-year-old "boy wonder" second baseman, had guided the Senators to their first pennant and World Series championship in 1924 and had the team in first place again in 1925. The Braves were floundering with shortstop Dave Bancroft at the helm, but the Cardinals were streaking after replacing Branch Rickey with second baseman Rogers Hornsby, and Veeck believed the Cubs could benefit by employing a manager who also played in the field each day.

The 33-year-old Maranville, one of baseball's premier free spirits, took over a seventh-place club with a record of 33–42 and proceeded to embarrass it on a regular basis. It didn't take Maranville long to display conduct unbecoming a major league manager, even for the "Roaring '20s." Maranville celebrated his first victory, a 10–5 decision over the Dodgers at Ebbets Field, by visiting a speakeasy and winding up an in altercation with a cab driver who thought Maranville should've tipped him for his service. Maranville thought otherwise.

Later in the season, Maranville doused the Cubs' traveling secretary, John Seys, with a bucket of water, and pranced through a Pullman car spraying the occupants with the contents of a spittoon. Those indiscretions didn't go unnoticed by Veeck. Nor did the fact the Cubs had fallen into last place.

Maranville's major league managerial career would be brief, ending on September 3. Maranville left his club in Boston and returned to Chicago to personally submit his resignation to Veeck, who made no effort to dissuade him. It's likely Veeck would've fired his manager had Maranville not stepped down voluntarily at his meeting with the team president.

"Maranville had failed to enforce discipline on himself he exacted from the players under him," explained Veeck.[1] Maranville would remain with the Cubs for the rest of the season, but Veeck was expected to trade him at the earliest opportunity. As it turned out, the Cubs didn't even bother to work out a trade for Maranville. The future Hall of Famer was sent to Brooklyn for the waiver price. His managerial record was 23–30. He never managed again, although, according to Maranville, he was offered the Boston Braves managing job by club owner Emil Fuchs in 1929 and declined it.

Former Pittsburgh manager George Gibson, a coach under both of Chicago's deposed 1925 managers, Killefer and Maranville, was appointed interim manager for the rest of the season. With some semblance of order restored, the Cubs won 12 and lost 14 with Gibson in charge for a final record of 68–86 and a basement finish, a half game behind Philadelphia.

1928

Boston Braves
Jack Slattery to Rogers Hornsby

Acquiring a player of the caliber of Rogers Hornsby would seem to be every manager's dream come true.

Unfortunately for Jack Slattery, the Boston Braves' trade for Hornsby, who was obtained from the New York Giants in January of 1928 for catcher Shanty Hogan and outfielder Jimmy Welsh, turned out to be the rookie skipper's worst nightmare. The acquisition of Hornsby essentially ended Slattery's managerial career before it had begun.

A Boston native, Slattery played 103 games in the major leagues over four years with Boston, Cleveland, Chicago and Washington in the American League and St. Louis in the National League between 1901 and 1909. He coached baseball at Tufts College, 1914–18; Harvard, 1919–24; and Boston College in 1925, '26 and '27. He resigned from the Boston College job when he was offered the Braves managerial position by club owner Judge Emil Fuchs in the fall of 1927. Boston had been managed by shortstop Dave (Beauty) Bancroft since 1924 and was coming off consecutive seventh-place finishes. Slattery wouldn't have to concern himself with Bancroft looking over his shoulder as the shortstop was given his release after the 1927 season and signed with Brooklyn.

Slattery would, however, have to deal with rampant speculation that his days as Braves manager were numbered that began the day Hornsby was acquired. Hornsby had managed the Cardinals to the 1926 World Series championship, and guided the Giants to a 22–10 record while substituting for John McGraw in 1927. Few believed that Fuchs had obtained Hornsby merely to play in the field. So pervasive was the speculation Slattery would be fired that Fuchs gave him a testimonial dinner in February of 1928, during which Slattery was reaffirmed as the "Braves manager in fact as well as in name." It escaped no one's notice that while Slattery may have been manager, Hornsby had been appointed team captain. It was assumed by baseball fans not only in Boston but around the country that a promotion for the Rajah was inevitable.

The Braves, despite the presence of Hornsby in their lineup, were sadly lacking in talent and began the season slowly. Their record stood at 11–20 on the morning of May 23, when what everyone regarded as inevitable became reality. Slattery submitted his resignation to Fuchs, who elevated Hornsby from team captain to manager.

Fuchs, in a floridly worded statement, said:

> Under the existing circumstances, based on our experience, best judgment and information as to conditions, we are constrained to accept the resignation of Mr. Jack Slattery as manager. It is our hope that he will remain with the Braves in a different department, one that may be more congenial and may give him further opportunity in the line of his vocation, at the same salary and terms as specified in his present contract.
>
> We have, after much persuasion, obtained the consent of Mr. Rogers Hornsby to accept the management of the Braves. We shall continue in our efforts to build up a fighting and winning team for Boston.[1]

Few believed Fuchs's claim that "much persuasion" had been necessary to convince Hornsby to accept the manager's job.

Despite having two future Hall of Famers in their starting lineup, first baseman George Sisler (who hit .340) and Hornsby (who led the NL in batting at .387), the 1928 Braves were a dreadful team who won 39 and lost 83 for their new player/manager. Rookie pitcher Ed Brandt led the league in defeats with 21, and Bob Smith and Art Delaney chipped in 17 losses apiece. The Braves finished seventh, with a record of 50–103, 44½ games behind pennant-winning St. Louis and 42½ behind New York, Hornsby's two previous clubs.

Mercifully for Hornsby, his stay in Boston was brief. Fuchs grew weary of his abrasive second baseman/manager after one season and passed him along to the Chicago Cubs in early November of 1928, in exchange for five players and $200,000, which the financially ailing Fuchs badly needed.

As for Slattery, the 31 games he managed for the Braves in 1928 were the sum total of his major league managerial career.

Chicago White Sox
Ray Schalk to "Lena" Blackburne

A pair of White Sox legends had failed to cleanse the stench of the Black Sox from Comiskey Park as the 1920s neared an end.

Kid Gleason, the feisty rookie manager whose heart, but not his fighting spirit, had been broken by the betrayal of eight of his players in 1919, stayed with the club through 1923. Johnny Evers piloted the White Sox in 1924, and future Hall of Famer Eddie Collins, Gleason's second baseman in 1919, took the job in 1925. Collins managed Chicago to a pair of fifth-place finishes in 1925 and '26, winning more games than he lost both seasons, but was replaced by former teammate Ray Schalk.

Chicago's 70–83 record under the ex-catcher in 1927 earned it another fifth-place finish, and the White Sox were languishing in sixth place, with a 32–42 mark, on July 4, 1928, when Schalk submitted his resignation to owner Charles Comiskey. White Sox fans had expected more from their team despite its six straight second-division finishes, and Schalk felt compelled to step down. The man known as "Cracker" said in his letter of resignation that he was doing so for the good of the organization, which was rebuilding with youth that Schalk felt would be better served by a different manager. Schalk never managed again and exited with a record of 102–125. He was replaced by coach Russell (Lena) Blackburne, who led the White Sox to a 40–40 record and fifth-place finish at 72–82.

Comiskey stuck with Blackburne in 1929, and Chicago dropped to seventh (59–93.) Blackburne was dismissed at season's end, and didn't manage in the major leagues again. His career record for a season and a half in Chicago was 99–133.

1929

St. Louis Cardinals
Billy Southworth to Bill McKechnie

Sometimes, even winning isn't enough.

Rogers Hornsby had managed the St. Louis Cardinals to their first National League pennant in 1926, then shocked the heavily favored New York Yankees in a seven-game World Series. For his trouble, Hornsby was traded to the New York Giants and replaced in the field by Frankie Frisch, the man he was traded for, and in the dugout by Bob O'Farrell. O'Farrell led the defending world champions to a second-place finish in 1927. That didn't satisfy Cardinals owner Sam Breadon, who fired O'Farrell and replaced him with "Deacon" Bill McKechnie, who'd managed the Pirates to the 1925 world championship but left Pittsburgh amid controversy following the 1926 season.

McKechnie's 1928 Cardinals won the pennant and faced the Yankees in a rematch of the 1926 World Series. Breadon expected the same result, but the Yankees had their revenge, flattening McKechnie's team in four straight games. Rather than fire McKechnie, however, Breadon demoted him to manager of St. Louis's top farm team in Rochester, New York. Rochester's manager, former major league outfielder Billy Southworth, was promoted to St. Louis.

The swap of skippers didn't have the desired results. The National League's defending champions were mired in fourth place, winners of 36 games and losers of 30, six games out of first, when they opened a 22-game road trip in Pittsburgh's Forbes Field on July 2. That trip produced only seven victories. By the time they returned to St. Louis on July 24, the Cardinals had fallen 13½ games behind the front-running Cubs, and Southworth was on his way to Rochester to replace McKechnie, who had been summoned to Sportsman's Park as Breadon reversed the swap of field bosses. McKechnie took over a team with a 43–45 record, but still in fourth place. St. Louis posted a 34–29 record for its new/old manager, but couldn't make up any ground in the standings, finishing fourth at 78–74 (Gabby Street won a game as Cardinals interim boss while McKechnie was en route from Rochester), 20 games in arrears of the pennant-winning Cubs.

McKechnie had had quite enough of Breadon after the 1929 season and accepted an offer from Judge Emil Fuchs to manage the Braves in 1930. Southworth would hone his craft in the minor leagues and return to the St. Louis dugout in 1940.

Pittsburgh Pirates
"Donie" Bush to Jewel Ens

Poor road trips proved to be the demise of two National League managers in 1929. St. Louis's disastrous eastern swing in July led to the demotion of Billy Southworth, and a weak visit to the east in August convinced Owen (Donie) Bush to quit as manager of the Pittsburgh Pirates.

Bush managed the Pirates to the 1927 pennant despite a feud with star outfielder Hazen (Kiki) Cuyler. Bush presented owner Barney Dreyfuss with an ultimatum of "it's Cuyler or me" after the Pirates were swept in the World Series by the Yankees, and Dreyfuss backed his manager.

Bush's Pirates fell to fourth in 1928, but he had the team in first place as late as July 23 of 1929 (56–31) before they dropped to second behind the onrushing Cubs (and their right fielder, Cuyler, who hit .360 and drove in 102 runs). A road trip that resulted in five wins and 12 defeats (including five losses to the sixth-place Phillies) sealed Bush's fate in Pittsburgh. Although it was widely believed that he still had Dreyfuss's support and was expected to return in 1930, Bush, with the Pirates 14½ games out of first, submitted his resignation on August 28. The manager said he had no hard feelings toward his players or Dreyfuss, but "simply desired to quit."[1]

Dreyfuss accepted the resignation, saying he liked and respected Bush and calling his ex-manager "a hard and faithful worker with the best interests of the club at heart."[2] Dreyfuss promoted coach Jewel Ens to interim manager and said Ens could keep the job with a strong September showing. The Pirates took to their new boss immediately, winning four straight games from the pennant-bound Cubs at Forbes Field to reduce their first-place deficit to 10½ games. It was as close as Ens could get his team to first place until the season's final day. The Pirates won 21 and lost 14 for Ens, finishing second with a record of 88–65.

Ens was rewarded with a new contract. He brought the Pirates home fifth in both 1930 and '31. That was the end of his career as a major league manager. His clubs won 176 games and lost 167.

Skeptics who doubted that Bush had suddenly lost his taste for managing as the result of one bad road trip, and suggested he'd actually been fired by Dreyfuss, had their case strengthened when Bush signed with the White Sox and guided them to a pair of seventh-place finishes in 1930 and '31. He resurfaced with Cincinnati in 1933 and was fired after finishing last. He never managed in the majors again, and left with a lifetime record of 497–529, with one pennant.

1932

New York Giants
John McGraw to Bill Terry

It was almost as if the Empire State building had toppled over.

Just six weeks short of 30 years on the job, New York Giants manager John McGraw announced his retirement on June 3, 1932. Since arriving in New York in July of 1902, McGraw had made the Giants into the flagship franchise of major league baseball and their home field, the Polo Grounds, became the most famous venue in the sport ... although by 1932, it had lost that distinction to nearby Yankee Stadium.

McGraw's health began to fail in the mid–1920s. He turned the team over to his coach, and former Baltimore Oriole teammate, Hughie Jennings, for 44 games in 1924, and surrendered the reins to Rogers Hornsby for the final 32 contests of the 1927 season. Trying to dispel rumors that his health would soon lead to his departure from the Giants' dugout, McGraw signed a five-year contract in 1931. But sinus problems continued to plague him, and he was frequently forced to remain in New York when the Giants went on the road. McGraw had been turning the team over to his coach, and former player, Dave (Beauty) Bancroft under those circumstances, and it was accepted that McGraw was grooming Bancroft, who had managed the Boston Braves from 1924 through 1927, to take his place when he retired. But no one expected that retirement to come so soon.

The final blow was delivered by McGraw's doctor, who told him that he could not travel with the Giants for the rest of the 1932 season. Being able to lead his team only at the Polo Grounds wasn't acceptable to an old warrior like McGraw, and he announced his retirement with the team in the unaccustomed position of last place with a 17–23 record. He didn't appoint Bancroft as his successor, however. McGraw surprised everyone by selecting Giants first baseman Bill Terry to take over as manager ... the club's first new manager in three decades.

McGraw chose Terry because "it was my desire that a man be appointed who was thoroughly familiar with my methods and who learned his baseball under me." McGraw said he'd be "on hand at all times, my health permitting, when needed" to advise Terry, but made it clear that Terry had "full, complete charge and control of the team and will have to assume entire responsibility therefor."[1]

Like everyone else, Terry had expected Bancroft to take over when McGraw stepped down. Terry said that when he agreed to take the job, McGraw "looked like a man who had had a 40-pound weight lifted from his head."[2] As for Bancroft's future with the Giants, all Terry would say was that a team couldn't have two bosses and "they know I'm the boss. I've already told them that."[3] Terry also said he'd ease up on the team. McGraw was a notorious control freak.

"I'm going to let them relax and see what they can do toward getting out of last place," said the new manager. "They won't have to report to the park at 10 in the morning, nor get to bed at any certain hour. All I'm going to ask is that they play good ball, and if they don't do that for me, they're out."[4]

In his column on June 4, sportswriter Grantland Rice, who had watched McGraw's entire career as New York manager, called him "the greatest showman baseball has ever known," and "the most aggressive leader I have ever known on a ballfield. With him, it was a case of win-win-win and no alibis ever counted."[5] Rice also pointed out that, for a guy with a public reputation as a hard-boiled SOB, McGraw had a sentimental side, particularly for old ballplayers who were down on their luck. Rice noted that McGraw found jobs with the Giants for 19th-century greats such as slugger Dan Brouthers and ace pitcher Amos Rusie (both now in the Hall of Fame) and said no old-time player ever approached McGraw for help and walked away empty-handed. Rice estimated that McGraw doled out over $100,000 of his own money to indigent ex-ballplayers.

McGraw assured Giants fans that he was retiring from managing, but not from the game. He said he'd retain his stock in the Giants and assist in the front office operation of the team. He'd be called out of retirement in July of 1933 to serve as manager of the first National League All-Star team. McGraw's National Leaguers lost to Connie Mack's American League stars, 4–2, on July 6. Babe Ruth, who'd transformed McGraw's beloved game of strategy into one of brute strength, much to McGraw's dismay, hit the home run that proved to be the difference in the game, played in Chicago's Comiskey Park.

McGraw managed 4,801 games in his illustrious career, all but 152 of them in the 20th century. His Oriole and Giant teams won 2,784 and lost 1,959. He was unquestionably the most influential manager of his era, and possibly the most influential manager of all time.

McGraw died on February 25, 1934, at age 60. He lived long enough, however, to watch Terry, his protégé, lift the Giants out of the cellar to a sixth-place finish in 1932 with a 72–82 record, and win the 1933 pennant. Terry's Giants defeated the Washington Senators in a five-game World Series. Terry won two more pennants, in 1936 and '37, but lost to the Yankees in the post-season both years. He retired as a player after the 1936 World Series defeat but managed the Giants through the 1941 season.

Terry's record with the Giants was 823–661.

Boston Red Sox
"Shano" Collins to Marty McManus

Shano Collins may have been the first manager to resign via telegram.

An outfielder who played 16 seasons in the major leagues, Collins was with the Chicago White Sox from 1910 through 1920 and the Red Sox from 1921 through 1925. Collins's Red Sox were in Cleveland on Saturday, June 18. They had lost the first two games of their four-game series with the Indians by scores of 9–3 and 9–2, which dropped Boston's record to an abysmal 11–44. Collins had stomached as much as he could and sent a wire to team president Bob Quinn, resigning effective immediately. Collins was hired prior to the 1931 season, the fifth manager Quinn had employed since assuming the team presidency. Collins's first Red Sox team finished sixth, the club's highest position in the standings since the 1924 team came in seventh. The 1931 Red Sox had snapped a streak of six straight basement finishes, but the club was firmly entrenched in the cellar in 1932 with no hope of escaping. It was more losing than Collins could handle.

"Feeling that I have done everything in my power to win, and not being able to accomplish anything," said Collins in his resignation telegram, "I feel it would be better for all concerned that I resign my position, thereby giving you the opportunity to find someone who can bring the club out of the terrible slump they have been in."[6] That person did not exist, because the Red Sox weren't in a slump. They were a bona-fide last-place team.

Quinn was startled by Collins's resignation. "It was all out of a clear sky to me," said the team president. "I had no inkling he was so discouraged until I talked to him [June 18] when he made it plain he couldn't keep going. I gave him every opportunity to reconsider."[7] Collins couldn't be dissuaded, so Quinn named shortstop Marty McManus the team's interim manager for the rest of the season. McManus said all he'd ask of his teammates was that they hustled for him. "If you do that, we'll still win a lot of ball games," he told his charges.[8] The Red Sox won 32 and lost 67 for McManus. They stayed lodged firmly in the American League's basement with a final record of 43–111.

Collins never managed in the major leagues again. In less than 1½ seasons, his Red Sox won 73 and lost 134. McManus managed the Red Sox through the 1933 campaign, finishing seventh with a record of 63–86. His lifetime managerial record was 95–153 with the wretched Red Sox.

Chicago Cubs
Rogers Hornsby to Charlie Grimm

In 1929, Rogers Hornsby helped the Cubs win the National League pennant. In 1930, with four games left in the season, Hornsby was selected by team president William Veeck to succeed Joe McCarthy, who lost his managerial job for failing to repeat as NL champions. The Cubs won all four games but finished second, two games behind Gabby Street's St. Louis Cardinals.

While McCarthy moved on to manage the Yankees in 1931, Hornsby managed the Cubs to an 84–70 record, good for third place, 17 games behind as St. Louis won again. Hornsby's Cubs were in second place, winners of 53 and losers of 46, five games behind the front-running Pittsburgh Pirates, when the team arrived in Philadelphia on the night of August 2, 1932. The Cubs had lost to the Dodgers at Ebbets Field that afternoon, and Veeck was in Philadelphia waiting for them. What he had to say to his manager couldn't wait until morning, and Hornsby was instructed to report to Veeck's room at the team's hotel.

After a brief discussion of the Cubs' situation, Veeck told Hornsby he'd been planning to make a managerial change for several weeks, and August 2 was as good a time as any, with the club still within striking distance of first place. Although the change was announced to the newspapers as a resignation, there is no doubt Hornsby was fired.

"We just thought the best interests of the club would be served by my retirement," Hornsby told reporters. "Mr. Veeck decided he wanted the move and it's perfectly all right with me. There's no ill-feeling or anything like that."[9]

"When I got in tonight I called Hornsby to my room and we talked the whole thing over," said Veeck. "I told him I wanted to make a change. I told him we should part as friends—but part."[10] In addition to firing Hornsby as manager, the Cubs released him as a player, but agreed to pay off the remainder of his $40,000 contract. Hornsby played in just

19 games in 1932, batting .224 with one home run and seven runs batted in. He didn't think he was washed-up as either a player or a manager.

"I still think I'm a good manager, and I hope to land a player-manager's job before next season," said the Rajah.[11] He had a little more to say about his "resignation," and his meeting with Veeck, on August 3. "Yes, there was some discussion about the way the team should be handled on the field, but when I'm the manager, I run the team. That's all I have to say. I think the Cubs are good enough to win the pennant and the World Series, and I hope they do."[12] Hornsby would get half of his wish.

Cubs owner P.K. Wrigley, who inherited the team from his father, William, in January of 1932, backed Veeck's decision to fire Hornsby. "Anything Veeck does is all right with me," said Wrigley. "It's Veeck's job to see that the Cubs win the pennant."[13]

Veeck entrusted the job of winning the pennant to first baseman Charlie Grimm, known to his teammates and fans as "Jolly Cholly." Grimm was taken by surprise by his promotion. "It came out of a clear sky to me. I didn't know a thing about what was going on until they told me I was it."[14] Grimm's easygoing style was just what the Cubs needed after nearly two full seasons working for the dour Hornsby. Chicago won 37 and lost 18 for its new manager, roaring past Pittsburgh and winning the pennant by four games. Grimm's magic touch didn't extend to the World Series as the Cubs were swept by McCarthy's Yankees, providing Marse Joe with a measure of revenge against Veeck for dismissing him during the waning days of the 1930 season.

Hornsby didn't find the player/manager job he wanted before the 1933 season, but he finished that season as the manager of the woeful St. Louis Browns. Grimm's Cubs fell to third place in 1933, trailing Bill Terry's Giants by five games. Jolly Cholly's long and successful career as a manager had just begun.

1933

Cleveland Indians
Roger Peckinpaugh to Walter Johnson

Walter Johnson found himself in an uncomfortable position on June 10, 1933.

The legendary Washington Senators pitcher and ex-manager had just been hired to manage the Cleveland Indians. He was replacing the man described as his closest friend in baseball, Roger Peckinpaugh.

Peckinpaugh, who had failed to lift the Indians higher than fourth place in five full seasons at the helm, spent his first day of unemployment on a golf course, relaxing with some of his former players. He was anything but bitter about his dismissal. "You're going to work for one of the greatest guys who ever lived, and I'll think less of you if you let him down," he admonished his golfing companions.[1] Unfortunately, the Indians didn't heed their former manager's warning.

No one had speculated that Johnson was in the mix for the Cleveland job, and some Cleveland writers questioned the judgment of general manager Billy Evans and team president Alva Bradley in choosing him to replace Peckinpaugh. Those writers looked back on

Johnson's four-year tenure with the Senators, which ended after the 1932 season, and labeled him a failure. If the only criterion by which a manager is measured is winning pennants, then Johnson had failed as Washington finished fifth, second, and third twice under his leadership. But Johnson's 1930–32 teams won no fewer than 92 games per season, while the best Peckinpaugh's Indians could do during the same stretch was 87 victories and three consecutive fourth-place finishes.

Johnson made no promises upon arriving in Cleveland. He candidly assessed the Indians' problem and his ability to correct it. "I understand the Indians aren't hitting," said the new manager. "That's too bad. I have no magical formula that will make them hit."[2] The 1933 Indians weren't hitting, and the problem was their home field. Mammoth Cleveland Municipal Stadium had no inner fence, and the outfield was roughly the size of the Grand Canyon. Pitchers loved the new park. Hitters despised it. Even Babe Ruth shuddered at the sight of the vast expanse and joked that outfielders should be allowed to use horses in order to patrol the huge pasture. Only balls hit directly down the right and left-field lines, where the stands were 320 feet from home plate, had a chance of leaving the park. Municipal Stadium's distant centerfield bleachers would forever remain unconquered.

The Indians' problem was that they were accustomed to cozy League Park and its 40-foot-high right field wall that stood a mere 290 feet from home plate. Fly balls hit 291 feet either cleared the wall or banged off it, becoming long singles, doubles and occasionally triples. Fly balls hit 291 feet in Municipal Stadium wound up in outfielder's gloves. It was assumed when the Indians left League Park in 1932 that they'd never

ROGER PECKINPAUGH: A shortstop who was the American League's MVP in 1925, Peckinpaugh became the youngest manager in modern major league history when he took over the Yankees in 1914 at the age of 23. He managed the Indians from 1928 until June of 1933, and again in 1941.

return. All of the team's 1933 home games were played in Municipal Stadium, and the club's offense suffered mightily as a result. Cleveland's first two games under Johnson's guidance resulted in 1–0 victories.

Johnson took over a team with a 27–25 record that displayed a "lack of pep," in the opinion of its president. The Indians won 48 and lost 51 for Johnson, finishing fourth once again with a mark of 75–76. Crowds that would've been small in tiny League Park looked even smaller in huge Municipal Stadium, so Bradley abandoned the new park on the lakeshore and moved the Indians back to League Park for 1934. Johnson remained as manager.

St. Louis Browns
"Reindeer" Bill Killefer to Rogers Hornsby

The last two weeks of July were eventful ones for St. Louis baseball fans.

On July 19, Browns manager Bill Killefer stepped down, knowing owner Phil Ball was likely to drop the axe on him shortly. At least, that was the way the Associated Press announced Killefer's departure. An AP story a week later, announcing Rogers Hornsby's hiring as Killefer's replacement, said that Killefer had, indeed, been fired by Ball. Whichever story was correct, Killefer was out and Browns coach Allen Sothoron took his place on an interim basis.

Killefer, the former manager of the Chicago Cubs, took over in St. Louis in 1930 and led the Browns to sixth-, fifth-, and sixth-place finishes, somehow managing to avoid the American League's cellar despite losing more than 90 games each season. Killefer and Ball had been at odds throughout the 1933 season, with Ball insisting he'd given Killefer enough talent to be higher in the standings than eighth, which was the club's position when Killefer either quit or was terminated. The Browns had won 34 and lost 57. "Reindeer Bill" never managed again and retired with a lifetime record of 524–622, his teams never finishing higher than fourth.

Sothoron's Browns won two and lost six while Ball searched for a permanent replacement for Killefer. He found his man in the same ballpark he owned and leased to the National League's Cardinals.

Hornsby hadn't found the player/manager job he hoped for after being fired by the Cubs in August of 1932, but he hooked on with his former team, the Cardinals, as a utility player for the 1933 season. Hornsby played in 46 games for the Cardinals and was batting .325 when his boss, general manager Branch Rickey, got him and Ball together. Rickey, who had no use for either Hornsby or Ball, apparently felt the two men deserved each other. Rickey wasn't concerned about losing Hornsby's bat as the Cardinals vied for the National League pennant, and Hornsby wanted to manage so badly he didn't mind leaving a contender for a doormat.

Ball signed Hornsby to a three-year contract on July 26, against the advice of American League president Will Harridge, who, for unspecified reasons, didn't want Hornsby to take over the league's worst team. "Teams that are too tame don't get very far," Hornsby said when introduced to the press as the new Browns boss. "On the other hand, there is no excuse for fighting or rough stuff."[3] Hornsby said he planned no immediate personnel changes and would keep Sothoron as a coach. He announced, "While I have a superficial knowledge of the St. Louis American League club, I want to have them in hand for some time so that I can familiarize myself with their style of play, and what they can do. I believe I have the nucleus of a good baseball club."[4]

There were 52 games left in the Browns' season when Hornsby took over. They won 19 and lost 33 and didn't budge from last place. Their final record was 55–96.

St. Louis Cardinals
Gabby Street to Frankie Frisch

It had worked once before.

In 1925, St. Louis Cardinals owner Sam Breadon had relieved his manager, Branch Rickey, of his duties and replaced him with the club's star second basemen, Rogers Hornsby. Hornsby got the team moving in the right direction and won the 1926 pennant and World Series, before agitating Breadon to the point that he traded Hornsby to the New York Giants a month after he'd won the world's championship.

Eight years later, Breadon's Cardinals were once again not playing well enough to suit their owner, so Breadon once again fired his manager, Charles (Gabby) Street. Unlike Rickey, whose record as a manager was undistinguished, Street had two pennants and a World Series title on his resume. Street's 1930 Cardinals, in the season of the ultra-lively ball, scored 1,004 runs en route to winning 92 games and edging Joe McCarthy's Cubs by two games for the NL crown. Connie Mack's Philadelphia Athletics, in the middle year of their three-year dynasty, defeated St. Louis in six games in the World Series. Street and the Cardinals had their revenge in 1931, beating the Athletics in seven games when Mack could find no answer for outfielder John (Pepper) Martin, who batted .500 and stole five bases to lead the Cardinals to victory.

Street's Cardinals plunged to seventh place in 1932 with a record of 72–82, but got off to a fast start in 1933 and were in second place on July 11. By July 23, a double-header split with Boston left the Cardinals in fourth place, eight games behind the Giants with a record of 46–45, and Breadon made a change. Street was fired and replaced by the team's star second baseman, Frankie Frisch. The man known as the "Fordham Flash" came to the Cardinals in the trade that sent Hornsby to the Giants in 1927 and had played on three St. Louis pennant winners. Breadon said he hoped Frisch's leadership would enable the team to emerge from the slump that had seen it fall from its season-high of 13 games above the .500 mark, achieved on June 18 and June 21, and get back into the pennant race.

"Of course, like all ballplayers, I have been ambitious to become a manager," said Frisch following his appointment, "and I am naturally pleased to get my opportunity. I haven't had much chance to plan as yet. I do think, though, that if our club comes out of its present hitting slump, we should go somewhere in this race."[5] Street wasn't bitter about his dismissal, although, understandably, he believed it was undeserved.

"Mr. Breadon gave me the job, and it was his to take away as he saw fit," said the former manager. "My baseball has been sound, as sound as during the years when we won. But I am leaving with the best of feeling for Mr. Breadon. He gave me a great chance when he made me manager, and I am grateful for it."[6] Street's managing days weren't over. He'd pilot the Browns to a seventh-place finish in 1938.

Frisch's Cardinals perked up, winning 36 and losing 26 to finish fifth with a final ledger of 82–71, half a game behind fourth-place Boston and 9½ in back of Bill Terry's pennant-winning Giants. St. Louis did manage to shake off the batting slump Frisch mentioned and led the National League in runs scored.

Breadon may have experienced déjà vu as the 1934 season progressed. Just as Hornsby had done in 1926, his first full season as manager, Frisch, in his first full season at the Cardinals' helm, led the 1934 "Gas House Gang" to the pennant and World Series championship.

1934

Chicago White Sox
Lew Fonseca to Jimmy Dykes

It didn't take Lew Fonseca long to add his name to the growing list of managers who'd tried and failed to restore the Chicago White Sox to their former place of prominence following the Black Sox scandal.

Fonseca, whose playing career began in 1921 with the Reds and included the 1929 American League batting title (.369 with the Indians), was promoted from player to player/manager to succeed Donie Bush after the 1931 season. Fonseca didn't do much playing, as Fonseca the manager wisely decided to keep a player who could generate batting averages of only .135 in 1932 and .203 in 1933 on the bench.

Fonseca's 1932 White Sox were horrible, finishing seventh with a record of 49–102. The White Sox were spared the cellar because the Red Sox were even worse, losing 111 games. Fonseca's 1933 White Sox improved and were merely lousy, winning 67, losing 83, and moving up a notch in the standings to sixth. Despite the improvement, rumors swirled around Chicago's spring training camp in 1934 that Fonseca was about to be replaced by Jimmy Dykes, the third baseman on Connie Mack's pennant-winning teams in Philadelphia in 1929, '30 and '31. As he'd done following his run of four pennants in five seasons from 1910

JIMMY DYKES: The third baseman on championship Athletics teams in 1929-30-31, Dykes spent 12 seasons managing the White Sox, then skippered the Athletics, Orioles, Reds, Tigers and Indians. The six clubs Dykes managed is the major league record (*Cleveland Press* collection/Cleveland State University).

through 1914, Mack broke up his 1929 dynasty, starting to sell off his star players in 1932. Dykes wound up in Chicago, batting .260 and establishing himself as prime managerial timber. Though team president Lou Comiskey denied Fonseca's job was in jeopardy, eyebrows were raised when Comiskey accompanied the White Sox on their second road trip of 1934. The club left Chicago with a 4–7 record and proceeded to lose a game in Philadelphia and three straight to the defending league champion Senators in Griffith Stadium. Eleven losses in 15 games was enough to convince Comiskey that a change was needed, and Fonseca was fired on May 8. As had been speculated all spring, Dykes took over.

"I can promise you plenty of fight," said Dykes upon his elevation to player/manager status.[1] The new manager's first order of business would be to restore the 1933 outfield of right fielder Evar Swanson, centerfielder Mule Haas and left fielder Al Simmons (the latter two, like Dykes, former members of Mack's champion Athletics.) The move would have to wait until Simmons recovered from a concussion suffered when he was hit by a thrown ball during a loss in Washington three days before Dykes became manager. The tinkering didn't help. Despite the presence of two future Hall of Famers (Simmons and shortstop Luke Appling) in their starting lineup, the White Sox finished eighth, winning 53 and losing 99 (49–88 for Dykes.) Dykes the player helped his manager's cause by hitting .268 with seven homers and 82 RBI.

Fonseca's career as both a player and a manager ended with his firing. His Chicago teams won 120 and lost 196. He wound up working for major league baseball in a public relations capacity. If you ever see an old baseball newsreel film from the 1930s or '40s, watch the opening credits. There will probably be one that reads, "Written by Lew Fonseca."

Pittsburgh Pirates
George Gibson to "Pie" Traynor

George Gibson's second tour of duty as manager of the Pirates didn't end any better than the first.

Gibson had managed the team he spent most of his playing career with from 1920 through the first 65 games of the 1922 season. He served as interim manager of the Cubs in 1925 and returned to the Pittsburgh dugout in 1932, replacing Jewel Ens. Gibson's 1932 Pirates started slowly, losing 16 of their first 24 games and finding themselves in eighth place as late as May 22. Then the tide began to turn, and Pittsburgh headed steadily toward first place, claiming the top spot on June 26 following a double-header sweep of Cincinnati. The Pirates' record peaked at 58–38 on July 28, and they held first place until August 11, by which time they'd fallen to just 10 games above the .500 mark. Pittsburgh wouldn't sniff first place again, but would rally in September to come in second, four games behind the pennant-winning Cubs, with a record of 86–68.

Gibson's 1933 Pirates bolted from the starting block like Jesse Owens and held first place until May 31 before descending as low as fifth in late August. Another torrid September was necessary in order for the Pirates to finish second again, five games in back of Bill Terry's New York Giants, with a record of 87–67. In 1934, Pittsburgh again got off to a fast start and was looking down at the rest of the National League on May 27, before beginning to fade. Gibson wouldn't be around to guide the Pirates to another furious finish.

Following a meeting with team president Bill Benswanger and secretary Sam Watters, Gibson "retired" as manager, giving way to his star third baseman Harold (Pie) Traynor. "Gibson is leaving us on the most friendly terms," said Benswanger, the son-in-law of long-time Pirates owner Barney Dreyfuss. "We both feel the change will be for the best interests of the club. The team has been going badly. Everyone knows that."[2] The Pirates had a record of 27–24 when Gibson "retired," having lost 16 of their last 27 games.

Traynor had been a Pittsburgh mainstay since 1922 and was the starting third baseman on the 1925 world's champions and the 1927 pennant-winners. He couldn't light a spark under the Pirates in 1934, however. The club won just 47 games and lost 52 for its new manager, finishing fifth with a record of 74–76. Traynor managed the Pirates through 1939.

If Gibson had "retired" as Pirates manager, without any persuasion from Benswanger, he made the retirement stick and never managed in the major leagues again. He quit with a record of 413–344 and three runner-up finishes to his credit.

Cincinnati Reds
Bob O'Farrell to Chuck Dressen

Bob O'Farrell had been fired after one season as manager of the St. Louis Cardinals, despite leading the club to a second-place finish with 92 victories in 1927. He had to wait seven years to be given a second chance, and he took command of a team with far less talent than the Cardinals had.

Cincinnati hadn't enjoyed a winning season since 1928, and O'Farrell wasn't able to break the streak. His team lost its first three games, alternated between sixth, seventh and eighth places through June 2, then dropped into the basement to stay on June 6. After 90 games, general manager Larry MacPhail had seen enough. He worked out a deal with the Nashville club of the Southern Association to obtain its manager, 35-year-old Chuck Dressen, who'd piloted the team to the first-half championship of the league's split season. Dressen had played for the Reds from 1925 until 1931, batting a career-high .292 in 1927 and .291 in 1928. He inherited a team with a 30–60 ledger from O'Farrell, who was given the option of sticking with the Reds as a catcher for the remainder of his contract, which ran through the 1935 season. O'Farrell, who'd seen action in 44 games in 1934, chose instead to be released and signed with the Cubs.

Cincinnati's problems were too numerous for Dressen to fix during what was left of the 1934 season. The Reds won one of every three games they played for O'Farrell, and they did just about the same for Dressen, winning 21 and losing 39. Burt Shotton won a game as interim manager between O'Farrell's departure and Dressen's arrival, giving the eighth-place Reds a final mark of 52–99. They finished 42 games behind the pennant-winning Cardinals.

O'Farrell never managed again. His season and a half managing the Cardinals and Reds produced a record of 122–121. Dressen's long career in various dugouts in the National and American leagues was just starting.

1935

Cleveland Indians
Walter Johnson to Steve O'Neill

Walter Johnson probably wished he stayed on his farm in Maryland.

Some players should be associated with one team and one team only. Johnson won 416 games pitching for the Washington Senators from 1907 through 1927 and 350 managing the Senators from 1929 through 1932. He was team president Alva Bradley's surprise choice to take over from the deposed Roger Peckinpaugh as manager of the Cleveland Indians in June of 1933. It was a bad fit.

Johnson's players failed to respond to his leadership, although the club improved from 75 victories in 1933 to 85 in 1934. And Cleveland's fans, for some unknown reason, took an immediate dislike to Johnson, as did the city's baseball writers. The situation deteriorated to the point that the *Cleveland Press,* in a bold-print front-page headline late in the 1934 season, demanded Johnson's dismissal. Bradley responded by signing his manager to a contract for 1935.

Lethargic play and a player insurrection that may have only existed in Johnson's mind doomed him in 1935. Johnson insisted veteran catcher Glen Myatt, an Indian since 1923, and veteran third baseman Willie Kamm had masterminded what he called an "anti-Johnson" bloc and were poisoning the minds of the club's young players. Both players were released as the fans howled their displeasure. By June, management had instructed the team's concessionaire at League Park to serve beer and soft drinks in paper cups only, fearing that the patrons would hurl glass bottles at Johnson when he left the home team's dugout.

Despite the chaos, the Indians moved into second place on June 20 and stayed there for 11 days. They got as close as 2½ games behind the front-running Yankees before five straight losses to the eventual champion Tigers, July 1 through July 4, sent them on a skid that cost Johnson his job.

Bradley's contribution to baseball was the oft-quoted bromide "I hire the manager, the public fires him." And there can be no doubt that Cleveland's fans fired Johnson. By Sunday, July 28, with the Tigers in town, Cleveland was 9½ games out of first. Only 5,000 fans were in League Park to watch the Indians battle the league-leaders, and, according to newspaper accounts, most of them were cheering for the visitors, who won the game.

Despite his personal fondness for Johnson, Bradley couldn't hold out any longer. He called the manager to his office on July 29 to give him the bad news. One of the reasons Bradley cited for making a change was the obvious fact that "the fans are mad at you."[1] Steve O'Neill, one of Johnson's coaches and a former Tribe catcher, would take over as manager immediately. Johnson stoically accepted his fate, but asked his boss for a favor. He explained that the Indians were scheduled for a six-game road trip to Chicago and Detroit and would probably lose several of those games. Johnson didn't think it would be right for O'Neill to start his new job on a losing streak.

"Let me take the club west, and the minute we get back to Cleveland, you can announce my resignation, no matter how the trip goes," said Johnson.[2] Bradley agreed. The Indians lost five of the six games and announced Johnson's resignation on August 5.

Bradley managed to keep a straight face as he told reporters that Johnson's resignation "has not been suggested or requested by me or, so far as I know, by any of the owners of the Cleveland club. It is with regret that I bow to his wishes."³ And Bradley was being truthful. He had not requested Johnson's resignation. He had fired Johnson, although he hadn't wanted to. He felt the fans had demanded it.

Said O'Neill of the opportunity the Indians had given him, "We've got to hustle, and beyond doing my best to make the boys hustle, I haven't any immediate plans. Walter Johnson had plenty of hard luck, and there wasn't much of anything he could do about it, but I have a pretty strong suspicion that there's going to be a turn for the better soon. We may not be pennant contenders anymore, but we're too good a ball club to be down in the second division."⁴

WALTER JOHNSON: Johnson pitched 20 seasons for the Senators, then won 350 games as their manager from 1929 through 1932. He spent two regrettable years managing the Indians from June of 1933 until August of 1935.

Bradley saluted the departing Johnson by saying, "Walter is one of the finest gentlemen I've ever met. He is a man who couldn't but be respected by everyone who really knows him. And as a manager? Well, who could have done better with the breaks he got? I've told Walter that I couldn't understand why he wanted to take everything that went with managing a ball club. But he's all courage, as he's proved to me often."⁵

O'Neill's Indians came alive after Johnson departed, winning 36, losing 23 and finishing at 82–71, in third place, 12 games behind the pennant-winning Tigers. The strong finish created hope that the 1936 Tribe could play at such a pace for a full season and contend for an elusive pennant. It also launched a long and successful career for O'Neill as a big-league manager.

Johnson never managed again. His career record as a big league skipper was 529–432, with one second-place finish.

1937

St. Louis Browns
Rogers Hornsby to Jim Bottomley

From all accounts, no one saw this one coming. Not even with the St. Louis Browns bouncing between seventh and eighth places since May 18. Even with his pathetic club jousting with the equally pathetic Philadelphia Athletics in an effort to stay out of the American

League's basement, Browns owner Donald Barnes steadfastly supported his manager, Rogers Hornsby. Until July 21.

Following a double-header loss to the Yankees at Sportman's Park that dropped the Browns 29 games behind the league-leaders with exactly half the season to go, Barnes issued a terse statement to the press: "For the best interests of the club, Rogers Hornsby has been relieved of the management, effective at once."[1] Barnes also fired Charlie O'Leary, Hornsby's top coach. Barnes brought former Cardinals manager Gabby Street in to replace O'Leary and promoted former Cardinal star "Sunny" Jim Bottomley, who was then a Browns coach, to succeed Hornsby for the remainder of the season. According to the Associated Press, the decision to change managers surprised even the Browns' top brass. Barnes, aside from his brief statement to the press, wasn't talking. Neither were Hornsby nor O'Leary.

Barnes did mention that Hornsby would not be paid for the rest of the season, due to a clause in his two-year contract extension, signed in 1935, which stipulated that Barnes owed him nothing if he was terminated. The contract paid Hornsby $18,000 per season.

Hornsby's tenure with the Browns, which ended just eight days short of four full seasons, had been rocky. In addition to the constant losing and tiny crowds at Sportman's Park (Hornsby's 1935 Browns played before just 80,922 spectators at home, an average of 1,051 per game), Hornsby found himself at odds with several of his players. He'd fined and suspended catcher Rollie Hemsley for breaking training rules during a road trip shortly before Barnes fired him. Hornsby had a fistfight with pitcher Dick Coffman in 1935 (Coffman was later released) and feuded with outfielder Julius (Moose) Solters, shortstop Lyn Lary and pitcher Paul Andrews in 1936. The trio was traded to Cleveland.

The Browns didn't improve for Bottomley, winning 21 and losing 56. Overall, St. Louis won just 46 games and lost 108, finishing 56 games out of first place and 9½ games behind seventh-place Philadelphia. It was Bottomley's first and last managerial job. Street would replace him for 1938. Hornsby's career as a major league manager wasn't over, although it wouldn't resume for 15 years.

Cincinnati Reds
Chuck Dressen to Bobby Wallace

It wasn't Chuck Dressen's fault that the Cincinnati Reds, with their 51–78 record, were in last place, 27½ games behind, after splitting a double-header with the Cardinals on September 12. Reds general manager Warren Giles admitted as much. But that didn't stop Giles from firing Dressen and coaches Tom Sheehan and George Kelly the next day.

"There have been many contributing causes to the failure of the Reds this season," Giles said in announcing Dressen's dismissal, "and by no means are we placing full responsibility on Charlie and his assistants."[2] To guide the Reds for the rest of the season, Giles chose the team's chief scout, Roderick (Bobby) Wallace, a former major league pitcher and shortstop whose career began with the Cleveland Spiders of the National League in 1894. The 64-year-old Wallace hadn't managed in the big leagues since 1912, when he was fired by the Browns after 40 games. The Reds showed absolutely no respect for Wallace and his lifetime of service to baseball and lost 20 of the 25 games he managed. Cincinnati staggered home in eighth place, its record of 56–98 leaving it 40 games behind the pennant-winning New York Giants.

Dressen would manage again. Wallace wouldn't. The future Hall of Famer's major league managerial record was a dismal 62–154.

1938

Chicago Cubs
Charlie Grimm to "Gabby" Hartnett

Winning a pennant … or two … only guarantees a manager a limited amount of job security. No fewer than three flag-winning managers, two of them multiple pennant winners, learned that the hard way in 1938.

The first to be let go was "Jolly Cholly" Grimm, who'd replaced Rogers Hornsby as the Cubs' manager in August of 1932 and led the team to a pennant … and a World Series loss in four straight games at the hands of the New York Yankees. Grimm's Cubs captured another pennant in 1935, only to lose a hard-fought seven-game World Series to the Detroit Tigers. Chicago finished second in 1936, five games behind the New York Giants, and played bridesmaid to the Giants again in 1937, finishing two games back.

Grimm's 1938 team started strongly and was in first place on June 7 before faltering. The Cubs plummeted to fourth place on June 29 and were just three games above .500 (38–35) on July 12. They then reeled off seven straight victories, but that wasn't enough to save Grimm's job. On July 20, the day after the streak ended with a loss to the Dodgers at Wrigley Field that dropped the Cubs 5½ games out of first, owner P.K. Wrigley made the switch.

"The decision to change was not a sudden one," said Wrigley, who had been accused of being not overly concerned with his baseball club. "I have been thinking about it for some time. In fact, I have thought about it so much that I have lost sleep, and have almost lost my appetite. Charlie Grimm has done a swell job, but I decided that a change would be best for the organization. Grimm gave us everything that he had, but the club has not done as well as we felt it should. I had decided a change would be of advantage to the club, and if anything was to be done, it should be done now. I believe the man who can do the most for the Cubs is Leo Hartnett."[1]

Hartnett agreed. "I am as happy as a kid with a new toy," exuded the new Cubs manager. "I only hope I'm as lucky as a manager as I have been as a ball player. If I am, we should do all right. I had no idea what was in the air, although the papers have been full of talk of a change. It's not the first time they've talked about it in print. I'm not figuring on any changes right away. One thing, I don't want my guys on the field until one o'clock before a game. They'll get tired enough playing ball."[2]

Grimm apparently hadn't read the newspapers Hartnett referred to. "We lost yesterday, but I didn't have any thought that Mr. Wrigley was planning to let me go. Today, he called me up to his … apartment and said we had better talk over the situation. The club is in fourth place now. He decided a change would help and I guess it will. Leo has everything it takes to make good, personality, ability and spirit. I'll stick around a few days and give Leo any help he needs. I don't know what I'll do, except I hope to stay in baseball."[3]

Grimm did stay in baseball. Before he could head for his home in the St. Louis area to unwind for awhile, he was hired by Chicago's WBBM radio to help broadcast Cubs games for the rest of the season.

Wrigley's decision to change managers proved to be brilliant. Just as the Cubs had rallied after Grimm replaced Hornsby in 1932, they got hot for Hartnett and surged past the Pirates and Giants to win the pennant by two games. The most important of the 44 games the Cubs won for Hartnett (against 27 losses) came on September 28 at Wrigley Field. Hartnett's famous "homer in the gloamin'" off Pittsburgh relief ace Mace Brown gave the Cubs a dramatic 6–5 victory and all but clinched the pennant. A 10-game late–September winning streak had kept alive the Cubs' streak of winning pennants every third year (1929, 1932, 1935 and 1938).

Unfortunately for Wrigley and Hartnett, the Cubs kept another streak alive in October. They were swept by Joe McCarthy's Yankees and lost their sixth straight World Series.

Hartnett's 1939 Cubs dropped to fourth place, and his 1940 team came in fifth. That was the end of his career as a manager. His clubs won 203 and lost 176. Grimm's career as a dugout strategist was merely on hold. He'd be summoned back to the Cubs dugout by Wrigley in 1944, and have the Cubs back in the World Series the next year.

Detroit Tigers
"Mickey" Cochrane to Del Baker

The second pennant-winning manager to feel the sting of his boss's guillotine in 1938 was Gordon (Mickey) Cochrane. Cochrane's career started in 1925, when he joined the Philadelphia Athletics. Connie Mack's club was slowly emerging from the abyss into which he'd plunged it in 1915. Mack was putting together the pieces of the team that would win three pennants and finish second three times from 1927 through 1932, and the man who came to be known as "Black Mike" was one of those pieces. Cochrane batted over .320 six times in his nine seasons with the Athletics and hit .400 in the 1929 World Series, which Philadelphia won from the Cubs in five games. When Mack sold off the players from his second dynasty, Cochrane found himself with Detroit in 1934. Tigers owner Frank Navin paid Mack $100,000 for Cochrane's contract. He was immediately named player/manager.

Cochrane's 1934 Tigers won the team's first pennant in 25 years but lost a nasty World Series to Dizzy Dean's St. Louis Cardinals in seven games, the seventh being an 11–0 Cardinals romp in Detroit's Navin Field. The Tigers won another pennant for Cochrane in 1935 and outlasted the Cubs in seven games in the World Series for Detroit's first world's championship.

Cochrane's playing career, which was winding down when he arrived in Detroit, ended in 1937 due to a beaning he suffered during a game in 1936. Cochrane played in just 44 games in '36 and 27 more in '37. He also was forced to hand the reins of the club over to coach Del Baker for significant periods (34 games in 1936 and 54 games in 1937) as he dealt with the effects of the beaning. Detroit finished second both years, far behind the pennant-winning Yankees.

Cochrane was a bench manager in 1938, and the Tigers were struggling in sixth place on July 21 when they launched an eight-game winning streak that pulled them back to the .500 mark at 46–46. They were still 12½ games out of first, however, and when the winning streak was followed by losses in five of the next six games, owner Walter Briggs decided to make a change. Baker was again placed in charge of the Tigers, but not on an interim basis.

Though Briggs declined to say Cochrane had been fired, Cochrane made it clear that he was. "It was agreed that he would no longer continue his connection with the Detroit baseball company," explained Briggs. "I sincerely regret the termination of our baseball relationship, both from a personal standpoint and because of the contribution which Mickey Cochrane made to Detroit and the club when he came here as manager and catcher five years ago. But it seems apparent to both of us that for the good of the club, and in justice to the supporting fans, a change should be made."[4]

Cochrane didn't have a lot to say, but what he said didn't sound at all as if the decision to change managers had been a mutual one between himself and Briggs. "There is nothing I can say except that I am out. I haven't had time to think of anything. I was told after the game [a 14–8 loss to Boston] that I was through. I want to get my bearings before I say anything."[5]

Detroit's new manager said he had no immediate plans to tinker with the Tigers' lineup. "Believe me, it was a distinct surprise when Briggs offered me the job of manager," said Baker. "I want to say that I never worked for a finer man than Cochrane and at no time did we ever have any trouble."[6]

Briggs defended his decision to fire a local hero. "This has not been an easy task for me to perform. When Charlie Grimm was fired as leader of the Chicago Cubs a few weeks ago, he said, 'That's baseball.' Cochrane said the same thing at our conference today."[7]

Many observers felt Cochrane, while a great leader on the field, wasn't an effective bench manager, and Baker may have proven that to be true, taking over a fifth-place team with a 47–51 record and guiding it to a 37–19 finish for an overall record of 84–70. Baker's 1939 club came home a lackluster fifth (81–73), but his 1940 Tigers won a tight pennant race with the Indians and extended Bill McKechnie's Reds to seven games before losing the World Series. Baker managed the Tigers through 1942.

Cochrane never managed in the major leagues again. He fashioned a record of 361–262 with two pennants, a world's championship, and two second-place finishes.

St. Louis Cardinals
Frankie Frisch to Mike Gonzalez

The third World Series-winning manager to get the axe in 1938 was Frankie Frisch, who, according to reports, was not so subtly shoved out the door by Cardinals general manager Branch Rickey, even though it was owner Sam Breadon who made the decision to dismiss the Fordham Flash after five years on the job.

Frisch couldn't duplicate the success of his rookie year as a manager. The 1934 "Gas House Gang" Cardinals won the pennant and the World Series. Frisch's next three St. Louis clubs finished second, second, and fourth.

Breadon said he didn't hold Frisch accountable for the Cardinals' 63–72 record, but "I believe a change in managers is necessary for 1939. Frank has been with us longer than any other manager since Branch Rickey. I do not blame him for the condition of the club this year. He has not done anything we can find fault with, and he has been a good manager."[8]

Frisch may have been the only manager in major league history to be relieved of his duties during a game. He was coaching at first base in the first inning of a game against Pittsburgh when his firing was announced. He walked off the field immediately, went into the Cardinals' clubhouse, and cleaned out his office. The usually talkative Frisch had nothing to say about his dismissal.

Breadon had signed Frisch for 1938 over Rickey's objections. He revealed that New York Giants manager Bill Terry had asked for permission to talk with Frisch after the 1937 season. "At that time, Rickey, Frisch and I had a meeting. We decided Frisch could go to the Giants if he could better himself. Two months later, however, Frisch signed a contract for 1938 with the Cardinals."[9]

Frisch was succeeded by one of his coaches, Mike Gonzalez, who led the Cardinals to eight wins and eight losses for a final record of 71–80 and a sixth-place finish.

Frisch wasn't through as a major league manager. He'd spend 9½ seasons managing the Pirates and Cubs, but would never again come close to the glory he had led the Cardinals to in 1934.

1940

St. Louis Cardinals
Ray Blades to Billy Southworth

Ray Blades was born too soon. Forty years too soon.

Blades believed a pitching staff was meant to be used, and he used his Cardinal staff liberally in 1939. Three of the four busiest pitchers in the National League were Cardinals, including Clyde Shoun, whose 53 appearances topped the league's hurlers. Rookie Bob Bowman's 51 appearances were third, and Curt Davis was fourth, pitching in 49 games. No St. Louis pitchers were to be found among the league leaders in complete games.

Blades's manipulation of his pitchers was considered deft by some and crazy by others in 1939, when his Cardinals finished second with 92 victories, trailing the pennant-winning Reds by five games. It represented an improvement of 11 games over the club's 1938 finish. But when the Cardinals faltered early in 1940, Blades's propensity for yanking his starters and using his bullpen became a joke, not only in St. Louis but around the National League.

On June 7, the day Blades was dismissed with the Cardinals in sixth place, sporting a record of 14–24, a creative writer with the Associated Press called him Ray (I Love a Parade) Blades and suggested his habit of using four and five pitchers per game had cost him his job. That would change when Billy Southworth took over.

"When I start a pitcher, I expect him to finish, unless he is batted out of the box or something unforeseen happens,"[1] said Southworth, sounding like most managers of his era, as he assumed command of the Cardinals for the second time. Coach Mike Gonzalez kept the seat warm until Southworth arrived, losing five of six games. St. Louis was in seventh place, 15½ games out of first, with a record of 15–29 when Southworth began his second tour of duty on June 14. He had the cure for what ailed the Cardinals, and led the team to 69 victories against 40 losses the rest of the way. As to Southworth's handling of his pitchers,

Shoun's 54 appearances again led the National League, but no other Cardinal hurler pitched in more than 38 games.

The Cardinals finished third (84–69) in 1940 and were on the brink of a dynasty. St. Louis would finish second, 2½ games behind Brooklyn in 1941, and Southworth would lead the team to three straight pennants from 1942 through 1944. The Cardinals would stun Joe McCarthy's Yankees in five games in the 1942 World Series, and defeat the Browns in six games in the only all–St. Louis World Series in 1944.

Blades would serve as the Dodgers' interim manager for one game in 1948, as the club waited for its new manager, Burt Shotton, to arrive following the resignation of Leo Durocher. The Dodgers won that game, giving Blades a lifetime record of 107–85. Gonzalez, in a pair of interim stints with the Cardinals, won nine games and lost 13.

1941

St. Louis Browns
Fred Haney to Luke Sewell

Not often had it been said during their 51-year existence that big things were expected from the St. Louis Browns, but that was the case in 1941. The team Fred Haney had taken over two years earlier improved from 43 victories in 1939 to 67 in 1940, and off-season trades for pitchers Johnny Allen, Denny Galehouse, Fritz Ostermueller and George Caster had Browns fans talking pennant ... well, at least talking first division as the 1941 season approached. The last time St. Louis had finished as high as fourth had been 1929, but the Browns were supposed to be the most improved team in the American League.

As the season opened, however, Haney's club looked a lot like the Browns who'd been the American League's personal punching bag for more than a decade. St. Louis lost seven of its first 10 games to fall into the AL basement, emerged for two days, then resumed its cellar-dwelling status until May 28. The club alternated between seventh and eighth place until June 4 when, despite consecutive victories over Washington that improved the Browns' record to an unsightly 15–29, owner Donald Barnes decided to make a change. Haney reportedly had expected to be fired on June 1, when the Browns returned from a 19-game road trip on which they'd won only six games. Barnes waited three days before dropping the axe.

The consensus was that former Browns catcher Rick Ferrell, who'd been traded to the Red Sox in 1933 and had returned to St. Louis from Washington on May 15 in exchange for pitcher Vern Kennedy, had been obtained to replace Haney as manager. Barnes selected a catcher as his new manager, but it wasn't Ferrell. Barnes asked the Cleveland Indians, who were in first place at the time, for permission to talk to coach Luke Sewell. Sewell joined the Indians in 1921 and became their regular catcher the following year. He was traded to Washington in 1933, moved on to the White Sox in 1935, and returned to Cleveland as a player/coach (mostly coach) in 1939. Sewell accepted Barnes's offer to manage the Browns. He left with the blessing of his former employer.

"I would have preferred that he stay on indefinitely," said Indians team president Alva Bradley, "but I told him I wouldn't stand in his way if he believed the Browns' proposition offered him a chance to better himself. He is a fine young man, and a smart one, and I believe he will make a good manager."[1]

Said Cleveland general manager C.C. (Cy) Slapnicka, "I don't believe St. Louis could have made a better managerial selection. I regret exceedingly that Sewell decided to leave us."[2] Tribe manager Roger Peckinpaugh had nothing but praise for his former confidant: "I wish Luke nothing but the best of luck. He has been an invaluable lieutenant to me and I'm going to miss him, but I'm glad he has got the chance to do what he wants to do."[3]

Haney was diplomatic after losing his first major league managing job: "I'm glad to see a fellow like Sewell get the job, and I'll bet the Browns wind up in fourth or fifth place."[4]

Sewell was going to give himself time to get thoroughly acquainted with his new team before making any dramatic changes. "I plan no revolutionary changes, and that goes for the coaches as well as the players," he said.[5] One of the Browns' coaches, Johnny Bassler, had been a teammate of Sewell's in Cleveland in 1940. Sewell said he believed he could fix the pitching problems that had plagued St. Louis through the first two months of the season.

The Browns didn't burn up the American League for their new manager, but they played better for Sewell than they had for Haney. St. Louis won 55 and lost 55 to finish sixth with a final record of 70–84, the team's best showing since its fourth-place finish of 1929. The Browns had accumulated some talent, and Sewell knew how to use it. Helped immeasurably by the wartime manpower shortage, Sewell would lead the Browns to their only pennant in 1944.

Haney's career as a manager wasn't over. He'd take over the Pittsburgh Pirates' dugout in 1953.

1943

Philadelphia Phillies
"Bucky" Harris to Freddie Fitzsimmons

There was a reason the Philadelphia Phillies were the first major league franchise to rack up 10,000 losses. After decades of penny-pinching ownership, first under William F. Baker, and then Gerry Nugent, who became notorious for selling the few talented players his Phillies had in order to be able to pay the players who were unfortunate enough to have to remain, the Phillies were sold to William Cox in 1943. Cox hired Bucky Harris, the former "Boy Wonder" who was appointed manager of the Washington Senators at the tender age of 24 and promptly won two pennants and a World Series, as his manager. Cox also gave Harris a seat on the Phillies' board of directors, of which Cox was chairman.

Harris had been trying for 17 years with the Senators, Tigers and Red Sox to duplicate the success of his first two seasons as a manager. His teams failed to finish higher than fourth. Cox, who served as his own general manager, gave Harris a club the owner was convinced was a contender. He needed only 90 games to decide he'd made a mistake by putting his team in Harris's hands.

The Phillies were in seventh place on July 27, 21½ games out of first. It was Harris's last day as manager. Earlier in the week, Cox had met with Brooklyn Dodgers pitcher/coach

"Fat" Freddie Fitzsimmons and offered him the Phillies' managing job. Fitzsimmons had won 217 games in a career that began with the New York Giants in 1925 and continued with the Dodgers in 1937. Fitzsimmons's 16–2 record led the National League in winning percentage in 1940, but by 1943 he was hanging on only because so many of baseball's best players were serving in the military. He'd won three games and lost four for Brooklyn when Cox asked if he'd be interested in managing the Phillies. Fitzsimmons said he would be.

Fitzsimmons "has been engaged as manager of the Phillies, to assume his duties before the night game in St. Louis tomorrow [July 28]," was all the brief statement released to the press said. Harris's name wasn't mentioned. Making matters worse for Harris, none of his fellow directors bothered to tell him he'd been fired before the statement was released to the newspapers. Harris wasn't personally notified of his dismissal until hours after the newspapers broke the story. The reason given by the board of directors was the standard "for the best interest of the successful operation of the club."

Fitzsimmons was released by the Dodgers and joined his new team. He called his hiring "a great honor" and said he was taking over a team that "has great possibilities." He also said, "I might try to do a little more pitching this year, if I am able."[1] He wasn't.

"This is the most shocking thing that has happened to me in my entire life. I do not understand it," said Harris.[2]

Cox hadn't put together a contender, and Fitzsimmons couldn't turn it into one. The Phillies won 26 and lost 38 for their new manager, finishing seventh with a record of 64–90, 41 games behind the pennant-winning Cardinals. Fitzsimmons's career as a major league manager would be brief. Harris's career had many years to go.

Cox's penchant for gambling would force baseball commissioner Kenesaw Mountain Landis to order him to sell the Phillies after the 1943 season.

1944

Chicago Cubs
Jimmie Wilson to Charlie Grimm

In sports, there's a tendency to seek the best and worst of everything. Based strictly on the numbers, it can be argued that Jimmie Wilson was among the worst managers in major league history.

Wilson, a catcher, broke into the major leagues with his hometown Phillies in 1925. He was traded to the Cardinals in 1928, as the team was on its way to the National League pennant. Wilson backstopped for three St. Louis championship clubs, including the 1931 World Series winners. Traded back to the Phillies after the 1933 season, Wilson's career steadily wound down until he played in just three games for the Phillies in 1938. He hooked up as a coach with Bill McKechnie's Cincinnati Reds in 1939, just in time to cash World Series checks that season and the next, as the Reds lost to the Yankees in 1939 but beat the Tigers in 1940. Wilson came out of retirement, at age 40, following the tragic suicide of Cincinnati catcher Willard Hershberger, to play 16 regular season games and catch six of the seven games against Detroit in the 1940 World Series, batting .353 and helping the Reds win their second world's championship.

Wilson managed the Phillies as well as playing for them from 1934 through 1938, never winning more than 64 games, losing at least 100 twice, and never finishing higher than seventh. Nonetheless, he was offered the Cubs managerial job after his heroic effort in the 1940 World Series.

Wilson's Cubs came home sixth, sixth and fifth in his three full seasons as manager, always losing more games than they won. In his eight full seasons as a big league manager, Wilson's clubs never posted a winning record. But a first-division finish was anticipated in 1944, and Chicago started the season with a victory in its opener against the Reds in Cincinnati. It was the last game Wilson would win as a manager.

Nine consecutive defeats followed, and on April 30, owner P.K. Wrigley summoned Wilson and Cubs vice president and general manager Jimmy Gallagher to his office. "We simply got together to see what could be done," explained Wrigley. "Wilson offered to resign, hoping his resignation might improve the club."[1] Wrigley accepted the resignation.

"If you can't win in baseball, you'd better get out, and I thought it would be the best thing for me to step out. I don't have any squawks of any kind. Both Wrigley and Gallagher have given me excellent treatment," said Wilson.[2]

Wrigley found Wilson's replacement in Milwaukee, where former Cubs manager Charlie Grimm had the Brewers in first place in the American Association. Grimm's Cubs didn't recover sufficiently from their dismal start to challenge for the pennant, but he moved them into the first division, although their record remained below the .500 mark. The Cubs were 74–69 under Grimm and 75–79 overall, losing one game for coach Roy Johnson while they waited for Grimm to take over. Chicago finished 30 games out of first place.

Things would be much different in 1945. Grimm would guide the Cubs to 98 victories and a pennant. They'd lose a rematch of the 1935 World Series to Detroit.

Wilson's managerial career was over. His record was a miserable 493–795. His teams won just 40 percent of their games.

1945

Philadelphia Phillies
Freddie Fitzsimmons to Ben Chapman

Hope for the seemingly hopeless Philadelphia Phillies arrived after the 1943 season in the person of Robert Carpenter, heir to the DuPont chemical company fortune. Carpenter bought the Phillies from William Cox, whose involvement with gamblers made commissioner Kenesaw Mountain Landis nervous. Unlike previous owners of the Phillies, Carpenter had cash and was willing to spend it to make his team relevant again in the National League.

Carpenter hired former major league pitcher Herb Pennock as his general manager. Pennock chose to keep the manager he inherited from Cox, "Fat" Freddie Fitzsimmons. The Phillies finished last in 1944 for Fitzsimmons, winning 61 and losing 92, and were plodding along in eighth place again in 1945 with an 18–51 record, 23½ games out of first place, when

Fitzsimmons came to the conclusion he was part of the team's problem. After a particularly demoralizing 9–1 drubbing by the Cardinals at Shibe Park on June 29, Philadelphia's third straight loss, Fitzsimmons resigned.

According to Pennock, Fitzsimmons believed stepping aside "would benefit the club."[1] Pennock's choice to replace Fitzsimmons was 36-year-old Ben Chapman, whose major league career began as an outfielder with the Yankees in 1930 and continued through 1941 with the Senators, Red Sox, Indians, and White Sox. Chapman returned to baseball during the manpower shortage in 1944 as a pitcher with Brooklyn and won five games. He was traded to the Phillies for catcher Johnny Peacock just two weeks before Fitzsimmons resigned.

Chapman had some managerial experience. He'd piloted the Richmond, Virginia, club of the Piedmont League in 1942 and 1944. With the Phillies, as a pitcher Chapman saw action in three games without a decision. As a manager, his record was 28–57. Added to Fitzsimmons's record, the Phillies won 46, lost 108, and finished last.

Fitzsimmons didn't manage in the majors again. His Phillies won 105 and lost 181.

Boston Braves
Bob Coleman to Del Bissonette

Bob Coleman's second tour of duty managing the Boston Braves wasn't any more successful than his first.

Coleman was selected by Braves owner Lou Perini to step in after manager Casey Stengel had been sidelined by an auto accident in the spring of 1943. Stengel's broken leg left him unable to open the season in the Boston dugout. Coleman's Braves won 21 and lost 25 before he turned the club back over to Stengel, who couldn't lift it out of sixth place. Coleman got the job permanently when Stengel was fired at the end of the year.

The Braves finished sixth again in 1944 (65–89) and were languishing in seventh place in 1945 when Coleman resigned. The team had been as much as two games over .500 on July 1 but was slumping, having lost 20 of 29 games since the season's high point. Braves third base coach and former major leaguer Del Bissonette took over a team with a 42–51 record on July 30. Coleman's contract ran through 1946, and general manager John Quinn said, after a brief vacation, Coleman would return to the team in a scouting capacity.

Bissonette's playing career, spent entirely in Brooklyn, spanned five seasons, from 1928 through 1931 and 1933. He retired with a lifetime batting average of .305 and brought some experience as a manager to his new position. Bissonette won the 1944 Eastern League pennant with the Braves' Hartford farm club. He didn't get much of a chance to turn the Braves around, but he did move the club up one position in the standings. Under Bissonette, the Braves were 25–34 to finish sixth with a record of 67–85.

Neither Coleman nor Bissonette ever managed again. Coleman's record was 128–165.

1946

New York Yankees
Joe McCarthy to Bill Dickey

Ironically, Joe McCarthy and the man who derisively called him a "push-button manager" resigned on the same day.

McCarthy had won his last pennant in 1943. World War II took its toll, talent-wise, on the Yankees as it did on every other club, although few people ever thought the day would come when New York would finish behind St. Louis, as in 1944, when the Browns shocked everyone by winning the pennant while the Yankees couldn't keep pace down the stretch and came in third. St. Louis finished ahead of New York again in 1945, although by only a half game as the Browns fell to third and the Yankees dropped to fourth.

McCarthy experienced health problems in 1946. He left the team in Cleveland on May 21 and returned to his home outside Buffalo, New York. On May 24, he officially stepped down as Yankees manager, a job he'd held with uncommon distinction since 1931. His reign had produced pennants in 1932, 1936–39, and 1941–43. McCarthy's Yankees lost only one World Series, in 1942, when they took the first game against the St. Louis Cardinals, and then dropped four in a row. They returned the favor the next year.

McCarthy's letter of resignation to general manager Larry MacPhail said, "It is with extreme regret that I must request that you accept my resignation as manager of the New York Yankees baseball club, effective immediately. My physician advises that my health would be seriously jeopardized if I continued, and this is the sole reason for my decision which, as you know, is entirely voluntary on my part. I have enjoyed our pleasant relationship and was hoping it would continue until we won the championship."[1]

MacPhail responded, "I have been extremely reluctant to accept your resignation, even though I understand the reason why you feel your retirement is best. I am glad to know your services are available to me and to the club in an advisory capacity and I hope you will feel safe to act in that capacity in a very short time."[2] MacPhail announced that catcher Bill Dickey, a Yankee since 1928 and a mainstay on nine pennant-winning teams, would succeed McCarthy.

The official announcement said Dickey would be "the manager of the Yankees for the remainder of the 1946 season and all of 1947."[3] But it didn't work out that way.

"It's going to be a pretty tough task for me to try to fill the shoes of the greatest manager in the history of baseball," Dickey said upon assuming command of the Yankees. "And while I am trying to do it, I'll continue catching as long as I feel that my playing services will help the club."[4] Dickey saw action in just 54 games and batted .261 in 1946, his final year as a player.

Dickey had the support of his teammates, according to pitcher Charlie (Red) Ruffing, Dickey's battery mate since 1930. "It was the logical choice and I know all of the players will co-operate with Bill to the limit," said Ruffing.[5] Dickey's teammates may have cooperated with him, but he wouldn't be satisfied with the cooperation he'd receive from MacPhail.

McCarthy, whose salary was reported to have been $40,000, visited Yankee Stadium on May 29 to say goodbye to his former players. He said he was still a Yankee, and expressed the opinion that the club would keep winning for Dickey as it had for him.

McCarthy was right. The Yankees won 57 and lost 48 for their new manager. Rather than managing through 1947, however, Dickey wouldn't last the season.

Chicago White Sox
Jimmy Dykes to Ted Lyons

It only seemed to frustrated White Sox fans who hadn't seen their team finish higher than third since 1920 that Jimmy Dykes had been the manager forever. Dykes had taken over in 1934 and guided the southsiders' fortunes for better than 12 years before handing in his resignation on May 24 ... the same day Joe McCarthy, the man he'd called a "push-button" manager, also resigned.

Like McCarthy, Dykes had missed time on the bench early in 1946, undergoing surgery for a stomach ailment late in spring training and not managing his first game until May 3. With the White Sox floundering in seventh place in late May with a 10–20 record, Dykes picked the wrong time to ask club president Grace Comiskey for a contract extension. According to the Associated Press, Dykes claimed to have received feelers from other teams interested in his services for 1947, and he wanted to know just where he stood with the White Sox. He found out. Mrs. Comiskey declined to offer him a contract for 1947 with 124 games left to be played in 1946, and the White Sox not doing well. Dykes quit. Mrs. Comiskey appointed former White Sox pitcher Ted Lyons as the club's new manager.

The hiring of Lyons was hailed as the most popular decision Mrs. Comiskey could have made. Lyons pitched 21 seasons for Chicago, tying Walter Johnson's record for pitching longevity with one team. Lyons's first move was to hire another former White Sox hurler, Urban (Red) Faber, as the team's pitching coach.

Lyons managed to coax a 64–60 record out of the White Sox for a fifth-place finish at 74–80. Lyons's 1947 club came in sixth, and his 1948 White Sox lost 101 games and finished last.

Although Dykes hadn't done much in 12-plus seasons in Chicago, he would prove to be in demand as a manager ... although none of the clubs that had reportedly contacted him hired him for the 1947 season, despite his availability.

St. Louis Browns
Luke Sewell to "Zack" Taylor

What have you done for us lately?

Even though Luke Sewell had accomplished the seemingly impossible, winning a pennant with the perpetual doormats known as the St. Louis Browns, it seemed inevitable that the team would sink back to its accustomed position in the league's nether regions, once the players who'd marched off to war came marching back, ready to resume their careers. Sewell brought his defending champions home third in 1945, but when "real" baseball returned in 1946, the Browns, as expected, sank back to the bottom of the American League.

The Browns had been below .500 since May 3. Sewell resigned on August 31, at a meeting with team owner and president Richard Muckerman. At least, that was how Muckerman announced it, using the standard "for the good of the club" reason. Pressed by reporters as to whether Sewell had really resigned or had been fired, Muckerman said only, "Well, the club is down, isn't it?"[6] The Browns were 53–71.

Sewell, whose contract ran through 1947, said the constant losing had been "preying on my mind. Maybe I did a little too much worrying about it. I said to Mr. Muckerman that if I was the difference in the club's winning or losing then I would step aside. The club was not the best to watch that I have ever seen, but I can say the majority of the players gave their best. I have no grievance against anyone. My days in St. Louis were happy ones."[7]

Muckerman promoted coach Jim (Zack) Taylor to finish out the season as manager. The Browns won 13 and lost 17 for Taylor, finishing seventh with a record of 66–88. Taylor returned to the coaching ranks in 1947, but took over the Browns again in 1948 and managed the club through 1951, never winning more than 59 games in a season or finishing higher than sixth.

Sewell was hired to manage the Reds with three games left in the 1949 season.

New York Yankees
Bill Dickey to Johnny Neun

The official announcement of Bill Dickey's hiring to succeed Joe McCarthy as New York Yankee manager stated that Dickey's contract ran through the 1947 season. It didn't, and Dickey wanted to know just what Larry MacPhail's plans for the future were as the 1946 season wound down.

Dickey confronted MacPhail on September 2 and was informed that, public pronouncements to the contrary notwithstanding, no decision had been made as to who would manage the Yankees in 1947, and no decision would be forthcoming until after the season. A week later, MacPhail hired former major league manager Bucky Harris as an "adviser." Dickey got the message and told MacPhail on September 11 he didn't want to be considered for the Yankees' managing job and that he preferred to leave immediately for his home in Arkansas. MacPhail accepted the resignation.

"I regret exceedingly leaving New York," Dickey said to reporters as he checked out of his hotel room in Detroit on September 12. "I have played only with the Yankees, and they will always be my team. I am very grateful to the fans in New York for the way they have treated me through the years. I am sorry my New York association ended just when it did. As Colonel MacPhail said in his statement, it is 'unfortunate' but the circumstances made no other action possible on my part."[8]

Coach Johnny Neun became the third New York manager of 1946. The Yankees won eight and lost six for a final record of 87–67, good for third place, 17 games behind the Red Sox. As Dickey anticipated, Harris was promoted from "adviser" to manager for the 1947 season.

Dickey never managed in the majors again. Neun would land the Cincinnati managerial job in 1947.

1948

New York Giants
Mel Ott to Leo Durocher

It was like the Statue of Liberty had sunk into New York Harbor.

In July of 1948, with his Giants continuing to flounder under the leadership of one of baseball's all-time "nice guys," manager Mel Ott, owner Horace Stoneham asked National League president Ford Frick to approach Dodgers general manager Branch Rickey and ask if Rickey would be willing to release manager Leo Durocher, one of baseball's all-time cantankerous cusses, from his contract. Rickey said yes.

The Dodgers were languishing in fifth place with a record of 35–37 at the All-Star break. Rickey had been less than thrilled with the job Durocher was doing with the defending champions, going so far as to ask the manager if he had quit on his team. When Frick called Rickey on Stoneham's behalf, the Brooklyn general manager was more than willing to let the Giants' owner negotiate with his manager. Rickey hoped Stoneham would make Durocher an offer he couldn't refuse, and Stoneham obliged. A contract calling for a $60,000 annual salary, running through 1949, did the trick. Durocher left the Dodgers to take over the hated Giants.

At his introductory press conference, Durocher emphasized that it was his decision to leave Brooklyn: "I was not dismissed. I resigned, and I feel great about it. The Giants have a great club and I know the players pretty well. I cannot say anything about changes yet, until after I talk it over with Mel."[1] Ott's Giants never finished higher than third (in his first season) and twice finished last ... although they were a game ahead of Durocher's Dodgers when Ott was relieved of his duties. It was a reference to Ott by Durocher that was eventually twisted into the famous expression "nice guys finish last."

Despite Durocher's seeming contempt for the icon he was replacing, Stoneham said it was Ott who suggested that Durocher be offered the Giants job. "Ott suggested that we attempt to get Leo," the owner explained. "So yesterday I called President Ford Frick of the National League and asked him to contact Rickey for me. Then I told Rickey that I would like to have Leo if he was available. I had been led to believe in the past couple of weeks that something was doing. I was agreeably surprised when Rickey gave me permission to talk to Durocher."[2]

Stoneham offered Ott a job in the Giants' front office. Ott accepted, but said he'd take a vacation before starting his new, and vaguely defined, duties. Rickey re-hired an old crony, Burt (Barney) Shotton, to replace Durocher. Shotton had managed the Dodgers to the 1947 pennant while Durocher was serving a year's suspension handed down by commissioner Albert (Happy) Chandler for associating with "undesirables."

Rickey announced, "I have great admiration, fondness and respect for Barney Shotton. Last season, I turned to him in a time of great stress, and he came through brilliantly. I again have turned to him in a time of great stress and feel confident that he will carry on the thorough job of which he has always been capable. We have been friends for 39 years and, while Barney is not as young as he once was, I hope our association will be long and mutually pleasant."[3]

The 63-year-old Shotton's Dodgers went 48–33 the rest of the way, finishing third, 7½ games behind pennant-winning Boston and almost catching second-place St. Louis. Durocher's Giants played only slightly better for him than they had for Ott, winning 41 and losing 38 for a final record of 78–76, good for fifth place.

Philadelphia Phillies
Ben Chapman to Eddie Sawyer

On the same day Leo Durocher ditched the Dodgers, another managerial change took place ... amid considerably less fanfare. Robert Carpenter's Philadelphia Phillies, possessors of seventh place with a record of 37–42, which wasn't bad as far as seventh-place records go, dismissed third-year skipper Ben Chapman.

"I want to put the facts on the line," said Carpenter. "We have decided to make a change. As a matter of fact, Ben and I decided between ourselves that a change might help."[4] Chapman didn't sound as if he and Carpenter agreed on the decision. Like Durocher, he wanted everyone to understand the circumstances surrounding his departure.

"I'm not a quitter. I was left out. Mr. Carpenter is the best friend I've ever had in baseball, and I appreciate everything he has done for me. I don't think we were doing so bad, 2½ games out of fourth place, considering the fact that we were going along with two Class A outfielders, two Class A infielders, and three Class B pitchers."[5] Chapman claimed his firing came as a complete surprise. He said three of his coaches and eight of his players wept openly when he told them Carpenter had dismissed him.

Chapman was replaced on an interim basis by Allen (Dusty) Cooke, described by the Associated Press as a close friend of Chapman's for 20 years. Cooke had been hired as a coach by the ousted manager in 1947. He held the reins for 16 games, winning eight and losing eight, while Carpenter looked for a new manager. He chose 37-year-old Eddie Sawyer, who was managing Philadelphia's Toronto farm team of the International League. Sawyer never played in the major leagues, but spent 11 seasons in the Yankees' system as a player and manager. The Phillies collapsed under Sawyer, winning 23 and losing 40 for a final record of 66–88 and a sixth-place finish, 25½ games behind the pennant-winning Braves.

Better days were ahead, however, for Sawyer and the Phillies. Chapman never managed in the majors again. His career record was 196–276.

Cincinnati Reds
Johnny Neun to "Bucky" Walters

Johnny Neun had compiled an impressive record managing in the New York Yankees' farm system. Neun started his managerial career in Akron, Ohio, in 1935 and eventually managed both of New York's top minor league clubs, Newark and Kansas City, before earning a job as a coach with the big club. Neun took charge of the Yankees for the final 14 games of the 1946 season, after Bill Dickey had resigned, winning eight and losing six. That earned him a shot with the Cincinnati Reds.

Cincinnati had fallen on hard times since winning consecutive pennants in 1939 and

1940, plus the 1940 world's championship. The manager who led the Reds to those titles, "Deacon" Bill McKechnie, had been fired with four games left in the 1946 season and Cincinnati in sixth place. Neun wasn't given a lot of time to turn things around.

Neun's Reds finished fifth in 1947 and were in seventh place when he was fired 100 games into the 1948 season. Cincinnati had won 44 and lost 56, and management decided pitcher Bill (Bucky) Walters, one of the last holdovers from the glory years under McKechnie, could pull the club out of its lethargy. Walters took the job reluctantly.

"I never cared for managing," Walters said after his brief career as a manager ended. "When I was pitching, I could go sit by myself in the clubhouse and nobody would bother me. But as a manager, I'd have to be ready to talk to the press after every game, win or lose."[6] In Walters's case, they were mostly losses. The Reds were 20–33 for their new manager to finish the 1948 season in seventh place with a record of 64–89. Cincinnati was in seventh place again in 1949 when Walters and his 61–90 record were fired and replaced by former St. Louis Browns manager Luke Sewell with three games to go.

Neither Neun nor Walters managed again after being fired by the Reds. Neun's career mark was 125–143. Walters's record was 81–123.

1949

Chicago Cubs
Charlie Grimm to Frankie Frisch

Charlie Grimm had served the Chicago Cubs well. "Jolly Cholly" played for Chicago from 1925 through 1936 and managed the club to pennants in 1932, 1935, and 1945. The only thing Grimm hadn't done was win a World Series for Chicago's north-side baseball fans. When it became clear that 1949 wasn't going to be the Cubs' year, Grimm was booted into the front office and given the title of vice president in charge of baseball.

The new man in charge of the Cubs on the field was former Cardinals and Pirates manager Frankie Frisch. After being fired by the Cardinals in 1938, Frisch caught on with Pittsburgh and managed there from 1940 through 1946. Frisch's 1944 Pirates finished second, a distant 15 games behind Frisch's old St. Louis club. None of Frisch's other Pirate teams finished higher than fourth, and Pittsburgh's management made a change after Frisch brought the team in seventh in 1946.

Frisch took over a last-place team with a record of 19–31 from Grimm and promised only that it would hustle like the Cardinals "Gas House Gang" teams that he managed from 1933 through 1938. Frisch may have delivered the hustle, but he couldn't deliver victories. The Cubs were 42–62 under the "Fordham Flash" and never budged from eighth place, winning 61 and losing 93.

Things wouldn't improve during the rest of Frisch's tenure in Chicago. Grimm would find himself back in the dugout in 1952 with the Boston Braves.

1950

Chicago White Sox
Jack Onslow to "Red" Corriden

Jack Onslow may have been too fiery for his own good. Then again, having to watch the Chicago White Sox play every day would've made anyone hard to get along with.

Onslow's major league career consisted of 40 games: 31 with Detroit in 1912, and nine with the Giants in 1917. He was given the job of reviving the White Sox after they'd lost 101 games for Ted Lyons in 1948 and achieved a slight improvement, moving the team from eighth place to sixth with a record of 63–91. But Onslow's boss, White Sox general manager Frank Lane, wasn't known for his patience, and with Chicago in the American League cellar on May 26, with a record of 8–22, Lane sent his manager packing. The Associated Press described Onslow as a fiery pilot and reported he'd had arguments with several players, which contributed to the White Sox' woes.

Onslow was replaced by one of his coaches, John (Red) Corriden, who was given the job for the rest of the season. His employment could extend into 1951, said Lane, if the White Sox showed marked improvement: "He is hired for the balance of the season. If he can prove himself, he will be permanent. We don't like to change managers."[1]

In addition to promoting the 62-year-old Corriden, the White Sox also made aging shortstop Luke Appling a coach and "adviser." Appling coached first base as the White Sox won Corriden's first game, 6–1, over Cleveland at Comiskey Park. Not many more victories followed, although Corriden did push the White Sox up to sixth place. They won 52 and lost 72 for a final record of 60–94, not nearly good enough to convince Lane to keep Corriden for 1952. Instead, Lane chose a former catcher named Paul Richards as his new manager, and together the two men presided over a new era on the south side.

Corriden didn't manage again. Neither did Onslow, whose lifetime record for 184 games was 71–113.

Boston Red Sox
Joe McCarthy to Steve O'Neill

Joe McCarthy gave it his best shot. But he didn't have any more pennants left.

McCarthy took a year and a half off to recover his health after resigning as Yankees manager in June of 1946. He was persuaded by Boston Red Sox owner Tom Yawkey to return to the dugout in 1948, after Joe Cronin, who'd led the 1946 Red Sox to the pennant and a near-miss in the World Series, moved upstairs to the front office.

McCarthy's Red Sox tied the Cleveland Indians for first place with a 96–58 record in 1948, then lost the American League's first one-game, winner-take-all playoff at Fenway Park, 8–3. Red Sox fans are still scratching their heads over McCarthy's controversial decision to start journeyman pitcher Denny Galehouse in that game. In 1949, the Red Sox took a one-game lead into their season-ending two-game series at Yankee Stadium and promptly lost both games, and the pennant, to Casey Stengel's team.

In late June of 1950, McCarthy, as he had been in 1946, was ordered by his physician to return home to Buffalo, New York, for a long rest. McCarthy was apparently in a testy mood as he got off the plane and took a swing at a photographer who tried to snap a picture of him in his less than robust condition. McCarthy responded to a query as to whether he'd return to the Red Sox later in the season by saying, "We'll talk about that later." He added, "Have you ever felt lousy?"[2]

McCarthy resigned the next day, May 23. He said he was "disgusted after three years of beating my brains in trying to lead the Red Sox to a title. When a man can't help a ball club anymore, it's time to quit. I'm sick and tired and I'm entitled to quit. I feel much better mentally tonight, now that the strain is off." McCarthy said he wouldn't take another managing job: "I've had enough. I just don't want anymore."[3]

Cronin didn't try to talk McCarthy out of resigning and gave the manager's job to coach Steve O'Neill. O'Neill's managerial resume included winning the 1945 World Series with Detroit.

"I'm sorry Joe had to step out," said the new Red Sox manager. "But I am very glad to get another job as manager. It feels mighty good to be back in managerial harness. This is quite a break for me."[4]

STEVE O'NEILL: Like many catchers, O'Neill became a coach and manager. His Cleveland, Detroit, Boston Red Sox and Philadelphia Phillies clubs won 56 percent of their games and never had a losing season.

The Red Sox responded well to O'Neill, who took over a team with a 31–28 record and guided it to 63 wins and 32 losses. Boston's 94–60 record was good for third place, four games behind Stengel's Yankees, who captured their second of five straight pennants. O'Neill's Red Sox came home third in 1951, but their 87–67 record wasn't good enough to save his job. He was replaced by former Cleveland manager Lou Boudreau.

McCarthy made his retirement stick. He never managed again. His career record showed 2,125 victories against 1,333 losses. McCarthy's teams won nine pennants and seven World Series. He finished second seven times and never brought a club home lower than fourth.

1951

Boston Braves
Billy Southworth to Tommy Holmes

The strain of managing a major league baseball team, and being expected to win every season, had taken its toll on Yankees and Red Sox manager Joe McCarthy. It also did a number on Billy Southworth.

After winning three pennants and two World Series with the Cardinals, Southworth accepted the challenge of managing the Boston Braves and led the team to its first pennant in 34 seasons in 1948. By August of 1949, Southworth had to temporarily surrender the Braves managerial post to coach Johnny Cooney in order to recover from what was described as a "near nervous breakdown." Southworth returned in 1950 to lead the Braves to a fourth-place finish, and the club was in fifth place, three games below the .500 mark, when Southworth again voluntarily stepped aside on June 19, 1951. Southworth told owner Lou Perini "somebody else could do a better job."[1]

Southworth admitted disappointment in his club's performance but insisted, "I'm not mad at anyone on the club. I just want to rest up for the remainder of the year."[2] Some of Southworth's players, however, were mad at him. He'd angered some members of the 1948 NL champions by reportedly claiming that he'd won a pennant with a team that belonged in the second division. The 1949 Braves, who finished fourth, voted their manager only a half-share of the post-season money they received, but were overruled by baseball commissioner Happy Chandler, who ordered that Southworth receive a full share ... even though he'd left the team in Cooney's hands in August.

Cooney wasn't interested in taking over the Braves in 1951, so Perini offered the job to recently retired outfielder Tommy Holmes, the manager of Boston's Hartford farm club. Holmes said, "The first I heard about the job was [June 17]. Mr. Perini called and asked if I'd take the challenge. I told him yes. I'm undecided about resuming playing for the Braves. If there's an opening I'll jump right back in. I have some ideas about the Braves outfield and there are certain hitting flaws I hope to correct."[3] Holmes knew a little something about hitting. His career batting average was .302, but he'd bat just .172 for the Braves in 27 games after taking over as manager.

Holmes said he planned no changes to the Boston coaching staff and offered the opinion that the Braves were "a sound ball club in need of a few base hits at the right time." Boston got enough hits at the right time to win 48 games for Holmes while losing 47. Their overall record of 78–76 placed them fourth.

Holmes wouldn't last through the 1952 season. Southworth never managed in the major leagues again. His career record was 1,044–704.

Chicago Cubs
Frankie Frisch to Phil Cavarretta

When Cubs owner P.K. Wrigley decided a change was needed with the team in seventh place under the guidance of Frankie Frisch in July of 1951, he turned to an old first baseman to reverse the team's fortunes.

This time, however, the Cubs didn't call upon Charlie Grimm once again. Wrigley turned to Phil Cavarretta when Frisch was fired or resigned (depending on the source) with a 35–45 record. Frisch's 1950 Cubs had placed seventh with a record of 64–89, and things were going no better in 1951 when the change was made. Cavarretta, a Cub since 1934 and the 1945 National League batting champion with a .355 average, actually fared worse than Frisch, leading the team to a 27–47 record and last-place finish. He'd manage the Cubs through 1953, winning 169 and losing 213. Cavarretta achieved the rare distinction of being fired in spring training of 1954, when he had the nerve to tell Wrigley the Cubs were lousy and could anticipate another long campaign. He was replaced by former Cub third baseman Stan Hack, who led a lousy team through another long campaign.

Frisch's career as a major league manager was over. He did enough winning early in that career with the Cardinals to finish with a winning record (1,138–1,078), one pennant and a world's championship. Frisch never again scaled the heights he reached in his first full season, 1934, when his "Gas House Gang" Cardinals won the World Series.

1952

Boston Braves
Tommy Holmes to Charlie Grimm

The Boston Braves dugout was no place for on-the-job training.
The record indicates that Tommy Holmes had been Braves owner Lou Perini's choice to succeed Billy Southworth in 1951. General manager John Quinn would've preferred a manager with more experience at the major league level, of which Holmes had none when he was hired. That was the reason Quinn gave for firing Holmes on May 31, 1952, and replacing him with veteran Charlie Grimm.

"We have a lot of regard for Tommy Holmes," said Quinn. "But we felt Holmes needed more experience. We selected Grimm because Charlie has had that experience and background, both as a manager in the majors and the minors."[1] Grimm brought 11 seasons of experience, all of them with the Chicago Cubs, to his new position in Boston.

Holmes took his dismissal in stride. "They are wonderful people," he said of Quinn and Perini.

> They probably hated twice as much telling me I was fired as I disliked hearing it. And it's no disgrace to be replaced by Charlie Grimm.
> They told me I needed more experience and apologized for bringing me up so soon. But I don't want them taking the responsibility for my performance. That was my responsibility. If I don't have the stuff, then naturally, that's all there is to it.[2]

Holmes must not have had the stuff, because he never managed in the major leagues again. His record for less than a full season as Braves boss shows a 61–69 record in 130 games. Boston was in seventh place with 13 wins and 22 losses, 13 games out of first place and mired in a four-game losing streak when Holmes was dismissed.

The Braves won 51 and lost 67 for Grimm, finishing sixth with a 64–89 record. More importantly, they attracted just 281,000 paying customers to Braves Field, almost 1.2 million fewer than the club drew during its 1948 National League championship season. Perini came to the conclusion that Boston couldn't, or wouldn't, support two teams and greener pastures beckoned to the west.

In March of 1952, Perini moved the Braves to Milwaukee. Grimm went with them.

St. Louis Browns
Rogers Hornsby to Marty Marion

Like father, like son.

In August of 1932, William Veeck the elder had seen enough of Rogers Hornsby's managerial style and dismissed him as skipper of the Cubs. In May of 1952, William Veeck the younger decided he didn't like Hornsby's style, either.

"I blew one. I shouldn't have signed him in the first place. I had the change in mind for some time,"[3] was Veeck's candid assessment of his decision to sign Hornsby to a three-year contract, at a reported $36,000 per season ... a sizable outlay of cash for the financially ailing Browns. Hornsby had fulfilled less than half a season of that contract when Veeck dismissed him on June 10.

Veeck determined that Hornsby was "unreasonable" in his dealings with the hired hands. "He doesn't consider them as individuals, only as players, something to be manipulated."[4] Hornsby fired back at his former boss, declaring that "no one is going to tell me how to run a ball club. I'm not going to go for any of his screwy ideas."[5]

The Browns were in seventh place with a 22–29 record, although only 7½ games out of first, when Veeck pulled the plug on Hornsby's second tour of duty with the club. The decision earned him the gratitude of his players, who presented him with a 24-inch silver trophy in the team's dressing room at Fenway Park to commemorate the event. The inscription read: *To Bill Veeck for the greatest play since the Emancipation Proclamation. June 10, 1952. From the players of the St. Louis Browns.* Pitcher Ned Garver made the presentation.

"No one is going to tell me how to run my ball club," Hornsby reiterated. "I think I did a good job. The boys played well for me. We got off to a good start and had the crowd with us in St. Louis, and that's what Bill wanted. I'm not sore at anybody."[6] The Browns were 9–6 and in first place on May 1 before retreating to their accustomed home in the second division. Hornsby said he wanted to manage again but would accept "a coaching job if necessary, and if it is the right one."[7] Hornsby hadn't managed in the major leagues since his dismissal by the Browns in 1937. He'd managed Seattle to the Pacific Coast League championship in 1951. He'd also managed Baltimore of the International League, Chattanooga of the Southern Association, and Oklahoma City and Beaumont of the Texas League. Major leaguers, however, apparently chafed under the type of conditions Hornsby's minor leaguers tolerated.

"It's better to have 25 players and no manager than just a manager," said Veeck. "Baseball is a team game. Things must be amicable and they weren't. I called Rogers Sunday and he said 'maybe you don't like my managing' and I said I didn't—that I'd come to Boston to talk with him. It's something I had to do."[8]

Hornsby's replacement, former major league shortstop Marty Marion, had been fired as manager by the Cardinals after the 1951 season, despite a third-place finish and 81–73 record. He said he signed with the Browns as a coach specifically because he didn't want to create the illusion that he wanted another shot at managing. "I'm really surprised. One reason I went with the Browns was because no one could say I was after the manager's job, not with an experienced fellow like Hornsby as manager." Marion planned no immediate changes, saying he wanted "a set ball club—a line-up that will be more or less the same every day. When the pitchers will pitch will be up to them. If a fellow tells me he can work better after three days' rest, he'll get three days' rest. If he needs four, he'll get four. I hope to have a regular rotation."9

The Browns may have felt liberated by the firing of the tyrannical Hornsby, but their performance didn't improve under Marion. St. Louis was 42–61 for its new manager for a record of 64–90 and a seventh-place finish. In 1953, their final season in St. Louis, they came home eighth for Marion with a record of 54–100.

Hornsby would have a major league managing job before the season ended.

Philadelphia Phillies
Eddie Sawyer to Steve O'Neill

Steve O'Neill should have been known as a doctor of baseball. He specialized in curing ailing teams. Only one of the teams O'Neill managed during his lengthy career didn't hire him in mid-season. He was hired to replace Walter Johnson in Cleveland in 1935; Joe McCarthy in Boston in 1950; and Eddie Sawyer in Philadelphia in 1952. Each club performed markedly better after O'Neill took over.

Sawyer, whose 1950 "Whiz Kids" won the Phillies' first pennant in 35 years, resigned on June 27, after a meeting with owner Bob Carpenter. At least, that's how it was announced to the press. Sawyer and Carpenter had been discussing a change in leadership for several days and came to the conclusion Sawyer's departure would be best for the club. The Phillies were in sixth place, 17½ games out of first, with a record of 28–35 when Sawyer stepped down. Sawyer would be retained, doing "special assignment scouting" for Carpenter.

Carpenter called Red Sox general manager Joe Cronin to ask about O'Neill's availability. O'Neill had been let go as Boston's manager despite a third-place finish and 87–67 record in 1951 and was serving as a scout. Carpenter was interested in O'Neill because Steve had signed several bonus-baby prospects for the Red Sox that Carpenter had wanted for the Phillies.

"Cronin telephoned me [June 26] at Louisville and told me that Carpenter was interested in me. He said it was up to me what I wanted to do."10 O'Neill wanted to manage and accepted Philadelphia's offer of a contract running through 1953. He signed the contract in his office in Shibe Park before the Phillies took on the New York Giants on June 28. The Phillies won, 7–2, for their new manager.

The 61-year-old O'Neill confessed to being "a little excited by it all. Everything's going to look the same around here for a little while anyway." O'Neill said he'd keep Sawyer's coaches, Benny Bengough, Cy Perkins, and Dusty Cooke, for the time being. He said he was taking over a club with the best pitching in major league baseball, strong defense, but lacking in power.

"Doc" O'Neill had the right prescription for what ailed the listless Phillies. Philadelphia went 59–32 under the old catcher to finish fourth with a record of 87–67. Sawyer tackled the "special assignments" given to him by Carpenter and bided his time. Phillies fans hadn't seen the last of him.

Detroit Tigers
"Red" Rolfe to Fred Hutchinson

Honesty was the order of the day in 1952. In a burst of candor rare for a team owner, Bill Veeck admitted he never should've hired the abrasive Rogers Hornsby to manage the Browns. In an equally rare moment of honesty, Detroit Tigers owner Walter (Spike) Briggs, Junior, admitted that firing his manager, Red Rolfe, probably wouldn't improve the team's dismal fortunes. But the fans demanded action, and he took a shot.

Rolfe was a stellar third baseman for the New York Yankees from 1934 through 1942, leading the American League in triples (15) in 1936, and in hits (213) and doubles (48) to complement a .329 batting average in 1939. Rolfe was the toast of Detroit in 1950, when he earned "Manager of the Year" honors from *The Sporting News* for keeping the Tigers on top of the AL for most of the season before succumbing to his former team, New York, and finishing second (95–59), three games back. A season and a half later, Detroit was in the AL cellar with a 23–49 record, and Rolfe was the least popular man in town. The Tigers held the distinction of being the only franchise in major league baseball which had never finished a season in last place, and Briggs wanted to keep it that way. He recommended to the club's board of directors on July 5 that Rolfe, and third base coach Dick Bartell, be dismissed.

"I want to tell you the board accepted my recommendation," Briggs said in announcing the firings. "We all appreciated the loyalty of Red and Dick and the fine job they've done. I doubt if there can be any improvement in the ball club, but we've got to find out."[11] Briggs offered the manager's job to first base coach Ted Lyons, who'd been fired as White Sox manager after the 1948 season. Lyons wasn't interested, so Briggs startled everyone by selecting Detroit's 32-year-old relief pitcher, Fred Hutchinson.

Hutchinson had spent his entire career with Detroit, beginning in 1939, serving in the military during World War II, and returning in 1946. Hutchinson won 18 games in 1947, 15 in 1949, and 17 in 1950. He was a rarely-used reliever in 1952, and would pitch in three games in 1953.

Briggs was right about the Tigers being beyond help. Hutchinson could do no more with them than Rolfe had. Just two years removed from chasing the Yankees down to the wire, Detroit finished last for the first time in club history, winning only 50 times while losing 104. The Tigers were 27–55 for Hutchinson, but the fans who demanded Rolfe's firing had been appeased, and Briggs retained his new manager for the 1953 season.

Cincinnati Reds
Luke Sewell to Rogers Hornsby

Luke Sewell had one miracle in him as a major league manager, and that had been achieved when he guided the St. Louis Browns to the 1944 American League championship. The Reds turned to Sewell to replace Bucky Walters with three games remaining in the 1949 season, and the best he was able to do in slightly more than 2½ seasons in Cincinnati were a pair of sixth-place finishes and a seventh-place standing (39–59), 26 games out of first place, on July 29, 1952. Following a double-header loss to the Phillies in Shibe Park, Sewell submitted his resignation to general manager Gabe Paul.

"When you don't win in baseball, the only thing to do is get out," explained Sewell succinctly.[12] Sewell got out of Cincinnati with a record of 174–234 and a career managerial mark of 606–644 ... including the one and only pennant in club history that Browns fans and their descendants will forever cherish. Paul immediately announced that Sewell would be replaced by another former Browns manager, Rogers Hornsby.

"Powel Crosley, Junior [the Reds' owner], and I decided on Rogers Hornsby to lead the Reds because we feel him to be the type best-suited to manage in our particular situation," said Paul. "I am confident he will do a good job."[13] Hornsby had been scouting for Cincinnati since his dismissal in early June by the Browns, but no announcement of his hiring had been made to the public. Hornsby was on a scouting mission when Sewell quit, and the Reds were placed in the hands of coach Earle Brucker until Hornsby could assume his duties on August 5. Cincinnati won three and lost two for Brucker.

The day before he took command, Hornsby was interviewed on a Cincinnati radio station and told his players what they could expect under his leadership:

> The players will set their own curfew rules and there will not be any detectives to watch them once those rules are made; however, I expect every player to live up to what he has promised.
>
> I do not pat a player on the back when he drives in a run, when he singles or when he gets a home run. He must not expect me to kiss him when he hits the all-needed home run. That's his job, otherwise he would not be in the major leagues. I don't pat guys on the back for what they are being paid to do. In that way, perhaps, I'm not a diplomat.
>
> Another thing: the player taken out of the game is not going to the showers. He is going to stay right there on the bench, whether he be a pitcher, catcher, or whatever position. By staying there, the removed hurler might learn what was done to stop a rally. The others, too, should learn what happened to the man who succeeded them. Men can't learn baseball in the showers.
>
> I believe the sacrifice bunt is one of the lost arts. We will try to regain it here.[14]

Cincinnati improved under Hornsby's whip, closing the season with a 27–24 record for another sixth-place finish at 69–85. The improvement didn't carry over into 1953, and by the middle of September, Hornsby had worn out his welcome, just as he'd done everywhere else he played and managed. Hornsby was fired by Paul with eight games to go and the Reds in sixth place, 35 games behind the first-place Brooklyn Dodgers, with a record of 64–82.

Cincinnati was Hornsby's last stop as a manager. His career record for 14 seasons was 701–812 with one World Series title, that being in 1926, his first full season as a manager.

1954

Philadelphia Phillies
Steve O'Neill to Terry Moore

It's rarely a good idea for a manager or coach in any sport to find himself working for a general manager who didn't hire him. Steve O'Neill learned that the hard way.

Roy Hamey's first major move as general manager of the Phillies was to relieve O'Neill of his duties on July 15. As had been the case in Cleveland and Boston previously, the Phillies had spurted after O'Neill replaced Eddie Sawyer midway through the 1952 season. The 1953 Phillies played well for O'Neill, finishing in a third-place tie with St. Louis with an 83–71 record. The 1954 Phillies were essentially treading water, and rumors that Hamey would make a change circulated for weeks before the general manager pulled the trigger.

The Phillies "just decided to change managers," explained Hamey. "The appointment of [Terry] Moore is a shot in the dark. I know that Terry has never managed before, but he's a young man. He has always been an alert, hustling ballplayer. It's the kind of spirit Terry always showed as a ballplayer that I want instilled into our team."[1] Moore patrolled centerfield for the Cardinals from 1935 through 1942, and again from 1946 through 1948. That tour of duty included world's championships in 1942 and 1946. Moore's only experience as a major league manager consisted of two weeks filling in for Marty Marion with the Cardinals in 1951. Nonetheless, Hamey decided he was the man to light a fire under the Phillies, who had apparently grown weary of working for a manager who wasn't afraid to express his opinions to his players. Moore was hired, among other reasons, because he was expected to be less direct with his players than O'Neill. He was described as "quiet and unassuming." His brief tenure in Philadelphia would prove to be anything but quiet.

"I hope you have better luck than I did," said O'Neill to his successor.[2] O'Neill departed with a 40–37 record and the Phillies in third place, 13½ games out of first. Philadelphia was the last stop in O'Neill's career as a major league manager. He retired with a career record of 1,040 victories against 821 defeats. His teams finished second three times, and his 1945 Tigers won the American League pennant and outlasted the Cubs in a seven-game World Series. O'Neill's teams never lost more games than they won.

Hamey didn't show much confidence in Moore, giving him a contract only for the remainder of the 1954 season. Expected to be "quiet and unassuming," Moore clashed with his players quickly. Soon after Moore took over, it was revealed that the Phillies had decided to keep tabs on their employees by assigning private detectives to monitor their off-field activities, with Moore's approval. The players, understandably, didn't appreciate being spied on. They won just 35 while losing 42 for Moore, whose contract wasn't renewed at the end of the year. He never managed in the major leagues again.

1955

St. Louis Cardinals
Eddie Stanky to Harry Walker

"The Hat" replaced "the Brat."

Eddie Stanky was in his fourth season as manager of the St. Louis Cardinals when owner August A. Busch, Junior, decided to move in a new direction. Stanky's 1952 and 1953 teams had finished third, but his 1954 Cardinals had slumped to sixth, and the 1955 club was in fifth place, 10 games out of first, with a record of 17–19 when Busch dipped into the Cardinals' minor league system for a new manager. Stanky, known during his playing days with the Cubs, Dodgers, Braves, Giants and Cardinals as "the Brat," gave way to Harry Walker, who was managing St. Louis's Rochester farm club. Walker, as a player with the Cardinals, Phillies, Cubs and Reds, earned the nickname "the Hat" for his habit of tugging on the bill of his cap before every pitch thrown to him.

"We just felt a change might make things work better,"[1] said Busch of the decision to replace Stanky with Walker. Busch said declining attendance, even though the Cardinals had St. Louis all to themselves with the departure of the Browns to Baltimore after the 1953 season, had nothing to do with his decision to fire Stanky. Stanky would be offered a job in the Cardinals' organization, in an as-yet undetermined capacity. He said he'd stay in baseball "if I have to go to a Class D league."[2]

Walker was in his fourth season as Rochester's manager. His 1954 team finished third, and Rochester was in third place again in 1955 when Walker was summoned to St. Louis. He was replaced in the Rochester dugout by his brother, Dixie, who had been a Cardinal coach under Stanky. Harry Walker was given a contract that would expire at the end of the 1955 season.

The Cardinals, said their new manager, "are a fine young club with a fine future and will go a long way."[3] They went the wrong way under Walker, dropping from fifth place to seventh. They won 51 and lost 67 for Walker for a final record of 68–86. Walker wasn't invited to return in 1956, but it wasn't the end of his managerial career.

Stanky wasn't finished as a manager, either, although a decade would pass before he'd get another chance to call the shots for a major league team.

1956

Milwaukee Braves
Charlie Grimm to Fred Haney

Milwaukee Braves owner Lou Perini had a terse reply when pressed by reporters about the status of his manager, the veteran Charlie Grimm. More specifically, the reporters pressured Perini to give Grimm a vote of confidence, which he refused to do. Perini said an announcement about the manager would be forthcoming, and it was made on June 17. Grimm stepped down after nearly four full seasons at the helm.

The normally talkative Grimm had little to say except, "Let somebody else take a shot at it."[1] Grimm's Braves had finished second, third and second since moving to Milwaukee in 1953. The 1956 club, with a 24–22 record, stood fifth when Grimm decided to give someone else a chance. That someone else turned out to be former Browns and Pirates manager Fred Haney, who'd been dismissed in Pittsburgh after the 1955 season and signed on with Milwaukee as a coach. Haney's three years in Pittsburgh had been even more miserable than the two and a fraction years he'd spent managing the Browns, if such a thing was possible. The Pirates were consistent under Haney, finishing last in 1953, '54 and '55, and never winning more than 60 games in a season.

"He's filling out Charlie's tenure. He's not assured of anything. Time will tell how far he'll go," said Perini.[2] Haney was reluctant to accept the promotion at first. He'd signed with the Braves with the understanding that if Grimm left, he'd leave with him. Haney knew nothing of Grimm's resignation until 20 minutes before the announcement was made public. He refused to take the manager's job until he spoke to Grimm. "When Charlie said 'Go ahead, I want you to take it,' I took it," explained Haney.[3] The new Braves boss said he'd keep coaches Charley Root and Bob Keeley.

Milwaukee had lost 12 of 17 games prior to Grimm's resignation, but snapped out of its slump quickly for Haney. The Braves won 68 and lost 40 the rest of the way to vault from fifth to second place with a record of 92–62. They chased the Brooklyn Dodgers down to the season's final day, finishing one game out of first place.

There is no better example of the fact that a manager is only as good as his players than the managerial career of Fred Haney. Haney's St. Louis and Pittsburgh clubs combined for 288 victories and 526 losses. When he was given talent to work with in Milwaukee, Haney brought the Braves home second in 1956 and won pennants in 1957 and 1958, with his '57 Braves winning the World Series from the Yankees. The Braves tied the Dodgers for first place in 1959, but lost the best-of-three playoff. The loss cost Haney his job.

Haney retired with a career mark of 629–757 that included two pennants, two second-place finishes, and a World Series title.

1957

Washington Senators
Chuck Dressen to "Cookie" Lavagetto

How different might baseball history have been had Chuck Dressen not been so stubborn? Or had Walter O'Malley been more flexible?

After guiding the Brooklyn Dodgers to consecutive pennants in 1952 and '53, Dressen demanded a multi-year contract. O'Malley stuck to team policy and signed Walter Alston to a one-year deal. Alston's Dodgers finished second in 1954 and won Brooklyn's only World Series title in 1955. Dressen was hired to manage the perpetually downtrodden Washington Senators.

Dressen, who was convinced he knew more about baseball than just about anybody, told his players, "Keep it close, boys, and I'll think of something." That belief was put to the test in Washington, where he no longer had Gil Hodges, Jackie Robinson, Pee Wee Reese, Carl Furillo, Roy Campanella or Duke Snider in his line-up, as he had in Brooklyn. Dressen's first two Senators teams finished eighth and seventh, and the 1957 club was buried in last place with a 4–16 record on May 6 when owner Calvin Griffith met with his manager in Detroit and told him a change was needed. Coach Harry (Cookie) Lavagetto, Dressen's top lieutenant in both Brooklyn and Washington, was selected to finish the season as Senators manager.

"I haven't gotten this much attention since 1947,"[1] Lavagetto cracked on his first day in charge. He was referring to the fourth game of the World Series, when his pinch-hit double in the bottom of the ninth inning broke up Yankee right-hander Floyd (Bill) Bevens's no-hitter and lifted the Dodgers to a 3–2 victory.

Lavagetto couldn't lift the Senators out of the American League's basement in 1957. They won 51 and lost 83 for a final mark of 55–99, a distant 43 games behind the first-place Yankees. Lavagetto's club finished last in 1958 and 1959 before inching up to fifth in 1960, the original Senators' final season in Washington. Lavagetto remained the team's manager as it became the Minnesota Twins in 1961.

Dressen would replace Fred Haney as Milwaukee's manager in 1960.

Pittsburgh Pirates
Bobby Bragan to Danny Murtaugh

Bobby Bragan had been the toast of Pittsburgh early in the 1956 season, his first as manager of the Pirates. A club little had been expected from found itself in first place on June 15, and the hiring of Bragan was being hailed as a masterstroke. The Pirates stayed in first place for only three days, however, and by season's end were seventh with a 66–88 record. Bragan's 1957 Pirates didn't tease their fans, stumbling out of the gate and falling into the cellar on May 19. The Pirates alternated between sixth, seventh and eighth places for the next 2½ months, and held seventh place with a 36–67 record when general manager Joe L. Brown fired Bragan on August 3.

"There were a number of reasons Bragan was released," said Brown. "I think it best just to say it was for the good of the team, now and in the future. Anything specific I might charge might be better left unsaid."[2]

The brash Bragan sounded as if he was happy to be finished with Pittsburgh and the Pirates: "I had a lot of jobs in baseball I'd be real bitter about losing, but I can't say the same about this one. It's a result of the oldest rule in the book. When a team doesn't win, the manager has to go, so I'm going. Brown felt it was time to change. It was obvious that our approach to the game clashed in many instances."[3]

Bragan was replaced by Pirates coach Danny Murtaugh, who took the job only after another Pirate coach, Clyde Sukeforth, had turned it down. Pittsburgh played better for Murtaugh than it had for Bragan, going 26–25 over the season's final two months, but still finishing seventh at 62–92. Murtaugh would become a mainstay in Pittsburgh, managing the Pirates for 15 seasons over three separate tours of duty.

Bragan, who wrote a magazine article about the insecurity of a baseball manager's job that would be printed across the country on August 18, had been fired for the first time. It wouldn't be the last.

Kansas City Athletics
Lou Boudreau to Harry Craft

Same record, same result.

Two days after Bobby Bragan was fired by Pittsburgh, Lou Boudreau was dismissed by the Kansas City Athletics. Like Bragan's Pirates, Boudreau's Athletics had a record of 36–67. Also like Bragan's Pirates, Boudreau's Athletics were in seventh place. Kansas City trailed the league-leading Yankees by a whopping 33 games.

Boudreau's dismissal was the first in-season managerial change in the history of the Athletics franchise, discounting the two occasions when Connie Mack turned the Philadelphia Athletics over to his son, Earle, in 1937 (for 34 games) and 1939 (for 91 games.) That's the way it works when the manager also owns the team, as Mack did. Arnold Johnson bought the Athletics from the Mack family after the 1954 season and moved the team to Kansas City in 1955, hiring Boudreau as his manager.

The Athletics finished sixth their first season in Kansas City, losing 91 games, and plunged to the cellar in 1956 with a 52–102 record. Johnson didn't see any improvement as the 1957 season dragged on, and, as owners usually do, he held his manager responsible. "Harry Craft is manager of the Kansas City Athletics for the balance of the season," Johnson announced on August 5. "Craft knows baseball. We'll see what he can do and what developments there are by the time the season ends before we worry about next season. We are disappointed in the showing of the club this year and we are hopeful of improvement. We want a winner. I'm for getting the club up in the league race. The fans like to win as I like to win."[4]

Boudreau had heard the rumors that his days in the Athletics' dugout were numbered, but he insisted he was surprised by the firing, calling it a "severe blow. I didn't think it actually would happen because of the happy situation in Kansas City and the spirit of the front office."[5] The situation Boudreau referred to was the fan support the club had enjoyed since relocating from Philadelphia.

In his autobiography, *Lou Boudreau: Covering All the Bases*, he described how he felt when general manager Parke Carroll gave him the bad news. "I told him nobody could have done better with the players we had. We'd scrapped our building program and wound up with as bad a team as we'd inherited from Philadelphia. But that didn't change anything and I was out of a job. I wasn't resentful because, the truth be told, the travel and the losing—especially the losing—were getting to me. In a way, I was relieved that it was over."[6]

Craft, after being encouraged by Boudreau to accept the Athletics' managing job, said the team had been in a "disorganized state. We have to relieve a lot of the tension on this club. Once we get these players loosened up, I think the Athletics will play the good brand of ball they're capable of playing."[7] The 42-year-old Craft had managed the Yankees' Kansas City farm team in 1953 and 1954. Those clubs undoubtedly possessed more talent than the team he inherited from Boudreau. He said he'd keep coaches Bob Swift and Spud Chandler.

The Athletics improved under Craft, winning 23 of their final 50 games to move up to seventh place with a 59–94 record. Craft's 1958 club finished seventh but won 73 games, the most for the franchise since 1952. The 1959 Athletics, also a seventh-place team, won just 66. Craft was fired after the season, but, like Boudreau, he wasn't through as a big league manager.

1958

Detroit Tigers
Jack Tighe to Bill Norman

After nearly 20 years in the Detroit organization, Jack Tighe was rewarded with the opportunity to manage the club in 1957. Tighe's Tigers finished fourth with a record of 78–76, but when the team got off to a slow start the following season, he wasn't given much time to right the ship. Detroit was in last place, 12½ games out of first, with a record of 21–28 after a 9–4 loss to Boston on June 9. It proved to be Tighe's final game as a major league manager.

"I made up my mind [June 8] that we had to make a change," explained general manager

John McHale. "I think our club has greater potential than it has shown to this point. That potential wasn't being realized, so we made the change for the good of everybody concerned."[1]

"I'm surprised to a degree, but not too much, though," said the deposed Detroit skipper. "You sit and wonder—if your club doesn't perk up you know there might be a change. Right or wrong, that's the way it has always been and will always be. I can't blame the Tigers. We're in last place and lost five of our last seven games. The way the club was going, I'd say a change was in order. I figured that if we didn't start moving I'd be called into the front office Monday morning as soon as we got home."[2]

Tighe wasn't afraid to criticize players he thought were just going through the motions. He'd accused some of the Tigers of laziness and not hustling. "I don't know what's wrong with the club," he admitted. "The morale has been good, but we just can't seem to get going."[3]

That was why Bill Norman, the manager of Detroit's farm team in Charleston, West Virginia, found himself in the Tiger dugout on June 11, calling the shots in a double-header against the Red Sox in Fenway Park. Norman had spent five years as a coach and minor league manager in the Detroit organization after serving as a coach with the St. Louis Browns in 1952 and '53. He joined the Browns after winning pennants at Wilkes-Barre in 1950 and '51.

"Many others were considered, but Norman's name kept coming up," said McHale. Said the new manager, "I'm surprised, happy and dog-tired. I'm coming in cold, and I'll need all the help I can get."[4] Norman said he'd retain all of Tighe's coaches.

The Tigers swept that June 11 twin bill from the Red Sox and won 56 games for Norman while losing 49. They finished in fifth place with an even-.500 record of 77–77. Norman would be back to start the 1959 season as manager. He wouldn't finish it.

Cleveland Indians
Bobby Bragan to Joe Gordon

"Bobby, I don't know how we'll get along without you. But starting tomorrow, we're going to try."

According to legend, at least in Cleveland, those were the words Indians manager Bobby Bragan heard on June 26, when he was called into general manager Frank Lane's office after a 2–1 loss to Boston. The loss dropped the Tribe's record under its first-year manager to 31–36. The 67 games Bragan managed are the fewest in team history for a manager who didn't have the word "interim" attached to his title.

"We are making this change with the hope there will be a general improvement in the club," said Lane. "In my opinion, Bragan was a sober, industrious manager, and he deported himself in a manner that caused no embarrassment to the Cleveland ball club. I simply feel that he wasn't able to cope with the situation here. Despite the injuries we have suffered, I feel that we should have better results. Personally, Bragan and I remain the best of friends. I think I was more shocked when I broke the news to him than he was."[5]

As had been the case with Bragan in Pittsburgh, "an accumulation of little things,"[6] in Lane's words, led to his decision to dismiss the manager after less than half a season on the job. The biggest strike against Bragan may have been that Lane inherited him when he replaced Hank Greenberg as Cleveland's general manager in November of 1957. Greenberg hired Bragan after firing manager Kerby Farrell following the Indians' plunge into the second division in '57. Shortly thereafter, Greenberg was fired and replaced by Lane. It would have been unseemly, even for Lane, to fire a manager who hadn't even managed one game. Lane, however, insisted that being Greenberg's choice didn't factor in his decision.

"I thought Hank made a good choice when he hired Bragan," said Lane. "I might have picked him for the job myself. I don't know."[7] Lane said he wouldn't embarrass Bragan by offering him another position within the Cleveland organization.

"I have no regrets," said Bragan before leaving town. "I think if certain things had worked out differently, I'd still be on the job. No use thinking about that now, though."[8] Bragan had been fired twice within a span of 10 months, but he'd be back in a major league dugout.

BOBBY BRAGAN: Bragan managed the Pirates, Indians and Braves, never finishing higher than fifth place. His 67 games in Cleveland in 1958 is the shortest stint in club history for a "non-interim" manager (*Cleveland Press* collection/Cleveland State University).

Lane selected former Indian second baseman Joe Gordon to replace Bragan. The choice was popular with fans who remembered Gordon as a key player on the Tribe's 1948 world's champions. Gordon had smacked 32 home runs and driven in 124 in his final productive season as a player. Gordon brought managerial experience to his new position, having piloted the San Francisco Seals to the 1957 pennant in their last year in the Pacific Coast League.

"This is quite an honor," Gordon said of his return to the major leagues. "I'll do my best, and I sure am happy to be coming back to Cleveland."[9] He signed a contract running through the 1959 season and said he'd keep all of Bragan's coaches.

"I know Joe pretty well and respect his ability. If I didn't think he could do the job, I wouldn't have made the change,"[10] said Lane, who now had his hand-picked manager in place. That didn't stop Gordon's two seasons from being a bumpy ride. His regime started out well enough, however. The Indians won 46 and lost 40 under their new manager to climb up to fourth place with a final tally of 77–76.

Philadelphia Phillies
Mayo Smith to Eddie Sawyer

Roy Hamey hadn't done much better with his second managerial hiring than his first one. Terry Moore lasted exactly half a season with Philadelphia after replacing Steve O'Neill in 1954, winning 35 games, losing 42, and having to deal with a player rebellion pertaining to the club's decision, with Moore's approval, to hire private detectives to tail the players and monitor their off-field activities. Hamey's second managerial hiring was almost as surprising as his first.

Mayo Smith had never managed in the majors when Hamey hired him to succeed Moore. Smith's 1955 Phillies finished fourth with a 77–77 record, his 1956 team dropped to fifth (71–83) and his 1957 squad also finished fifth with 77 wins and 77 losses. The 1958 Phillies started slowly, then won six straight between July 1 and 6 to vault from seventh place to fourth in the tightly-bunched National League. Although their record was just 37–36, the Phillies were only 3½ games out of first after the winning streak. Unfortunately for Smith, the Phillies followed the brief spurt by losing nine of their next 12, and fell into the cellar (although only 7½ games back). Philadelphia had a 39–45 record when Smith was fired on July 18.

"We needed a change," said Hamey. "No one thing tipped the scale. I just thought we needed a change."[11]

"Nobody feels good about being fired, but that's the way baseball is, and that's the risk you take. I have no definite plans but certainly hope to remain in baseball,"[12] said Smith of his dismissal. He'd bounce back quickly, being named manager of the Cincinnati Reds for the 1959 season.

Hamey's third managerial hire with Philadelphia was as surprising as his first two. Hamey turned to Eddie Sawyer, who'd managed the Phillies to the 1950 pennant and then was fired two years later. Asked why he was re-hiring a manager the team (but not Hamey) had fired once already, Hamey responded, "Eddie had a good record when he was here."[13] Sawyer signed a contract running through the 1959 season. He wouldn't assess the team he was taking over from Smith, but he didn't do any better with it than his predecessor had. The Phillies were 30–40 under their new manager and finished in last place with a record of 69–85.

Sawyer's 1959 team was worse, coming home last again with a 64–90 record. He quit after managing the Phillies to a loss in the opening game of the 1960 season. Sawyer's career managerial record, compiled entirely with Philadelphia, shows 390 victories and 423 defeats, one pennant and one third-place finish. Those were the only seasons Sawyer's teams won more games than they lost.

Cincinnati Reds
"Birdie" Tebbetts to Jimmy Dykes

"For the good of the team," or derivatives thereof, is a phrase that has been used often in this text. Owners and general managers have used it to explain why they fired their managers. Managers have used it to explain why they resigned. This is another case of the latter.

George (Birdie) Tebbetts, as so many former major league catchers have done, became a coach and later a manager after his playing days were finished. Tebbetts spent 14 years in the majors with the Tigers, Red Sox and Indians, retiring after the 1952 season. He was hired by Gabe Paul to succeed Rogers Hornsby as manager of the Reds in 1954 and earned "Manager of the Year" honors when his 1956 team finished third with a 91–63 record, a mere two games behind the pennant-winning Brooklyn Dodgers. The Reds fell to fourth in 1957 and were floundering in seventh place with 52 wins and 61 losses on August 14 when Tebbetts resigned after a double-header sweep at the hands of the league-leading Milwaukee Braves.

"I have resigned my job as manager of the Cincinnati Reds baseball club," Tebbetts announced. "This was not an easy decision to make because I have always felt that a manager should never quit. I am not resigning because of my feeling that I am not doing the job properly, but solely because, in my heart, I believe that it is better for the Cincinnati baseball club that someone succeed me."[14] The fans had turned against Tebbetts, jeering him every time he stepped out of the dugout, and he felt that had a negative effect on the team.

It was the players, in Paul's opinion, who were responsible for the Reds' position in the standings, not the manager. Paul said Tebbetts was the victim of poor pitching, poor hitting and injuries. He sympathized with his manager and said of Tebbetts's resignation, "If I were Birdie, I'd do the same thing."[15] There's no indication that Tebbetts's resignation was coerced or encouraged by Paul. Tebbetts had a contract running through the 1959 season.

Paul plucked Jimmy Dykes from the Cincinnati coaching staff to finish out the season. Dykes hadn't managed since being fired by the Baltimore Orioles after a miserable 1954 season during which the transplanted St. Louis Browns lost 100 games in their new home. Dykes accepted the challenge and guided the Reds to a 24–17 record the rest of the way. The team came in fourth at 76–78, but the strong finish wasn't enough to entice Paul to give Dykes the manager's job for 1959. Dykes was dismissed and latched on as a coach on Danny Murtaugh's staff in Pittsburgh.

Tebbetts would be back on a major league bench in 1961. Despite feeling that a manager should never quit, he would resign from two more manager's jobs.

St. Louis Cardinals
Fred Hutchinson to Stan Hack

St. Louis general manager Bing Devine didn't expect Stan Hack to resurrect a lost season for the Cardinals. He simply wanted to get the season over with and entrusted Hack with that responsibility.

Fred Hutchinson was in his third season as Cardinals manager in 1958. His first club had finished fourth and his 1957 team came in second, resulting in great expectations for 1958. St. Louis was in second place, just a game and a half out of first, as late as July 12, but could get no closer to the top spot and soon sank to the National League's cellar on August 3, as rumors began to swirl that Hutchinson was on his way out. When Hutchinson couldn't stop the slide, the rumors became fact on September 17. The Cardinals' record was 69–75, and they trailed the league-leading Braves by 17½ games, their largest deficit of the season.

"No, I didn't get a raw deal," Hutchinson said to reporters. "This is just baseball."[16] Hutchinson had a job lined up managing the Seattle club of the Pacific Coast League in

1959. Hutchinson's coaches, Terry Moore (a former Cardinal star) and Al Hollingsworth, were also fired. So was third base coach Hack, who was coaxed into managing the team for its final 10 games before cleaning out his locker. The Cardinals won three and lost seven for their lame-duck interim manager, to finish with a record of 72–82.

Hutchinson didn't manage Seattle for long. His greatest success was ahead of him. Hack never again managed in the majors. His record with the Cubs and Cardinals was 199–272.

1959

Detroit Tigers
Bill Norman to Jimmy Dykes

Fifteen losses in 17 games is a lousy way to open a baseball season. Such a start cost Bill Norman his job.

The Tigers were off to their worst start since the 1920 team lost its first 13 games when general manager Rick Ferrell relieved Norman of his duties on May 2. Norman hadn't even managed the Tigers a full season's worth of games when Ferrell decided to make a change lest the Motown fans lose interest before Memorial Day. "I have no criticism of Norman except he couldn't pick the club up," said Ferrell. "I feel another manager can jell this club. The potential of the Detroit club has not been realized. [Jimmy] Dykes is an experienced big league manager. I always liked his style. He's aggressive and has a big league background."[1]

The emotions of Detroit's old and new managers were, understandably, vastly different. Norman was reported to be in tears in his office. "I didn't quit, gentlemen, I was fired," he told his former players. Norman wasn't so shocked, or distraught, that he couldn't look at the situation pragmatically: "I guess I'll go back home. They'd better pay me for the rest of the season, though!"[2]

Dykes was ecstatic at being given another opportunity to manage in the major leagues. The Tigers would be the fifth club he'd piloted. "I thought I was all through as a manager. I never dreamed another chance would come up, but I'm thrilled that it did."[3] Dykes signed a one-year contract and said he'd keep Norman's coaches, Billy Hitchcock, Willis Hudlin and Tommy Henrich.

Norman's former players filed into his former office to say their goodbyes. Harvey Kuenn, who, 23 years later, would become a major league manager himself, was particularly outspoken in defense of his ex-boss. "It was a bum rap. Bill Norman didn't get a chance. It was the players' fault, it wasn't Bill's fault at all. He didn't even get a chance to manage a full season. He was for us all the way. You couldn't find a better one."[4]

Despite Kuenn's ringing endorsement, the players who cost Norman his job won as many games for Dykes in one day (2) as they'd won for Norman in three weeks. The Tigers greeted their new manager by sweeping a double-header from the Red Sox on May 3. Detroit went on a 30–10 tear for its new manager, climbing from 13 games below the .500 mark on the day Norman was fired to five games over at 32–27 on June 15. The team that once stood at 2–15 had vaulted into third place, just 1½ games out of first. The Tigers couldn't keep up such a torrid pace and eventually dropped out of the race. They still won 74 and lost 63 for

Dykes, finishing fourth with a record of 76–78. Ferrell rewarded Dykes with a contract for the 1960 season.

Norman never managed in the major leagues again. His career record for 122 games was 58–64.

Boston Red Sox
"Pinky" Higgins to Billy Jurges

Joe Cronin. Joe McCarthy. Pinky Higgins?

Ted Williams said Mike (Pinky) Higgins was the best manager he'd played for since joining the Boston Red Sox in 1939. That included Cronin, who'd led the Red Sox to the 1946 American League pennant, and McCarthy, who managed Boston from 1948 through 1950. Williams lauded Higgins on the day he was dismissed by owner Tom Yawkey after 4½ seasons in charge of Yawkey's team. Higgins, a stand-out third baseman with the Athletics, Tigers and Red Sox from 1930 through 1944 and 1946, had posted winning records every year since taking over the Red Sox from Lou Boudreau in 1955, finishing fourth twice and third twice, although Boston never seriously challenged the Yankees for the pennant. Higgins's 1959 Red Sox were in eighth place with a 31–42 record when Yawkey decided that a new manager was needed.

"It was a tough thing to call him and tell him a change at this time might be beneficial to the ball club," explained Yawkey. "I don't think anyone likes to tell anyone else he's through. To me, it's always been unfair, when a club is going poorly, for maybe a combination of reasons, the manager usually takes the rap. It might be his fault. It might not."[5] It might or might not have been Higgins's fault that Boston was 9½ games out of first place on July 2. Yawkey needed to create the impression that he was doing something about it, so he fired Higgins.

To replace Higgins, Yawkey chose former National League shortstop Billy Jurges, who spent 17 years with the Cubs and Giants. Jurges had played on Chicago's pennant winners in 1935, 1938 and 1945. He'd managed in the Cleveland Indians' farm system and was a coach with the Washington Senators when Yawkey decided he was the man to get the Red Sox moving in the right direction. The Senators were two notches higher in the standings than Boston when Jurges was hired.

The Red Sox may have needed a new voice to respond to. Jurges led Boston to a 44–36 record the rest of the way and lifted the team from eighth place to fifth with a 75–79 record. Managing proved to be too much for Jurges's nerves, however, and he wouldn't last until the All-Star break in 1960.

Cincinnati Reds
Mayo Smith to Fred Hutchinson

Mayo Smith wasn't out of work long. But it wasn't long before he was out of work again.

After being fired by the Phillies midway through the 1958 season, Smith was picked by Gabe Paul to manage the Cincinnati Reds, replacing Jimmy Dykes. Dykes hadn't impressed

Paul despite guiding the Reds to a 24–17 record following the unexpected resignation of Birdie Tebbetts in August of 1958, and he wasn't offered a contract for the following season.

Smith, coming off 3½ unimpressive seasons with the Phillies, managed the Reds until the All-Star break in 1959. Paul took advantage of the three-day break to change managers for the third time in less than one calendar year. Smith's Reds held first place for one day (May 9) but quickly went south and, after losing a double-header to the Dodgers in Los Angeles on July 5, arrived at the All-Star break in seventh place, 10½ games behind, with a record of 35–45. Paul didn't think the Reds could erase the deficit under Smith's leadership and fired him on July 8. In a statement to the press described by the Associated Press as "terse," Paul didn't even resort to the time-honored explanation that Smith was being released for the good of the club. He simply announced that Smith was no longer manager and that Fred Hutchinson was. No explanation for the change was given.

Hutchinson was managing the Seattle club of the Pacific Coast League when he was summoned to Cincinnati. He left a minor league team in last place to join a major league team in next-to-last place. Paul had whiffed on his choices of Rogers Hornsby and Smith to manage the Reds, but he made a solid selection in Hutchinson. Cincinnati was a team on the rise, and Hutchinson led them to a 39–35 record for the rest of the 1959 season. The Reds finished sixth with a final record of 74–80.

Cincinnati would struggle to a sixth-place finish with a 67–87 record in 1960, then exploded into contention in 1961, winning the city's first pennant since 1940.

There was a pennant in Smith's managerial future as well. He would lead Detroit to the 1968 pennant and a victory over St. Louis in the World Series in the final season before divisional play began.

1960

Chicago Cubs
Charlie Grimm to Lou Boudreau

You can't relive the past.

Chicago Cubs owner P.K. Wrigley gave it his best shot after dismissing manager Bob Scheffing following the 1959 season. Who better to revive the team's sagging fortunes and return it to its glory days than "Jolly Cholly" Grimm, who'd managed the Cubs to pennants in 1932, 1935 and 1945? But Grimm was 61 years old in 1960, and the competitive fires

LOU BOUDREAU: Hall of Fame shortstop who talked the Indians' board of directors into hiring him as manager at the age of 24. Boudreau was the American League's MVP while managing the Tribe to the 1948 World Series title. He also managed the Red Sox, Athletics and Cubs (*Cleveland Press* collection/Cleveland State University).

may not have burned as brightly as they once did. Or he may have realized that he'd taken on a hopeless case. When he offered the manager's job to Lou Boudreau, general manager John Holland explained, "Charlie said he was reading a magazine at three in the morning with the lights off. His nerves were shot, and he couldn't take any more of the way the team was playing."[1] Grimm's Cubs stumbled through 17 games before he realized he'd made a mistake by giving up the club vice presidency to return to the dugout. He tendered his resignation, which Wrigley accepted.

"We didn't get off to a very good start," Wrigley said of the last-place Cubs, whose record was 6–11 when Grimm relinquished the manager's job for the final time. "Charlie could have led the club to great heights—he has done it before—but he appeared to be getting himself down in the dumps and I didn't want to see him take a beating. The choice of Boudreau was common sense as far as I can see. The logical choice was someone who had been watching the National League teams as well as the Cubs. Boudreau has been doing just that for two years. He certainly was the natural choice."[2]

Boudreau had been watching the Cubs finish seventh, fifth and fifth under Scheffing from the relative safety of the radio broadcast booth. He enjoyed his job, but at age 43, he was still, in his heart, a manager. "It is a thrill to be managing in your hometown," said the Cubs' new bench boss. "You get some different observations from the radio booth, and I have some ideas about the Cubs. I don't want to make any changes, however, until I have talked with the players."[3] One of Boudreau's ideas was to serve as Chicago's third base coach. Grimm returned to his vice president's desk in the Cubs' front office.

Grimm wouldn't have been able to lead the Cubs to the "great heights" Wrigley spoke of, and neither could Boudreau. Chicago won 54 and lost 83 for the former shortstop to finish in seventh place with a 60–94 record, 35 games behind the pennant-winning Pirates. Wrigley had grown weary of watching a parade of managers fail to restore the Cubs to the glory days of the 1930s and decided a new approach was needed. Rather than a manager, Wrigley's 1961 Cubs would employ a "college of coaches," with each coach serving as the head man for a limited period of time. Holland and Wrigley wanted Boudreau to be one of those rotating coaches. Boudreau wanted no part of an arrangement he was convinced would fail. Fortunately, his old job was waiting for him in the team's radio booth. He never managed again. His Cleveland, Boston, Kansas City and Chicago squads won 1,162 games and lost 1,224 with one pennant and one world's championship.

Boston Red Sox
Billy Jurges to "Pinky" Higgins

Charlie Grimm, a veteran of 13 full seasons and parts of four others as a major league manager, wasn't the only pilot whose nerves were worn to a frazzle by the demands of the job in 1960. Billy Jurges had only 122 games under his belt when he was seen "acting extremely nervous," in the words of Boston trainer Jack Fadden, before, during, and after a 12–3 drubbing the Red Sox endured at the hands of the second-place Indians in Fenway Park on June 7. Jurges was examined by team doctor Ralph McCarthy and consulting physician Richard Wright and ordered to take a "complete rest."

Red Sox general manager Bucky Harris announced that Jurges was leaving the team indefinitely to follow his doctor's orders. Although Harris possessed the credentials to run the team in Jurges's absence, he instead named 68-year-old coach Del Baker the interim manager. Harris offered no clue as to how long Jurges might be gone, but insisted the club had no intention of replacing him permanently, even though Boston was in eighth place with a 15–27 record.

On June 9, Jurges was fired. He was succeeded by the man he'd replaced the previous season, Mike (Pinky) Higgins. Higgins didn't sign a contract, but worked under a "gentleman's agreement" with owner Tom Yawkey. The agreement didn't specify how long Higgins would serve as Boston's manager. "Mike Higgins knows the players and he can move right into the assignment,"[4] said Yawkey of his decision to bring back the manager he'd reluctantly fired less than a year earlier.

Higgins's second tour of duty with the Red Sox lasted through 1962. Boston won 48 and lost 57 for its new/old manager in 1960, finishing seventh with a mark of 65–89 (the Red Sox were 2–5 for Baker). The 1961 Bosox finished sixth, and the 1962 edition came in eighth (which was no longer last place, thanks to the addition of two expansion clubs in 1961). Higgins's career managerial record was 560–556 with a pair of third-place finishes. The Red Sox were the only team he ever managed.

Jurges's career as a major league manager spanned just 122 games. The Red Sox won 59 and lost 63.

San Francisco Giants
Bill Rigney to Tom Sheehan

Win or else.

That was the ultimatum Bill Rigney faced when San Francisco Giants owner Horace Stoneham signed him to a one-year contract for the 1960 season. The Giants had just moved into their new ballpark on Candlestick Point, and Stoneham wanted to celebrate the occasion with a World Series in October. Rigney's marching orders were to win the National League pennant or look for employment elsewhere at season's end. As things turned out, Rigney didn't have to wait that long.

Rigney had been a utility infielder with the New York Giants from 1946 through 1953. He played in 44 games and batted .232 for the Giants' 1951 pennant winners and succeeded the manager of that club, Leo Durocher, in 1956. Rigney's first two Giant teams finished with losing records, but the club had finished third in 1958 and '59 after moving to San Francisco. Stoneham thought the Giants were poised to win it all in 1960, and Rigney had them in first place, with a record of 25–14, as late as May 29. The club was second, four games out of first place, after being swept at home by the league-leading Pirates in mid-June. Stoneham had expected the Giants to make their move during that showdown series, and the losses cost Rigney his job.

"It wasn't necessarily that Rigney wasn't managing well, but something had to be done,"[5] explained Stoneham, who did something. He replaced Rigney with 64-year-old Tom Sheehan, the head of the Giants' scouting department, who had no major league managerial experience.

"We played bad for several days and then worse for several more,"[6] Rigney said, assessing the home stand that led to his dismissal. The Giants continued to play bad for Sheehan, posting a 46–50 record for the interim manager and slipping from second place to fifth with a record of 79–75.

Rigney didn't have to look very hard to find another job. He was hired to manage the expansion Los Angeles Angels of the American League in 1961 and led the team to a third-place finish in 1962—an astounding accomplishment for a team in its second season of existence.

Sheehan never managed again.

Cleveland Indians/Detroit Tigers
Joe Gordon to Jimmy Dykes to Joe Gordon

JOE GORDON: Hall of Fame second baseman had the distinction of being hired, fired, re-hired and re-fired by Frank Lane in Cleveland, then wound up working for Lane in Kansas City the next year ... briefly. Gordon also managed the Tigers and was the first manager of the Royals (*Cleveland Press* collection/Cleveland State University).

Clevelanders who thought they'd seen everything in 1959, when general manager Frank Lane fired manager Joe Gordon, only to re-hire him the next day, found out they were wrong on the morning of August 3, when they turned on their radios or televisions or opened their newspapers to discover the mercurial Lane had managed to top even himself by exchanging managers with the Detroit Tigers.

For the record, while most baseball history books call it a trade of managers, it wasn't. Managers' and coaches' contracts aren't transferable as player contracts are, so Lane couldn't, technically, trade Gordon for Detroit skipper Jimmy Dykes. As Dykes himself put it, "This was no trade. It was just a case of a couple of guys getting fired and getting fielded on the first bounce by a couple of other guys."[7] More specifically, it was a couple of general managers whose clubs were going nowhere (although the Cleveland club Dykes would take over was just six games out of first place with 59 games remaining) deciding to shake things up and get some publicity in the process.

The idea of swapping managers, strangely, wasn't Lane's. It started with

Tigers general manager Bill DeWitt about two weeks before the transaction took place. DeWitt and Lane were talking shop, and both mentioned that they weren't happy with their managers. DeWitt suggested that he'd hire Gordon if Lane would hire Dykes, and both clubs could reap a bonanza of free publicity. Lane agreed.

"If I thought the change wouldn't be an improvement, I wouldn't be making it," Lane insisted the day the swap was announced. "We have a good ball club. Dykes is a solid guy. He has the ability to snap teams out of their troubles. He did it last year with the Tigers. I'm hoping he'll do it here. I'm not blaming Gordon," Lane said of the manager he'd hired, fired, re-hired and fired again. "He did the job to the best of his ability. I would have kept him on until the end of the season, at least, if this opportunity didn't present itself. Our team is tense," Lane said of the fourth-place Indians, who'd been in second, just 1½ games behind the leader, as recently as July 17. "It's pressing. Gordon hit a roadblock. Night after night he'd say to me, 'What should we do now, boss?' To me, that was a clue. We both realized it. I think Jimmy, who is a solid guy, is the settling influence we need now."[8]

"I'm bringing no magic to Cleveland," said Dykes. "If I had any, I would have used it on the Tigers. I knew I was finished in Detroit, so when this switch proposition was made I figured what the hell, I might as well try something new. I was looking around for something else anyhow."[9]

The Indians didn't improve for Dykes, going 26–31, dropping out of the pennant race, and coming in fourth with a record of 76–78. Nonetheless, one of Lane's final acts as general manager was re-hiring Dykes for the 1961 season. The Tigers didn't improve for Gordon, either, also winning 26 and losing 31 to finish sixth at 71–83. Gordon signed a contract running through 1961 with the Tigers, but resigned at season's end and took the managerial job in Kansas City.

1961

Minnesota Twins
"Cookie" Lavagetto to Sam Mele

Calvin Griffith, the adopted son of Clark Griffith, who'd been affiliated with the Washington Senators as manager and then owner since 1912, was expecting big things when he moved the Senators from the nation's capital to the Twin Cities of Minneapolis-St. Paul for the 1961 season. So was manager Harry (Cookie) Lavagetto, particularly after the Senators had jumped from eighth place to fifth in 1960, the club's last season in Washington.

The renamed Twins got off to a good start in their new home, winning nine of their first 12 games. They were in second place, two games out of first, as late as May 20. Then the club nosedived, winning just one of its next 17 contests, and was in the midst of a 13-game losing streak when Griffith ordered Lavagetto to return to Minneapolis on June 6.

"I am telling Cookie to come back to the Twin Cities," explained Griffith. "I am not calling him home to fire him. I just want to get him away from the ball club for a week. Take his mind off the team ... play golf for a while. Call it a vacation if you want. I want to discuss personnel changes on the team with him. He definitely will resume as manager when the club returns from this road trip in a week. What has happened to the team is not Cookie's fault. Our second-line pitchers have failed miserably. When we get good second-line pitching, our hitting fails. There is nothing a manager can do about it."[1]

While Lavagetto was "vacationing," coach Sam Mele took control of the Twins and led them to a 2–5 record on the rest of their eastern road swing. As Griffith had promised, Lavagetto was back in the dugout when the club returned to Metropolitan Stadium on June 13, and his return was celebrated by his players with an 8–6 win over Kansas City. Three victories and six losses later, Griffith summoned Lavagetto to his office again. The Twins had a record of 25–41. The personnel change the owner had in mind this time was a new manager.

Lavagetto, in Griffith's words, "did a fine job as manager of this club since he took over in May of 1957, but recent failures of the team caused him to be disheartened. In the hope that this might pump new life into the club, in which I still have a lot of faith, we are making the change in manager. We have a good, sound ball club right here. The big thing is to try to snap the club out of its losing complex."[2] Griffith hoped Mele could do just that.

Mele, a former outfielder with the Red Sox, Senators, White Sox, Orioles, Reds and Indians from 1947 through 1956, had joined Lavagetto's Washington coaching staff in 1958. He said he planned no drastic personnel moves, and any changes in personnel would have to be discussed with Griffith. Mele managed to coax a 45–49 record out of the Twins the rest of the way, moving them from ninth place to seventh with a final mark of 70–90, and was retained for 1962.

Lavagetto didn't manage in the majors again. His record with the Senators and Twins was 271–384.

Kansas City Athletics
Joe Gordon to Hank Bauer

As the saying goes, truth is stranger than fiction.

After being hired, fired, re-hired, and fired again by Frank Lane in Cleveland, Joe Gordon, after two forgettable months managing in Detroit, accepted the job of managing the Athletics after the 1960 season. Soon afterward, the Athletics were purchased by insurance executive Charles O. Finley, who needed an experienced general manager to run his ball club. He hired Lane. Gordon was destined to be fired ... again ... but it wasn't Lane who dismissed him. It was Finley.

"I was the one who made the move and I think the heat should be taken off our general manager," said Finley on June 19, as he announced Gordon's dismissal. "One thing became obvious to me. [Lane and Gordon] liked each other, but they seemed to have trouble working together. Now, I could have ignored this, but that would have been stupid. It seemed to me that one or both should go. Lane has been invaluable to me. He has taught me a lot about baseball, but I discovered he was trying to please Gordon and myself. I'm not going to rest until we win a pennant, and this is the reason I instigated this move to replace Gordon with Hank Bauer."[3]

The 38-year-old Bauer had spent his entire career with the Yankees before being dispatched to Kansas City, New York's favorite trading partner, in 1959. The deal sent a young outfielder named Roger Maris from the Athletics to the Yankees. Bauer would continue to patrol the outfield for Kansas City until Lane could acquire someone to replace him and allow him to be a bench manager.

"Hank will be the kind of manager the players will respond to," said Lane. "We don't expect him to make .300 hitters out of .250 hitters, but I believe we might get better results out of the change."[4] Bauer signed a contract to manage through the 1962 season.

"This is a helluva surprise,"[5] said Gordon, who insisted he had no idea why he was fired. The Athletics had won 26 and lost 33 under his direction. Gordon wouldn't manage again until 1969, when he took on the thankless job of managing an expansion team ... the Royals, who replaced the Athletics after Finley moved them to Oakland in 1968.

If Bauer was the type of manager Kansas City's players would respond to, it wasn't the type of response Finley, Lane or Bauer wanted. The Athletics promptly went into the tank for their new manager, winning just 35 games while losing 67 and finishing ninth with a record of 61–100. Bauer's 1962 team also finished ninth (72–90), and the parade of managers Finley would employ during his two-plus stormy decades as owner of the Athletics had begun.

St. Louis Cardinals
Solly Hemus to Johnny Keane

It cost the St. Louis Cardinals the services of infielder Gene Freese to acquire Solly Hemus from the Philadelphia Phillies, with the intention of making Hemus their manager. Freese spent one year in Philadelphia before being traded to the Cubs. Hemus spent 2½ years in St. Louis before being fired.

Hemus's 1959 Cardinals finished seventh with 71 victories. The 1960 squad leapt to third with an 86–68 record, and similar if not better results were expected in 1961. When general manager Bing Devine found his team in sixth place with a 33–41 record on July 6, he fired Hemus and replaced him with Hemus's top assistant, Johnny Keane.

"If you don't win, you don't stay," said the deposed manager. "I have no hard feelings. It's just the way baseball is. I have no baseball job in sight, but I would like to return to managing."[6] In addition to firing Hemus and promoting Keane, Devine made second baseman Red Schoendienst, who was in the twilight of a Hall of Fame career, a Cardinal coach, and added Vern Benson, manager of St. Louis's Portland farm club of the Pacific Coast League, to the coaching staff. Benson replaced Darrell Johnson, who was reassigned in the shake-up.

St. Louis was 47–33 for Keane, finishing sixth with a record of 80–74. Hemus had a long coaching career ahead of him, but he'd never earn another shot at managing in the major leagues. His lifetime record was 190–192.

Baltimore Orioles
Paul Richards to Luman Harris

Paul Richards knew how to build a winner.

Richards never played in more than 100 games in a season during his eight-year career with the Dodgers, Giants, Athletics and Tigers from 1932 through 1935 and 1943 through 1946. Like many catchers, Richards was a keen student of the game, and after years of floundering aimlessly, Chicago White Sox general manager Frank Lane chose Richards to help him pull the club from the throes of mediocrity in 1951. Richards's Chicago teams finished fourth, third, third, and third again, increasing their victory totals from 81 to 86 to 94 from 1951 to 1954. Richards left the White Sox with eight games remaining in the 1954 season to accept the job as manager/general manager of the pathetic Baltimore Orioles, who had formerly been the pathetic St. Louis Browns.

With Richards at the helm, both in the front office and the dugout, the Orioles gradually emerged as a contender, finishing second in 1960 with an 89–65 record. They were in third place in 1961 with a 78–57 mark when Richards accepted the challenge of molding one of the National League's expansion clubs, the Houston Colt .45s. Since the Orioles had been no better than an expansion club when Richards took over, he seemed like the perfect choice to build a winner in Houston.

Richards had been expected to finish the season with the Orioles before taking the Houston position, but instead resigned on September 2, leaving the team in the hands of coach Luman Harris. Baltimore won 17 and lost 10 for Harris, holding third place with a record of 95–67. The good showing wasn't good enough to earn Harris the Oriole managing job for 1962. He'd follow his mentor, Richards, to Houston.

Richards wasn't finished as a manager. Bill Veeck lured him from retirement to pilot the White Sox to a 64–97 record in 1976. His lifetime record was 923–901.

Milwaukee Braves
Chuck Dressen to "Birdie" Tebbetts

Lou Perini finally got his man.

Two seasons after succeeding Fred Haney, who'd won a pair of pennants and gotten the Milwaukee Braves into a play-off for a third, Chuck Dressen hadn't been able to put Milwaukee back on top of the National League. Dressen's 1960 Braves finished second, and his 1961 club was in third place with a 71–58 record when general manager John McHale informed him that he'd decided not to offer the manager a contract for 1962 and not to let him finish the 1961 campaign.

McHale's choice to succeed Dressen was former Cincinnati Reds manager Birdie Tebbetts, who was named a Braves vice-president shortly after resigning the Reds job in 1958. Tebbetts found the front office just wasn't where he belonged, that he "found myself as a baseball man getting farther and farther away from the things I love most. I just wasn't happy being so far away from the field."[7] Tebbetts said the Braves had both the best organization and the best team in baseball.

"Mr. Perini has been trying to hire Birdie as manager since 1946," said McHale, who didn't explain why Perini didn't hire Tebbetts when he was available in 1959, when he needed a replacement for Haney and Tebbetts was working in an office right down the hall. "Charlie Dressen did pretty good job for us the last two years, but when Birdie became available, we wanted him."[8]

Dressen was surprised by his firing but said, "These things have happened before and are part of baseball. But I was more surprised when I was told Tebbetts was going to become manager. I thought he was going to be president."⁹ Dressen's managerial career wasn't over yet. He'd take over the Tigers in June of 1963.

Tebbetts, who was signed through the 1963 season, he guided Milwaukee to a 12–13 record over the final 25 games of 1961. The Braves dropped from third to fourth with a final record of 83–71.

1963

Washington Senators
Mickey Vernon to Gil Hodges

Managers, so the saying goes, are hired to be fired. Especially managers of expansion teams. Rarely is an expansion team's first manager allowed to stick around long enough to reap the rewards of his hard work when (if?) the team finally becomes a contender. Mickey Vernon wouldn't be the exception to that rule.

Vernon, a two-time American League batting champion, spent the majority of his 20-year big league career, spanning 1939–1960 with a year off during World War II, with the original Senators. When Calvin Griffith moved the Senators to Minneapolis-St. Paul after the 1960 season, the AL placed a new franchise in the nation's capital. Vernon, whose career had just ended with a nine-game stint in Pittsburgh, was tapped to manage it despite having no previous experience.

As with all expansion clubs, the "new" Senators had to make do with players the existing teams decided they could part with, and the best Vernon could do in 1961 was a tie for ninth place with Kansas City. Washington's 61 victories were nine fewer than the 70 racked up by the expansion Los Angeles Angels under veteran skipper Bill Rigney. Rigney's Angels then stunned the baseball world by posting an 86–76 record in their sophomore year, finishing third. Vernon's Senators lost 101 games and finished 10th, trailing even lowly Kansas City by 11½ games.

When the Senators started slowly in 1963, Vernon was shown the door. Vernon's final game was a 4–3 loss to the White Sox at D.C. Stadium (later Robert F. Kennedy Stadium) that dropped the Senators' record to 14–26. The Senators' new manager would be former Dodgers first baseman Gil Hodges, who, like Vernon, had never managed before. Hodges played for the expansion New York Mets in 1962 and suffered through their abominable 120-defeat season. When he accepted the job on May 21, he was on the disabled list with a knee injury. The Mets released him to allow him to take the Senators post.

"I expect Gil to get our club hustling," said general manager George Selkirk. "I don't anticipate that he'll achieve the impossible. Hodges was acquired with a long-range program in mind. It was not a pleasant task to replace Vernon. But we reached the point where I believe that new blood was needed."¹

Hodges knew nothing about the club he was going to manage. "I haven't seen the team play, except for three or four innings this spring in St. Petersburg, Florida."² He said he would retire as a player.

Washington was 42–79 for Hodges, finishing last for the third straight season with a record of 56–106 (the team lost a game for interim manager Eddie Yost). Hodges's Washington teams would finish ninth, eighth, eighth and sixth before he returned to the National League to manage the Mets in 1968.

Vernon never managed in the major leagues again. His lifetime record was 135–227. The new Senators never would become a contender.

Detroit Tigers
Bob Scheffing to Chuck Dressen

Beware the dreaded vote of confidence.

While Detroit general manager Jim Campbell hadn't given his good friend and manager, Bob Scheffing, a vote of confidence as the team struggled in 1963, he did say he wouldn't make changes simply for the sake of making changes. Shortly afterward, Campbell fired Scheffing, who had led the Tigers to 101 victories in 1961 and 85 more in 1962.

"I felt a complete change was needed," explained Campbell. "It was in the best interests of the club and there were a lot of little reasons. We just needed a completely different atmosphere. I made up my mind on [June 16] after we lost that double-header to the Yankees."[3] And Campbell meant a complete change. Coaches Phil Cavarretta, Tom Ferrick and George Myatt were also dismissed. Detroit's new manager, 64-year-old veteran Chuck Dressen, would be permitted to choose his own assistants.

Dressen had been scouting for the Dodgers since being fired by Milwaukee in September of 1961. He took over a ninth-place team with a 24–36 record. "I want my players to run like hell and slide like hell. I've got to get a little pep in them," he said. "I think we can move up. In spring training, they looked like a first division club. I think they can still finish there."[4]

Dressen couldn't lift the Tigers into the first division, but he did get them to play winning baseball. Detroit won 55 and lost 47 for Dressen to move from ninth place to fifth with a record of 79–83. The Tigers were the last club Dressen would manage. He'd be forced to retire for health reasons early in the 1966 season with the Tigers owning a record of 16–10. Dressen's career record was 1,008–973 with two pennants.

1964

Kansas City Athletics
Ed Lopat to Mel McGaha

After having just one manager from 1901 through 1950, because manager Connie Mack also owned the team and wasn't about to fire himself no matter how bad things got, and never changing managers during the season until 1957, the manager's office in Kansas City's Municipal Stadium, and later in the Oakland Alameda County Coliseum, should've been equipped with the proverbial revolving door during Charlie Finley's ownership of the Athletics.

Former Yankee pitcher Ed Lopat became the latest manager to pay the price for failing to make Finley's team a contender when he was fired on June 11. Lopat had replaced his longtime Yankee teammate, Hank Bauer, as Athletics manager in 1963 and guided the team to a ninth-place finish, winning just 73 games. The '64 Athletics weren't even winning one of every three contests. They were 17–35 when general manager Pat Friday told Lopat his services were no longer needed.

"It's easier to change the manager than five or 10 ball players," rationalized Lopat. "You don't develop players like scrambling eggs. This is a young ball club and it takes time. There is no other way."[1] Finley, however, wasn't a patient man. He and Friday determined that a change was in order.

"The ball club wasn't going well, didn't seem to jell. Some attitudes developed that we didn't think would change without a change in leadership,"[2] said Friday, who chose Athletics coach Mel McGaha to succeed Lopat. McGaha had left the Athletics four days earlier to manage the club's rookie league team in Wytheville, Virginia. He was en route after having dropped his family at their home in Louisiana when he got the call to go to Cleveland, where the Athletics were playing. It was also where McGaha started his managerial career, guiding the Indians to a sixth-place finish in 1962.

The 37-year-old McGaha (pronounced McGAY-HAY) said he planned "nothing drastic. I intend to put the nine best men available on the field. When I talk of the best nine men, I mean the pitchers, too."[3] McGaha was taking a subtle slap at Cleveland writers who'd criticized his handling of the team's pitching staff during his year at the helm. Specifically, the writers hadn't liked his use of starting pitchers in relief roles.

McGaha was asked if he thought he was better equipped to handle the rigors of managing than he'd been as a first-year skipper. "I felt I was equipped then," he answered. "You should pick up something in this business every day. I know I learned a lot about pitchers from Eddie Lopat." McGaha said he didn't plan to make any changes to Kansas City's coaching staff "for now."[4]

McGaha had no more success with the talent Friday and Finley had accumulated than Lopat had. The Athletics wobbled through the rest of the season with a 40–70 record to wind up 10th, winning 57 and losing 105.

McGaha would start the 1965 season as Kansas City's manager. He wouldn't finish it. Lopat wouldn't manage in the majors again, leaving a record in less than a season and a half with Kansas City of 90–124.

Houston Colt .45s
Harry Craft to Luman Harris

The nearly impossible job of managing an expansion team claimed its second victim on September 19. Mickey Vernon lasted just two and a fraction seasons managing the expansion Senators. Harry Craft almost made it through three full seasons as bench boss of the Houston Colt .45s.

General manager Paul Richards fired Craft with just 13 games remaining in the 1964 season and the Colt .45s, who'd soon be renamed the Astros when they moved into their new stadium, the Astrodome, leading only the pitiful New York Mets in the standings. The Colts had won 61 games and lost 88 and trailed the league-leading Phillies by 28½ games when Craft was relieved of his duties. He went out a winner, as the Colts defeated the Mets, 3–2, in his final game.

Richards chose former major league pitcher Luman Harris to succeed Craft and signed him to a contract running through the 1966 season. Harris's only managerial experience consisted of 27 games with Baltimore in 1960, after Richards had resigned to accept the general manager's post in Houston. Harris had been a coach for 13 seasons, all of them under Richards, first with the White Sox, then the Orioles, and finally the Colts.

Houston won five and lost eight for Harris, including a 1–0 victory over the Dodgers on September 27, the final game the team would play in Colt Stadium, the makeshift 32,600-seat facility built for the Colt .45s. Houston finished ninth with a record of 66–96, 27 games out of first place.

Craft's major league managing career was over. He compiled a record of 360–485 with the Athletics, Cubs (as "head coach"), and Colt .45s.

1965

Kansas City Athletics
Mel McGaha to Haywood Sullivan

Mel McGaha's Kansas City Athletics posted a pathetic .364 winning percentage after he replaced Ed Lopat in June of 1964. The 1965 Athletics made that number look good by comparison.

A record of 5–21, with 10 of the losses coming before the home folks in Municipal Stadium, a seven-game losing streak, and last place in the American League standings were all owner Charlie Finley could stomach. Finley fired McGaha on May 15, replacing him with 34-year-old Haywood Sullivan. Sullivan spent seven years catching at the major league level, including three (1961–63) in Kansas City. He was managing the Vancouver club of the Pacific Coast League when Finley made him the youngest manager in the big leagues. Sullivan signed a contract running through the 1966 season.

Sullivan had no more luck with the Athletics than McGaha had ... or Lopat before him, or Hank Bauer before him. Kansas City's record for its youthful new manager was 54–82, and the team never budged from the American League's basement. Their overall record of 59–103 left the Athletics 43 games behind the league champion Twins.

Sullivan's contract ran through 1966, but Finley dumped him after less than a full season to sign veteran pilot Alvin Dark. Sullivan never managed in the major leagues again. McGaha, whose career record for 160 games in Cleveland and 136 games in Kansas City showed 123 wins and 173 defeats, never managed in the majors again, either.

Chicago Cubs
Bob Kennedy to Lou Klein

Shakespeare wrote, "A rose by any other name would smell as sweet." In Wrigley Field, a manager by any other name, given the players on the Cubs roster, would continue to produce sour results.

Phil Wrigley abandoned his rotating "college of coaches" after the 1962 season. The experiment produced a seventh-place finish (in an eight-club league) in 1961, and a ninth-place finish (in a 10-club league) in '62, with records of 64–90 and 59–103. Wrigley replaced Charlie Metro, the last of the college of coaches, with Bob Kennedy for 1963, but he declined to call Kennedy the Cubs' manager. He was, instead, the team's "permanent head coach," and he did something no other Cubs boss had done since Charlie Grimm in 1946: he led the team to a winning record. Thanks largely to the presence of the bumbling Colts and Mets, the Cubs won 82 games despite finishing seventh. Their 82–80 record was the best in National League history for a club so low in the standings ... although the league had consisted of 10 clubs for just two seasons. Chicago reverted to form in 1964, sliding to eighth place with a record of 76–86, and occupied ninth place with 24 wins and 32 losses on June 14 when Kennedy was dismissed in favor of Lou Klein. Klein had won 17 and lost 24 as one of the rotating "college of coaches." He managed four different Cubs farm clubs, and was Chicago's first base and batting coach under Kennedy.

The Cubs showed no improvement under their new "head coach," winning 48 and losing 58 to finish eighth, ahead of only the Astros and Mets, with a record of 72–90. Klein would never manage in the majors again. His record with the Cubs for less than a full season's worth of games was 65–82. Kennedy would manage the 1968 Oakland Athletics to a record of 82–80, the Athletics' first .500-plus season in 16 years. He would be rewarded for the accomplishment by owner Charlie Finley with a pink slip. Kennedy's record for three full seasons and part of a fourth as a big league manager was 264–278.

New York Mets
Casey Stengel to Wes Westrum

"I'll never make the mistake of being 70 years old again," Casey Stengel said on the October day in 1960 when he was fired by the New York Yankees. Owners Del Webb and Dan Topping said Stengel had retired, but Stengel saw it differently, explaining to the scribes he often referred to as "my writers" that his bosses made it clear he was not welcome to return in 1961. It was exactly that kind of wit that prompted the Mets to hire Stengel as their first manager. In addition to his baseball knowledge, the Mets were counting on a river of "Stengelese" to distract the writers, and the fans, from the fact that the Mets were going to be a horrible team for a long time. They lived up to that lowly expectation.

The 1962 Mets remain the worst major league team of the modern era, losing 120 games. Seasons of 111 and 109 defeats followed. They never threatened to vacate last place. Stengel's Mets were mired in 10th place on July 23, 1965, when he suffered a serious hip injury requiring surgery. He turned the team over to coach Wes Westrum with a record of 31–64. Originally, Westrum was to serve as interim manager until Stengel returned to the bench. But the 75-year-old's recuperative powers weren't up to the task, and Stengel retired on August 30.

Casey needed a cane to navigate his way to the podium at the press conference at which he announced an end to a 56-year career as a player and manager. "I want it understood that nobody put pressure on me to resign. I was the one who hired Westrum to replace me, didn't I? While I was disappointed with the club, I certainly was not disappointed with the public, which stood by me and the club. I'll never forget them, and I hope to pay them back by coming up with a couple of good, young players that will help the club in the future."[1]

Westrum won just 19 games while losing 48 as New York staggered to another 10th-place finish with a 50–112 record. The Mets moved out of the cellar for Westrum in 1966, finishing ninth with 66 wins and 95 losses.

As was mentioned earlier in this book with Fred Haney, Stengel's long career proved that a manager is only as good as his players. Stengel's Brooklyn Dodger clubs won 148 and lost 251 from 1934 through 1936. He moved on to Boston and managed the Braves to 373 wins and 491 defeats from 1938 through 1943. As manager of the expansion Mets, Stengel won just 175 games while losing 404. But from 1949 through 1960, his Yankees won 1,149 games while losing just 696, for an average record of 96–58. New York won 10 pennants and seven World Series for Stengel, whose overall record as a major league manager was 1,905–1,842. His 12 seasons with the Yankees earned him a plaque in the Hall of Fame.

1966

New York Yankees
Johnny Keane to Ralph Houk

The most unusual managerial change in baseball history wasn't the swap of skippers engineered by the Indians and Tigers in 1960. It was the defection from one pennant winner to another by Johnny Keane in October of 1964.

With another also-ran finish apparently in the offing, St. Louis Cardinals owner Gussie Busch fired general manager Bing Devine and was waiting for the end of the season to dismiss Keane, his manager. But the Cards took advantage of Philadelphia's epic September collapse to win the pennant, and then beat the Yankees in the World Series. The Yankees had roared from behind to pass the Orioles and White Sox in the season's closing days and win their fourth straight pennant and the first for manager Yogi Berra.

New York had decided to fire Berra at the end of the season, and the World Series loss allowed them to follow through with that plan. Busch couldn't fire a manager who'd won a world's championship and arranged a press conference to announce Keane's re-hiring. Keane had a surprise for Busch and resigned. He signed with the Yankees, replacing Berra. He couldn't have made a worse decision.

The Yankees and their new manager never clicked. Keane was an outsider and an old-school disciplinarian. Berra, try as he may to assert his authority in his only season as manager, was still good old Yogi to his former teammates, many of whom believed they won the pennant in spite of him rather than because of him. Keane's rules rubbed his new players the wrong way. In addition, the Yankees were simply an old ball club. Berra had coaxed one last pennant out of a group of stars on the downside of their careers. The decline began, however, on Keane's watch, and he'd pay the price.

Keane's 1965 Yankees sank to sixth place in the American League, 25 games behind the pennant-winning Minnesota Twins, with a record of 77–85. It was the Yankees' first losing season in 40 years. Keane was given a second chance in 1966, but it didn't last long. New

York dropped 16 of its first 20 games when club president Dan Topping ordered general manager Ralph Houk to fire Keane. Keane was informed of his dismissal while the Yankees were in Los Angeles for a series with the Angels on May 7.

Topping's memo to Houk, who had managed the Yankees to consecutive pennants in 1961–62–63, read: "I have decided that we simply must make a change, despite our efforts and hopes to snap out of this. As discussed, Johnny Keane will be relieved immediately, and you are appointed manager of the Yankees on a four-year contract through November 1, 1969. Internal management moves will be made in the near future to relieve you of your general manager duties, per your request."[1]

"In all the years I've been with the Yankees, Houk is the best manager we ever had," said Topping. "This club is not as bad as its record. Right now, it looks like a long row to hoe, but the Yankees should be a first-division ball club ... and maybe even better."[2]

The deposed manager, said Topping, is "a fine gentleman, but I don't think he ever got to know these fellows. He got off on the wrong foot last year with the unfortunate injuries to our ballplayers, and once the snowball started rolling, he couldn't stop it. When Keane saw our top guys ... players like [Mickey] Mantle and [Roger] Maris and [Elston] Howard ... they were 90 percent under the weather physically. He never saw them play baseball like they can. But Ralph knows them all, they respect him, and he can get the best out of them."[3]

"I have the best interests of the Yankees at heart, and I had no alternative but to do it," Houk said of carrying out Topping's directive. "I don't want to call him a failure, but something had to be done. Keane is my man. I don't believe he failed."[4]

Keane's top assistant, coach Vern Benson, who came to the Yankees with him from the Cardinals, was also fired. Houk's contract called for a raise from his $50,000 per year salary as general manager to $70,000 per season.

Topping was kidding himself about the 1966 Yankees being a first-division club, or possibly better. The dynasty was over, much to the delight of Yankee-haters from coast to coast. Houk's former players welcomed him back and may have played with more enthusiasm than they'd displayed for Keane, but that didn't keep the Yankees from dropping into the American League cellar for the first time since 1912, with a record of 70–89. They won 66 and lost 73 for Houk.

Keane didn't live long enough to get another chance to manage in the major leagues. He died in January of 1967 at age 55.

Cincinnati Reds
Don Heffner to Dave Bristol

It isn't often that a coach from a last-place team is chosen to manage an expected pennant contender. But it happened in 1965, when the Cincinnati Reds fired Dick Sisler and plucked Don Heffner off the staff of the New York Mets to succeed him. Heffner had managing experience in the minor leagues, and apparently that had been enough to convince Reds general manager Bill DeWitt that he was the man to lead Cincinnati to the promised land.

It didn't take DeWitt long to change his mind. Eighty-three games into the 1966 season, DeWitt decided a change was necessary. "It is with deep regret we announce that Don

Heffner has been relieved of his duties as manager of the Reds," said the statement DeWitt had written.

> While we feel that Heffner, who is a dedicated baseball man, did a good job, we believe a change is in order at this time. I have talked to Don from time to time about his status with the club and always found him fair and understanding.
> Dave Bristol has been appointed interim manager and will take over immediately. It is our plan to seek a permanent manager as soon as is feasible. While we are greatly disappointed with the showing of the Reds to date, we still feel that we have a much stronger club than the won and lost record indicates. The second half of the season, we believe, will be more interesting and exciting for the enthusiastic fans of Cincinnati and the area.[5]

The 33-year-old Bristol managed the San Diego Padres of the Pacific Coast League in 1964 and '65. He was hired by the Reds as a coach for 1966 and took over a team in eighth place with a 37–46 record. He couldn't steer the team back into the pennant race, but his 39–38 record earned him the full-time job. Cincinnati finished seventh, with a record of 76–84, 18 games behind the pennant-winning Dodgers.

Bristol managed the Reds through the 1969 season, finishing fourth, fourth, and third. Heffner's half-season with Cincinnati was his only big league managerial experience.

Atlanta Braves
Bobby Bragan to Billy Hitchcock

Looking to make a splash in their first season in Atlanta, Braves manager Bobby Bragan brashly predicted his club would win the 1966 National League pennant. When Bragan didn't deliver, he suffered the fate of most managers of disappointing clubs.

Bragan had managed the Braves since 1963, winning at least 84 games a year but never finishing higher than fifth. That wouldn't be good enough in a new city with a new ballpark. The Braves were spinning their wheels in seventh place with a 52–59 record, 12½ games out of first, when Bragan was fired on August 9.

"We owe it to the fans of Atlanta to finish just as high as we can," said general manager John McHale in announcing the managerial switch. "We waited this long, hoping Bobby could get the club moving. All the evidence pointed to the fact that he couldn't."[6] Bragan was replaced by 50-year-old Billy Hitchcock, the former manager of the Baltimore Orioles who was in his first season as a coach for the Braves.

"Naturally, I had aspirations to manage again," said Hitchcock of his second chance to run a major league club. "Anytime you have been in baseball 28 years, naturally you want to be a manager again."[7] Hitchcock's 1962 Orioles finished seventh with a record of 77–85. His 1963 team improved to fourth at 86–76, but that wasn't good enough to earn Hitchcock a third year at the helm.

"I don't plan to make any startling changes," said Hitchcock. He said he'd try to straighten out the Braves' pitching problems by "putting confidence in my pitchers and giving them responsibility."[8] McHale expressed confidence in his new manager because "he knows our talent and personnel as well as anyone."[9]

Bragan's dismissal had been rumored for weeks. "Nobody likes to be fired, but this was no surprise. Nobody ever treated me better than the Braves, although our experience in

Milwaukee and Atlanta was a stormy one," he said. Bragan had run afoul of the fans in Milwaukee for his vocal support of the decision to move the team to Atlanta, and, despite the fact he was a native southerner from Birmingham, Alabama, the fans in Georgia never took to him. As for the on-field problems that got him fired, Bragan said, "We're just the same team we were last year. High-scoring, but unable to stop the other team from scoring more."[10] It was Hitchcock's job to correct that problem.

Hitchcock did get the Braves turned around, winning 33 games and losing 18. The spurt gave Atlanta a winning record on the season at 85–77, and lifted the team to fifth place. The momentum didn't carry over to 1967, as the Braves stumbled to a seventh-place finish with a 77–82 record that cost Hitchcock his job. He never managed in the big leagues again. His career record showed 274 wins and 261 losses.

Bragan was through as a major league manager as well. His career ledger was 443–478, and none of his clubs finished higher than fifth.

Cleveland Indians
"Birdie" Tebbetts to George Strickland

It started so promisingly for Birdie Tebbetts and the 1966 Indians. After finishing fifth with an 87–75 record the previous year, and watching attendance rise at Cleveland Municipal Stadium by nearly 300,000, the '66 Indians broke from the starting gate like Secretariat, tying the American League record with 10 consecutive victories and standing at 14–1 on May 5. Cleveland was winning with pitching, posting six shutouts in its first 15 games. The Indians held on to first place until June 7, fell to second briefly, returned to first just as briefly, and then began a descent on June 14 that Tebbetts would be unable to halt.

By August 19, the Indians, their pennant hopes shattered, were in fifth place with a record of 65–57, trailing first-place Baltimore by 14 games. On a Friday night in Municipal Stadium, Leon Wagner's 10th-inning home run gave the Tribe a 3–2 victory over the White Sox. It was Tebbetts's last game as a major league manager, and he exited a winner. He interrupted the celebration in the clubhouse to tell his stunned players that he was quitting.

Sounding much as he did when he resigned as manager of the Reds in 1958, Tebbetts said, "I'm doing what I think is best for baseball in Cleveland. I came here happy and I'm leaving the same way. I have no complaints and no gripes. It's just that I believe a fresh start would be the best thing for everybody. I am very proud of the job I have done. If it were not for the phenomenal year Baltimore is having, we'd be in contention. But I have to do what I think is right. I want to stay in baseball. I don't care how."[11]

Cleveland's fans were told at the time that Tebbetts and general manager Gabe Paul met on the afternoon of August 19 and the manager expressed a desire to resign. "I was to decide when it was to become effective," Paul was quoted by the newspapers. "During the game I decided it was best for all to do it immediately."[12] Tebbetts told a somewhat different story years later.

"I told Gabe, 'Look, I think you're a so-and-so, and you think the same of me. I don't want to take the team on the road again, so why don't you let George take over?'"[13] George was coach George Strickland, who'd filled in for Tebbetts for the first 72 games of the 1964 season while the manager recuperated from a heart attack. Paul later expressed the opinion that Tebbetts's health problem had robbed him of some of the fire and feistiness he'd shown while managing the Reds and Braves. Paul was more than willing to let Strickland manage the Indians for the rest of the 1966 season. Just days after Strickland was named interim manager, it was revealed that he'd turned down an offer to replace Al Lopez as manager of the White Sox after the 1965 season. Strickland had played for Lopez in Cleveland from 1952 through 1956.

"My idea of managing was to let the players do the job for me," said Strickland of his first stint as Cleveland's interim manager. "I never let them forget that everything depended on what they did. I didn't try to kid them or myself that I was a smart manager. It was a good experience for me, but from now on it's the real thing. The next 39 games will tell."[14] Strickland sounded as if he wanted to succeed Tebbetts on a full-time basis, but the players let him down. The Indians won just 15 and lost 24 to finish fifth with an 81–81 record. Strickland was let go at season's end, the third manager Paul had fired since taking over the Indians' front office in 1961. There's little doubt that he would've fired Tebbetts had Birdie not beaten him to the punch.

Neither Tebbetts nor Strickland ever managed again. Strickland's record for two terms as Cleveland's interim pilot showed 48 wins and 63 defeats. Tebbetts's ledger with Cincinnati, Milwaukee and Cleveland was 748–705. His best year was 1956, when the Reds finished third, two games out of first, and he was named "Manager of the Year."

Boston Red Sox
Billy Herman to Pete Runnels

Another season spent deep in the American League's second division led to another change of managers in Boston. The Red Sox were in ninth place with a record of 64–82 on September 9 when the axe fell on Billy Herman. Herman had been a Red Sox coach for five seasons before his promotion to manager in 1964. His 1965 Red Sox had lost 100 games and barely managed to finish ahead of Kansas City. With the decision to fire him having already been made, general manager Dick O'Connell chose not to wait until after the season.

"Although the Red Sox have played more exciting baseball under Billy Herman this year, we think a change was necessary to ensure that the club will continue to climb in the American League standings," said O'Connell.[15]

"I think Billy did the best job he could," said owner Tom Yawkey. "However, I think a change was in order."[16] Herman was replaced on an interim basis by Pete Runnells, a former batting champion who'd joined the Red Sox staff as a coach when Herman became manager. Runnells said he didn't plan any changes during the remaining 16 games of the season. The Red Sox would win eight and lose eight for Runnells to finish another ninth-place season with a record of 72–90. Runnells wasn't a candidate to manage the Red Sox in 1967.

Herman never managed in the major leagues again. He left behind a record of 189–274, which included a seventh-place finish with Pittsburgh in 1947.

1967

Minnesota Twins
Sam Mele to Cal Ermer

Sam Mele won the battle but lost the war.

Mele had barely survived the 1966 season, when his defending champion Twins fell 19 games out of first place in early July, but rallied to finish second. The Twins' coaching staff, meanwhile, had been splintered by a dispute between Billy Martin and his former Yankee teammate, pitching coach Johnny Sain. Sain's methods of coaching pitchers were unusual, but they got results, and Sain was given a lot of credit for Minnesota's 1965 pennant. Maybe more credit than Mele thought was deserved. The battle lines had been drawn, with Mele and Martin on one side and Sain and coach Hal Naragon on the other. The Twins' other coach, Jim Lemon, tried to remain neutral.

The manager went to owner Calvin Griffith at the end of the season and essentially issued an edict of, "It's Sain or me." Griffith sided with Mele and fired both Sain and Naragon. Both men signed with Detroit for 1967. The loss of Sain didn't sit well with Minnesota's pitchers, and Mele knew he had to keep the Twins in the pennant race in 1967 to prove he had been right to demand Sain's ouster.

Minnesota was chugging along at a .500 pace on June 9, six games out of first, when Griffith dismissed Mele and replaced him with Cal Ermer, the manager of the Twins' Denver farm club ... bypassing Martin. It was assumed that Martin had been hired as Mele's heir apparent, but Martin wound up eventually taking Ermer's place in the Denver dugout. Griffith apparently liked the fact that Ermer had managed 11 of the players on Minnesota's roster somewhere in the club's farm system.

A change, said Griffith, "would be in the best interest of the ball club. Sam did a great job for us. Mele in the past has done a terrific job for us, but I thought there had been an accumulation of certain things. I thought there were certain things that should have been done that weren't done."[1] Griffith admitted that he'd considered firing Mele when the Twins fell 19 games out of first place in 1966. "I had certain things on my mind, but the club turned around and started winning."[2] Griffith, whose only income was derived from baseball, had to be more conscious of the bottom line than some other owners and confessed that Mele's two-year contract, signed after the 1965 season, played a part in his keeping his job. Ermer wouldn't get a two-year deal.

Mele admitted to feeling the pressure to win before the season began. "I know I am under pressure to win this season or else. And I know he won't wait long to make the decision."[3] Griffith didn't, firing Mele after 50 games, before the club was too far behind for a change in managers to make any difference. And replacing Mele with Ermer made a big difference.

The Twins improved markedly for their new manager, going 66–46 the rest of the way and finding themselves in the thick of the tightest American League pennant chase since 1948. Minnesota, Detroit, Chicago and Boston each entered the final weekend of the season with a chance to grab the flag. The pennant was Minnesota's to lose, as the Twins had taken over first place on September 2 and held it until September 30, when they arrived in Boston for a season-ending two-game series with the Red Sox. Boston trailed by one game and needed a series sweep to win its first pennant in 21 years. The Red Sox got it, winning Saturday's game 6–4 and Sunday's game 5–3. When word arrived from Detroit that the Tigers had lost the second game of their double-header to the California Angels, eliminating the possibility of a tie and a one-game playoff, the Red Sox were champions.

Ermer earned a one-year contract to pilot the Twins in 1968. The team fell to seventh at 79–83 and Ermer was fired. Martin was promoted from Denver to begin perhaps the most interesting managerial career in major league history in 1969. Ermer's career record shows 145 wins and 129 losses.

Mele never managed in the big leagues again. His Twins won 524 games and lost 436, with one pennant.

Pittsburgh Pirates
Harry Walker to Danny Murtaugh

When in doubt, call Danny.

That was what Joe L. Brown had done in 1957, when he parted ways with Bobby Bragan and coach Clyde Sukeforth had turned down the job. By 1960, Murtaugh's Pirates were world's champions, defeating Casey Stengel's last Yankee club in the strangest World Series ever played. New York outscored Pittsburgh 55–27 over the seven games, but still managed to lose.

Murtaugh's Pirates finished sixth, fourth, sixth and eighth between 1961 and 1964, and he retired at the end of the '64 season. Harry "The Hat" Walker took over and guided the Pirates to a pair of third-place finishes (with 90 and 92 victories) in 1965 and '66. With Sandy Koufax having been forced to retire due to arthritis after the 1966 season, taking his 27 victories with him, the Pirates were heavy favorites to dethrone the Los Angeles Dodgers as National League champions in 1967.

With the Pirates stuck in neutral at 42–42 on July 18, Brown fired Walker and coaxed Murtaugh out of a comfortable retirement. "Just one more hit a day, that's all it would have taken," lamented Walker. "I don't know what I'll do now. Maybe play a little golf. This is the first time I ever had a paid vacation in my whole life."[4] Walker blamed the Pirates' failure to take charge of the National League race on poor hitting and low morale.

Murtaugh said he was back only because Brown had asked him to manage the club, and he would not be a candidate to manage Pittsburgh in 1968. He stated, "I don't have any ideas about the club yet, so I'm just going to have to observe for a while."[5] Murtaugh wasn't very familiar with the team, having seen only three Pirates games all season. Pittsburgh played .500 ball for Murtaugh, just as it had for Walker. The Pirates won 39 and lost 39 for their interim skipper to finish at 81–81, in sixth place, 20½ games behind pennant-winning St. Louis. True to his word, Murtaugh stepped down when the season ended.

It wouldn't be too long before he'd get another phone call from Joe L. Brown.

Kansas City Athletics
Alvin Dark to Luke Appling

During their lamentable 13-year existence, the Kansas City Athletics were a poor excuse for a major league baseball team. The Athletics never once won more games than they lost in a season while they were headquartered in the Middle West, but by 1967, with the club's stadium lease about to expire and owner Charles O. Finley planning to move the team to Oakland, the Athletics had begun to piece together a semblance of a respectable ball club and employed a capable manager in Alvin Dark. Cleveland general manager Gabe Paul, who coveted Dark for his Indians, said Dark should've been named "Manager of the Year" for bringing the 1966 Athletics home in seventh place with 74 victories. Even though the '67 Athletics were back in the accustomed position of 10th place, with a 52–69 record, on August 20, Finley was prepared to sign Dark for two more years when chaos broke loose.

The Athletics were in Washington when the players met to discuss Finley's suspension of pitcher Lew Krausse for what the owner termed "conduct unbecoming a major league player" on a recent team flight. The result of that meeting was the release to the press of a statement criticizing Finley and accusing him of undermining the team's morale by using informers (whom the players did not identify) to spy on them.

"We the players feel that if Mr. Finley would give his fine coaching staff and excellent manager the authority they deserve, these problems would not exist,"[6] read the statement, which was issued on August 19. Finley read the statement and said, "This compels me to withhold the announcement of a two-year Dark contract until further consideration."[7] Finley then summoned the club's top brass, including general manager Ed Lopat, Dark, player representative Jack Aker, and broadcaster Monty Montgomery to his hotel room in Washington, where they met until the wee hours of the morning August 20. Rather than emerging from the meeting with a new contract, Dark emerged without a job.

The hours following the meeting, with that afternoon's game rained out and thus not available to provide a distraction, became a case of "he said, she said." First, the players issued another statement, in response to Dark's firing. "We, the players, feel a deep, personal loss at the firing of Alvin Dark. We feel this action is the result of the public statement of August 19."[8]

Dark told Finley he knew nothing of the players' original statement. Finley countered that Aker told him the players read the statement to Dark before releasing it to the press, and the manager gave it his blessing. Aker responded that while he had read the statement to Dark, the manager had no response to it. Finley added that

ALVIN DARK: A former infielder on pennant-winning Braves and Giants clubs, Dark managed the San Francisco Giants to their first pennant and won a flag and World Series title across the bay in Oakland in 1974. Also managed in Kansas City, Cleveland and San Diego (*Cleveland Press* collection/Cleveland State University).

Dark told him that if the players had consulted him about the statement he would "certainly have made every effort to prevent it because it had no basis in fact."[9] Aker "refuted that," according to the Associated Press account of the three-ring circus going on in Washington.

Ultimately, Finley fired Dark because "I am convinced he had lost control of his ball players."[10]

"I'm not upset about being fired," a tearful Dark said to his former players. "That's part of baseball. I hate to leave you kids. Good luck." Dark tried to continue but choked up. Asked if he thought it was the players' statement that led to his firing, he answered, "I think it did. I had to back up my players. Everything in their statement was correct."[11]

On August 21, Dark issued a statement of his own in an effort to clear the air. Dark admitted to knowing of the players' statement and okaying it before they gave it to the press. He called the players action "the most courageous thing I have ever seen. With courage of this type, these boys are potential pennant winners and Mr. Finley should be proud of them."[12] Dark was right on the money about the players he left behind being potential pennant winners, although a few more pieces would have to be added before the Athletics broke through in 1972.

Coach and general assistant Luke Appling had been with the Athletics since 1964, and was placed in charge for the rest of the season. The Hall of Fame shortstop won only 10 of the 40 games he managed, and Kansas City finished 10th in its final season in the Midwest, with a record of 62–99. With a guarantee from the American League of an expansion team to replace the Athletics in 1969, the baseball fans of Kansas City were relieved to be finished with Finley and the circus-like atmosphere he created.

Dark landed on his feet. A manager of his caliber was in high demand, and he signed to manage the Indians in 1968. Cleveland's third-place finish would be its highest since 1959. Appling wouldn't manage in the major leagues again.

New York Mets
Wes Westrum to "Salty" Parker

Wes Westrum could read the handwriting on the wall.

Although Casey Stengel hadn't done much as Mets manager from 1962 through 1965, and couldn't have been expected to with the material he was given, he was still a legend, at least in New York City, and Westrum had the always difficult task of following that legend. Westrum elevated the Mets out of the National League basement for the first time in 1966, winning 66 games, finishing ninth (because Leo Durocher's Cubs somehow managed to finish 10th), and earning the manager a new contract for 1967.

With the Mets back in the cellar in September of 1967, and with Westrum having not yet been offered a contract for 1968, the manager grew weary of waiting and submitted his resignation. "I came to the conclusion that the strain of waiting, in addition to the mental and physical strain of managing, had become increasingly severe, and that maybe the whole thing had developed into a blessing in disguise,"[13] said Westrum in announcing he'd taken the burden of deciding his fate out of management's hands.

"Under the conditions, and knowing baseball and being around the game for 26 years, if you don't improve your standing, certain things have to be done," said Westrum. The Mets hadn't improved their standing from 1966 to 1967, and the whole "lovable losers" shtick that had worked for Stengel was no longer acceptable to the front office or the fans. Westrum had a pretty good idea what management was planning for the coming season. "If I didn't show it, I can assure you the strain of losing had become difficult to endure, after the club had encouragingly gotten to within two games of the [seventh-place] Dodgers in late July." Since almost passing the Dodgers on July 22, the Mets had won 20 and lost 40.

"We were deep in the process of making a decision about Wes when he came to us,"[14] said M. Donald Grant, chairman of the board. Westrum's resignation was accepted with no effort made to talk him out of it. Coach Francis (Salty) Parker was appointed interim manager for the season's final 11 games, of which the Mets won four to finish with a mark of 61–101, 40½ games out of first.

1968

Philadelphia Phillies
Gene Mauch to Bob Skinner

Differences with a team's star player have been the downfall of many major league managers.

Gene Mauch had managed the Phillies since 1960. He survived the team's monumental collapse in 1964, when it blew a 6½-game lead with 12 to play and lost a pennant that was seemingly in the bag. As he entered the 1968 season, his eight years at the helm were the most of any Phillies manager, as were his 646 victories. No other Phillies manager had posted six straight winning seasons, as Mauch had. But Mauch was having trouble with temperamental slugger Richie Allen, Philadelphia's best player.

Allen would hit 33 homers and drove in 90 runs in 1968, and few players posted such numbers in the "year of the pitcher." Management thought Allen was capable of even better production if he got along with his manager, so with the team in fifth place with a record of 27–27 on June 14, Mauch was fired and replaced by Bob Skinner. Skinner was managing Philadelphia's top farm club in San Diego and had won the 1967 Pacific Coast League title. He was signed through the 1969 season.

The Phillies regressed under Skinner, posting a 48–59 record and plummeting to eighth place with a final mark of 76–86 (winning one game for interim manager George Myatt while Skinner was en route from San Diego). Skinner wouldn't fulfill his contract.

Mauch was back in a big league dugout in less than a year. He was hired to manage the expansion Montreal Expos for the 1969 season.

Houston Astros
Grady Hatton to Harry Walker

The Houston Astros were taking "the year of the pitcher" to ridiculous extremes.

The Astros, in the words of beleaguered manager Grady Hatton, "hadn't hit since spring training."[1] Houston was mired in a six-game losing streak during which it had scored no more than three runs in any single game (and that just once) when Hatton was relieved of his duties.

The ugly numbers showed Houston with a team batting average of an anemic .222, and the Astros had scored a National League-low 174 runs, an average of just 2.85 per game. What does such an offensively-challenged team do to try to turn things around?

Fire the manager and promote the batting coach. Harry Walker, hired by the Astros to tutor their hitters after being fired by Pittsburgh in 1967, was apparently not being held accountable for Houston's miserable offense and took over as manager of a 10th-place team with a 23–38 record on June 18. Walker, a career .296 hitter in five full major league seasons and parts of six others, admitted he couldn't rejuvenate Houston's offense immediately.

"The hitting isn't going to come overnight," said the new Astros boss. "You can't push a button and say, 'We're going to do it.' I'd just like to get some of the hits we got in Pittsburgh. I hope I'm lucky enough to find some boys like I had there."[2]

Walker didn't find anyone who could hit like some of his Pirates had, but the Astros managed not to finish last in either team batting average (.231) or runs scored (510). They did, however, finish last in the standings, winning 49 and losing 52 for Walker for an overall record of 72–90.

Hatton never managed in the majors again. His career record, all with Houston, was 164–221.

Baltimore Orioles
Hank Bauer to Earl Weaver

Earl Weaver made Hank Bauer nervous, and for a good reason.

Bauer, a two-time "Manager of the Year" award winner with Baltimore (for finishing third in 1964 and first in 1966), was forced to make sweeping changes to his coaching staff after the defending World Series champions plunged to sixth place in 1967. Among the coaches hired was Earl Weaver, who'd made a name for himself managing in Baltimore's farm system. Bauer could feel Weaver's hot breath on the back of his neck.

Bauer's Orioles had a 43–37 record at the All-Star break in 1968, but trailed the league-leading Tigers by 10½ games. He was fired the day before the season resumed. "It wasn't much of a surprise," said Bauer. "Somebody has to take the blame and I'm the guy. Our pitching has been going good, but the hitting has been bad. You have to expect things like this in baseball. The Orioles have treated me fine. I have no bitterness."[3] Bauer's $50,000 per season contract was to expire at the end of the year. He said he had no immediate plans for another job in baseball.

Bauer took a verbal slap at Weaver, who replaced him as Baltimore's manager. Noting Weaver had only been given a contract running through the end of the season, Bauer cracked, "They must not have too much faith in him, either. I know I would've named Billy Hunter. He knows the players better." Bauer admitted he didn't want Weaver on his coaching staff. "I didn't want him around. I was knifed in the back once before."[4]

Bauer was referring to the 1962 season, when his former Yankee teammate, Ed Lopat, was hired as Kansas City's pitching coach. Bauer felt Lopat had undermined him and resigned at season's end. Lopat took over as manager.

General manager Harry Dalton said he hired Weaver because "I think he's a winner. He's very aggressive. He's a battler."[5] Weaver said he didn't think the pennant race was over. "I still feel we are a pennant contender. I don't think first place is unrealistic, even though we are 10½ games out."[6]

Weaver's Orioles couldn't overhaul the Tigers, who won 103 games and then captured the World Series, but his 48–34 record earned him a contract for 1969. Weaver would manage Baltimore through the 1982 season.

Bauer's days as a major league manager weren't over. He'd hook up with his old boss, Charlie Finley, in Oakland in 1969.

Chicago White Sox
Eddie Stanky to Al Lopez

Just days after Eddie Stanky told Hal Lebovitz of the *Cleveland Plain Dealer* that former White Sox manager Al Lopez was enjoying retirement far too much to return to baseball, Lopez returned to baseball. He replaced Stanky, who was fired July 12.

Stanky's 1967 White Sox had led the American League through much of the summer and were in first place as late as August 24. They were the first team to fall by the wayside in the furious four-way pennant chase and finished fourth, three games behind Boston.

A few days after the interview with Lebovitz, White Sox owner Arthur Allyn announced Stanky's resignation, although, in the same statement, Allyn used the term "relieved," as in relieved of his duties. "Eddie and I met for two hours today [July 12] and he resigned in the best interest of the team," said Allyn. "We remain the best of friends, and there is no rancor on either side. To say he was relieved 'under fire' is too emphatic. We've been waiting for a turn of events after our poor start, but it never came."[7] Poor start is an understatement. Stanky's White Sox opened the season with 10 consecutive losses. Since then, Chicago had played almost .500 baseball for a record of 34–45 when the change was made.

"Things happened quickly, and we decided it was best for myself, my family and the organization," explained the ex-manager. "As of now, I am still with the organization, but I could change my mind overnight."[8] Stanky's contract ran through 1971, and he said he'd be paid provided he didn't take another job in baseball.

Lopez had only been in charge of the White Sox for 11 games following Stanky's departure when he was hospitalized for what was originally reported to be a stomach ailment. That ailment turned out to be appendicitis. He was sidelined for 34 games, not returning to the bench until August 22. Chicago won 12 and lost 22 for interim manager Les Moss in Lopez's absence, and posted a 15–21 record for Lopez through the end of the season. All told, for Stanky, Moss and Lopez, the White Sox won 67 and lost 95, finishing in eighth place, 36 games behind the Tigers.

1969

Chicago White Sox
Al Lopez to Don Gutteridge

Fifteen years of managing in the major leagues were all Al Lopez could stand.

The White Sox had a record of 8–9 when the 60-year-old Lopez resigned on May 2, on the advice of his doctor. On top of the appendectomy, he'd suffered an undisclosed stomach ailment in November of 1968 and had been under a doctor's care ever since. "I've been on pills since then and I've got to get off of them," said Lopez. "I've tried to stick things out, but the condition isn't getting any better."[1] Lopez would return to his Florida home for treatment, but he'd stay on the White Sox payroll as a vice president. He turned the managing duties over to coach Don Gutteridge, who was appointed manager for the rest of the season.

Lopez's 15 full seasons and parts of two others managing the Indians and White Sox earned him election to the Hall of Fame in 1977. He won pennants in Cleveland in 1954 and Chicago in 1959, making him the only American League manager to deny Casey Stengel a pennant between 1949 and 1960. Lopez's teams finished second 10 times, and his career winning percentage of .584 is the ninth-best of all time.

Gutteridge's White Sox won 60 and lost 85 for a final record of 68–94, good for fifth place in the six-team American League West. He'd be retained to manage Chicago in 1970, but wouldn't finish the season.

California Angels
Bill Rigney to "Lefty" Phillips

Bill Rigney survived longer than any other expansion manager.

As the 1969 season opened, Rigney was still at the helm of the California Angels, the only manager in the team's eight-season history. Rigney had been rumored to be on the way out in September of 1968, with the club floundering in eighth place. Instead, Angels general manager Dick Walsh strongly backed his manager and signed Rigney to a two-year contract. Walsh, however, expected significant improvement in 1969, and when the Angels staggered out of the starting gate, Rigney became the last of the original expansion managers to be shown the door.

California was in sixth (and last) place in the newly created Western Division of the American League with an 11–28 record, losers of 10 games in a row and 12 games out of first on May 27. Before the first game of a home stand, Rigney was replaced by Harold (Lefty) Phillips. Angels owner Gene Autry called the decision to cut ties with the team's first manager "one of the toughest decisions I've had to make in the history of the Angels."[2]

"It is the position of my own and of management that this is not a sixth-place club in the Western Division of the American League," said Walsh in announcing Rigney's dismissal. "We waited for the ship to right itself and it finally became time that a decision had to be made. We would either forgo the entire season or make a change."[3] Walsh chose not to pull the plug on 1969 just 39 games into the season. Phillips was hired for the remainder of the season only, and took over a club with a .216 batting average, the lowest in the major leagues.

"The first thing we're going to do is work on fundamentals," announced the new manager. "A repetition of base running, fielding, and all-around baseball. I realize you can't make a .300 hitter out of a .210 hitter, but twice during the last road trip a pitcher could have scored on singles by Jim Fregosi but they stopped at third. Fregosi and Ruben Amaro are the only guys on the club who really know how to play baseball."[4]

Phillips got an improved performance out of the club, posting a 60–63 record and earning a contract for 1970. The Angels finished 71–91, third in the weak Western Division, in which only two of the six clubs played better than .500 baseball.

Rigney wasn't out of work long. He was hired to manage the Minnesota Twins for the 1970 season.

Philadelphia Phillies
Bob Skinner to George Myatt

Bob Skinner didn't think his bosses had his back. So he turned his back on the Philadelphia Phillies on August 7.

"All he told us was that under the present conditions, he did not feel like continuing on the job," said Phillies general manager John Quinn as he announced Skinner's resignation. "The straw that broke the camel's back was the handling of Richie Allen."[5]

Skinner cited a "lack of support from the front office" when he met with reporters to explain his side of the story. "There is no way, in my opinion, that a manager can win in Philadelphia without having complete control of all the players, without exception. I feel I've done a great job, but I have too much pride. I am a winner, and I want to be with a winner, and you can't win this easy. Allen has been a big factor in our losing and there is very definitely disharmony on the club. Now I know what Gene Mauch went through."[6] Mauch had been fired in 1968 after several run-ins with Allen, the Phillies' temperamental slugger.

Skinner claimed Allen appealed all fines and other disciplinary action taken against him directly to owner Bob Carpenter and said Carpenter had canceled a fine Skinner had imposed on Allen for missing two games in New York earlier in the season.

Carpenter said he regretted Skinner's decision and denied any interference in the handling of the club on the field. As for Allen, the owner said, "Whatever I did in the Allen case, I did for the benefit of the Philadelphia ball club."[7]

Coach George Myatt took over a club with a 44–64 record for the remainder of the season, and led it to 19 victories and 35 losses. Philadelphia finished fifth in the National League's Eastern Division, ahead only of Mauch's expansion club in Montreal. Myatt's brief managerial career (20–35) was over. Skinner would manage one more game, as an interim skipper with the San Diego Padres in 1977. Skinner's teams won 93 and lost 123.

Oakland Athletics
Hank Bauer to John McNamara

It was often said of Kansas City/Oakland Athletics owner Charles O. Finley that he changed managers as often as most men changed socks. So Finley's decision to dismiss Hank Bauer late in the 1969 season didn't surprise anyone.

Bob Kennedy managed the Athletics in 1968, their first season on the west coast, and led the team to an 82–80 record, the franchise's first winning year since it was located on the east coast in 1952. That didn't satisfy Finley, and he gave Bauer a second crack at managing the Athletics in 1969. Bauer managed the club in Kansas City in 1961 and '62, quitting after the 1962 campaign.

Bauer kept the youthful Athletics nipping at the heels of the Minnesota Twins most of the season. Oakland held first place as late as Independence Day, and was within 1½ games of the front-runners on August 20 before tailing off. The Athletics were still in contention beyond Labor Day, but fans in Oakland weren't responding to the team as Finley hoped they would. He had one eye on the standings and one on the bottom line when he fired Bauer on September 18. Oakland was still in second place but had fallen nine games behind the Twins with a record of 80–69.

Finley gave no specific reasons for changing managers yet again, saying only he'd been considering firing Bauer for quite a while, and had discussed the situation with the manager several times. The Athletics' new skipper was John McNamara, who'd been a coach on Kennedy's staff in 1968 and was retained when Bauer was hired. McNamara had 14 seasons of minor league managerial experience, nine of which were spent in the Athletics' farm system. Finley said he originally planned to allow Bauer to finish the season, but changed his mind to give McNamara a taste of managing at the major league level. He signed a contract through the 1970 season.

Oakland won eight and lost five for McNamara to finish in second place, one of just two clubs to win more games than it lost in the American League West in 1969. Oakland's 88–74 record left it nine games behind Minnesota.

Bauer's managerial career had reached an end. He won 594 and lost 544, with a pennant and world's championship to his credit.

1970

San Francisco Giants
Clyde King to Charlie Fox

The San Francisco Giants were in a rut.

The Giants had finished second five years in a row, and owner Horace Stoneham was tired of it. The first four runner-up finishes were earned with Herman Franks at the helm. Stoneham replaced Franks with former major league pitcher Clyde King for the 1969 season, hoping King could get the Giants over the hump in the newly created National League Western

Division. The best King could do was another second-place finish (90–72), and the Giants were struggling in fourth place in 1970 with a 19–23 record on May 23, after losing a 5½ hour, 17–16 slugfest to the fifth-place San Diego Padres. The defeat left San Francisco just one game ahead of the second-year expansion club, which had lost 110 games in 1969, and Stoneham had seen enough. He met with King after the game and fired him.

"I talked to Clyde and told him I thought we could improve the situation, or whatever you want to call it, if we changed managers," said Stoneham. "Clyde was quite upset. I feel for him and realize it came as quite a shock. But it wasn't a snap decision. I discussed it with club officials the last couple of weeks and we reached a decision this morning."[1] Stoneham turned the club over to Charlie Fox, whose 28 years in the Giants organization included three games behind the plate for the club in 1942. That was the extent of Fox's major league career.

Fox was managing the Giants' Phoenix farm club in the Pacific Coast League when he was summoned to San Francisco to replace King. It was the second time in less than a year Fox had taken over for King, having succeeded him in Phoenix when King was named manager of the Giants. "I plan no changes until I have a chance to observe the club for awhile," Fox said. "I was surprised to be named manager of the Giants."[2] Fox had Phoenix on top of the PCL's west division when he was promoted.

The Giants responded favorably to their new manager, winning 67 and losing 53. They moved up to third place with a final record of 86–76, but finished a distant 16 games behind the division champion Cincinnati Reds. When the Reds slumped in 1971, Fox guided the Giants to the division title with a record of 91–71. They lost the League Championship Series to the Pittsburgh Pirates in four games.

King's career as a manager was put on hold until 1974, when he took over the Atlanta Braves in mid-season.

Kansas City Royals
Charlie Metro to Bob Lemon

Being the manager of an expansion club isn't an easy task. Being the second manager isn't a lot easier.

When Kansas City returned to the American League in 1969, after a hiatus of one season, former Cleveland, Detroit and Kansas City Athletics manager Joe Gordon was chosen to guide the fortunes of the Royals. Gordon was satisfied that he'd done all he could after one year on the job and resigned in September, after leading the team to a fourth-place finish with a respectable 69–93 record. Gordon was succeeded by Charlie Metro, who'd been the last of the "college of coaches" with the Chicago Cubs in 1962. It was good training for managing a second-year expansion team, although the Royals were far better organized than Phil Wrigley's Cubs had been when Metro took over ... and probably had better players.

Metro didn't get much of a chance to show what he could do in Kansas City. He was fired only 52 games into the 1970 season. The Royals were in fifth place with a 19–33 record when Metro was sacked on June 9 and replaced by his pitching coach, former Indians ace Bob Lemon. Lemon's minor league managing career began in Hawaii of the Pacific Coast League in 1964 and included stops in Seattle and Vancouver, British Columbia. Lemon's

1966 Seattle Rainiers won the PCL championship, and his 1969 Vancouver club finished tied for second. He accepted the job as Kansas City's pitching coach when Mel Harder retired.

"I have hoped for a long time to get back to the major leagues ... as a manager," Lemon told reporters. "We have a good bunch of boys. I hope to put it together and win some ball games the rest of the way. We're long on talent and short on experience. I hope to find that the team has aged a couple of years since we got back from that trip."[3] The Royals had just returned from a nine-game journey to Washington, New York and Boston. They lost eight of those games, paving the way for Metro's firing and Lemon's promotion.

Lemon said he planned "no major changes in the club at this time. I found out about this only last night. You're supposed to sleep on these things. Well, I didn't sleep a bit last night." He was asked if he'd given any thought to hiring a new pitching coach. "The way I've been going, maybe I ought to go out and get somebody," he answered.[4]

Lemon's Royals didn't exactly catch fire for their new boss, winning 46 and losing 64. Kansas City finished fourth with a 65–97 mark, a regression from its first season. The Royals moved up to second (85–76) in 1971 and slid back to fourth (76–78) in 1972. Lemon was fired after the season.

Metro's managerial career was over, and he offered a lament. "It is almost impossible for a manager to be an honest man and keep his job. At the very least, a manager—if he's going to keep his job—has to be something of a con man, and I'm not very good at that."[5] In just over one full season's worth of games, Metro's Cubs and Royals combined for 62 victories and 102 defeats.

Chicago White Sox
Don Gutteridge to Chuck Tanner

Al Lopez had bailed out just in time.

Lopez's successor, Don Gutteridge, had gotten the White Sox off to a respectable start in 1970. The Chisox were just two games below .500 on May 6 before the bottom fell out. With Chicago in last place, 31 games behind the division-leading Twins, with a record of 49–87, newly appointed club executive vice president Stu Holcomb was dispatched to Oakland on September 2 by owner John Allyn to tell Gutteridge that he wouldn't be offered a contract for 1971. Gutteridge told Holcomb that he preferred to be relieved of his duties immediately, and coach Bill Adair was appointed interim manager. Holcomb said Chicago's manager for 1971 would be introduced at a press conference on September 14.

Holcomb's choice to pilot the White Sox was former major league outfielder Chuck Tanner, whose eight-year career had been spent with the Braves, Cubs, Indians and Angels. Other than the appointment of a new manager, the major news to come from the press conference was the hiring of Johnny Sain to be Tanner's pitching coach. Sain had tutored the Twins' pitchers when they won the 1965 pennant, and was in charge of the Tigers' staff when they won the 1968 world's championship. He was available because his unorthodox methods often put him at odds with the manager. Tanner, as a rookie skipper, wasn't afraid of adding Sain's strong personality to his staff. The White Sox were in the process of losing 106 games in 1970, and Tanner knew the improvement he was expected to produce had to start with the pitching.

Chicago was 4–6 under Adair and 3–13 for Tanner, for a mark of 7–19 after Gutteridge resigned.

Gutteridge knew his days as White Sox manager were numbered as early as July. "We've got some problems here, but we've got nobody in particular to blame them on. So I'll be the guy to get fired," he said.[6] And he was. Gutteridge's career major league managerial record was 109–172.

1971

Cleveland Indians
Alvin Dark to Johnny Lipon

The reason the Cleveland Indians fired Alvin Dark on July 30 wasn't complicated.

"In view of recent events, we felt that a change was advisable at this time," newly reinstated general manager Gabe Paul explained. "We just weren't winning. We hope this helps us start winning."[1]

Those recent events found the Indians in last place in the Eastern Division with a record of 42–61 after having flirted with the .500 mark in late June. Dark's firing ended a chaotic period during which financially strapped owner Vernon Stouffer shook things up by demoting Paul to team president and adding Paul's responsibilities as GM to Dark's duties as field manager. The experiment failed miserably.

Chimed in Stouffer, "We are looking now to having more unity. Johnny Lipon will give us this. Alvin did a great job for us, helping us put together this young team. We need more communication all the way around."[2]

Lipon said, "Alvin had unity. But I intend to encourage discussion. I plan to talk to the young players a little more than most managers. I want the lines of communication open at all times. This is important."[3]

"Sometimes a team does better when you make a change or you don't make it," concluded Paul, who was no stranger to changing managers. He'd fired Jimmy Dykes, Mel McGaha and Joe Adcock since coming to Cleveland in 1961, and would likely have fired Birdie Tebbetts had Tebbetts not quit first. "Winning games is what counts. We hope we start winning."[4] The Indians didn't. They were 18–41 under Lipon and finished sixth with a wretched record of 60–102. Lipon was dismissed at season's end. His temporary stewardship of the Indians would be his only shot at managing in the major leagues.

Dark would return to the dugout in 1974, when Charlie Finley hired him to manage the two-time world champion Athletics after the defection of Dick Williams.

1972

San Diego Padres
Preston Gomez to Don Zimmer

San Diego's puzzling decision to fire Preston Gomez a mere 11 games into the season raises the question: why did Padres general manager Buzzie Bavasi allow Gomez to start the season in the first place?

Bavasi knew Gomez from their days with the Los Angeles Dodgers. Gomez had been a coach for the Dodgers from 1966 through 1968 before Bavasi selected him to manage the expansion Padres in 1969. Gomez's first club lost 110 games, the second lost 99, and the third dropped 101 games. Each finished in the basement of the newly created NL Western Division. Nonetheless, Gomez was retained for 1972. What Bavasi saw as the Padres lost seven of their first 11 games that convinced him a change was needed wasn't specified when he met with the media to announce the switch from Gomez to Don Zimmer on April 27. It was the earliest in-season managerial firing in modern major league history.

"The meeting was very amicable," said Bavasi of the get-together at which he relieved the manager of his duties. "I explained to Preston why I thought a change of managers was necessary at this time. After 12 years' association with Preston, I continue to consider him an exceptionally qualified baseball man, and I told him he would have a job in my organization any time he desired."[1] Not, however, with the Padres. At least, not as manager.

The Padres' new manager was former major league infielder Don Zimmer, who had managed San Diego farm clubs in 1969 and '70. Zimmer spent the 1971 season as a coach on Gene Mauch's staff in Montreal. He was familiar with the perils of an expansion team, having played briefly for the worst such team of all time (14 games with the 1962 Mets before being liberated via a trade to Cincinnati.) The bottom line was the Padres lacked talent and performed no better for Zimmer than they had for Gomez, winning 54 and losing 88. San Diego finished last for the fourth straight season with a record of 58–95, but Zimmer returned as manager in 1973.

Gomez would be hired to manage the Astros in 1974.

Milwaukee Brewers
Dave Bristol to Del Crandall

Milwaukee manager Dave Bristol closed the clubhouse door and sternly lectured his players following a 9–3 thumping at the hands of the Red Sox in Fenway Park on May 27.

"I've never closed the clubhouse after a game," Bristol said afterward. "I told the players that we had to play a little baseball, that I never had a team that didn't, and I wouldn't stand for it now."[2]

After Bristol met with his players, owner Allan (Bud) Selig met with his manager. The meeting lasted until 2:30 the following morning, and when it ended, Bristol was out of a job. Selig's statement announcing the dismissal said it was done very reluctantly, but "a change at this time will benefit the whole Milwaukee organization ... we are pleased to have such a capable and well-known man as Del Crandall to take [Bristol's] place."[3]

Crandall, a former catcher who spent most of his career in Milwaukee, was in his second season managing the Brewers' Triple-A farm club in Evansville, Indiana. Before that, he'd managed Albuquerque of the Texas League in the Dodgers organization, winning the 1970 championship.

Bristol was in the final year of his contract. He'd signed a two-year deal in 1970, and the contract was extended by a year in 1971. Cleveland general manager Gabe Paul wanted Bristol to replace Alvin Dark (or, more accurately, Dark's interim replacement, Johnny Lipon) in the Indians' dugout in 1972, but Milwaukee denied him permission to talk to Bristol.

"Nobody likes to be fired, but something has to happen when you don't win enough," said Bristol. "But managing in the major leagues is the only place to be—and I'll be back."[4] Bristol left for his successor a last-place club with a 10–20 record that showed little improvement for its new manager. The Brewers split a pair of games for interim skipper Roy McMillan, and then went 54–70 under Crandall's direction. Milwaukee finished last with a record of 65–91.

Crandall led the Brewers to three straight fifth-place finishes before being fired with one game left in the 1975 season. Bristol had vowed to manage again and did, being hired by Ted Turner's Atlanta Braves in 1975.

Minnesota Twins
Bill Rigney to Frank Quilici

Baseball was Calvin Griffith's business. His only business. And with corporate behemoths like Anheuser-Busch owning the Cardinals and CBS owning the Yankees, Griffith was finding it increasingly difficult to compete financially. Money had been the main reason Griffith moved the Washington Senators to Minneapolis–St. Paul in 1961, and with the Twins slipping since their 1970 American League Western Division title, he didn't like what he saw when he looked at the bottom line.

Minnesota's attendance had fallen below 1.1 million for the first time in 1971, as the team dropped from first to fifth place. The turnstiles were spinning even more slowly in 1972, even though the club was playing better than .500 ball for manager Bill Rigney. A four-game losing streak that left the team with a 36–34 record, 9½ games behind division-leading Oakland, inspired Griffith to change managers on July 6.

"The most important reason for making this change was that the players weren't reacting on the field," explained the Twins' owner. "Too many were nonchalant. I'm just hoping Frank will have better luck the second half of the season."[5] Former Twins infielder Frank Quilici was named as Rigney's replacement. Quilici had been with the Minnesota organization for 11 years. He played 405 games for the Twins from 1965 through 1970, including 56 games during the 1965 pennant-winning season.

"I think as far as I'm concerned, we can have the Twins making a little luck," said Quilici. "Something I've learned from a lot of guys, including Calvin and our friend Billy Martin, is that you've got to have a lot of pride. We've got to get it all together."[6]

"You know, I've had a couple of sleepless nights," said Griffith of his decision to change managers. "I decided on my way to work that we couldn't stand another year like last year."[7] The Twins were 74–86 in 1971 and drew 941,000 fans to Metropolitan Stadium.

"Calvin said we are not selling any tickets, and he wants to go with a local man," said Rigney.[8] Griffith's only means of making money was selling tickets, and he hoped Quilici's popularity with the fans would help. It didn't. The Twins won 41 and lost 43 for Quilici and finished in third place with a record of 77–77. They trailed Oakland by 15½ games. Attendance fell to 798,000.

Quilici managed the Twins through 1975, finishing third, third and fourth. His career record as a manager would be 280–287. Rigney would conclude his managerial career with the Giants in 1976. He'd retire with a mark of 1,239–1,321 and one division championship.

Philadelphia Phillies
Frank Lucchesi to Paul Owens

The Phillies had gotten steadily worse since hiring Frank Lucchesi as their manager after the 1969 season. Lucchesi, who never played in the major leagues, led Philadelphia to a fifth-place finish in 1970, with a record of 73–88. He followed that with a sixth-place finish at 67–95 in 1971, and the Phillies had the worst record in the major leagues (26–50) in July of 1972 when owner Bob Carpenter decided to make a change.

"I guess it's the same in politics, war, and everything else in life," said Carpenter. "You can't change the army, so you change the general."[9] Carpenter's new general was Paul Owens, who had been appointed general manager in June of 1971. Owens had served as a minor league player, scout, manager and farm director before taking control of the Phillies' front office 13 months before he replaced Lucchesi in the club's dugout. Owens would finish out the year while Carpenter searched for a new manager.

Lucchesi attended the press conference at which his demotion from manager to special assignment scout was announced and was reported to be visibly upset. His eyes were red when he spoke to reporters afterward. "I'm upset and hurt, but I have to take some of the blame for the team's poor showing," he admitted.[10]

The showing didn't improve much for Owens. Philadelphia won 33 and lost 47, staying firmly entrenched in last place with a final mark of 59–97.

Both Lucchesi and Owens would manage again. Lucchesi would be hired by the Texas Rangers in 1975. Owens would return to Philadelphia's front office at the end of the 1972 season and put together clubs that would win division titles in 1976, 1977, 1978 and 1980, plus the 1980 pennant and World Series. He found himself in uniform again in 1983.

Chicago Cubs
Leo Durocher to "Whitey" Lockman

To borrow a phrase used frequently by the occupant of the White House at the time, President Richard M. Nixon, Cubs' owner Phil Wrigley wanted to make one thing perfectly clear.

"Leo was not fired," said Wrigley on July 25 when he announced that Leo Durocher would no longer be managing the Chicago National League club. Durocher and Wrigley met for three hours and "Leo agreed with me it was best for his own sake and in the club's best interest to step aside at this halfway mark [the All-Star break]. If Leo was fired, he wouldn't be on the payroll as a consultant." Both men felt a change was needed "before we got into another hassle, and with the newspapers calling Leo a disturbing influence, and with letters and phone calls telling me our Cub players are just putting in a day's work. If there has been any friction between Leo and the players this year, then Leo's decision will allow the players to find out if they are pennant contenders." The hassle and friction Wrigley mentioned referred to a player insurrection Durocher managed to survive in 1971.

As for the decision to replace Durocher with Carroll (Whitey) Lockman, a coach who'd been with the Cubs' organization since 1965, Wrigley said, "I told Leo, let's put a man in charge who has been looking at all the talent we have in our system."[11] Lockman spent 15 years in the major leagues with the Giants, Cardinals, Orioles and Reds. He'd played for Durocher in New York from 1948 through 1955. Lockman's only experience as a manager had been in the minor leagues.

"We have a good team and we'll have a shot at winning the pennant if we work hard at it,"[12] said Lockman of his new assignment. He took over a fourth-place team with a 46–44 record and steered into a second-place finish, winning 39 and losing 26. The Cubs' final record of 85–70 left them 11 games behind the Eastern Division champion Pirates. Lockman would return as Cubs manager in 1973.

Durocher wouldn't stay with Chicago as a consultant for long. He'd be back in a major league dugout within a month.

Atlanta Braves
Luman Harris to Eddie Mathews

The Braves decided to test the theory that star players generally don't make good managers when they appointed their first base coach, Eddie Mathews, to replace Luman Harris on August 7. Harris was in his fifth season with Atlanta, having managed the Braves to the first-ever National League Western Division title in 1969 with a 93–69 record. The Braves then ran into the buzz saw that was the Miracle Mets and were swept in the first-ever National League Championship Series. It was all downhill for Harris from there.

Atlanta finished fifth in 1970, third in 1971, and was in fifth place when Harris was fired after 104 games in 1972. He declined to comment on the club's decision to replace him with Mathews, who'd spent the first 15 years of his 17-year career with the Braves. Mathews hammered 512 homers in those 17 seasons, and with Hank Aaron had formed one of the most potent 1–2 offensive punches in baseball history.

Said Mathews of the 47–57 club he took over from Harris, "We're going to fly real low and slow. We're going to put the same club out there and evaluate the team as a whole. We are going to explore the attitudes of the players and get back to basic fundamentals. I have the green light as far as the ballplayers on the playing field go."[13] Mathews lifted the Braves from fifth place to fourth, their 23–27 record for their new manager giving them an overall mark of 70–84. The slight improvement earned Mathews a full season at the helm in 1973.

Harris's career as a big league manager had reached its conclusion. His teams won 466 games and lost 488 with one division title.

Houston Astros
Harry Walker to Leo Durocher

Harry Walker had navigated a tightrope throughout his tenure as manager of the Houston Astros, which began 61 games into the 1968 season. The Astros hovered around the .500 mark each year but didn't seriously challenge for the National League's Western Division championship. It came as a surprise to some that Walker was re-hired by the Astros late in the 1971 season. It came as a bigger surprise that he was fired in August of 1972, with the Astros 13 games above .500 and in second place, albeit a distant second to Sparky Anderson's "Big Red Machine" in the Western Division.

The biggest surprise of all was Houston general manager Spec Richardson's choice to replace Walker: Leo Durocher. Less than a month after stepping down as Cubs manager (although the Associated Press story of Durocher's hiring by Houston claimed he had been fired by Phil Wrigley), Durocher took over the Astros, signing a contract running through 1973.

Richardson said once he decided to dismiss Walker, Durocher was the only candidate he considered to replace him. "He's an outstanding man," Richardson said of the Astros' new boss. "He has fire, and he might be just what we need to win the pennant." Richardson also had perfunctory praise for the man who was no longer managing the Astros, calling Walker "one of the most dedicated baseball men I've ever known."[14]

Walker never managed in the major leagues again. His record in five full seasons and four partial seasons with the Cardinals, Pirates and Astros reads 630–604 with two third-place finishes, both in Pittsburgh.

Houston was just 16–15 for its new manager (compared to 67–54 for Walker) and finished second at 84–69 (winning one game for interim manager Salty Parker.) The Astros were 10½ games behind the division-winning Reds.

Durocher's 1973 Astros finished fourth with an 82–80 record, after which he called it a career. Twenty-four years of managing produced 2,009 victories against 1,709 defeats. Durocher's teams won three pennants and one World Series. He was elected to the Hall of Fame in 1994.

1973

Detroit Tigers
Billy Martin to Joe Schultz

The first week of September 1973 was a bad one for major league managers. Three of them lost their jobs within six days.

Billy Martin was the first to get the axe. Martin won the first-ever American League

Western Division title with Minnesota in 1969 before angering Calvin Griffith and earning his first pink slip. He was hired by Detroit for the 1971 season and coaxed a division title out of an aging roster in 1972. The Tigers lost a five-game League Championship Series to the Oakland Athletics. It was the last hurrah for the team that had been an American League contender since 1967 and won the 1968 World Series, although it appeared as late as August 14, 1973, that Martin might direct the club to another division championship. The Tigers were in first place with a 66–53 record before fading, and had fallen to third, 7½ games behind, when Martin made the decision that cost him his job.

On August 30, with the Tigers on the short end of a 3–0 shutout fashioned by Cleveland's Gaylord Perry, whose stock-in-trade was the illegal spitball, an infuriated Martin ordered two of his pitchers to retaliate by tossing spitballs at Cleveland batters late in the game. The stunt earned him a suspension from American League president Joe Cronin.

"I'm telling the truth," said Martin, admitting he'd ordered his pitchers to throw illegal pitches. "[Perry's] lying. Where's the justice?"[1] Martin never returned to the Tiger dugout. He was fired by general manager Jim Campbell on September 2.

"He has done an outstanding job on the field, between the foul lines, but there were other extenuating circumstances," said Campbell. Those circumstances caused "a breakdown of efficiency of the entire organization. There was a breakdown in some policy matters, a misunderstanding about Billy making some remarks about the commissioner of baseball and the American League president's office, Detroit executives and minor league players, and other things."[2]

"They did what they thought was right, and I did what I thought was right,"[3] was all Martin had to say about his firing. He was replaced for the rest of the season by coach Joe Schultz, who had been the first and only manager of the ill-fated Seattle Pilots. Schultz managed the Pilots to a last-place finish with a 64–98 record in 1969, the franchise's lone season in Seattle. He led the Tigers to a 14–14 record in September and they stayed in third place, finishing with 85 wins and 77 losses. Schultz never managed again and concluded his career with a record of 78–112.

Despite two firings under dubious circumstances, Martin remained very much in demand. He wouldn't be out of a job long.

Pittsburgh Pirates
Bill Virdon to Danny Murtaugh

Danny Murtaugh meant it when he said he wasn't a candidate to manage the Pirates in 1968 when summoned from retirement by general manager Joe L. Brown to replace Harry Walker in 1967. Larry Shepard got the job.

When Brown fired Shepard after two lackluster seasons, he again turned to Murtaugh. The genial Irishman managed the Pirates to the National League's Eastern Division crown in 1970 and the World Series championship in 1971, after which he looked forward to a well-earned permanent retirement from managing. No such luck.

Murtaugh's protégé, former Pittsburgh outfielder Bill Virdon, took over following Murtaugh's third retirement and won the 1972 Eastern Division title but lost a hard-fought five-game League Championship Series to Cincinnati. In 1973, the Pirates floundered, as did every club in the Eastern Division. Pittsburgh plunged into the division cellar on June 24, 10½ games out of first place, and then rallied back to the .500 mark by July 29. The Pirates moved into second place on August 12 and stayed there, occasionally with a sub-.500 record, but never more than three games out of first, through September 5. Virdon, in Brown's opinion, wasn't capable of getting the team over the hump. On September 6, Murtaugh's phone rang. Again.

Murtaugh was serving as Pittsburgh's director of player acquisition and development. "He was shaken," said Brown. "There was almost 30 seconds of dead silence and then he came back and said 'Why?' I gave him my reasons, and he said he'd have to think it over."[4] Murtaugh thought it over, and as much as he regretted replacing the man he'd personally groomed for the job, he agreed to come to the Pirates' rescue one more time.

As for the reasons he dismissed Virdon, Brown said, "The fact that a change has been made indicates something. In some areas, he has not done what I thought he should do."[5] The Murtaugh magic wasn't enough to boost the Pirates to another division title in 1973. The club was 67–69 when the new manager took over and 80–82 when the season ended, 2½ games behind the Mets, whose 82–79 record was the worst for a division winner up to that time.

Virdon tried to find some solace in his firing. "They say you're not a manager until you're fired at least once," he joked.[6] He would bounce back quickly and have a long career as a big league skipper.

Murtaugh managed the Pirates through the 1976 season. He won division titles in 1974 and '75 but lost the League Championship Series both years. His 1976 Pirates finished second to the Phillies with 92 victories. He wouldn't be available to rescue the Pirates from any more jams, however. Murtaugh died on December 2, 1976, at age 59. He managed Pittsburgh for all or part of 15 seasons between 1957 and 1976, winning 1,115 games and losing 950. His clubs won two pennants, two World Series championships, and four division titles.

Texas Rangers
"Whitey" Herzog to Billy Martin

Major league baseball wasn't catching on in Dallas-Fort Worth.

Fans weren't swarming to Turnpike Stadium to watch Bob Short's transplanted Washington Senators play. The renamed Texas Rangers had drawn just 662,000 fans in 1972, a mere seven thousand more than had watched the Senators play in their final season at RFK Stadium. A 100-loss season, and the players' strike that preceded it, didn't help matters. The 1973 Rangers were on their way to another 100-defeat campaign, with home games attracting an average of about 8,000 spectators, when Short caught a break.

Short hired Dorrel (Whitey) Herzog, a former major league outfielder who'd labored for the Senators, Athletics, Orioles and Tigers with minimal distinction from 1956 through 1963, to replace Ted Williams as manager. Herzog was given a two-year contract and a mandate to build the Rangers into a team that more than 8,000 Dallas-Fort Worth residents would want to pay to watch per game.

Herzog's Rangers spent the 1973 season looking up at the rest of the American League's Western Division, falling into last place on April 20 and staying there. Texas had the worst record in the major leagues at 47–91 on September 7 when two managers with division titles on their resumes, Billy Martin and Bill Virdon, suddenly became available. Short fired Herzog.

"I was under the impression that I had a two-year contract and was in a position of trying to build a ball club," said the deposed manager. "When Short kept coming into the clubhouse and laughing after every defeat, I assumed the won-loss record was secondary and I managed accordingly."[7] Short apparently saw things differently, attributing Herzog's demise after less than a year on the job to the team's record and what he termed its "unartistic performance on the field."[8] Martin was hired to change that.

"This speaks, as of this date, of the success of the franchise in Texas," said Short at the press conference announcing the club's new manager. "I know he will win."[9]

"I can make no great promises," said Martin. "I think we have a fine club here. I've been beaten by them. They have good speed and good arms. We will be trying to win the rest of the season. Winning is everything."[10] Martin knew how it felt to lose to the pathetic Rangers. His Tigers lost their season series to Texas in 1973, seven games to five.

Taking over the Rangers with 23 games left on the schedule, Martin won nine and lost 14. Texas finished last with a record of 57–105.

Herzog's standing in the baseball community wasn't damaged by the quick hook he got in Texas. He was named manager of the Kansas City Royals in 1975.

1974

California Angels
Bobby Winkles to Dick Williams

With a few notable exceptions, such as Don Coryell in the NFL and Dr. Jack Ramsay in the NBA, the record shows that successful college coaches have rarely duplicated that success in the professional ranks. For whatever reason, major league baseball clubs, unlike their football and basketball brethren, haven't often dipped into the collegiate coaching pool in search of managers. When they have, the results haven't been pretty.

Such as 1928, when the Boston Braves convinced Boston College coach Jack Slattery to give it a shot with the pros. Slattery lasted all of 31 games before being replaced by Rogers Hornsby. Or in 1972, when the California Angels coaxed Bobby Winkles, the highly successful head baseball coach at Arizona State University, to forsake the collegians and accept a coaching position at the major league level. Winkles had coached a number of players who'd achieved big-league stardom, among them Reggie Jackson, and in 13 years at the Arizona State helm, his teams won three national championships. If anyone had the credentials to make the jump from college to the pros, and do it successfully, it was Winkles.

After one year as a coach, Winkles was promoted to succeed Del Rice as California's manager after the 1972 season. The Angels finished fourth in 1973 with a 79–83 record, 15 games behind Oakland, and Winkles found himself at odds throughout the season with Frank Robinson, his designated hitter. Robinson and Bob Oliver constituted just about all the offense the Angels were able to muster. Robinson slammed 30 homers and drove in 97 runs; Oliver contributed 18 homers and drove in 89. No other Angel hit more than eight home runs or batted in more than 57 runs. It would be Robinson's last productive year.

The relationship between manager and designated hitter remained strained in 1974, and after a fast start (8–3), the Angels hit the skids. California had fallen to last place with a 30–44 record when Winkles was fired on June 27. "We were not playing well, losing 18 of our last 24 games," said general manager Harry Dalton. "After a good start, we started losing. We're in the entertainment business, and I don't think we were entertaining on the field."[1]

Robinson was noncommittal about the change in managers many people thought he was at least partially responsible for. "I don't know if the change will be good or not. That's something that remains to be seen, but the club wasn't playing well. We made trades last winter that helped the ball club and then we got off to a good start ... then started losing. You can't fire 25 players, so you fire the manager."[2]

Robinson didn't try to avoid discussing his differences with Winkles. "It's something that goes back to last season. He felt I was needling, riding too hard on two or three players, and he said he wanted me to stop. He said I yelled too much at umpires. I'm a stubborn guy and so is he and we just never got together."[3]

Winkles left no doubt as to why he thought he was dismissed. "I was fired for my inability to manage Frank Robinson. The main reason I was fired was not my ability to manage the team, I just could not handle Frank Robinson properly. It was my fault that I didn't handle him right. I've never questioned his ability as a ball player. I know he wants to manage, but I don't think he ever intentionally did anything to jeopardize my job."[4] Winkles, who had taken a pay cut to leave Arizona State and join the pros, emphasized the word "intentionally." Robinson responded by insisting he'd never caused trouble for any of the managers he'd played for in 18 seasons in the major leagues: "No, no way was he fired because of me."[5]

Aside from his problems with his star player, Winkles said there were other reasons Dalton let him go. "He called me into his office one time and said something about three areas I could improve upon," said Winkles. "One was to set up a definite pattern for the bullpen; another was to make a few more moves, percentage moves within the ball game, such as batting right-handers against left-handers and so forth; and I think the third involved getting the most out of my players."[6]

Winkles admitted that a few of his players didn't want to play for him, but said there was no unusual dissension on his club. He said he hoped to stay in the major leagues.

As Winkles mentioned, Robinson wanted to manage and made no secret of it. He trained during the off-season by managing the Santurce Crabbers in Puerto Rico's winter league, but Dalton didn't consider him as Winkles's replacement. Not with Dick Williams available. Williams had resigned as Oakland's manager after leading the club to a second straight World Series title in 1973, due to a dispute with owner Charlie Finley. He signed a contract running through the 1977 season. Dalton declined to say whether Williams would be paid more than the $70,000 per year he was getting in Oakland. Dalton did say, "He is a well-paid manager."[7]

The Angels did no better for Williams than they had for Winkles. California won 36 and lost 48 under Williams to finish last with a record of 68–94.

Winkles got his wish to stay in the major leagues. He'd take over as manager of the Athletics in 1977.

San Francisco Giants
Charlie Fox to Wes Westrum

After winning the National League West for Charlie Fox in 1971, the Giants slumped to fifth place in 1972, as many of the players who'd made them contenders since 1965 grew old.

The Giants rallied for a third-place finish in 1973 with a record of 88–74, 11 games behind Cincinnati. They occupied fifth place, 17½ games out of first and just one game in front of the last-place Padres, when Fox resigned on June 28. Fox had been criticized for being too "old school" and not being able to get along with the club's younger players. He insisted the criticism had nothing to do with his decision to quit, and owner Horace Stoneham said he put no pressure on his manager to step down.

"There's been a lot of bad press that didn't help," Fox admitted. "But we're not winning, we're not drawing and the feeling was possibly a change would help. There was no pressure to quit aside from that feeling."[8] Fox stayed with the organization and switched jobs with Wes Westrum. Westrum became the Giants' manager and Fox replaced him as the team's major league scout. Westrum joined the Giants as a coach in 1968 after resigning as Mets manager and became a scout in 1972.

"I think we'll win some ball games," he said. "I'll just be observing for a while. Then I plan to sit down with Mr. Stoneham and we'll work it out."[9] The Giants did win some ball games for Westrum, but not enough to lift the club out of fifth place. San Francisco was 38–48 under its new manager to finish with a record of 72–90.

Westrum managed the 1975 Giants to a third-place finish with a record of 80–81. He was dismissed at season's end and his career record as a major league manager shows 260 wins and 366 losses. His final season was his most successful.

Fox would manage twice more, taking over at Montreal in 1976 and the Cubs in 1983, both on an interim basis.

Atlanta Braves
Eddie Mathews to Clyde King

Like most superstar players who become managers (and, when you get right down to it, like most managers in general), Eddie Mathews was found wanting by the Atlanta Braves after roughly two years on the job.

In 1973, Mathews's only full season at the helm, Atlanta had finished fifth with a record of 76–85, despite leading the National League in runs scored, thanks largely to the presence of three 40-home run hitters (Hank Aaron, Davey Johnson and Darrell Evans) in Mathews's line-up. The Braves showed minimal improvement in 1974, holding fourth place with a 50–49 record after losing the final game before the All-Star break to Pittsburgh. It was also the final game of Mathews's career as a manager. He was informed of his firing minutes after the game by general manager Eddie Robinson, who wasn't pleased that the team he'd put together was 14 games out of first place.

"After long and very careful consideration and in-depth analysis of our team this year,

I've reluctantly come to the conclusion that a change in managers has to be made," said Robinson.[10] Mathews insisted he had no clue that his job was in jeopardy.

"I didn't have an inkling this was going to happen. But it's over and done with. I'm sure it wasn't done on the spur of the moment. It took some thought. I asked [Robinson] for a reason and he said, 'We're not winning.' I told him, 'I'm sorry I didn't do a better job.' When you don't win, you don't stay around too long."[11]

Aaron wasn't pleased with the firing of his longtime teammate. He said Mathews's dismissal was "a blow to me personally. I thought he did a heck of a job. I've seen many managers fired, but this one touched me personally." Aaron said he'd take over for Mathews "if the Braves offered me the job. I'd feel compelled to take it simply because there are no black managers in the major leagues. I have said previously that I wasn't interested in managing the Braves or any other team. But since my name was injected into the conversation by Eddie Robinson, I've changed my mind."[12]

Robinson had already chosen former Giants manager Clyde King to replace Mathews, but he added, "If Hank indicates after this season that he desires to be a manager and the time comes to change managers again, I think certainly that Hank would have to be considered."[13] After King's hiring was announced, Aaron expressed annoyance that the Braves didn't consider his brother Tommie for the job. Tommie Aaron was managing Atlanta's farm club in Savannah, Georgia.

Said King, "My number one problem is righting the club. We've got some talent, but we have to be consistent."[14] Atlanta showed a spark for its new boss, going 38–25 the rest of the way for a final mark of 88–74 and a third-place finish. King wouldn't make it through the 1975 season.

Mathews never managed in the major leagues again. His lifetime record was 149–161.

Chicago Cubs
"Whitey" Lockman to Jim Marshall

The All-Star break seemed like a good time for Whitey Lockman to relinquish the job of managing the Chicago Cubs to the man being groomed to succeed him.

The Cubs were in fifth place with a 41–52 record, but only seven games out of first in the tightly bunched National League Eastern Division, when Lockman stepped down on July 24. He resumed his job as director of player development, thereby making him at least somewhat responsible for the success of his replacement, coach Jim Marshall. Marshall had been promoted to Chicago's coaching staff following the 1973 season, which he'd spent managing the Cubs' Triple-A farm club in Wichita, Kansas. Marshall had been a minor league manager in the Cubs' system for six years. He won "Manager of the Year" honors with Wichita in 1972.

All Marshall had to say upon his ascension to the top job was that events were moving so quickly he didn't know what to say. His Cubs won 25 and lost 44 the rest of the season, falling to sixth place with a record of 66–96. He'd stay with the Cubs through 1976, winning 75 and losing 87 both seasons and earning a pink slip. Marshall re-emerged in Oakland in 1980 during the waning days of the Charlie Finley ownership. The Athletics won 54, lost 108, and drew just 306,000 fans to their games. Marshall was fired at season's end. His career managerial record was 229–326.

Lockman's brief career as a manager ended when he returned to the Cubs' front office. In one full season and parts of two others, his teams won 157 and lost 162.

1975

Texas Rangers
Billy Martin to Frank Lucchesi

Billy Martin beat Brad Corbett to the punch.

Looking haggard after 48 hours without sleep, Martin announced his firing as manager of the Texas Rangers on July 22 to the media two hour before Corbett's press conference. "I've been fired," said Martin. "My top assistant, Frank Lucchesi, is taking over."[1]

"I recognize this will cause trauma with the fans," said Corbett, who had purchased the club from Bob Short in 1974 and immediately antagonized Martin by installing himself as general manager. "The fan reaction will be tough. As a student of the game, Billy was one of the finest. But there are causes for his firing beyond his won-loss record. There was no one particular thing. What sometimes works for veteran players does not work for young players. Sometimes a manager gets too much credit when he wins and too much criticism when he loses. Billy certainly made a contribution to this franchise."[2]

Corbett declined to say whether Martin's criticism of the Rangers' new management led to his firing. "He wants to call the shots," beefed Martin. "One year in baseball and all of a sudden he's a genius. People want a 'yes man,' somebody who says 'yes, sir.' Well, you can't win doing it that way." Martin said of Corbett's involvement in personnel matters, "It had to cost me control of my players."[3]

Martin felt the last straw had been his opposition to Corbett's trade of outfielder Willie Davis to the St. Louis Cardinals. "Corbett accused me of one thing—disloyalty. One thing, I'm not disloyal. You can kill me before accusing me of being disloyal. I have proved my way is a winning way. A man has got to stand up for his convictions. I'm happy about one thing. I brought Texas a winner. I brought Texas a million fans. And Texas finally got to see some baseball. I don't think I can come back into baseball, but, of course, I'm saying that without any sleep in two days."[4]

Martin had brought a winner to Dallas-Fort Worth. He'd taken over a club that finished in last place in 1973 with 105 losses, and led it to second place in the American League West the next year with an 84–76 record. But the magic was missing in 1975. The Rangers, after occupying first place in early May, had slid to fourth with a record of 44–51 when Martin was dismissed. Fired along with him were coaches Art Fowler and Charlie Silvera.

Lucchesi didn't want to take the Rangers job, even after being given Martin's blessing. His son changed his mind, explaining it would give him a chance to show those who criticized the way he handled the Philadelphia Phillies that he was a good manager. Lucchesi couldn't fight that argument. Texas went 35–32 the rest of the way, and Lucchesi was retained for 1976.

Martin may have thought his managing days were over, but he was mistaken.

Kansas City Royals
Jack McKeon to "Whitey" Herzog

The Kansas City Royals were in second place in the American League West in late July, but general manager Joe Burke didn't like the way his team was playing, and neither did owner Ewing Kauffman. Burke was given a mandate by Kauffman to "do whatever you think is necessary to get the ball club back on the right track."[5]

"What was necessary," Burke explained at the press conference announcing a change in managers, "was the firing of Jack McKeon. There were two considerations. There really was no real rapport between Jack and the team and the team with Jack. And Jack's rapport with the news media was not good. This thing has been bothering me for the last couple of months."[6]

McKeon's relationship with his players had been strained since he'd asked management to fire popular batting coach Charley Lau after the 1974 season. Lau was demoted to the position of minor league batting instructor, and several players responded by making it clear they no longer wanted to play for McKeon. As of July 24, they no longer had to. Burke replaced McKeon with California Angels coach and former Texas manager Whitey Herzog.

Herzog, who lived near Royals Stadium, said he "couldn't be happier. I've always thought about managing the Royals ... or the New York Mets. That was my goal. I think we have a good ball club. Outside of Cookie Rojas and Harmon Killebrew, this ball club is relatively young. I think we've got players who can play better than they've been playing. There's not much difference between the Royals and the A's. We're not out of this yet. We're still in the race. Oakland hasn't had a real losing streak yet."[7] Kansas City had a record of 50–46 and trailed the Athletics by 11 games when Herzog assumed command.

Herzog's first move was to reinstate Lau as batting coach. "The one guy in the American League who can steal your sign,"[8] Herzog said of the famed batting instructor.

The Royals played well for Herzog, winning 41 and losing 25. They never seriously threatened the Athletics, although they climbed to within 4½ games of the leaders on September 6. Kansas City finished second with a record of 91–71.

Herzog's evaluation of his new team was accurate. The young Royals were a club on the rise, and emerged as the new power in the American League West. Herzog managed the club to division titles in 1976, '77 and '78.

McKeon joined Finley's Athletics and became their manager in 1977.

New York Yankees
Bill Virdon to Billy Martin

"How do you do it?" Cleveland manager Frank Robinson asked Billy Martin when they exchanged line-up cards at home plate in Shea Stadium on August 2. The Indians had opened their road trip on July 22 in Arlington, the same day Martin had been fired by the Texas Rangers. Less than two weeks later, as the Indians concluded the same trip, there was Martin in New York pinstripes, discussing the ground rules with Robinson and the umpires.

Although Martin expressed the opinion (or fear) that he wouldn't be returning to baseball after being fired by the Rangers, the third time he'd been given the heave-ho from a big league managing job, it was probably inevitable that he'd find his way to New York. The Yankees were the only team Martin ever really wanted to play for (although he wore six different uniforms during his 11-year career), and the Yankees were the only team he really wanted to manage. In his heart, Billy Martin was a Yankee.

New York general manager Gabe Paul admitted that he started thinking about firing his manager, Bill Virdon, and hiring Martin the day Brad Corbett fired him. Virdon had been the American League's 1974 "Manager of the Year" for piloting the Yankees to an unexpected second-place finish in the Eastern Division, but New York was spinning its wheels in 1975 with a record of 53–51 in early August, and that wasn't acceptable to owner George Steinbrenner. Paul replaced Virdon with Martin "in the best interest of the club. We're not saying anything derogatory about Bill Virdon, no way."[9]

As for Martin's track record of clashing with management, Paul said, "If a guy can't learn from the experience of three jobs, then he's not very smart. And I think Billy is very smart."[10]

Unlike in Texas, where Martin chafed at having personnel decisions made by Corbett, in New York he'd be answering to Paul, a veteran executive whose experience dated back to the 1950s. "All my duties here are as manager. I'll expect to have something to say on personnel, but only as a consultant."[11]

Martin promised Yankee fans to give arch-rival Boston a run for the division title. New York trailed the Red Sox by 10½ games with only five head-to-head matches remaining on the schedule. The Yankees didn't play much better for Martin than they had for Virdon, winning 30 and losing 26 for a final ledger of 83–77. That was good for third place, 12 games behind the Red Sox.

As for Virdon, he'd earned enough respect managing the Pirates and Yankees to make sure his stay on the unemployment line was brief.

New York Mets
Yogi Berra to Roy McMillan

Anything the Yankees could do…

In the fierce battle for headlines in the Big Apple, the Mets had to do something to counter the Yankees' blockbuster hiring of Billy Martin. So they responded with a managerial change of their own.

"He didn't sound surprised," said Mets board chairman M. Donald Grant when he told a press conference that he'd phoned manager Yogi Berra to inform him that he was no longer manager. "This has been under consideration for a long time. We just felt we had to make a change. We were wondering if we were getting the most of our material. I don't mind saying that I personally felt this season we had a very strong team. When you love a team like we do, you have to take action. Maybe the players will feel they got a shot in the arm."[12]

Martin had a proven track record of providing a shot in the arm to a new team. Roy McMillan did not. McMillan spent 16 seasons playing shortstop in the major leagues, the last three with the Mets. His managerial experience consisted of piloting the Mets' Visalia, California, and Memphis farm teams, plus two games as Milwaukee's interim manager in

1972. He'd been a coach with the Brewers and the Mets. He took over a club on a five-game losing streak, the last two games being a pair of shutout losses to the Montreal Expos in a double-header at Shea Stadium which convinced Grant that Berra had to go. The Mets were 56–53 and trailed first-place Pittsburgh by 9½ games.

"I was stunned," said McMillan. "I had never given it a thought." Then, sounding much like the manager he replaced, McMillan added, "Even after the last five games, we can still win this thing. We won't be out of it until we are mathematically eliminated."[13] Yogi put it somewhat differently, but the sentiment was the same.

The Mets got less out of their talent under McMillan than they did under Berra. New York was 26–27 for its caretaker manager to finish third at 82–80, 10½ games out of first. McMillan never managed in the major leagues again and sported a career record in a pair of interim stints of 27–28.

Berra spent his first day of unemployment playing golf on the same course he'd played on the day the Yankees had informed him of his dismissal in 1964. He'd rejoin his former team as a coach and, later, as manager.

Houston Astros
Preston Gomez to Bill Virdon

It was August 18. Three days had passed since the Houston Astros had been mathematically eliminated from contention in the National League West, thanks to the juggernaut Cincinnati Reds, who were on their way to 108 victories. Houston had a record of 47–80 and manager Preston Gomez found himself in the unenviable position of working for a general manager who hadn't hired him. Tal Smith, who apprenticed in the Yankee front office, had replaced Spec Richardson on August 7. Gomez wanted to know where he stood with the new regime and asked for a meeting with Smith. Gomez got his answer at that meeting. He was fired.

Houston's new manager was Bill Virdon, who was back in the National League after a brief hiatus in the Yankees' dugout. "I know we can't win the pennant this year," said the Astros' new boss. "When I was hired at Pittsburgh and New York, I was expected to win. But there are things we can do right away here, and next year could be different. I think it's in my favor to come in the last 30-odd games and get some idea of what we have. I couldn't discuss any specific problem areas we have right now because they might not be accurate. I do know they have some talent on the team. There are some things we can do that will help right away."[14] Virdon's contract ran through the 1976 season.

Smith explained why he hired Virdon: "I have had the opportunity to closely observe Virdon's managerial capabilities the last two seasons, and we are delighted to obtain his services to direct the Astros on the field."[15] Smith said he had no input into the discussions that led to Virdon's firing by the Yankees because he was negotiating with the Astros to replace Richardson at the time.

Virdon settled in for an extended stay in Houston. The Astros played .500 ball over their final 34 games of 1975, but still finished last with a record of 64–97.

Gomez wasn't quite finished yet as a major league manager. He'd resurface in Wrigley Field in 1980.

Atlanta Braves
Clyde King to Connie Ryan

Clyde King had provided the Atlanta Braves with a quick pick-me-up after replacing Eddie Mathews in 1974. But the 1975 Braves didn't exhibit the same spark, so on August 30, general manager Eddie Robinson made another switch. King was fired with Atlanta in fifth place with a record of 58–76. The Braves trailed the rampaging Reds by 31½ games.

"We're making a move toward next year, and [Connie] Ryan, who is a firebrand type manager, will give us a fresh viewpoint of our team," said Robinson. Ryan was a former major league infielder who played for the Giants, Braves, Reds, Phillies and White Sox from 1942 through 1954. Robinson said of 1976, "Several candidates are being considered. We have a building program ahead of us, and we are getting after it."[16] Firebrand or no, the Braves knew Ryan, who had been a special assignment scout before replacing King, was simply minding the store for the rest of the season, and they played like it. Ryan's record was 9–18. Atlanta's final record was 67–94, good for fifth place, ahead of only the Astros.

King would join the Yankees organization and become one of the parade of men who managed (briefly) for George Steinbrenner. Ryan would hook up with the Rangers and manage them for six games in a pair of interim stints in 1977.

1976

Boston Red Sox
Darrell Johnson to Don Zimmer

Darrell Johnson found out how Jake Stahl felt.

In 1913, with the Red Sox floundering, Stahl was fired as manager in mid-season, despite having won the 1912 World Series. In 1976, with the Red Sox floundering, Johnson was fired as manager in mid-season despite having won the 1975 pennant and going toe-to-toe with Cincinnati's "Big Red Machine" before losing in seven games.

Injuries scuttled the 1913 Red Sox. Johnson's club may have been undermined by ill feelings resulting from contentious contract negotiations with three star players. Whatever the reason, the defending American League champions were staggering along in fifth place in the Eastern Division with a 41–45 record, trailing the first-place Yankees by 13 games, when general manager Dick O'Connell dismissed Johnson.

"We know the club has not played up to its capabilities this year," explained O'Connell. "Therefore, a change at this time, we hope, will make for improvement. We cannot blame everything on Darrell Johnson, but it's easier to change managers than the team, which would be practically impossible."[1]

Johnson wasn't surprised by O'Connell's quick hook. "The way the team's been going, I don't blame Dick O'Connell or the Red Sox one bit," said the departing manager. "In my opinion, it was time for a change. But I wouldn't change anything I did one bit."[2] Johnson was asked if the salary squabbles between O'Connell and catcher Carlton Fisk, shortstop

Rick Burleson and the American League's reigning Rookie of the Year and Most Valuable Player, Fred Lynn, had soured the atmosphere in Boston's clubhouse.

"I really couldn't say," he answered. "It would be common sense to say we knew it was there, but to what degree it hurt, I don't know. We're not scoring the way we're capable of, the way we did last year."[3]

Zimmer joined the Red Sox as a coach in 1974, after two miserable seasons managing the San Diego Padres. His spot at third base was filled by longtime Red Sox organization man Eddie Popowski. Boston won 42 and lost 34 for the man known as "Popeye" and finished third with a record of 83–79. Zimmer would be retained for 1977.

Johnson was hired by the owners of the Seattle Mariners to manage their expansion club in 1977.

California Angels
Dick Williams to Norm Sherry

The Angels wanted Dick Williams so badly they signed him to a 3½-year deal to replace Bobby Winkles in 1974. A year and a half remained on that deal when Williams was given the boot by owner Gene Autry in late July of 1976.

"It was the unanimous opinion that the team will not reach its full potential without a managerial change at this time,"[4] said the Angels' owner and board chairman of a meeting between himself, club president Red Patterson, and vice president and general manager Harry Dalton. The Angels finished last for Williams in 1975 with a record of 72–89, and a 7–5 loss in Cleveland in the final game of a road trip sent them crashing back to the cellar with a record of 39–57 on July 22. These weren't the results Autry expected from a manager who'd won three division titles, two pennants and two world's championships with Oakland, plus a pennant in Boston.

The Angels were in almost open revolt against the gruff Williams, and tempers nearly boiled over on the team bus back to Anaheim Stadium from the airport after the trip on which California won four and lost five. Williams had banned loud music on the bus, but several players were reported to be playing their portable stereos full blast when the manager, from his seat in front, barked, "Quiet, all you winners."[5] Bill Melton, a former American League home run champion on the downside of his career who'd bat just .208 for the Angels, didn't appreciate his manager's delicate sarcasm and went nose-to-nose with Williams before they were separated. Williams was fired within hours of the altercation.

Coach Norm Sherry, a former back-up catcher with the Dodgers and Mets from 1959 through 1963, was named to succeed Williams "because he knows these young players and how to get along with them,"[6] in the words of Patterson. The Angels played as if they were relieved to be rid of Williams, going 37–29 for Sherry to finish fourth with a mark of 76–86. Sherry was asked to return in 1977.

Williams would return to the diamond in 1977 as well. He'd be calling the shots for the Montreal Expos.

Montreal Expos
Karl Kuehl to Charlie Fox

The reason the Expos were in the market for a new manager for 1977 was that the experiment of naming a longtime scout with limited managerial experience had backfired in 1976. Karl Kuehl started managing in 1959, at Salem, Oregon, of the Northwest League. But Kuehl's career as a minor league manager had been relatively brief. He joined the Houston Astros as a scout in 1963, scouted for the Seattle-Milwaukee organization in 1969–70, and moved on to Montreal as a scout from 1971 through 1975. Someone in the Expos' front office decided that 12 years as a scout qualified Kuehl to manage in the major leagues ... and manage a club sorely lacking in talent.

Montreal fell into the National League East basement on May 29 and stayed there. The team was in the midst of a streak of 17 losses in 19 games when Kuehl was fired on September 3. He was replaced by former Giants manager Charlie Fox, who'd been serving the Expos as a special assignment scout. His new special assignment was winning a few games before the curtain came down on the 1976 season. The Expos were 43–85 and trailed the first-place Phillies by 38 games when Fox took over. Knowing there was nothing he could do with the talent on the field, Fox tried to shake things up by moving first base and batting coach Larry Doby to a seat in the dugout. Ron Piche took Doby's place in the coach's box. Fox may have wanted Doby on the bench where he could talk to each batter after his trip to the plate. Or Doby may have spent the season's final month as the forerunner of today's bench coach.

The Expos were 12–22 for Fox to finish with an appalling 107 losses against just 55 victories. Dick Williams had a huge task ahead of him when he took over at the end of the season. He proved to be up to it.

Kuehl never managed in the major leagues again. Fox would do another interim managing stint in 1983.

1977

San Diego Padres
John McNamara to Alvin Dark

Baseball seasons were getting pretty monotonous in San Diego.

Since their creation in 1969, the Padres had finished sixth, sixth, sixth, sixth, sixth, sixth, fourth and fifth in the National League West. The only signs of improvement had come with John McNamara as manager in 1975 and 1976, when the Padres vacated the division basement for the first time, winning 71 and 73 games, respectively. That didn't stop general manager Buzzie Bavasi from firing McNamara on May 28, with San Diego in fourth place, 14½ games out of first.

Bavasi's choice to replace the most successful manager in the franchise's brief history was Alvin Dark. Dark hadn't managed since 1975, when his Oakland Athletics won 98 games en route to their fifth straight American League West championship. The three-time defending

World Series champions were shocked by the Red Sox in three straight games in the League Championship Series, and that was all for Dark. He was coaching first base for the Cubs when he got the call from San Diego.

"We have always respected Alvin's abilities over the years, and have always felt he was one of the best managers in the game," said Bavasi.[1] Dark's resume included two pennants and a world's championship.

"Buzzie called me last night and I thought about it all night before I finally made my decision this morning. I hate to leave a good club like the Cubs, but I'm happy to get back to managing. I don't have any idea of what I will do. We haven't discussed any contract and I've made no decision as to who my coaches will be."[2]

Dark left a first-place Cubs team with a record of 27–14 for a Padres team with a record of 20–28. San Diego celebrated the arrival of its new manager by sweeping a double-header from San Francisco and briefly moved into third place, within striking distance of the .500 mark. But the Padres needed more than a new manager, and soon skidded back to their accustomed position of fifth place, with a final record of 69–93. Despite his record of 48–65 with the Padres, Dark was retained for 1978, probably because he'd signed a contract through 1979. The length of the pact notwithstanding, Dark achieved the extremely rare distinction of being fired in spring training the following year.

New York Mets
Joe Frazier to Joe Torre

Joe Frazier didn't get much of a chance to show what he could do.

The former outfielder, whose claim to fame was leading the National League in pinch-hits with 20 for the 1954 St. Louis Cardinals, was hired to manage the Mets for the 1976 season and guided the club to a third-place finish. New York's 86–76 record placed it a distant 15 games behind the Eastern Division champion Phillies, but represented a four-game improvement over the club's 1975 showing. When the bottom fell out early in 1977, the Mets wasted no time showing Frazier the door.

"The time has come for a change," said general manager Joe McDonald on May 31. McDonald's club was in sixth place with a 15–30 record and looked listless while losing a double-header to Montreal at Shea Stadium the day before. "Frazier was dealing with a difficult time. He was placed in a situation where it was difficult to get all the players to pull together. You only have to look at the standings."[3]

Rather than promoting a member of Frazier's coaching staff to replace him, McDonald offered the job to aging first baseman Joe Torre, a native of Brooklyn. Torre had been the 1971 National League MVP with the Cardinals, leading the league with a .363 batting average and 137 RBI. He was traded to the Mets in 1974. Torre would serve as a player/manager, at least for the time being.

"I can only hope the team responds," said the new Mets boss. "It makes an awfully long year to quit in May."[4] It was an awfully long year for New York's National League fans. The Mets were 49–68 for Torre, finishing in last place with a record of 64–98 while the Yankees were winning a world's championship.

Oakland Athletics
Jack McKeon to Bobby Winkles

The 1977 season was Charles O. Finley's 18th as owner of the Athletics. When Finley fired Jack McKeon just 53 games into the season, it marked the 15th time he'd made a change in the dugout in those 18 years.

McKeon was hired to replace Chuck Tanner, who survived one year in Oakland and finished second. Many of the players who'd paced Oakland to 87 victories departed through free agency. Tanner then bolted himself, signing with Pittsburgh. Finley, however, did receive some compensation for the loss of his manager. The Pirates surrendered catcher Manny Sanguillen to the Athletics in exchange for Finley's releasing Tanner from his contract.

McKeon's decimated Athletics were in fifth place, just 6½ games out of first, with a record of 26–27 when Finley dismissed him on June 10. He plucked former Angels manager Bobby Winkles off the San Francisco Giants' coaching staff to replace him. "If you go into a managing job worrying about longevity, you're in trouble,"[5] said Winkles, who'd lasted just 1½ seasons with California.

Winkles said he had no trepidation about working for a mercurial owner like Finley. He said he knew why Finley had fired McKeon one-third of the way through his first season on the job. "Yes, we talked about the reasons, but that's between Mr. Finley and me. If I do a good job, I think I can continue managing here for some time."[6]

Winkles didn't do a good job, at least not according to the won-lost record. The Athletics tanked for their new manager, winning just 37 and losing 71 and finishing last despite the presence of the expansion Seattle Mariners in the American League Western Division. Oakland's 63–98 record placed it half a game behind the Mariners.

Finley, however, was satisfied with Winkles and retained him for 1978.

Cleveland Indians
Frank Robinson to Jeff Torborg

If Ted Bonda was given a mulligan, he would've kept Frank Robinson as his manager.

The first African American to be hired to manage a major league team on October 3, 1974, became the first African American manager to be fired on June 19, 1977. The Indians had won two straight games but were languishing in fifth place in the American League East with a 26–31 record, eight games behind the leader.

"This has been hanging over our head for some time," said Robinson. "But after the last couple of days, I thought things were getting better."[7]

"Ted and I talked and both of us felt the time had come to make a change," explained general manager Phil Seghi, who'd been badgering Bonda for permission to fire Robinson since September of 1976. "We felt it was necessary to make a change to maintain what I call the climate of our ball club so that we can go ahead for the rest of the season. There was some uneasiness and some unrest, and we felt that we had to do something."[8]

Bonda praised the ex-manager: "I thought Robinson did a good job as manager, but there were conditions beyond his control that dictated this move. Some of the players seemed to resent him, and some of the media stories were unfair to him. Those are the conditions I mean."9

Robinson was replaced by Jeff Torborg, a former teammate with the Angels who joined the Tribe's coaching staff in 1975. Torborg, who spent most of his career as a back-up catcher for the Dodgers, said, "I have always wanted to manage, but never at the expense of a friend. But Frank assured me he understood, urged me to take the job, and said he's sure I can do a good job."10 Torborg's contract ran through 1978.

Torborg took over a team on a two-game winning streak and added seven more consecutive victories to it. The nine-game streak gave Cleveland a 33–31 record on June 24, good for third place. It represented the season's apex, and soon the Indians were once again floundering in the lower portions of the Eastern Division. They finished sixth with a record of 71–90. They won 45 and lost 59 under Torborg's direction.

Bonda looked back on his years as Indians owner and regretted firing Robinson. "I wanted to keep Frank, but I caved in to too many pressures, from the media and the fans, as well as from ... well, my associates."11

Robinson would continue his managerial career in San Francisco in 1981.

Texas Rangers
Frank Lucchesi to Eddie Stanky to Billy Hunter

After taking his son's advice to accept the Texas Rangers managing job in July of 1975 in order to show his many detractors in Philadelphia, where'd he'd had little success managing the Phillies, that he was a good manager, Frank Lucchesi guided the Rangers to a fifth-place finish in the American League West in 1976 with a record of 76–86. The Rangers were in fourth place through the first 62 games of the 1977 season with a mark of 31–31 when Lucchesi, in the words of Texas's general manager Eddie Robinson, was "promoted to administrative assistant."12

Robinson's choice to replace Lucchesi was Eddie Stanky, the former Cardinals and White Sox manager who'd spent the past eight years as head baseball coach at the University of South Alabama. "I can't really tell you why he wants to come back," admitted Robinson. "That's a good question and I really don't know. I suppose he feels he has something to prove."13 Stanky signed a contract to manage the Rangers through the 1978 season.

"Despite position, age or health, I haven't lost my zest for the game," explained Stanky. "That's why I'm coming back. I had no idea of getting back into professional baseball until some of the Texas executives flew down [June 20] and offered me the job."14 Stanky departed Mobile, Alabama, for Minneapolis, where he led the Rangers to a 10–8 victory over the Twins on June 22. Thus ended Stanky's comeback.

Stanky called Robinson from the Minneapolis-St. Paul airport at 8:15 in the morning on June 23 and resigned. Robinson asked Stanky to hang on until the two men could discuss the matter face-to-face, but Stanky refused. "No," he told a stunned Robinson, "I've made my decision and there will be no second thoughts." Stanky said he began doubting the wisdom of his hasty decision to leave his home in Alabama on the flight to Minneapolis to join the Rangers. After just one day on the job he felt "lonesome and homesick." One night alone in a Minneapolis hotel room convinced him he'd made a mistake.

"The attitude of the ballplayers was great," Stanky said. "There was a lot of jumping up and down after Wednesday's victory. I would have stayed if I didn't have to go to my room alone each night."[15] The 60-year-old Stanky returned to his job at the University of South Alabama, and Robinson resumed his search for a manager. Coach Connie Ryan was appointed interim skipper and was thought to have the inside track for the permanent job but told Robinson he didn't want it. Robinson turned to Baltimore Orioles coach Billy Hunter, whose only managerial experience had been with Bluefield, West Virginia, of the Appalachian League in 1962 and '63. Hunter's Bluefield teams won the league championship both seasons. He'd been a coach with the Orioles since 1964, so he came to the Rangers with a winning pedigree.

"I'm accepting the job because I think the Texas Rangers have a contending team,"[16] said the Rangers' fourth manager within seven days time upon his arrival in Arlington. The length of Hunter's contract wasn't revealed, but it was known he'd signed for more than one year.

Hunter proved to be an inspired choice. The Rangers won 60 and lost 33 the rest of the way to vault into second place with a record of 94–68 (they were 2–4 for Ryan), eight games behind Kansas City. Texas fell to third in 1978, trailing the Royals by five lengths, and Hunter was fired with one game left in the season. He never managed in the major leagues again and departed with a record of 146–108.

Stanky and Ryan were finished as managers as well. Stanky's career record was 467–435, and Ryan, in a pair of interim managing assignments, won 11 games and lost 22. Lucchesi would manage again, briefly, 10 years later.

California Angels
Norm Sherry to Dave Garcia

Gene Autry wanted a return on his investment.

Arbitrator Peter Seitz's historic 1975 ruling invalidating the reserve clause had opened the door to free agency, and Autry was the first big spender. Autry lavished $4.5 million worth of contracts on outfielder Joe Rudi and infielder/outfielder/designated hitter Don Baylor from Oakland, and second baseman Bobby Grich of Baltimore. Autry had owned the Angels since their creation in 1961 and hadn't even sniffed a post-season berth. He expected the additions of Rudi, Baylor and Grich to change that.

The pressure was on Norm Sherry to win. The Angels had responded well to Sherry after he replaced the abrasive Dick Williams in July of 1976, but the roster with the large payroll wasn't tearing up the American League West at the halfway point of 1977. With exactly 81 games in the books, the Angels were in fifth place with a record of 39–42. Kansas City wasn't running away with the division as it had the year before, so Autry and general manager Harry Dalton decided to change managers while the season could still be salvaged. Sherry was fired and replaced by coach Dave Garcia on July 11.

"We feel our team is definitely a contending club and has the capability of moving into the middle of the pennant race in the second half of the season," said Dalton, who hadn't enjoyed the success in Anaheim that he'd enjoyed in Baltimore. "We felt that these changes would help us accomplish this."[17] The second change was the dismissal of pitching coach Billy Muffett, who was replaced by former big league catcher Andy Etchebarren.

Garcia signed a contract running through 1978. His first move was hiring his former boss in Cleveland, Frank Robinson, as the Angels' batting instructor. Garcia had coached for the Indians in 1975 and '76 before resigning to take a position much closer to home.

Garcia, Robinson and Etchebarren couldn't rally the Angels, who were 35–46 in the season's second half. They finished a disappointing fifth with a record of 74–88.

1978

St. Louis Cardinals
Vern Rapp to Ken Boyer

If the St. Louis Cardinals had selected Ken Boyer to succeed the retiring Red Schoendienst in 1976, the tumultuous 1977 season never would have happened.

Boyer, a former Cardinal third baseman and the National League MVP during St. Louis's world championship season of 1964, was among the candidates considered when Schoendienst stepped aside after 12 years at the St. Louis helm. Instead, the Cardinals promoted Vern Rapp on the basis of his successful record compiled in the club's minor league system. Rapp soon discovered that managing minor leaguers and managing major leaguers were two entirely different propositions.

Rapp's old-school discipline and "my way or the highway" attitude quickly alienated his players in St. Louis. Despite a season of tension in the dugout, the Cardinals improved their record under Rapp, jumping from fifth place to third and winning 11 more games than they did in Schoendienst's final season. But the resentment against Rapp continued to fester in 1978, and when the Cardinals lost 11 of their first 17 games, owner August A. Busch, Junior, decided to cut his losses and fire his manager. Rapp got the word after a 7–2 victory over the Expos in Montreal on April 25.

"They decided something during the day, apparently prior to the game, but I was notified afterwards. We had a very tough week. Unfortunately, there was a press leak by one of the radio stations in St. Louis involving a dispute with Ted Simmons," said Rapp. The dispute with Simmons, the Cardinals' hard-hitting catcher, was just the latest in an ongoing series of confrontations with his players, and was the straw that broke the camel's back and led to Rapp's dismissal.

"I have no regrets," insisted the ex-manager. "I'm sorry I didn't have enough time. I've been knocked down before."[1]

Busch turned to Boyer to calm the nerves in the Cardinal dugout. "After consideration of a number of candidates, we have come to the conclusion that Ken Boyer is the best choice available. We are confident that he will bring to the job the same skill and dedication that made him an outstanding player and minor league manager," said the owner.[2] Boyer was managing the Cardinals' Rochester farm team of the International League when he replaced Rapp.

Boyer restored a semblance of harmony to the Cardinals, but their play in the field didn't improve. St. Louis was 62–81 for its new manager, finishing fifth in the NL East with a record of 69–93.

Rapp's unhappy experience in St. Louis didn't prevent him from getting another shot at managing. He was hired to pilot the Cincinnati Reds in 1984. He didn't last long in Cincinnati, either.

Oakland Athletics
Bobby Winkles to Jack McKeon

Most, if not all, of the managers Charles O. Finley fired as owner of the Kansas City/Oakland Athletics thought they'd done a good job for their cantankerous boss. Bobby Winkles thought so, too, but didn't think Finley agreed and beat the owner to the inevitable punch by resigning on May 23.

Ironically, Finley was pleased with Winkles's work. The Athletics had collapsed after Winkles replaced Jack McKeon in 1977, but Finley kept him anyway, and Winkles had the surprising Athletics in first place in the AL West with a record of 24–15 when he stepped down. He informed Finley of his decision in a phone call three hours before a game against the Milwaukee Brewers at Oakland Alameda County Coliseum. The resignation was effective the moment Winkles hung up.

"He gave as his reason for resigning that he did not think I was satisfied with the manner in which he was managing the team," said Finley. "I stated to Bobby personally [May 21] and again by telephone today [May 23] that I thought he had done an outstanding job and gave him every assurance that I wanted him to continue managing the A's. I personally am sorry to see Winkles leave and am certain the entire personnel of the ball club feel the same way."[3] Finley said he asked Winkles's coaches, McKeon, Red Schoendienst, and Lee Stange, to plead with him to reconsider. After phoning Finley, Winkles left the stadium without comment.

Maybe Winkles realized that the Athletics were playing over their heads and would soon plummet back to Earth, at which time Finley would undoubtedly have blamed his manager for the plunge in the standings and replaced him. Winkles's major league record for one full season and portions of three others was 170–213.

The Athletics were playing beyond their ability early in 1978, and they quickly returned to form for their new manager, McKeon, who had remained with the Oakland organization after being fired as manager the season before. The Athletics won 45 and dropped 78 for McKeon, falling from first place to sixth with a final ledger of 69–93. Finley fired McKeon a second time at the end of the season.

California Angels
Dave Garcia to Jim Fregosi

There could be no excuses in Anaheim in 1978.

Injuries to a pair of expensive free agent acquisitions, Bobby Grich and Joe Rudi, had torpedoed the Angels in 1977. Grich and Rudi were back at full strength in 1978, and the Angels broke from the gate quickly, winning 18 of their first 27 games. California occupied first place in the AL West for three days in late May, but a four-game losing streak dropped the club's record to 25–20. Owner Gene Autry and executive vice president Buzzie Bavasi didn't care that the team was still just one game out of first place. They decided to pull the plug on mild-mannered manager Dave Garcia.

"It's always difficult to replace a manager," said Bavasi, who had plenty of experience replacing managers while with the Padres, "particularly one as nice a guy as Dave Garcia. However, I'm sure Dave understands our problem."[4] If Garcia didn't, Autry spelled it out for him.

"We felt that the Angels needed more motivation, and that [Jim] Fregosi is the type of individual to fill that bill," said the owner.[5] Fregosi had been an original Angel, playing in 11 games during the team's inaugural season of 1961. He stayed with the team through 1971 before being traded to the Mets. Fregosi was still active as a player in 1978, playing in 20 games for Pittsburgh before being tapped to succeed Garcia with absolutely no managerial experience.

Despite the handicap of having to obtain on-the-job training, Fregosi led the Angels to a 62–55 record. California finished tied with Texas for second place, five games behind Kansas City, with a mark of 87–75. Fregosi and the Angels would break through in 1979, winning the franchise's first division title.

Garcia would be back in a major league dugout in 1979, returning to Cleveland as a coach for Jeff Torborg, and then replacing him as manager.

Chicago White Sox
Bob Lemon to Larry Doby

In 1947, when he owned the Indians, Bill Veeck made Larry Doby the first African American player in the American League. In 1978, when he owned the White Sox, Veeck made Doby the league's second African American manager.

Veeck insisted his decision to fire another of his former Cleveland players, Bob Lemon, was no reflection on Lemon's ability as a manager. Lemon managed the White Sox to an unexpected third-place finish in the AL West with 90 victories in 1977, but the team started slowly in '78 and Veeck felt the need to shake things up. The White Sox were in fifth place with a 34–40 record, but only 5½ games out of first, when Veeck made the change on June 30.

"Let me emphasize this was an amicable and mutual decision," Veeck announced. "But we felt that the club was not making any real progress, and that maybe we could stir things up a little bit, to help the overall fortunes of the ball club. Maybe I didn't do my job as well as I could have in putting the club together. But we felt we had a potential we weren't quite reaching and we thought maybe this could help. We're dealing in generalities here. Larry is very thorough, and I just think that in this case it may be a change in philosophies and approach we're after."[6]

Doby found the moment bittersweet. "I was surprised and somewhat saddened to a certain degree," said the Sox' new boss. "Bob and I have been friends since 1947. Although it's a happy moment for me, it's still not as happy as you would like for it to be. We had a long talk today and, of course, the first thing he said to me was, 'Don't feel that way, because we're still friends and these things happen in baseball.' If I'm around long enough, it will happen to me."[7]

Doby had made no secret of his ambition to manage. He'd coached for Montreal from 1971 through 1973 and again in 1976. He'd spent a year coaching with his old team, the Indians, in 1974, and was disappointed when Cleveland selected Frank Robinson to break the managerial color barrier. Doby thought the job should have been his.

Veeck did more than change managers. He also fired pitching coach Stan Williams, but neither move helped the White Sox achieve the potential Veeck erroneously thought the team had. The White Sox didn't play well for Doby, winning 37 and losing 50 the rest of the way. Chicago finished fifth with a record of 71–90. Veeck didn't retain Doby for 1978, and Larry never got another chance to manage in the major leagues.

As for Lemon, his dismissal by the White Sox would soon prove to be the biggest break of his career.

New York Yankees
Billy Martin to Bob Lemon

As early as the day Billy Martin was hired to replace Bill Virdon as manager of the New York Yankees in August of 1975, some pundits in the Big Apple predicted his tenure would end badly. And they were right. But what a ride the Yankees enjoyed in between.

Martin's Yankees won the team's first pennant in 12 years in 1976, only to be steamrolled by the juggernaut Reds in the World Series. Buoyed by the acquisition of Reggie Jackson, a player coveted by owner George Steinbrenner but not necessarily by Martin, the Yankees won another pennant in 1977 and defeated the Los Angeles Dodgers in a six-game World Series. The Yankees were on top of the baseball world for the first time since 1962, and Martin was the toast of New York. But even as the Yankees were rolling toward their first world's championship in 15 years, rumors abounded during the summer of 1977 that Martin's job was in jeopardy. His relationship with Jackson was contentious, as was his relationship with the demanding Steinbrenner. It all exploded in 1978.

Martin suspended Jackson for insubordination, and the two nearly came to blows in the visitors' dugout in Fenway Park and had to be separated. The seething anger that permeated the Yankee clubhouse spilled over in Chicago's O'Hare Airport as the club awaited its flight to Kansas City on July 23. In the presence of two New York newspaper reporters, Martin verbally unloaded on Jackson and Steinbrenner. The remarks were printed in the next day's papers, and Martin denied them. His resignation followed.

"Billy needed to resign for health reasons," said team president Al Rosen, who made it clear that had Martin not done so, he would have been fired. "I couldn't let any employee of the Yankees say things like that about the front office." As for Martin's denials, Rosen said, "I'm absolutely satisfied that Billy made the comment."[8] Martin departed with New York in second place with a 52–42 record, trailing Boston by 10 games.

Rosen chose his former Cleveland teammate, Bob Lemon, to succeed Martin. Rosen correctly surmised that Lemon's easygoing manner was just the prescription for a team whose nerves had been stretched to the breaking point by the ongoing Martin/Jackson/Steinbrenner melodrama.

"I'm trying to come in with an open mind," said Lemon, who was scouting for the White Sox before getting the call from Rosen. "I have no wild plans. I'm not here to experience what the problems have been. I go by the way a person treats me, not by the way they treated anybody else. I'm not worried about what's gone on; in fact, I don't even know what the heck went on here."

The new manager injected a much-needed note of humor into his hiring. "I don't know whether Al's going to put me on a weekly, daily or monthly contract."[9] Upon donning a New York uniform, Lemon told his charges to simply relax and play ball as best they could. They followed their new manager's lead and tore up the American League the rest of the way, winning 48 games and losing 20 to overcome Boston's double-digit lead in the standings and tie the Red Sox for first place after 162 games.

The Yankees won the playoff game, the League Championship Series, and the World Series. Lemon would return in 1979, but, like most of Steinbrenner's managers, he wouldn't finish the season.

1979

Detroit Tigers
Les Moss to "Sparky" Anderson

Five division titles, three pennants and two World Series championships. Managers with that kind of resume don't stay unemployed long. And George (Sparky) Anderson didn't.

Cincinnati Reds general manager Dick Wagner stunned the baseball world when he fired the man whose "Big Red Machine" dominated the National League from 1970 through 1976. But the Reds finished second in 1977 and 1978. Trades and free agency broke up that old gang of Anderson's, and Wagner decided a new manager was needed for a new era of Cincinnati baseball. Anderson sat at home in southern California waiting for the phone to ring. There was no doubt that it would. The question was which club would be the first to offer the most successful manager of the 1970s a job.

The offer came from the Tigers, who fired manager Les Moss on June 12. Moss had managed in the Tiger organization for 11 years, winning three minor league pennants and never finishing lower than third. He was chosen to replace Ralph Houk after the 1978 season and took over a club that finished fifth in the AL East with an 86–76 record. Detroit general manager Jim Campbell didn't show much confidence in Moss and signed him for just one year. Moss made it only one-third of the way through that contract.

Detroit was mired in fifth place with a 27–26 record when Campbell fired Moss and replaced him with Anderson. "This change was dictated by circumstances," explained Campbell. "I regret that things just did not work out with Les, who earned his chance to manage in the major leagues."[1] Campbell didn't offer any details as to the "circumstances" that dictated Moss's firing, but most likely it was a matter of Anderson's being available and the Tigers' wanting to grab him before another team in search of a new manager made an offer.

"I'm not saying that Sparky Anderson is going to turn everything around," said the new boss of the Bengals, "and I don't want any fan thinking that because I'm walking in there lightning is going to strike. The only way it's going to strike is when we as a group get our thing together and we all get a feeling for each other. When good things get going, everything spreads."²

Anderson didn't magically turn things around in Detroit. The Tigers remained in fifth place, winning 56 and losing 50 for their new manager. But Anderson had the luxury of time, which Moss did not. It took a five-year contract to lure Anderson to the Motor City. By his sixth year with the Tigers, Anderson had the club in the World Series.

Despite his impressive minor league record, Moss never managed in the majors again. In two brief stints as interim manager of the White Sox, and 53 games at the helm of the Tigers, his teams won 39 and lost 50.

New York Yankees
Bob Lemon to Billy Martin

New York's prodigal son came home early.

It had been announced at the 1978 Yankees old-timers' game that Billy Martin would return to manage the club in 1980, at which time the newly hired skipper, Bob Lemon, would become general manager. That announcement came as news to both Lemon and club president Al Rosen, neither of whom was informed of it before it was announced to a packed house at Yankee Stadium. Lemon shook off the surprise to rally the disorganized Yankees to win a second consecutive World Series.

When the Yankees broke slowly in 1979, George Steinbrenner decided to welcome Martin back sooner than scheduled. New York was in fourth place with a 34–31 record when Steinbrenner summoned Martin back to Yankee Stadium. "The past few days have been extremely difficult for all of us. Bob Lemon is a very close personal friend and a fine man," said Steinbrenner. "He and I sat together in Texas to discuss the entire situation. He was in agreement with my assessment and felt as I did that in the best interests of the team, perhaps a change was in order. We will welcome him into our front office family."³

According to Lemon, Steinbrenner "suggested a change and I said okay. I think an owner should have a prerogative of a change. I might have felt differently if I was 10 games in front. I know it isn't anything against me. It's just something to get the club going."⁴ Lemon's placid acceptance of his firing may have stemmed from the death of his 26-year-old son, Jerry, in a car accident in Arizona shortly after the 1978 World Series. Many observers said he appeared to be distracted and may have lost his desire to manage.

"Billy is prepared to take command of the team [June 19]," Steinbrenner said in a statement announcing the change. "I am hopeful that he will be able to turn the ball club around and make a run at the championship."⁵ The Yankees improved under Martin, going 55–40 the rest of the season, but still finished fourth with a record of 89–71. They didn't make a run at the championship, winding up 13½ games behind Baltimore.

Despite his agreement with Steinbrenner, Martin didn't manage the Yankees in 1980. He was dismissed for slugging a marshmallow salesman who'd goaded Martin by making disparaging remarks about the Yankees in a hotel bar in Bloomington, Minnesota, shortly after the 1979 World Series.

Cleveland Indians
Jeff Torborg to Dave Garcia

The Indians wanted Bob Lemon to come home.

Lemon's strong right arm won 207 games for the Indians in a Hall of Fame career from 1946 through 1958. His success as a manager with the Royals, White Sox and Yankees had caught their attention, and when Lemon was fired by George Steinbrenner on June 18, Cleveland team president Gabe Paul, who was back with the Tribe after working for Steinbrenner from 1973 through 1977, wasted no time making him an offer to manage the Indians ... but not until 1980.

Much to Paul's dismay, Lemon didn't jump at the opportunity to return to the only team he ever played for. He asked for time to consider the offer, which didn't stop the Indians from foolishly holding a press conference on July 1 to announce that the job was Lemon's if he wanted it. That didn't sit well with the man who currently had the job of managing the Indians, Jeff Torborg, who announced on July 2 that he was resigning, effective at season's end. An agitated Paul asked Torborg why he didn't resign immediately. An equally agitated Torborg replied that he was neither a quitter nor a fool. He wasn't about to forfeit the money the Indians owed him through the remainder of the season by walking away from the job.

The Indians played as they might have been expected to play for their lame-duck boss, and Paul and general manager Phil Seghi put a stop to the farce on July 23. Third base coach Dave Garcia was named interim manager, and Seghi stressed that he'd serve only until the end of the season, by which time the Indians would have an answer from Lemon, who was still being paid by Steinbrenner and in no hurry to make a decision.

Garcia took over a sixth-place team with a 43–52 record that was understandably confused (and probably amused) by the farcical situation it was in, and led it to 10 consecutive victories. The Tribe played .500 ball after that to finish with an 81–80 record, but remained in sixth place.

Lemon decided to stay with the Yankees. Garcia's 38–28 record as interim manager earned him the job for 1980. Paul and Seghi spent the season's final two months wiping egg off their faces.

Torborg's managing career wasn't over, nor was Lemon's.

Chicago White Sox
Don Kessinger to Tony LaRussa

A combination shortstop and manager named Lou Boudreau had led Bill Veeck's 1948 Cleveland Indians to a world's championship. Veeck named his shortstop, Don Kessinger, to succeed Larry Doby as manager of the White Sox in 1979, hoping history would repeat itself. It didn't.

The White Sox hovered around the .500 mark through the middle of June, within striking distance of the division lead, before sliding to a record of 46–60 on August 2. Kessinger met with Veeck and expressed a desire to quit. "He said that for the best interests of the club and the fans, a change was indicated. And you know he's not a fellow given to hasty decisions, and I obviously had to respect what he wanted to do. He felt it required some kind of a shock to shake the athletes from the lethargy into which they had apparently fallen," said the owner.[6]

In addition to resigning as manager, Kessinger retired as a player. Shortstop Harry Chappas was recalled from Triple-A to take his spot on the roster. To replace Kessinger as manager, Veeck selected former major league infielder Tony LaRussa. LaRussa's career consisted of 132 games over six seasons with the Athletics, Braves and Cubs. He was managing Chicago's Des Moines farm club at the time of his promotion.

"We've been very pleased with Tony's performance at Knoxville and Des Moines," said Veeck. "The Des Moines club has stayed close despite the fact we took all their pitching staff." Veeck noted that Kessinger was "very low-keyed" and LaRussa was "quite the opposite."[7]

The White Sox split their remaining 54 games for LaRussa, finishing fifth in the AL West with a record of 73–87. It was the beginning of a Hall of Fame managerial career for LaRussa. Kessinger wouldn't manage in the majors again.

Philadelphia Phillies
Danny Ozark to Dallas Green

Danny Ozark managed the Phillies to NL East titles in 1976, '77 and '78. But they'd fallen to the NL West champions in the League Championship Series each year, and when injuries reduced the Phillies to an also-ran in 1979, Ozark was fired on August 31.

"This change is an organizational move that owner Ruly Carpenter and I decided to make after two or three days of deliberation," said general manager Paul Owens, announcing Ozark's dismissal. "We were disappointed in the way the club has performed the past few weeks and felt that something had to be done."[8]

It appeared early in the season that the signing of former Cincinnati Red Pete Rose as a free agent would have the desired effect. Owens believed Rose, who often bragged of playing in more games his team won than any modern player, would provide the spark the Phillies needed to win a pennant and the first World Series in the franchise's 96-year history. The Phillies sprinted from the starter's block and were in first place as late as May 23. Then injuries and sub-par years from some key players took their toll, and Philadelphia had sagged to fifth, with a record of 65–67, when Ozark was released. He was replaced by Dallas Green, a former big league pitcher who won 20 games over eight seasons with the Phillies, Senators and Mets. Green was serving as Philadelphia's director of minor leagues and scouting when he was tabbed as interim manager.

Green said he expected his players "to grind it out for the next 30 days, and as professionals look in the mirror and see if they can't accomplish something with pride and dignity."[9] The Phillies were 19–11 for Green, finishing fifth with a record of 84–78. Owens was sufficiently impressed to name Green the club's manager for 1980, and the Phillies responded with a division title, a pennant, and the first World Series victory for a franchise whose origin dated back to 1883.

It had been a long time coming.

San Francisco Giants
Joe Altobelli to Dave Bristol

If ever there was a run-of-the-mill change in managers, this was it. Out-of-town newspapers buried the story in the back pages of their sports sections.

Joe Altobelli's major league career consisted of 166 games as an infielder and occasional outfielder with the Indians and Twins in 1955, 1957 and 1961. He was hired to manage the San Francisco Giants after their second dismissal of Bill Rigney following the 1976 season. The Giants finished fourth in the NL West in 1977 with a record of 75–87, improved to third at 89–73 in 1978, but dropped back to fourth in early September of 1979. The Giants had won just 16 games while losing 31 since the All-Star break, and owner Bob Lurie, who was having attendance problems, resorted to the age-old remedy for an ailing ball club. Altobelli was fired and replaced by veteran manager Dave Bristol.

A brief press release announcing the change said there was no inciting incident, but rather that Altobelli had been fired due to the club's 61–79 record.

The Giants won 10 and lost 12 for Bristol to finish the season fourth with a 71–91 record. Although Bristol was announced as the team's interim manager, he was hired for 1980 and guided the team to a fifth-place finish at 75–86. That ended Bristol's undistinguished managerial career. His teams won 657 games and lost 764. A third-place finish with Cincinnati (89–73 in 1969) was the best any of his teams could muster.

Altobelli would join Earl Weaver's coaching staff in Baltimore and be anointed to succeed Weaver upon his retirement in 1982.

1980

St. Louis Cardinals
Ken Boyer to "Whitey" Herzog to "Red" Schoendienst

Ken Boyer probably understood how Frankie Frisch felt.

When the Cardinals fired Frisch as their manager in 1938, the announcement was made during a game with the Pittsburgh Pirates. Frisch heard the announcement while coaching at first base. He walked off the field, cleaned out his office, and left the ballpark.

When the Cardinals fired Boyer in 1980, they did so between games of a double-header at Montreal's Olympic Stadium on June 8. St. Louis lost the first game, 6–4, its fourth straight defeat. Boyer was met in the clubhouse by general manager John Claiborne, who informed him that a change in managers was being made, effective immediately. Coach Jack Krol managed the Cardinals to a 9–4 loss in the nightcap. It dropped St. Louis's record to 18–34. The team was last in the NL East, trailing the division-leading Expos by 12½ games, when Boyer's successor, Whitey Herzog, took the reins the next night in Atlanta. The Cardinals responded with an 8–5 victory over the Braves.

"I don't think we're a last-place club," said Herzog. "Things have happened and I'm not blaming anybody. We just have to right it."[1] Herzog was available because he'd been fired by the Royals in October of 1979. Three straight division titles (and three straight losses to the Yankees in the League Championship Series) weren't enough to save his job when Kansas City fell to second place.

Herzog couldn't steer the Cardinals back into contention, but they were 38–35 for their new manager when he was kicked upstairs on August 29. Herzog was appointed general manager, succeeding Claiborne, who was fired on August 18. Coach Red Schoendienst was named interim manager for the balance of the season and won 18 while losing 19. Under three managers, the Cardinals finished fourth with a record of 74–88.

After the season, Herzog decided the best available manager for 1981 was a fellow named Whitey Herzog and re-hired himself. It proved to be a wise choice, as he led the Cardinals to pennants in 1982, 1985 and 1987, plus the 1982 World Series title.

Boyer never managed in the major leagues again. In one full season and parts of two others, his Cardinals won 166 games and lost 190. St. Louis had finished third with a record of 86–76 in 1979, Boyer's only full season on the job.

Chicago Cubs
Preston Gomez to Joe Amalfitano

Once a Dodger, always a Dodger.

After unsuccessful stints as manager of the Padres and Astros, Preston Gomez was back on the coaching lines for Los Angeles (from which he'd been plucked to manage San Diego in 1969) when he was hired by the Cubs for the 1980 season.

Gomez's Cubs got off to a decent start but fell below the .500 plateau on May 18 and stayed there for the rest of the season. Injuries to slugger Dave Kingman and catcher Barry Foote didn't help matters, and the Cubs were in last place with a record of 38–52 when general manager Bob Kennedy accompanied the team to Los Angeles, where it began a 10-game road trip on July 25. Before the first game in Dodger Stadium, he fired Gomez.

Coach Joe Amalfitano was appointed interim manager for the second time in less than a year. Amalfitano had taken over when Herman Franks quit with seven games remaining in the 1979 season. Seventy-two games remained in 1980, and it was believed that with a strong showing, the Cubs could remove the "interim" tag from their new boss's title. Chicago was even worse under Amalfitano than it had been under Gomez, but despite winning just 26 and losing 46, Kennedy retained him for 1981.

Gomez was through as a big league manager. His career record was 346–529. His highest finish was fourth with the 1974 Astros.

Seattle Mariners
Darrell Johnson to Maury Wills

Before a 1978 exhibition game against Cleveland, Seattle Mariners coach Vada Pinson said the second-year franchise no longer considered itself an expansion team. Despite Pinson's optimism, the Mariners racked up 104 defeats in their second season and 95 more in their third. Seattle started well in 1980 and was just three games behind American League West leader Kansas City on Memorial Day before reverting to its previous form. The Mariners' 65th defeat, on August 3, cost manager Darrell Johnson his job.

Team president Dan O'Brien announced the firing and introduced former major league shortstop Maury Wills as Seattle's new field boss. Wills had played on four pennant-winning Dodger teams, and led the National League in stolen bases six times, including a big league record 104 thefts in 1962.

Wills had made no secret of his desire to manage, but what led O'Brien to believe he was ready to take over in Seattle's dugout isn't clear. Although Wills had done some coaching with the Dodgers, he had no managerial experience north of the border. He'd managed in the Mexican League, and some of his strategy during his brief tenure with the Mariners gave observers the impression he thought he was still there. Wills signed a contract running through 1982.

The Mariners were in sixth place when Wills took over on August 5 and fell to seventh by losing their first game for their new manager. They stayed in seventh place the rest of the way, winning only 20 and losing 38 for a final mark of 59–103.

Wills would be fired before Memorial Day of 1981.

Minnesota Twins
Gene Mauch to Johnny Goryl

When a manager or coach is fired in professional sports, it is often said by the party doing the firing that the players need to "hear a new voice." The phrase may have originated with Gene Mauch.

A 3–2 loss to Detroit at Metropolitan Stadium on August 24 dropped the Minnesota Twins' record to 54–71. They were in fourth place in the AL West, 26½ games out of first. The players packed their bags for a road trip that began in Cleveland the following day. Mauch stayed behind.

"For a lot of years, I threw a lot of words to a lot of players," said Mauch in announcing his resignation. "They were words which meant a lot to me; words like pride, dedication and responsibility. It's time for these players to hear some new words from a new voice. I hate the word 'quit' and I don't think that's what I'm doing. I'm not satisfied that I'm making contribution enough to stay around, and it irritated me to the point that I suggested to Calvin Griffith that it would probably be good for the team to function in a new atmosphere. He agreed."[2] Mauch said he didn't feel comfortable with the role he was playing in the ball club's progress ... or possibly lack of progress. He had managed the Twins since 1976, never finishing higher than third.

Coach Johnny Goryl was given the task of managing the Twins for the rest of the year. His fresh voice seemed to have a positive influence on a club that may have grown weary of Mauch's intensity. Minnesota won 23 and lost 13 to finish the season in third place with a 77–84 mark. Griffith liked what he saw and retained Goryl for 1981.

Minnesota was the third club Mauch had managed. He soon made it four.

1981

Seattle Mariners
Maury Wills to Rene Lachemann

Maury Wills wasn't the first former player to be hired as a manager without any significant experience. But he may have been the worst.

Dan O'Brien realized he'd made a mistake by hiring Wills to replace Darrell Johnson in August of 1980 and moved swiftly to correct it. The Mariners were off to the poorest start in their five-year history with a 6–18 record when O'Brien dismissed Wills on May 6. Former major league catcher Rene Lachemann, whose career lasted three years and 118 games with the Kansas City/Oakland Athletics from 1965 through 1968, was chosen to replace him. O'Brien wouldn't make the mistake of hiring a manager with no experience (unless Wills's time in the Mexican League is considered) again. Lachemann was managing Seattle's Triple-A farm club in Spokane when he was promoted.

"This is not something new to Lach and I, because we've talked about his desire to become a major league manager on a number of occasions," said O'Brien as he introduced the Mariners' new bench leader. "I don't know of anyone who has worked harder or deserves the opportunity more."[1]

As to why the switch was made, O'Brien explained, "A manager is no better than his players. You have to have a cohesive performing unit and that happens when talent takes over and you start to play and start to win. That wasn't happening." O'Brien said the firing was "not only in [Wills's] best interests, but those of the club. It was best that we change the picture."[2]

Wills wasn't dismissed "for lack of an all-out effort. I can't say enough about how cooperative he was to work with, how sensitive he is to people, perhaps too sensitive."[3] O'Brien said he believed Wills had been given a fair shot, even though he managed just 82 games. His record of 26–56 spoke for itself, even for a club as weak as the Mariners.

Pundits nationally absolved O'Brien of any blame for a quick hook, saying Wills was "a complete disaster" and "overmatched as a manager." Major league general managers apparently agreed, as none gave Wills a second chance.

Lachemann helmed the Mariners for just 33 games before the players' union went on strike in June. Seattle was 15–18 for Lachemann (21–36 overall) before the work stoppage and 23–29 after the players returned, for a season's record of 44–65. Such an aberrational year was hardly a fair test of Lachemann's ability, and he was retained for 1982.

Minnesota Twins
Johnny Goryl to Billy Gardner

Johnny Goryl's fresh voice turned sour quickly.

The same Minnesota players who'd closed the 1980 season with a rush to earn Goryl full-time employment staggered through April and May of 1981. The Twins were in sixth place with an 11–25 record, on an eight-game losing streak, and losers of 10 of 11 when Goryl was given his walking papers after an 8–2 loss to Milwaukee on May 25.

Owner Calvin Griffith wasn't overly confident his new manager, Billy Gardner, could fix what was wrong with the Twins. "It was our thought that hopefully, possibly, a change in managers at this time might redirect the team and get it going again. It's a good team. It didn't take us long to decide on Billy. He's experienced as a manager. He managed 12 years in the minors, won five pennants and was manager of the year three times."[4] Gardner also had 10 years' playing experience, as an infielder with the Giants, Orioles, Twins, Senators and Red Sox from 1954 through 1963.

Griffith was wrong about his Twins. They weren't a good team. But they weren't as bad as they were playing for Goryl. They won just six and lost 14 for their new manager before the strike (for a record of 17–39) but perked up afterward, going 24–29 in the season's second half for a final overall mark of 41–68. Gardner would be back in 1982.

Goryl had many years ahead of him in baseball, but none as a manager. His career record for 72 games was 34–38.

California Angels
Jim Fregosi to Gene Mauch

Less than two years after leading the Angels to their first post-season appearance, Jim Fregosi was out of work.

Fregosi's 1980 club was decimated by injuries and slipped from an 88–74 record and a division title to 65–95, the worst record in the franchise's history. Fregosi was given a chance to reverse the Angels' fortunes in 1981, and with owner Gene Autry continuing to spend liberally to acquire talent via free agency, he expected the downturn to be brief. California was treading water through Memorial Day, and Autry decided a change was necessary. He looked no further than the team's front office to find a replacement for Fregosi: Gene Mauch, the recently hired director of player personnel.

"Jimmy has been a friend of mine for years," said Autry. "However, we have to think of the best interests of the club, and for this reason we think a change is necessary."[5] Fregosi had claimed not to be worried about his job in early May, but soon afterward Autry began publicly questioning his manager's ability to motivate his players.

"I'm thankful for the opportunity Gene and [general manager] Buzzie Bavasi gave me to manage over the last three years," Fregosi said in departing. "I just wish the team had played better. I think they're an outstanding group of men, and I wish them all the best of luck the rest of the season."[6]

The Angels were 22–25 when Mauch took over. They won nine and lost four before the strike and went 20–30 after it. Overall, California won 51 and lost 59. Autry brought Mauch back in 1982 and was rewarded with a 93–69 record and the AL West championship—the first of only two titles Mauch won in 26 seasons of managing.

Fregosi's managing career was far from over, and it would include a pennant.

Kansas City Royals
Jim Frey to Dick Howser

Had there been a "Rookie of the Year" award for managers, Jim Frey would have won it.

All the first-year skipper of the Royals did was lead the team to 97 victories, the AL West title, and a satisfying three-game sweep of George Steinbrenner's Yankees, possessors of the best record in baseball, in the League Championship Series. Frey ran out of magic in the World Series, as the Royals were defeated by a Philadelphia club on a mission to win the first world's championship in its 97-year history. Still, Frey appeared to have a long and prosperous stay ahead of him in Kansas City.

That stay lasted less than a year. The defending champions fell flat on their faces as the 1981 season began, losing 10 of their first 13 games to fall into last place on April 30. With only a baker's dozen games played, the Royals were already a staggering 11 games out of first place. And things never improved. When the players went on strike, the Royals had won 20 games and lost 30. With a chance to right the ship and earn a play-off spot by winning the "second half" title in the west, Kansas City was a mediocre 10–10 on August 29, when general manager Joe Burke dismissed Frey following a 2–0 loss to Toronto at Exhibition Stadium.

Burke described Frey as being "stunned" by the news that he would be replaced by Dick Howser, the manager he'd defeated in the 1980 League Championship Series. Frey said, "Thank you for having me here. I like the organization. I have nothing to say now, or will I have in the future, except admiration for the Royals."[7]

Howser signed a three-year contract ... the longest pact the Royals had ever given a manager. He said the most important element in managing was "winning—but sometimes that's not enough."[8] He was referring to his dismissal by Steinbrenner after winning 103 games and the AL East in 1980. Nothing but a World Series title satisfied Steinbrenner, and Howser had failed to produce one.

Howser got the stumbling Royals turned around. They won 20 and lost 13 under his direction, and their 30–23 record was good enough to grab the "second half" title in the west. The first-half champion Oakland Athletics were guaranteed a spot in the expanded post-season tournament, and they dispatched Kansas City in three straight games. Oakland pitching held the Royals to a paltry two runs in sweeping the series.

Frey would be hired to manage the Cubs in 1984.

New York Yankees
Gene Michael to Bob Lemon

Above all else (except winning), George Steinbrenner demanded loyalty from his employees. When he didn't get it, heads rolled.

In the final week before the players' union went on strike in June, the Yankees had grabbed first place in the AL East and held it on the final day of play before the work stoppage. They were declared the "first half" champions and were guaranteed a place in the post-season tournament baseball's brain trust put together. Thus, with the exception of gaining home field advantage in the first play-off round, New York had little to play for when the game resumed on August 10. That didn't stop Steinbrenner from finding fault with Gene Michael's managing, as he'd found fault with all the managers he'd hired before Michael. The former major league shortstop grew weary of the constant nagging from the owner's office and, in late August, delivered an ultimatum: fire me or back off!

Steinbrenner considered Michael's tantrum an act of both disloyalty and insubordination. He demanded an apology, and when none was forthcoming, he granted his manager's wish. Michael was replaced by Bob Lemon on September 6. Back for a second tour of duty, Lemon said, "Usually, when you make a change like this, it's because the team's not winning. But I'm just going to hope they keep playing like they have been. There's nothing to be turned around."[9] The Yankees were 15–12 in the "second half" when Michael was relieved of his duties.

Steinbrenner signed Michael to a three-year contract to succeed Dick Howser in 1980. He called dismissing him the hardest decision he'd had to make as owner because he considered Michael "like family."

"I don't want to say he's better off," said Howser, observing the latest developments in the Bronx Zoo from the safety of his office at Royals Stadium, "but when the guillotine is over your head, it's better to have it happen. His head's been on the block for a long time. Sometimes, it's a relief. In my case, it was."[10]

As for why Lemon accepted a job from a boss who had dismissed him once, the new Yankee manager replied, "I was never known to be too smart."[11] Lemon managed the Yankees past Milwaukee in the divisional play-off and past Billy Martin's Oakland club in the League Championship Series. New York took the first two games from the Dodgers at Yankee Stadium in the World Series; then, in a startling reversal of form, lost four in a row, including game six in New York, 9–2.

Steinbrenner seethed, but he retained Lemon for 1982. Like Lemon, Michael would also return for another tour of duty with the Yankees.

Montreal Expos
Dick Williams to Jim Fanning

Rumor had it George Steinbrenner still had his eye on Dick Williams.

One day after Steinbrenner fired Gene Michael, Montreal Expos president and general manager John McHale fired Williams, despite the fact the club was in the thick of the race for the "second half" championship of the NL East. Or maybe because of it.

"We're floundering around," said McHale. "It's a funny season. We still have a chance to win. But the way we're playing, I didn't think we could win under the circumstances."[12]

Rumors were circulating that Steinbrenner had made a surreptitious offer to Williams to manage the Yankees in 1982. Such contact would have violated baseball's tampering rules. McHale said the stories had no bearing on his decision to dismiss Williams. "We made up our mind before the story surfaced. I don't think that's a healthy thing to be going on. I just didn't think the club could win the way we're playing. We lack discipline and direction."[13]

Williams was in his fifth season in Montreal. His 1977 and '78 teams finished with losing records, but in 1979 and '80 the Expos finished second. Montreal's 95 victories in 1979 left it three games behind Pittsburgh, and its 90 wins in 1980 came up one game short of the Phillies. The Expos were in third place when the strike began in 1981, and had a record of 14–12 in the "second half" when McHale changed managers.

Williams responded to the accusation that his team lacked discipline by saying, "I don't know. Since baseball has no more reserve clause, it's not like it used to be. It's tougher for a manager to do what he wants. I might be wrong, but I feel that way."[14]

Montreal's new manager was Jim Fanning, its general manager from 1969 through 1976, and the team's farm director when he was placed in charge by McHale. Fanning had no managerial experience, but McHale thought he'd have a better personal relationship with the players than Williams.

The Expos went 16–11 for Fanning and won the "second half" title with a record of 30–23. Montreal eliminated the "first half" champion Phillies in a five-game divisional play-off before falling to the Dodgers, also in five games, in the League Championship Series.

Fanning managed the Expos to a third-place finish in 1982, then returned to the front office. Williams would manage in 1982 also, but in San Diego, not New York.

1982

New York Yankees
Bob Lemon to Gene Michael

Bob Lemon probably should have been grateful for the 14 games he got.

Yankees owner George Steinbrenner was reportedly livid after his club won the first two games of the 1981 World Series and then collapsed, losing four in a row. Steinbrenner planned to fire Lemon right then and there, but calmed down and announced at baseball's winter meetings in December that Lemon would return in 1982 and would be given a full season at the helm. He'd then retire, and Gene Michael would take over in 1983 and manage the Yankees for three seasons. That was the plan, anyway.

Lemon didn't even make it through April. As he put it, "I thought this time it would go nine innings, but I never got out of the first inning. The man felt a change was needed, so why wait? But, 14 days? I had a bad spring. Why didn't he fire me this spring?"[1]

The Yankees were 6–8 when Steinbrenner terminated Lemon's second tour of duty in pinstripes. The only consolation, according to Lemon, was that he was dismissed "softly ... he didn't yell at me for a change." Lemon expanded upon the experience of managing for Steinbrenner:

> It's great here during the game. Before and after the game is the toughest part. During the game is great. You have the best horses.
> In 44 years I've had about everything you can have in this game, and all good things. This is just one of the few tough moments. I've had so many good times that offset this, it won't bother me long.[2]

Lemon would return to his job as a west coast scout for the Yankees. His managerial days were over. Lemon's teams compiled a record of 430–403.

Michael was asked why he was willing, as Lemon had been the previous September, to return to the dugout for an owner who'd fired him once. Managing the Yankees, said Michael, was "addictive ... or like hitting your head against a wall."³ The master plan had been for Michael to replace Lemon in 1983. He wouldn't survive 1982.

Milwaukee Brewers
"Buck" Rodgers to Harvey Kuenn

Milwaukee general manager Harry Dalton gave the usual reasons for firing Bob (Buck) Rodgers.

Rodgers managed the Brewers to the second-half championship of the American League East in the 1981 strike season. Milwaukee lost to the Yankees in the divisional play-off. That earned Rodgers a one-year contract extension, but when the Brewers played lethargically into early June of 1982, Dalton took action.

Milwaukee had lost 14 of 21 games to fall to fifth place with a record of 23–24 on June 2, when Dalton fired his manager. "The main reason for the change is that the club has not played up to what we think its potential is," said Dalton, sounding like a lot of general managers announcing a change in field managers. This time, however, Dalton was correct. The Brewers were underachieving. "We have a club which we legitimately believe is strong enough to be a contender, and we have not played in that fashion for the last three weeks or so."⁴

Dalton hoped Harvey Kuenn, the 1959 American League batting champion who'd played for the Tigers, Indians, Giants, Cubs and Phillies in a 15-year career, could change that. Kuenn had been Milwaukee's batting coach since 1971, and the players liked him. Kuenn was only appointed Milwaukee's "interim" manager; however, Dalton said he would be "a full manager in every sense. The 'interim' simply means that at some point we will have someone else come in to handle this ball club. However, the duration of this interim period is open-ended. It could well go through the end of the 1982 season."⁵

It did. The Brewers got their act together for Kuenn and stormed to the top of the division, then hung on for a one-game margin over Baltimore with a 95–67 mark. Milwaukee was 72–43 under Kuenn.

The Brewers lost the first two games of the League Championship Series to Gene Mauch's Angels in Anaheim before winning three in a row at County Stadium to capture the franchise's first pennant in its 13th season of existence. The joy ride ended when the St. Louis Cardinals beat the Brewers in a seven-game World Series.

Kuenn returned in 1983. The bubble burst and Milwaukee dropped to fifth place with a record of 87–75. Kuenn was fired at the end of the year and never managed again. His career record was 160–118 with one pennant.

Rodgers wasn't finished managing by a long shot. He was hired to pilot Montreal in 1985.

Cincinnati Reds
John McNamara to Russ Nixon

John McNamara's Reds had done something unique in 1981. Despite compiling the best record in the major leagues, the Reds didn't qualify for the post-season tournament.

That wouldn't have been possible in any season except 1981, when the strike by the players' union turned the game topsy-turvy. The Reds' overall record of 66–42 broke down into a 35–21 mark before the strike, and 31–21 after. Neither was good enough to top the National League West in either half of the season. The Reds watched the post-season tournament on television despite having won more games than any other major league club.

The 1982 Reds were a vastly different ball club from the 1981 edition. Gone were third baseman Ray Knight, and outfielders George Foster, Ken Griffey, and Dave Collins. Pitcher Tom Seaver's victory total plunged from 14 to five, and Tom Hume's declined from nine to two. General manager Dick Wagner thought he'd given McNamara a contending club in 1982, but the results on the field said otherwise. So Wagner did what most general managers would have under the circumstances. With Cincinnati in sixth place, he fired his manager.

"A managerial change is never an easy move to make," said Wagner. "The bottom line is that in this case I feel we are a better ball club than our record of 34–58 indicates. It's an extremely tough decision because McNamara has worked hard. We have 70 games remaining in our season, and our work is cut out for us."[6] Coach Joe Amalfitano, who joined the Reds after being fired as manager of the Cubs after the 1981 season, was also let go.

McNamara was replaced by coach Russ Nixon, a former major league catcher who'd toiled for the Indians, Red Sox and Twins. Nixon managed in the Cincinnati farm system from 1970 through 1975 before joining Sparky Anderson's coaching staff. "I'd like to get back in the winning habit. I don't think anybody here accepts it, but I think we've found ways to lose. It's going to be an aggressive club. If we don't have power, we're going to have to win games otherwise."

Nixon said he deserved the opportunity to see what he could do with the Reds. "In winter ball, I've done just about everything. I think I do deserve it."[7]

Cincinnati continued to lose with Nixon in charge. The Reds were 27–43 for their new boss, finishing a distant sixth with 61 wins and 101 losses. They were 16 games behind fifth-place Houston. Despite not being able to turn things around, Wagner decided Nixon had earned a full season in command and retained him for 1983. McNamara would resurface in Anaheim in 1983, hired by Gene Autry to replace the retired Gene Mauch.

Texas Rangers
Don Zimmer to Darrell Johnson

In 1976, Don Zimmer had replaced Darrell Johnson as manager of the Boston Red Sox. In 1982, Johnson replaced Zimmer as manager of the Texas Rangers.

Zimmer was released by the Red Sox with seven games left in the 1980 season and hooked on with the Rangers in 1981, managing the club to 57 wins and 48 losses during the strike-abbreviated campaign. Texas was in sixth place with a 38–56 record on July 26 when owner Eddie Chiles fired Zimmer, then had the nerve to ask him to stick around and manage the next two games against Milwaukee before Johnson took his job. For some reason not stated in newspaper accounts of the change in managers, Zimmer agreed. The Rangers lost both games for their lame-duck manager, so Johnson inherited a team with a 38–58 record on July 30.

Zimmer also attended the press conference at which Chiles announced his dismissal.

"Don didn't do anything wrong," the owner told reporters who wanted to know why the move had been made. That raised Chiles's Texas dander. "We are not a public business," he responded. "We are not a government agency. You're not entitled to know everything we do!"

Chiles was then asked why he chose Johnson as the Rangers' new manager. "That's my business!" he barked.[8] That ended the press conference. Before it concluded, Zimmer, despite the fact his team was 20 games below .500, professed to having no idea why Chiles fired him.

Johnson had more to say to the press than the man who hired him. "One of the main things we have to do is evaluate the team's personnel and still try to win as many games as possible. I never saw a thing that Zimmy did that I thought was wrong."[9] The Rangers won 26 and lost 40 for Johnson for a final record of 64–98. Texas finished sixth in the AL West, 29 games behind the division champion Angels.

Johnson didn't manage in the major leagues again. In five full seasons and portions of three others with Boston, Seattle and Texas, his teams won 472 and lost 590, with one pennant.

Zimmer had a lot more managing ahead of him.

New York Yankees
Gene Michael to Clyde King

Clyde King hoped he could do for the Yankees what Bob Lemon had done in 1978.

Amid another season of stress and turmoil, Gene Michael had been fired for the second time in less than a year on August 4. Since taking over from Lemon, Michael had won 44 games and lost 42. The Yankees were an even 50–50 when King, the former manager of the Braves and Giants, took over.

"I think we still have a chance to win, and I think the players think so," said King.

> This club is only eight games out. Remember in 1978, we were 14 games out and won everything. Most of you think we had a better club then, and I'm not saying you're not right, but I think we've got a good enough team. What I'd like to do is just get into the boat and steer it out into the calm where everybody can get their heads together and perform to what they're capable of doing without causing instant malfunction. I think we've had some of that. I'd like to create an atmosphere here where the players will love to come to the ball park and love to be in the clubhouse instead of dragging their feet in.[10]

King was serving as a special assignment scout when he was tapped by George Steinbrenner to replace Michael. "I know it's not what you want to do, but I'd like you to do this for me," said the boss.[11] King, who had been the Yankees' pitching coach for five weeks earlier in the chaotic season, said he'd be glad to return to scouting at season's end. Steinbrenner said he might manage the Yankees in 1983. King said he'd prefer scouting, although he told reporters, "I want to make sure you understand this—I do not dislike managing."[12]

King guided New York to a 29–33 record the rest of the way. The Yankees finished fifth, their lowest finish since 1969, the first season of divisional play. New York's 79–83 record was its first losing mark since 1973. All thoughts of King's managing the Yankees in 1983 vanished when Oakland fired Billy Martin after the 1982 campaign.

King managed only one full season (1969) in the major leagues. His clubs won 234 and lost 229. Michael wouldn't manage for Steinbrenner again, but his career as a field boss wasn't over.

Houston Astros
Bill Virdon to Bob Lillis

Before the season began, Bill Virdon declared the 1982 Astros to be "the best team I ever had in Houston."[13] That included the 1980 NL West champions who lost a hard-fought League Championship Series to the Philadelphia Phillies, and the 1981 team that captured the "second half" West title before losing to the Dodgers in the post-season tournament.

Virdon's Astros weren't performing up to the expectations of their manager or the team's owner and board chairman, John McMullen, in early August. Houston hadn't been above .500 since the third game of the year, and with the club in fifth place with a 49–62 mark on August 9, Virdon was dismissed.

"We made the decision that we were going to need a new manager next year," explained McMullen, "and in the interest of both the ball club and Bill Virdon, this seemed to be the appropriate time."[14] Virdon was replaced by coach Bob Lillis, whose Houston roots ran deep. Lillis, an infielder, had been plucked by the Astros from the St. Louis Cardinals in the expansion draft that created the team in 1962. He spent six years playing for the Astros, then joined the team's coaching staff in 1973. Virdon described him as "one of the best people I know, and without a doubt the best coach anyone could have."[15]

Lillis said the change in managers surprised him. "I'm still trying to recover. I have deep feelings for Bill. He's a gentleman and a pro."[16] The Astros showed some improvement for Lillis, winning 28 and losing 23 for a final record of 77–85. He couldn't move them out of fifth place, however. Lillis managed the Astros through 1985, winning 276 and losing 261.

Virdon signed to manage the Expos in 1983.

1983

New York Mets
George Bamberger to Frank Howard

The first time George Bamberger resigned from a major league managing job, he did it for his health. The second time, he did it because he didn't need the aggravation.

Bamberger stepped down as Milwaukee's manager late in the 1980 season. He'd managed 92 games after recuperating from heart bypass surgery and decided he wasn't up to the rigors of the job in his present condition. A year later, Mets general manager Frank Cashen persuaded Bamberger to end his retirement. Cashen had been Baltimore's general manager while Bamberger served as Earl Weaver's pitching coach, and the man known as "Bambi" relented.

Baltimore's pitching staff had been among the best in baseball during Bamberger's years there. But the 1982 Mets had no Jim Palmers, Mike Cuellars, or Dave McNallys on their staff. Bamberger didn't have the cure for New York's pitching woes, and the Mets finished last in the NL East with a 65–97 record. A discouraged Bamberger wanted to quit at season's end, but Cashen talked him into returning in 1983.

The Mets sputtered from the start in 1983, and Bamberger again told Cashen in early May that he wanted to resign. Cashen counseled patience. But with New York in sixth place, dragged down by the worst record in the major leagues at 16–30, Bamberger called Cashen on June 1 and repeated his desire to step down. Cashen asked Bamberger to think it over for a few more hours, but Bamberger was not to be denied. He walked away from the job and was replaced by former Dodgers and Senators slugger Frank Howard, who had coached for him in Milwaukee as well as with the Mets.

Bamberger insisted his current state of health played no part in his decision to resign. "There's nothing wrong with me now. But if I continue with this job another four months, there might be. I had ulcers once, and I don't want to get them back. The thing is, I don't need this. I'm going on 58, and I don't need the job."[1]

Howard, who'd managed the Padres to a 41–69 record during the strike-marred 1981 season and was fired immediately afterward, was appointed interim manager for the rest of the season. "I know what people think," said the Mets' new manager. "Why would he be so dumb or naïve as to accept the job only for the rest of the season? But I feel I owe the Mets the courtesy of taking it for the rest of the season, and if that's what they want, I'm not worried about the future."[2]

Howard's tenure as Mets manager was brief. New York did no better for him than it had for Bamberger, winning 52 games and losing 64. The Mets finished last with a record of 68–94, and Howard was fired at the end of the season. He never managed in the majors again, and his career record was 93–133.

Bamberger would be lured out of retirement a second time. He'd return to Milwaukee to manage the Brewers in 1985. He led the team to a pair of sixth-place finishes and was fired with nine games left in the 1986 season. His career record as a manager was 458–478.

Seattle Mariners
Rene Lachemann to Del Crandall

One former big league catcher with minor league managing experience hadn't turned the Mariners around. Owner George Argyros hoped another one would.

Rene Lachemann had moved the Mariners up to fourth place in 1982, the highest finish in the team's six-year existence, with a record of 76–86. But Seattle slid backward in 1983, and Argyros fired Lachemann with the club in last place, 13½ games behind first-place Texas, on June 26.

According to Argyros, Lachemann "has the right qualities to make a good major league manager under the right set of circumstances. It has nothing to do with my personal feelings toward Lach. We expect the team to play to its potential, and we don't think it has. We felt we had to make a change."[3] Argyros acknowledged the Mariners were still in their infancy and needed "careful handling," which he believed new manager Del Crandall could provide.

Crandall had managed the Brewers from 1972 through 1975 and had spent the past six seasons at the helm of the Dodgers' Triple-A Albuquerque farm club of the Pacific Coast

League. He took over a team with a 26–47 record and minus veteran pitcher Gaylord Perry and shortstop Todd Cruz, both of whom were released when Lachemann was fired. The 44-year-old Perry had given Seattle some positive publicity when he won the 300th game of his career in a Mariner uniform in 1982, but he was alleged to be responsible for some clubhouse tension thanks to negative remarks about a few of his young teammates. Perry was 3–10 when he was cut loose.

The Mariners won 34 and lost 55 for Crandall and finished seventh, with an overall mark of 60–102. Although Crandall signed a three-year contract, he wouldn't last through the 1984 season.

Philadelphia Phillies
Pat Corrales to Paul Owens

Few managers lose their jobs with their clubs in second place, two games out of first.

That was where Pat Corrales had his Phillies on July 18, but their 43–42 record didn't satisfy team president Bill Giles or general manager Paul Owens. Corrales, who spent most of his major league playing days backing up Hall of Famer catcher Johnny Bench in Cincinnati, was fired and replaced by Owens for the rest of the season.

"There is something wrong with this club," Giles said bluntly, "and Paul and I have knocked around the idea of making a change. We both felt [Owens] would be the best person to run the club for the rest of the season. Next year, he'll return to his role in the front office."[4] Owens had been with the Phillies since 1965, and their general manager since 1972. It was the second time he'd been called on to manage the Phillies on an interim basis. Owens had stepped in to finish the 1972 season after Frank Lucchesi was fired.

Philadelphia took control of the division with Owens at the helm. The Phillies' 47–30 record lifted them to the eastern title with a mark of 90–72, and they upset the favored Dodgers in the League Championship Series to win their second pennant in four years. But Owens could squeeze no more from an aging club, and Philadelphia was beaten by Baltimore in the World Series in five games.

Giles was so pleased with Owens's work in the dugout that he scrapped the plan to hire a new manager for 1984. Owens brought the Phillies home in fourth place with an 81–81 record and never wore a uniform again. His career record as a manager was 161–158, with one pennant.

Corrales, who had managed Texas in 1979 and '80 before taking the job in Philadelphia, would find employment before the month was out.

Cleveland Indians
Mike Ferraro to Pat Corrales

Mike Ferraro's brief career as manager of the Indians started badly and never got better.

After 3½ seasons under the leadership of the grandfatherly Dave Garcia, Gabe Paul decided the Tribe needed a young firebrand of a manager and chose Ferraro, whose big league career consisted of exactly one year's worth of games (162) spread over four seasons with the Yankees, Mariners and Brewers between 1967 and 1972. The 38-year-old Ferraro had been a coach with the Yankees, and his experience with New York wasn't adequate preparation for the monumental task that awaited him in Cleveland, where the Indians hadn't been serious contenders since 1959.

Shortly before spring training began, a routine physical examination discovered that Ferraro had a cancerous kidney which required immediate surgery. Once the season began, he had differences with several players, including pitchers Lary Sorensen and Rick Sutcliffe, and third baseman Toby Harrah, who admitted point-blank, "I don't like Ferraro and he doesn't like me."[5]

The Indians crept above the .500 mark briefly in mid–May, but soon were back in their accustomed position of sixth place in the AL East, where they seemed to have established permanent residency. They fell to seventh in early June, although, in the tightly bunched eastern division, they were just 4½ games out of first, but any thoughts of contention were soon revealed to be a mirage. A stretch of six victories and 16 losses following the All-Star break dropped Cleveland's record to 40–60 on July 30. Ferraro's brush with cancer seemed to sap him of the enthusiasm that had attracted Paul to him, and he was fired with the team in the midst of a series in Toronto.

"We felt a change was advisable," said Paul. "I don't want to discuss Mike. He is a fine young man. This was a very hard decision for me. I think the Indians are a much better team than their record shows. I want the players to do the best they can. All I know is what I see. I don't think we were playing up to our potential."[6] The Indians contacted recently dismissed Phillies manager Pat Corrales on July 29 to sound him out as to his interest in taking over the team. He flew to Toronto and signed a contract through 1984 the next day.

"Pat Corrales is a good manager, the best we could get at this point. We are excited about him,"[7] said Paul of his new bench boss. Ferraro, who had a multi-year contract with the Yankees, was bitter about Paul's quick hook. "I gave up something good to come here," he moaned. "It feels like I've been stabbed in the back."[8]

The season was beyond salvaging, but the Indians improved for Corrales, going 30–32 the rest of the way. They never budged from seventh place, and lost 92 games while winning 70.

Ferraro would have another brief trial as a major league manager, taking over in Kansas City in 1986 when Dick Howser was diagnosed with brain cancer and forced to resign. The Royals won 36 and lost 38, giving Ferraro a career record of 76–98.

Chicago Cubs
Lee Elia to Charlie Fox

It was the rant heard all over Chicago.

After another Cub loss early in the 1983 season, second-year manager Lee Elia lit into fans who'd spent the afternoon loudly expressing their opinion of his club's playing and his managing ... notably the infamous "bleacher bums." Said the frustrated manager, "Eighty-five percent of the people are out making a living. The other 15 percent come out to Wrigley Field to boo my team."

There was plenty to boo about Elia's Cubs. Chicago had finished fifth in the NL East in 1982 for the man whose playing career consisted of 95 games for the Cubs and White Sox in 1966 and '68. In 1983, the Cubs lost 10 of their first 12 games and spent the rest of the season unsuccessfully trying to climb out of the hole they'd dug for themselves. On August 22, general manager Dallas Green fired Elia and replaced him with former Giants manager Charlie Fox. The Cubs were in fifth place with a 54–69 record at the time.

"I told the players they are not playing the kind of baseball [they] should be playing this time of year," said Green, who had taken over Chicago's front office in 1982, "and told Elia that he was not managing up to his capabilities. We've got to win 20 just to get to 74 victories, where we were last year [the Cubs had actually won 73]. We've got a better baseball team than we've had here in some time. Unfortunately, the manager has to take the brunt of it."[9]

Green felt Elia had been too much of a player's manager: "If something doesn't work, you've got to try something different. Lee has his own thinking as to what has to go on in the clubhouse. That philosophy is what you get hired or fired for."[10]

Fox had been Green's top assistant in 1983 and was appointed on an interim basis. Green stated, "He's the manager. What happens in the next 39 games will determine what we will do. Let's finish 1983 first."[11] Green expected Fox, who'd been fired by San Francisco for being too tough on his players, to crack the whip.

If the Cubs didn't perform up to the new manager's expectations, Fox warned, "they will hear from me. My philosophy is we can disagree without being disagreeable. I was never tough. I like to have a little fun, and the only way to have fun is to win."[12]

Fox didn't have much fun managing the Cubs. His record was 17–22, and the team finished fifth with a 71–91 mark. He wasn't retained as manager for 1984, and his career record with San Francisco, Montreal and Chicago was 377–371, with one division title.

Elia would resume his managerial career with Philadelphia in 1987.

1984

Oakland Athletics
Steve Boros to Jackie Moore

Billyball was a hard act to follow.

After three years of Billy Martin's aggressiveness on the field (and off, which led to his dismissal), the new owners of the Oakland Athletics turned to scholarly Steve Boros to guide their club in 1983. Boros, who held a degree in English from the University of Michigan, managed the Athletics to a fourth-place finish with a 74–88 record in his first season, and had the team briefly in first place early in 1984. Oakland's 15–11 record was good for the top spot on May 2, but 13 losses in the next 18 games followed. Club president Roy Eisenhardt and vice president of baseball operations Sandy Alderson decided the Athletics had become a reflection of their manager, and that Boros wasn't sufficiently assertive. He was fired on May 24.

"There was a feeling on the part of the front office that, in light of the way the club had not only performed, but the attitudes and lack of aggressiveness that the players had demonstrated, that there was a need for a change of leadership,"[1] said Alderson in announcing the shift in managers.

"The team is not playing up to its ability across the board," added Eisenhardt. "We're losing ball games we should have won. I believe we have a good ball club, but we're not playing like a good ball club, and before the gap gets too wide, I had to make a change."[2]

Boros, said Alderson, "reacted very well, professionally. He expressed disappointment, but also recognition that this is part of the game. Very often a change of managers can be a catalyst to an improvement in the club. We all respect Steve, but this had to be done."[3] Pitching coach Ron Schueler was also fired, replaced by former Athletics pitching coach Wes Stock.

The change from Boros to first base coach Jackie Moore didn't serve as a catalyst for the Athletics. Moore, who caught 21 games for Detroit in 1965 and managed in the low minor leagues in 1968, 1969 and 1975, took over a team with a 20–24 record, but was only 2½ games out in the weak AL West. Moore kept the club in contention until mid–August, although Oakland would never reach the .500 mark the rest of the year. The Athletics finished third with a mark of 77–85, seven games behind Kansas City. The Royals' record of 84–78 was the poorest ever for an American League division champion. Alderson and Eisenhardt saw enough that they liked about Moore to retain him for 1985.

Boros, whose major league career as an infielder spanned 1957–1965 with the Tigers, Cubs and Reds, would be hired to manage San Diego in 1986.

San Francisco Giants
Frank Robinson to Danny Ozark

Frank Robinson had changed his mind.

Robinson called managing "a pain in the derriere" shortly before he was fired by the Indians in 1977. Just about anyone managing the disorganized, cash-poor Indians during that era would probably have come to the same conclusion. But when a second chance was offered, he jumped at it.

Robinson replaced Dave Bristol as manager of the Giants in October of 1980 and led the team to a 56–55 record during the strike-interrupted 1981 campaign. The Giants battled the Braves and Dodgers down to the wire in the NL West in 1982, finishing third at 87–75, two games behind Atlanta. Robinson's Giants fell to fifth in 1983 and were in sixth place, 22 games out of first, when owner Bob Lurie made a change on August 4.

"It was a very difficult decision, but it was up to management to make it," said the owner. "We just didn't get the consistency we needed."[4] Robinson's firing would hit Lurie in the bank account, as the manager was under contract for two more seasons.

"I did everything physically possible and everything mentally possible to get the players to play up to their capabilities," insisted Robinson. "I don't think I've gotten the best out of some of them, totally. Some gave everything they had; but as a 25-man unit, no."[5]

Robinson was replaced by his third base coach, former Phillies manager Danny Ozark. He said he was "totally surprised" by the turn of events and recalled his firing by Philadelphia in 1979: "It's a little different circumstances, but I felt then like I'm sure Frank does now. I feel good about it, naturally, being able to manage again, but I feel bad for Frank. He took it hard. He's a sensitive person."[6]

Said Lurie of his interim manager, Ozark "is an experienced major league manager who knows how to win and is the best man for the job right now. I'm confident he can lead the club to a respectable finish over the last two months of the season."[7]

Ozark won his first game with the Giants and said afterward he didn't think he'd done anything that Robinson wouldn't have under the same conditions. "Everybody manages about the same," he confessed.[8] San Francisco was 24–32 for Ozark, finishing the year in fifth place with a 66–96 record, trailing the division champion Padres by 26 games. He wouldn't be asked back for 1985, and his major league managing career was over. Ozark's Philadelphia and San Francisco clubs won 618 games and lost 542. His Phillies captured three NL East titles.

Robinson would manage again.

Cincinnati Reds
Vern Rapp to Pete Rose

The "Cincinnati Kid" was coming home.

Since owning baseball's best record, but failing to make the playoffs, in 1981, the Reds had fallen apart. What did they have to lose by offering the manager's job to Cincinnati's favorite son, Pete Rose? Rose was wasting away on the Montreal Expos' bench, so when his agent approached the Reds about making him their player/manager, Cincinnati was receptive.

On August 16, the Reds, with a 51–70 record, fired manager Vern Rapp. Rose was introduced as the Reds' player/manager. He brushed aside speculation that his hiring was a publicity stunt and said he was more concerned with winning than with breaking Ty Cobb's record of 4,191 career hits, which was within Rose's grasp. He had stroked his 4,000th hit with Montreal earlier in the season.

Rose also insisted that he was qualified to manage the Reds, despite having no experience: "I know as much about baseball as any manager. There's only so much baseball you can learn. What do you think I was doing when I was sitting on the bench, eating popcorn and looking at the chicks in the stands? I pay attention. When a game's over, I can tell you every pitch."[9] Rose said he felt he could inject a dose of enthusiasm in the fifth-place Reds. "I really think a club can take on a manager's personality. If you have a fiery manager, you have a chance to have a fiery team. If you have a subdued manager, you can have a subdued team. I want them to sit down with me and have breakfast in the coffee shop and talk to me like I was a player," Rose continued. "I don't want them to be afraid of me. I'm just like them. I've got two arms and two legs." He then added slyly, just so no one forgot, "And 4,000 hits."[10]

Rapp exited Cincinnati quietly, saying only that he wasn't angry about being fired. He skippered exactly 300 major league games, winning 140 and losing 160.

Rose took over a team in a free-fall. Since June 26, the Reds had won 16 games and lost 30. Cincinnati showed some life under its new manager, winning 19 and losing 22 to finish with a record of 70–92. It remained in fifth place.

Rose returned to manage the Reds, and break Cobb's record, in 1985.

Montreal Expos
Bill Virdon to Jim Fanning

There's no time like the present.

Bill Virdon's short tenure in Montreal didn't result in the swan song he, or the Expos, had hoped for.

Despite the talent on hand, Virdon's Expos won four fewer games in 1983 than Jim Fanning's team won the previous year, finishing third at 82–80. The slippage continued in 1984. Although Virdon kept the Expos on the fringe of contention, they were never closer to first place than 6½ games after the All-Star break. With the team in fifth place, losers of six straight games, with a record of 64–67, team president John McHale fired Virdon on August 30.

"I have no ill feelings about it," Virdon said after getting the news. "I partially created the situation myself. I had already told them that I wasn't planning on managing next year. That had to give them some food for thought."[11]

It did. McHale told Virdon he didn't see how the manager could hide his lack of enthusiasm for his job from his players during the season's final month and terminated him immediately. Fanning was again summoned from the front office to finish the year, in the interest of maintaining continuity. "He'll be here next season as a member of the Montreal baseball club," explained McHale. "The press release says he will manage until the end of the season. That's as far as it goes, and that's as far as we go."[12]

Fanning talked to the press after meeting with the players: "I appreciated their frustration. I impressed on them that they are capable of winning a lot of games. They should have some fun and enjoy themselves. I don't think you'll see any drastic changes."[13] Montreal went 14–16 for Fanning in September, finishing fifth with a record of 78–83. It was the last time the Expos would call on Fanning to leave his desk job, and his career managerial mark was 116–103, with "half" of a division title to his credit.

Virdon was finished as a major league manager. His Pirate, Yankee, Astro and Expo clubs won 995 and lost 921 with 2½ division titles. The "half" titles for Virdon and Fanning were during the strike-split season of 1981.

Seattle Mariners
Del Crandall to Chuck Cottier

Who's captain around here?

Less than two weeks before he was fired as manager of the Seattle Mariners, Del Crandall had been given a ringing endorsement by club owner George Argyros. However, Argyros, an activist owner who had been accused of being a bit too active by Mariners fans, had hired Chuck Armstrong as the team's president, and Armstrong hired Hal Keller as general manager. Neither had been around when Argyros hired Crandall, and when Argyros gave Crandall his vote of confidence, he made it clear that Armstrong and Keller were running the Mariners and had the final say. And they said they wanted a new manager on September 1.

After being three games below .500 and 4½ games out of first place in the weak AL

West on June 17, Seattle had won just 27 and lost 41 to fall 10½ off the pace. Crandall was dismissed despite a contract that ran through the 1986 season. He was replaced by Seattle's third base coach, Chuck Cottier. Cottier had four years' experience managing in the Angels' minor league system, where his teams had won 287 games and lost 197. He was in his third season coaching the Mariners when he was promoted, and the club won 15 and lost 12 on his watch. He was retained for 1985.

Crandall was through as a big league manager. His Milwaukee and Seattle teams were 364–469, and never finished higher than fifth place.

1985

New York Yankees
"Yogi" Berra to Billy Martin

Yogi Berra got two more games than Bob Lemon got.

There had been widespread speculation that George Steinbrenner would fire Berra after the 1984 season. The Yankees finished third with an 87–75 record, 17 games out of first. But Steinbrenner issued a statement that no changes would be made for 1985, and Berra (and many others) interpreted that to mean he'd be given a full season to try to return New York to the top of the heap. Steinbrenner even questioned the rampant changing of managers that had accompanied the new era of free agency. "I just can't understand all these teams changing managers they way they do," lamented the man who had changed managers more often than anyone, except for Charles O. Finley. "The lack of stability is alarming. It's startling to me how many teams changed managers this year. It's getting so that you can't even make news any more when you make a change."

Steinbrenner admitted, "I put a lot of pressure on my managers in the past to win at certain times. That will not be the case this spring."[1] But the spring of 1985 turned out to be no different from any other spring during the Steinbrenner regime, and when the Yankees started slowly and found themselves in last place with a 6–10 record and losers of six of their last seven games, Berra was fired on April 28.

The statement distributed by New York's public relations department and attributed to Steinbrenner read, "The action was taken by the Yankees, and we felt it was in the best interests of the ball club."[2] Prior to firing Berra, Steinbrenner admitted that he and his manager had different philosophies as to how a team should be run. He also said he wished Berra were more of a disciplinarian. But he insisted those differences wouldn't result in a change in managers.

Rumors about his future had swirled for days, and Berra said he wasn't surprised to be let go: "He's the boss. I had an inkling when you hear it everyday. This is a good club. They'll get it together. They'll be all right. Did I have a chance? He must have thought so."[3]

The Yankee who took Berra's firing hardest was infielder Dale Berra. The Yanks had traded for Dale in 1984 so he could play for his father. "I don't want to say anything. That's just baseball. That's the way the game is today."[4]

Berra was replaced by Billy Martin, who'd been a New York scout since being fired by

Steinbrenner after the 1983 season. The Yankees were a blazing 91–54 for Martin, but their overall mark of 97–64 fell 2½ games short of the Toronto Blue Jays. The second-place finish didn't save Martin from being fired yet again at the end of the year.

Berra's neighbor in New Jersey, Houston Astros owner John McMullen, who once owned a piece of Steinbrenner's Yankees, hired Berra as a coach. He helped rookie manager Hal Lanier lead the Astros to the NL West title in 1986. But he never managed again. His career record with the Yankees and Mets was 484–444 with two pennants and two seven-game World Series losses.

Texas Rangers
Doug Rader to Bobby Valentine

Doug Rader's managerial career started well but ended badly.

Rader spent the bulk of his 11-year playing career as an infielder with Houston. He took over the Rangers in 1983 and had the team in first place as late as July 21 (although with a record of just 48–45) before the club slid to third place with a mark of 77–85, 22 games behind the White Sox. Chicago closed the season with an amazing 52–19 run, while Texas won 29 and lost 40 over the same span.

Texas plopped into the AL West cellar in 1984 with just 69 victories and was off to a miserable start in 1985 when owner Eddie Chiles and general manager Tom Grieve made a change.

Rader was fired on May 17, after an agreement was reached with Mets coach Bobby Valentine to take over the Rangers, who'd won just nine games while losing 23. Valentine was a former major league infielder/outfielder with the Dodgers, Angels, Padres, Mets and Mariners from 1969 through 1979. "I met [May 16] with Eddie Chiles and put my cards on the table," said Valentine, who was leaving the team with baseball's best record to manage the team with the worst. "There were certain things I wanted, like three years and a restructuring of the chain of command. They put no cards on the table. I'd say the deal is set."[5]

Valentine knew it would take time to turn the Rangers around and received the three-year contract he wanted. He also told Chiles and Grieve that he wanted to report directly to Grieve and not team president Mike Stone, a business associate of Chiles's.

"Managing is something I will do and must do, either in the near future or the distant future," said Valentine.[6] The future turned out to be immediately, but the Rangers performed no better for their new manager than they had for Rader. Valentine's Rangers were 53–76 for a final record of 62–99 and a last-place finish. He boosted the team into second place in 1986 and stayed in Arlington until 1992.

Rader's career as a manager wasn't over. He'd serve as interim manager of the White Sox for two games in June of 1986, between the dismissal of Tony LaRussa and the hiring of Jim Fregosi, and he'd be hired as skipper of the Angels in 1988.

Baltimore Orioles
Joe Altobelli to Earl Weaver

How does one replace a legendary manager?

Joe Altobelli did it by winning the World Series. Altobelli took over in the Baltimore dugout after Earl Weaver's 14-year run and guided the Orioles past Philadelphia in the 1983 World Series. He would've been wise to quit while he was ahead.

Altobelli's encore was a fifth-place finish (85–77) in 1984, and with the club plodding along in fifth place at 29–26 on June 13, 1985, owner Edward Bennett Williams asked Weaver to come out of retirement to make things right again.

Altobelli spoke to general manager Hank Peters that day, as rumors circulated that he was to be replaced, and was told to "hang tough." But the decision belonged to Williams, and the rumors became fact the next day. Noting that Weaver had rejected offers to manage several other clubs since stepping aside after the 1982 campaign, Williams said, "I think he came back out of loyalty to the organization."[7]

Altobelli was bitter about the firing. "I thought this was a class operation," he told reporters, "but I guess I was sadly mistaken."[8] Altobelli would serve as interim manager of the Cubs for one game in 1991. His career record was 437–407, with one pennant and a World Series title.

Weaver had no magic wand to wave to turn the Orioles into contenders. The '85 Birds were a mediocre team and won 53 while losing 52 for their new manager. Baltimore came in fourth at 83–78, 16 games out of first place. Weaver managed again in 1986, then retired permanently. His career record was 1,480–1,060, with four pennants and a world's championship.

Minnesota Twins
Billy Gardner to Ray Miller

One lousy series may have done Billy Gardner in.

Gardner's Twins trailed Kansas City by two games when they arrived in Cleveland for a four-game series that would end the 1984 season. The Twins blew a 10–0 lead in the first contest and were easy pickings for the Indians in the remaining three games. The Royals won the division, and the hangover seemed to affect Minnesota into 1985.

The Twins were in sixth place with a 27–35 record, 7½ games out of first, on June 21, when Gardner was dismissed. "The situation had become such that we felt it was in the best interests of the club to make a change," said team president Howard Fox. The decision to fire Gardner and replace him with Baltimore pitching coach Ray Miller was made after "a very difficult and trying time. Maybe you and the rest of us have been disappointed at the way our ball club has performed. We made a decision [that] we need to change."[9]

The difficult and trying time Fox referred to had begun on May 20, when the Twins were in second place with a record of 21–16. Since then, they'd won just six games and lost 19. Miller was expected to reverse the slide.

"I know what it takes to win, and hopefully I'll be able to apply that here," said the new Twins' boss. "This is a team that has a chance to win now and win in the future."[10] Miller pitched for a decade in the minor leagues after signing with San Francisco in 1964. He was Baltimore's minor league pitching instructor from 1974 through 1977 before taking the job as pitching coach on the big league level in 1978. Miller coached five 20-game winners with the Orioles: Jim Palmer, Mike Flanagan, Steve Stone, Scott McGregor and Mike Boddicker.

Miller had slightly more success with Minnesota than Gardner did. The Twins split their 100 remaining games and finished tied with Oakland for fourth place with a record of 77–85. He wouldn't make it through the 1986 season.

Atlanta Braves
Eddie Haas to Bobby Wine

It was the opportunity Eddie Haas had worked a lifetime for, and the Atlanta Braves had high hopes for him.

The Braves selected Haas, who joined the organization while it was in Milwaukee in 1958 (playing in 41 games, 29 as a pinch-hitter) and remained a Brave ever since, as their manager for 1985, succeeding the fired Joe Torre. Haas had been a successful minor league manager, but didn't seem comfortable at the major league level. And the players, many of whom played for Haas in the Braves' system, didn't respond to him.

Atlanta's brain trust realized quickly that promoting Haas had been a mistake. With the team in fifth place, 22 games out of first, its record 50–71 and riding a six-game losing streak, Haas was mercifully relieved of a job he proved to be unsuited for. One week after owner Ted Turner said no changes would be made during the season, general manager John Mullen got the order from the top to fire the manager.

"We've been discussing the possibility of making a change for a few weeks," said Mullen. "I don't think Ted needs to give a reason. We've continued to lose games. I guess he just decided to do it."[11]

Haas was replaced on an interim basis by Atlanta's third base coach, Bobby Wine. Wine had been a good-field, no-hit shortstop for the Phillies and Expos from 1960 through 1972, and a coach for the Phillies from 1973 through 1983. "Lots of things can happen in six weeks," said the new skipper. "We've got nowhere to go but up. The players have been embarrassed about the way things have been going. We're not going to die."

As most new managers do, Wine promised an aggressive approach. "We might run into some outs, but we're going to be aggressive. We're going to try to generate some excitement and get the team moving. I can't guarantee we'll win 40 games in a row, but I think we're going to be competitive."[12]

Atlanta didn't win 40 games in a row, but it won its first five for Wine before reverting to its losing ways. The Braves were 16–25 under Wine, finishing fifth with a record of 66–96. Neither Haas nor Wine ever managed in the major leagues again.

San Francisco Giants
Jim Davenport to Roger Craig

Two organization men felt the sting of the executioner's guillotine in 1985.

The opportunity to manage in the major leagues that Eddie Haas spent 27 years in the Braves organization to achieve proved to be too much for him, and he was fired after just 121 games. In San Francisco, the same chance finally came to Jim Davenport, who had served the Giants as a player and coach for 27 years. Davenport was chosen to succeed interim manager Danny Ozark for the 1985 season. Haas and Davenport assumed command of weak teams and spent the season fighting each other to stay out of the NL West cellar. Haas was winning the battle when he was fired on August 26. Davenport hung on until September 18, when he fell victim to a regime change.

A week earlier, Giants owner Bob Lurie had hired former Yankees and Astros team president Al Rosen to fill the same position in San Francisco. Rosen fired Davenport, whose Giants were in last place, 29 games behind their arch-rivals, the Dodgers, with a record of 56–88. Rosen selected former major league pitcher, manager and pitching coach Roger Craig to replace Davenport. Craig had retired after helping the Tigers win the 1984 World Series as their pitching coach, but jumped at the chance to manage. Craig led San Diego to an 83–79 record and a fourth-place finish after replacing Alvin Dark in spring training in 1978, but was fired after the Padres slipped to fifth with 93 losses the next year. The Giants were 6–12 for Craig to complete the 1985 season with a record of 62–100 and a basement finish.

Davenport's only chance to manage in the major leagues lasted all of 134 games.

1986

Seattle Mariners
Chuck Cottier to Dick Williams

It was a bad year to be a manager in the AL West.

The first manager to be fired was Seattle's Chuck Cottier, who was let go by club president Chuck Armstrong on May 8. The Mariners were in sixth place with a 9–19 record, seven games behind the division leaders.

"This is the toughest decision I have ever had to make," said Armstrong, sounding much like other team presidents who felt compelled to change managers. "I have a great deal of respect for Chuck as a manager and person. Unfortunately, the club's current standing in the American League West is far below our expectations. This fact has moved us to seek a new direction."[1]

Armstrong was asked if he was in the market for a hard-nosed disciplinarian to serve as a contrast to the easygoing Cottier. "I think you look for that as a prerequisite for any manager you hire," was the response.[2] Speculation centered on Billy Martin, who was at liberty and was favored by Mariners owner George Argyros. Martin's track record scared some members of Seattle's front office, and Argyros agreed to accept Dick Williams instead. Williams was out of work after having resigned as manager of the Padres in spring training. He got a three-year deal from Argyros worth $200,000 per season, plus bonuses based on attendance and victories.

"It's possible I may be over-demanding for some players, but I'm not hired to be a nice guy," said Williams. "I'm hired to win baseball games. There's no reason you have to make excuses for a ball player. I'm here for one purpose—to produce a contender and a winner. I think this ball club has great potential, and I'm proud to be associated with it." Then, in a seeming contradiction of what he'd just said, Williams added, "If there's one thing this ball club needs right now, it's to have a positive attitude. I'm going to tell the players to relax and go out and have a good time."[3]

Cottier didn't comment on his dismissal, but from the east coast, his friend Rene Lachemann did. Lachemann had rebounded nicely after being fired by the Mariners in 1984. He was coaching third base for a Red Sox team that was headed for the World Series. Lachemann hired Cottier as a coach when he was managing in Seattle and took a verbal jab at Mariners management. Noting that Williams was Seattle's fifth manager in the six years Argyros had owned the team, Lachemann said, "I know management at one time used the thing that patience is for losers. Well, I believe you have to be patient in this game."[4]

Williams may have urged his players to relax and have a good time, but they played no better for him than they had for Cottier. Seattle was 58–75 under its hard-nosed disciplinarian manager to finish last with a record of 67–95. Cottier's brief career as a major league manager was over. The Mariners were 98–119 on his watch.

Chicago Cubs
Jim Frey to Gene Michael

Jim Frey's managerial magic wore off quickly.

As a rookie manager with Kansas City in 1980, Frey led the Royals to the World Series, where they lost to Dallas Green's Philadelphia Phillies. Frey was fired during the "second half" of the strike-shortened 1981 season.

Green left Philadelphia to take over the Cubs' front office in 1982, and he remembered Frey when he was looking for a manager after the 1983 campaign. In his first season in Chicago, Frey did the seemingly impossible: he steered the Cubs to the NL East championship and their first post-season appearance in 39 years. The Cubs won the first two games of the League Championship Series in the friendly confines of Wrigley Field, then blew three straight to the west champion Padres in San Diego to lose the pennant.

Injuries wiped out the Cubs' 1985 season. At some point during the year, all five Chicago starting pitchers were sidelined. The club was healthy in 1986, but continued wandering aimlessly while the Mets made a shambles of the division race. With the Cubs already 16½ games out of first place on June 11, Frey was fired.

"I think he did everything in his power to help the players and get the organization back on the winning track," said Green. "Unfortunately, whatever he was doing at this stage of the game wasn't getting the job done. The baseball players know how I feel about this change—I'm not very happy about it, and I told them in no uncertain terms how I feel they contributed to it."[5]

Green said he wouldn't forget how Frey guided the Cubs to their first division championship, "and I don't think anybody in Chicago should forget it." However, "for the good of the baseball team and the good of the fans, we had to make a change."[6]

Frey was upset over his dismissal. "It's something I'm very disheartened by. I wanted to stay here a long time. I wanted to stay here and win." Green, said the deposed manager, "didn't really give me any reason other than the performance of the team, and I don't think you need any reason other than that. Our performance has been disappointing, and he decided to let me go, in hopes that would improve the team."[7]

Frey was replaced by current Yankees third base coach, and former manager, Gene Michael. "Gene is a baseball guy," explained Green. "When I was going through my mind as to who was available, Gene stuck out like a sore thumb. He's been through pennant races and he's managed a club that was always under the media spotlight. He's certainly shown he can handle all the pressure of managing and has always produced. I called George [Steinbrenner] and told him I had a favor to ask of him, and he knew exactly what I wanted. George gave Gene the highest praise and told me, 'I think he's your man, your kind of guy.'"[8]

Michael assumed command of a club with a 24–34 record and no chance of challenging the rampaging Mets, who were on their way to 108 victories. The Cubs won 46 and lost 56 the rest of the way, coming in fifth with a 70–90 mark. He was invited back for 1987, but he wouldn't be around for the finish.

Despite having two division titles and a pennant on his resume, Frey didn't manage again. His Royals and Cubs teams won 323 games and lost 287.

Chicago White Sox
Tony LaRussa to Jim Fregosi

Ken Harrelson made one of the more unusual transitions in baseball history.

The man known as "Hawk" during his eight-season playing career with the Athletics, Senators, Red Sox and Indians had some interesting ideas as to how to run a ball club. He expressed those opinions on the air as a broadcaster for the White Sox, and got the chance to put his theories into practice when he was named general manager after the 1985 season.

Harrelson wasn't enamored of Tony LaRussa, who had some unorthodox ideas of his own and had been applying them since becoming Chicago's manager in 1979. Those ideas had paid off in 99 victories and a division title in 1983. The White Sox sagged to fifth in 1984, but rebounded to third in 1985. When Harrelson's '86 team started slowly, he demonstrated some traditional thinking by firing his manager. On June 20, with Chicago wallowing in sixth place with a 26–38 record, he dismissed LaRussa.

"This is not a personality conflict but a baseball decision," said the rookie general manager. "We have almost a hundred games to play, and we feel we still have a chance to contend in our division."[9] Harrelson also fired pitching coach Dave Duncan and replaced him with former major league pitcher Dick Bosman, who was serving in that capacity at Triple-A Buffalo.

LaRussa's successor was former Angels manager Jim Fregosi, who was managing the Cardinals' Louisville farm team. Fregosi, since being dismissed by California in 1981, had spurned offers to manage the Indians, Pirates and Mariners because he questioned their commitment to winning. He had no such qualms about taking over the White Sox.

"The team is 9½ games out," said Fregosi. "That's nothing. I don't see any reason we can't turn things around and compete in our division. This is a young club, there's talent here. There's some speed, there's defense, and there's power. We have to put it all together."

Fregosi said he was "more qualified to manage this time. The biggest difference is that when you are a player, you think you can manage. There's a lot more to managing than what goes on between the white lines. I learned to teach in the minor leagues. A lot of it is trial and error." Fregosi described himself as a "player's manager, as long as the players do what I want. If not, then I become a disciplinarian. The biggest part of managing is motivation. When I first managed the Angels, I had a lot of players I played with. Everybody matures. I won't get close to the players, but I will back them."[10]

Fregosi posted a slightly better record than LaRussa had, winning 45 and losing 51. The White Sox finished fifth with a ledger of 72–90. Harrelson soon returned to the broadcast booth, but Fregosi stayed in the White Sox dugout through the 1988 season, racking up two more fifth-place finishes.

Oakland Athletics
Jackie Moore to Tony LaRussa

Ken Harrelson probably did Tony LaRussa a big favor.

The White Sox were treading water when Harrelson fired LaRussa in late June, making him available to take over the up-and-coming Oakland Athletics in early July. A 15-game road losing streak proved to be the undoing of manager Jackie Moore, who was dismissed on June 26. The Athletics were in sixth place with a 29–44 record, and Moore was replaced on an interim basis by coach Jeff Newman while speculation swirled as to who Oakland's next manager would be. That speculation centered around the newly unemployed LaRussa, who took the job on July 7. Oakland was 2–8 for Newman while the details of LaRussa's new job were being negotiated.

LaRussa brought Dave Duncan with him as pitching coach. Duncan would remain LaRussa's right-hand man through 10 seasons with the Athletics and 16 more with the Cardinals. Under their new manager, the Athletics won 45 and lost 34, jumping from seventh place to third with a final record of 76–86.

Moore didn't manage in the major leagues again. His Oakland teams won 163 games and lost 190.

Minnesota Twins
Ray Miller to Tom Kelly

When Ray Miller arrived in the Twin Cities to take over the Twins in mid-season of 1985, he said he "knew how to win." He didn't get a whole lot of opportunity to prove it.

Miller's Twins were last in the AL West with a 59–80 record, 21½ games behind the division-leading Angels, when he was fired on September 12. "Unfortunately, it's typical of baseball that when a team goes badly, the manager gets fired," said the man who made the decision to fire the manager, club president Howard Fox. "I'll never ask a manager not to try his best. I don't want to finish in last place. I do want [new manager Tom Kelly] to find out some things about our younger players. Ray was under extreme pressure that he had to win every ball game to make sure he'd be back next year, so he may not have played his younger players."[11]

Miller responded:

> You're hired to be fired. My epitaph is the stat sheet and the record. It's absolutely asinine for any manager not to put the best players on the field every day, because the name of the game is winning. It's very unfair to me. I have done everything that was asked of me. I was hired and told to put the best ball club on the field every day. If they told me that they were out of the race and wanted me to put the young guys in and wanted to tell me that putting young guys in wouldn't affect my status as manager, of course I would have played the young guys.

I asked for an everyday left-fielder which, in turn, would have strengthened my bench, and I didn't get it. I asked for a bullpen stopper, but there aren't many of them around, and I didn't get one. I asked for more speed, and I didn't get it.[12]

Said Fox bluntly, "Ray Miller has been given every support."[13]

Kelly, an infielder whose major league career was limited to 49 games with the Twins in 1975, led Minnesota to a 12–11 record over the season's final 23 games. The Twins finished fifth with a mark of 71–91. Kelly would lead the Twins to a World Series title in 1987, and another in 1991.

Miller, who had been a hot managerial prospect before taking the Minnesota job, didn't get another chance to prove he knew how to win for 12 years. He took over a Baltimore club that had played in the League Championship Series in 1996 and '97, and promptly guided it to a pair of sub-.500 seasons in 1998 and '99. Miller's career record was 266–297.

1987

Philadelphia Phillies
John Felske to Lee Elia

One man's pushover is another man's whip-cracker.

When John Felske, a former major league catcher whose career consisted of 54 games with the Cubs and Brewers in 1968, 1972 and 1973, was named manager of the Phillies for the 1985 season, the question asked by some was whether he would be tough enough on his players. After watching Felske lead Philadelphia to fifth- and second-place finishes his first two years on the job, the answer, in the opinion of club president Bill Giles, was no. The Phillies were fifth with a record of 29–32 on June 18 when Felske was released. He was replaced by coach Lee Elia, the former manager of the Cubs.

"This is very emotional," said Elia upon assuming command of the Phillies. "I had a strong relationship with Felske. This is never an easy situation."[1] Elia had managed in Philadelphia's minor league system from 1975 through 1980, and coached for the club in 1980 and '81 under Dallas Green. When Green took the job as general manager of the Cubs, he hired Elia as his manager in 1982 and fired him in '83, after which the Phillies welcomed him back.

Elia signed a contract to manage Philadelphia only through the end of the season, but Giles said, "Hopefully, we'll have him around for many years in the future."[2]

Mike Schmidt, the Phillies' elder statesman at third base, was among Felske's detractors and approved of the switch. "He was a kind, thoughtful and sensitive man," said Schmidt of his former boss, "but in order for us to turn it around, a change had to be made."[3]

Elia promised "no miracle changes or changes of any consequence immediately. There's no one singular thing that might be a catalyst."[4] Felske was let go partly because he was perceived as not being tough enough. He rarely argued with umpires and refrained from publicly criticizing his players. Ironically, Elia had been fired by the Cubs because Green thought he was too much of a "player's manager." Giles was counting on Elia to put the hammer down on the underachieving Phillies.

There wasn't much difference record-wise between Felske's Phillies and Elia's Phillies. Philadelphia was 51–50 for its new manager to finish the season fourth with a mark of 80–82. That was good enough to earn him a contract for 1988.

Felske didn't manage in the major leagues again. His career record was 190–194.

Cleveland Indians
Pat Corrales to "Doc" Edwards

Don't believe everything you read in the newspapers. Or magazines.

There it was on the cover of *Sports Illustrated* in the spring of 1987. INDIAN UPRISING, read the headline. BELIEVE IT! CLEVELAND IS THE BEST TEAM IN THE AMERICAN LEAGUE!

The problem was, even the magazine's editors didn't believe it, and years later admitted as much. But it seemed like a good way to sell magazines, touting the long-suffering Indians as likely American League champions.

The Indians had won 84 games in 1986 and led the league in runs scored, but a horrid pitching staff torpedoed any chance the Tribe had of contending in 1987, and manager Pat Corrales was fired the day after the All-Star Game, with the team in last place. The Indians had a 31–56 record. Not exactly what was expected from *Sports Illustrated*'s "best team in the American League."

"It had nothing to do with one certain game," said general manager Joe Klein. "It had nothing to do with the hitting or pitching. We just didn't win enough games. The won-loss record at the major leagues is the most visible thing."[5]

Speculation about Corrales's job security began when the Indians lost 10 of their first 11 games. Pitching coach Jack Aker took the fall for the club's 5.59 earned run average and was fired on July 1. The players began fighting among themselves, and a grotesque 17–0 loss to the White Sox at Municipal Stadium on July 5 gave the fans the distinct impression the club had quit on its manager, leaving Klein and team president Dan O'Brien little recourse but to dismiss Corrales for appearances sake, if no other reason.

Corrales was replaced by bullpen coach Howard (Doc) Edwards, who was promoted for the rest of the season. Edwards spent the 1962–1965 seasons as a second-string catcher with the Indians, Athletics and Yankees, and then returned for 35 games with the Phillies in 1970. He looked at his 75-game audition as the chance of a lifetime.

"I love Pat Corrales. I have mixed emotions about getting the job because he was fired. But I've waited 13 years for this. I think Pat understands. I think Pat would be happy because one of his guys has taken over for him." As to his plans for the rest of the season, Edwards said, "I want them to be loosey-goosey, to have some fun. We didn't have the kind of life in the clubhouse that we had last year. If you can get life back in there, maybe it will carry out into the field. What I really want is for them to get their respect back. This team earned a lot of respect last year."[6]

Corrales left Cleveland without commenting on his firing. He never managed in the major leagues again, and posted a career record with Texas, Philadelphia and the Indians of 572–634.

The Indians won 30 and lost 45 under Edwards. They finished last in the AL East with 61 wins and 101 losses. Edwards was re-hired for 1988.

Kansas City Royals
Billy Gardner to John Wathan

Billy Gardner took over the Kansas City Royals under trying circumstances.

Dick Howser, the popular manager who'd led the Royals to the 1985 world's championship, took a medical leave of absence midway through the 1986 season, when he was diagnosed with a brain tumor. Coach Mike Ferraro took the reins for the rest of the season, but when Howser was forced to resign in the winter of 1987, management chose Gardner, the former manager of the Twins, as Howser's permanent replacement.

The AL West was wide open in 1987. Minnesota's 85 victories would win the division, so the Royals were justified in believing they were still very much in the race with a record of 62–64 on August 25, the day Gardner was fired. "It is our belief this club still has an opportunity to win the pennant with the talent and the commitment that it has,"[7] said general manager John Schuerholz in announcing the change in managers. Gardner was replaced by former Royals catcher John Wathan, who was then managing the team's Triple-A farm club in Omaha. Wathan wasn't Scheuerholz's first choice for the job. Hal McRae, Kansas City's designated hitter since 1976 who played in just 18 games in 1987, his final season, turned the position down.

Wathan spent his entire 10-year playing career with the Royals. His final season had been the world championship year of 1985. "Even though I have limited experience as a manager, I think the way I played the game, and the way I studied the game, is in my favor. I regard this as a golden opportunity. I have confidence in my ability that I will be back to manage next year. But I feel bad getting the job this way. Billy was like a father to me in the minors."[8] The 37-year-old Wathan's Omaha club had a record of 62–70 when he was promoted.

Kansas City won 21 and lost 15 for Wathan, but its 83–79 record left it three games short of a division title. As he'd anticipated, however, Wathan did show enough to his bosses to be retained for 1988.

Gardner was finished as a major league manager. His Minnesota and Kansas City teams won 330 games and lost 417.

Chicago Cubs
Gene Michael to Frank Lucchesi

Apparently Gene Michael wasn't Dallas Green's kind of guy after all.

Michael may have stuck out like a sore thumb among the list of available candidates to succeed Jim Frey as manager of the Cubs in 1986, and he may have gotten a ringing endorsement from George Steinbrenner, but the smart money said he was on his way out in September of 1987 when he beat Green to the punch and resigned.

Michael's Cubs were fifth in the NL East with a record of 68–68 when he was interviewed on a Chicago radio program on September 7 and said, "A week ago, I decided I don't want to come back [in 1988] but only because nobody has asked me. So I'll just say I don't want to come back. I'll qualify it by saying the coaches and players have been outstanding."[9]

What Michael didn't say spoke volumes. It wasn't a resignation, but Green interpreted it as such, and Michael was out, effective immediately. Green turned to former Philadelphia and Texas manager Frank Lucchesi to guide the Cubs through the final three weeks of the campaign.

"Frank understands that this is for 25 games and no longer,"[10] said Green, removing Lucchesi as a candidate for the permanent job. He said he didn't appoint first base coach John Vukovich as interim manager because he didn't think it would be fair to place Vukovich under that kind of pressure, knowing that he wanted the job.

"He explained it to me, and I understand completely," said Vukovich, who had managed the Cubs for two games between the departure of Frey and the arrival of Michael. "Certainly I want the job. Who wouldn't?"[11]

Green explained that hiring Lucchesi "will give us time to gather our thoughts and give us time regarding a managerial decision. We'd like to make a decision before the winter meetings ... but we won't make a decision before we're completely satisfied."[12]

Given the circumstances, it wasn't surprising that the Cubs sleepwalked through the 25 games Lucchesi managed, winning eight and losing 17. They finished last with a record of 76–85. It was an ignominious end to Lucchesi's managerial career. His Philadelphia, Texas and Chicago clubs won 316 and lost 399.

1988

Atlanta Braves
Chuck Tanner to Russ Nixon

Chuck Tanner got a lot of mileage out of one great season.

At the time of his (forced) retirement, Tanner stood 20th on the all-time major league managerial victory list with 1,352. As the 1988 season opened, he'd managed 18 years with the White Sox, Athletics, Pirates and Braves. Only once had a Tanner-managed club qualified for the post-season: 1979, when his Pirates won the NL East, the pennant, and the World Series. He managed Pittsburgh through 1985, leaving town after a cellar finish with 104 defeats.

The Braves signed Tanner to a five-year contract in 1986, but after producing sixth- and fifth-place finishes in his first two seasons in Atlanta, he was on a short leash as the 1988 campaign began. When the Braves lost their first 10 games, the leash grew shorter. With the team in sixth place, having won just 12 while losing 27, Braves general manager Bobby Cox relieved Tanner of his duties on May 23.

"We appreciate the many contributions that Chuck and his staff have made over the last few years, but we felt it was time for a change," said Cox's simple statement.[1] He opted for a thorough house-cleaning, firing coaches Willie Stargell, Al Monchak, Bob Skinner and Tony Bartirome in addition to Tanner.

Atlanta's new manager was Russ Nixon, the former Cincinnati skipper who was managing the Braves' Class-AA affiliate in Greenville, South Carolina, at the time of his promotion.

The 1988 Braves were simply a bad ball club and performed no better for Nixon than they had for Tanner. Atlanta was 42–79 for its new manager, finishing the season in the NL West basement with a record of 54–106. Nonetheless, Cox kept Nixon around for the 1989 season.

San Diego Padres
Larry Bowa to Jack McKeon

Larry Bowa had been a feisty player during his 16-year career with the Phillies, Cubs and Mets from 1970 through 1985. It was his combativeness that attracted the Padres to him when they needed a replacement for Steve Boros, who was fired after a fourth place finish in 1986. So it shouldn't have surprised anyone when Bowa refused to go quietly when he was dismissed after less than a year and a half on the job.

San Diego's record of 16–30 placed it ahead only of Atlanta in the NL West when Chub Feeney, the former San Francisco Giants executive and National League president, who'd taken over the Padres' front office after the 1987 season, terminated him on May 28. "It was a tough decision, but it was necessary," said Feeney.[2] The Padres had just arrived in New York to begin a series with the Mets, who were leading the NL East, when Bowa was fired. His disposition wasn't helped by the fact that he was told of his dismissal by a sportswriter an hour before he got the call from Feeney telling him his services were no longer required.

"If you're fired by a Frank Cashen [the Mets' GM], you get worried," said Bowa. "They're pretty knowledgeable baseball people. But if you're fired by these people, you don't worry about it. They said, 'We think we're better than a 16–30 ball club.' I said, not with Tony Gwynn out for two weeks, Chris Brown out for nine games, and John Kruk out."[3] Gwynn was the Padres' right-fielder who'd lead the NL with a .313 batting average in 1988. Brown was the starting third baseman, and Kruk a valuable utility player.

Bowa said he knew his days as manager were numbered when Feeney was hired as the club president. "As soon as he came in last year, I knew he wanted me out. I'm pleased with what I accomplished in a year. I learned a lot fast. I learned you should be having a little input on things. I've been in baseball all my life. I'll be back."[4] And he would be, as manager of the Phillies, the club he spent most of his playing career with.

Bowa was replaced in the dugout by San Diego's general manager, Jack McKeon, who made it clear his assignment was temporary. "At the end of the season, I go back to being GM only. They enlisted me. I didn't ask them. I never solicited the job. Larry's a high-class kid. I think he did a good job. Sometimes, business decisions enter into it."[5]

McKeon's Padres went 67–48 the rest of the way to finish third with a record of 83–79. The front office made a business decision to retain McKeon as field manager for 1989.

Seattle Mariners
Dick Williams to Jim Snyder

What began with a bang ended with a whimper.

No one, except possibly for Dick Williams himself, had expected him to lead the

"Impossible Dream" Boston Red Sox from ninth place to first in the summer of 1967. Williams moved on to Oakland and won three division championships, two pennants and two World Series titles. He bombed as manager of the California Angels, redeemed himself by guiding the Montreal Expos to within a whisker of the playoffs, and led the San Diego Padres to their first division title and pennant in 1984. The Seattle Mariners were the sixth and final club Williams would manage.

The Mariners finished fourth in 1987, Williams's first (and only) full season at the helm, with a record of 78–84. He seemed to have the franchise headed in the right direction, but when Seattle started slowly in 1988, Williams was dismissed despite a $200,000 per year contract running through the following season.

"We decided that the time had come to make this change in the interest of the current season as well as for the future,"[6] said Mariners president Chuck Armstrong, who was getting used to making such statements. Williams was the third manager Armstrong had fired. He also dismissed Seattle's third base coach, and Williams's friend and confidant, Ozzie Virgil. Williams was replaced on an interim basis by first base coach Jim Snyder.

"Dick Williams had his way of doing things. I'll do things the Jim Snyder way," said Seattle's new manager. "I've managed before and I have my ideas. I've always been an aggressive type. I've always tried to force the game."[7]

Snyder took over a sixth-place club with a 23–33 record and led it to a 9–16 mark over its next 25 games. That was good enough for Armstrong, who announced on July 14 that Snyder would stay in command through the end of the season. The Mariners won 45 and lost 60 for Snyder, and finished last in the west with a ledger of 68–93. Snyder never managed in the majors again.

Neither did Williams, whose six clubs won 1,571 and lost 1,451 with four pennants and two World Series titles.

New York Yankees
Billy Martin to Lou Piniella

By June of 1988, the whole thing was getting monotonous.

George Steinbrenner hired Billy Martin. Martin got on Steinbrenner's nerves. Steinbrenner fired Martin. Steinbrenner re-hired Martin, then re-fired him. It happened in 1978, 1980, 1983, 1985, and, for the final time, in 1988.

As usual, off-the-field transgressions helped cost Martin his job on June 23, but the biggest problem may have been Martin's chaotic use of his starting pitching rotation. He used pitchers as both starters and relievers, leaving them unable to establish regular work routines. Martin was well aware of the ever-present rumors.

"If they want to fire me, that's their prerogative," he snarled. "If they want me to go tomorrow, I'll leave. I'll pack up and won't say a word." He added a word of warning to Steinbrenner. "If they fire me, I won't come back again as manager. I'm sick and tired of being accused of being a drunkard."[8]

Steinbrenner fired Martin and coaches Art Fowler, Clete Boyer and George Mitterwald with the Yankees in second place with a record of 40–28. The dismissal followed a 2–7 road trip that knocked New York out of first place. Martin's replacement was Lou Piniella, who'd managed the Yankees to second- and fourth-place finishes in 1986 and '87.

"I feel terrible for him," said Piniella of the man he succeeded. "It's tough to replace somebody. I know how hard he worked at this job. Without the injuries the team suffered, I'm sure he wouldn't have had road trips like the last one."[9]

The Yankees played listlessly for Piniella, winning 45 and losing 48. They sank from second place to fifth with a record of 85–76. Perhaps the only thing that prevented Martin from returning for a sixth tour of duty with the Yankees was his death in a car accident on Christmas night of 1989. He was 61 years old.

Martin was a winner, and his love/hate relationship with Steinbrenner was one of baseball's most bizarre chapters. Martin's Minnesota, Detroit, Texas, Oakland and New York teams won 1,253 games and lost 1,013. He won five division titles, two pennants and one World Series.

Boston Red Sox
John McNamara to Joe Morgan

But for one strategic gaffe, John McNamara might have been the man to crush the "Curse of the Bambino." Had McNamara replaced gimpy first baseman Bill Buckner with Dave Stapleton in the bottom of the 10th inning of the sixth game of the 1986 World Series at Shea Stadium, with the Red Sox leading the favored Mets, 5–3, Buckner wouldn't have been on the field to allow Mookie Wilson's ground ball to roll through his legs, scoring Ray Knight with the winning run and setting New York up to defeat the disheartened Bostonians in the seventh game.

With the Red Sox fighting for a chance to return to the World Series in July of 1988, team president Jean Yawkey decided McNamara had to go. Boston entered the All-Star Break with a 43–42 record, trailing the first-place Tigers by nine games, when Yawkey decreed the need for new leadership. McNamara was dismissed "on the basis that a change in leadership was necessary if the Red Sox are to make a serious attempt at winning the Eastern Division title," read the official statement.[10]

The players were informed of the switch from McNamara to third base coach Joe Morgan as they reported to Fenway Park for a game against Kansas City. Morgan himself was given no advance notice. General manager Lou Gorman simply told him, "You're the manager," when he arrived at the ball park. Morgan took the job with no assurance he'd be the manager beyond the last game of the season.

"I have in mind the thought of some possible candidates who could be replacements," Gorman said. "Certainly, we'll give Joe Morgan consideration. But we'll look around and take time to find the right guy to run the club."[11] As it turned out, Gorman didn't have to look any further than the home team's dugout in Fenway Park.

The Red Sox went on a tear for Morgan, winning 12 in a row, losing one, and then ripping off another seven consecutive victories to move into first place, albeit for just one day. Boston battled Sparky Anderson's Tigers the rest of the way, taking over the top spot on September 4 and never letting go. The Red Sox won 46 and lost 31 under Morgan. Their 89–73 record was a game better than Detroit's and two games better than Toronto's. Despite being swept in the League Championship Series by western titlist Oakland, Morgan was rehired to manage the Red Sox in 1989.

Morgan managed the Bosox through the 1991 season. His 1990 club's 88–74 record was good for another division title. Again, Boston was broomed in the League Championship Series by Oakland. Morgan's major league managerial record was 301–262, with a pair of division championships. His Red Sox were 0–8 in the playoffs.

McNamara hungered for another shot at managing. He got it in Cleveland in 1989.

1989

Toronto Blue Jays
Jimy Williams to "Cito" Gaston

It took the Toronto Blue Jays, American League expansion class of '77, a dozen years to make their first in-season change in managers. And it turned out to be a stroke of genius.

Toronto achieved its first winning season in 1983. The Blue Jays won the AL East under manager Bobby Cox in 1985 and, after Cox departed to take the general manager's job in Atlanta, almost won the division again in 1987. Jimy Williams's club had a one-game lead over Detroit with three games to play, but was swept by the Tigers the final weekend of the season and finished two games back, with an impressive 96 victories.

Toronto fell to a third-place tie in 1988 amid numerous squabbles between Williams and his players, notably George Bell, Lloyd Moseby and Jesse Barfield. It came as a surprise to many observers that the Blue Jays brought Williams back for 1989, but he didn't stick around long. Toronto stumbled to a 12–24 start, and Williams was fired on May 15.

"It was an organizational decision," said general manager Pat Gillick. "We didn't think the club was responding to Jimy in the manner it should. From an organizational standpoint, we needed to make a change. Our problem hasn't been the attitude. It's been production. We just haven't had enough wins. We thought we put all our problems behind us in 1989. The carryover from the 1987 season was over, and the attitude was much better after 1988. We thought Jimy was maturing as a manager, but sometimes the best laid plans don't work out."[1]

Williams was replaced on an interim basis by Toronto's batting coach, former major league outfielder Clarence (Cito) Gaston. Gaston spent 11 years with the Braves, Padres and Pirates and compiled a .256 career average. Gillick made it clear Gaston would be an interim manager. He'd been burned once promoting a coach, and he wasn't going to let it happen again: "Jimy was a coach with us before we made him manager. We think that hurt him. We don't want to make the same mistake twice."[2]

The Jays continued to flounder for the first month under Gaston's leadership, but Gillick saw something he liked and eventually removed the "interim" tag from Gaston's title. Toronto had inched to within three games of .500 and seven games of first place at the All-Star break, then distanced itself from the rest of the division in the second half, winning 47 and losing 28. The Blue Jays won 77 and lost 49 after Gaston replaced Williams and took the division title with an 89–73 record. Toronto bowed to Oakland in the League Championship Series, but Gaston returned in 1990.

New York Yankees
Dallas Green to Bucky Dent

Former Phillies manager Dallas Green became the second person with no previous ties to the Yankees to be hired by George Steinbrenner to direct the ball club. Green's 1980 world's championship with Philadelphia, plus the two division title winning teams he built as general manager of the Cubs, convinced Steinbrenner he was the man to return the Yankees to the top of the American League.

By midsummer, Steinbrenner had grown disenchanted with Green. By late August, Green met the same fate as all of Steinbrenner's previous managers. "I have nothing critical to say about Dallas Green," said Steinbrenner on August 18, the day he fired another manager. "Some things I did disappointed him, and things he did disappointed me. But we're close friends."[3]

Steinbrenner flew to Detroit to meet with Green at the team's hotel. At that meeting, Green was informed that four of his coaches were about to be fired. "That's not the way to do it," Green said. "That's not the baseball way to do it, and you're not going to do it here. It's only going to lead to more agitation. Why don't you just fire the manager, and then make all the coaching changes you want?"[4] Steinbrenner promptly fired Green and coaches Charlie Fox, Pat Corrales, Lee Elia and Frank Howard.

"It had nothing to do with coaching changes," Steinbrenner explained. "I came here [to Detroit] on the basis of what was happening with the relationship. I just felt I wanted to make a change. I felt we had been friends for a lot of years—some 30 years—and it started getting personal. I was beginning to read in the papers he was saying a lot of personal things. I told him it was very disappointing to me. He was upset with me, and I was upset with him. Life's too short for that."[5]

Green said he'd taken the Yankee job to feed his ego. "The reason I took the New York thing was the city, and the Yankees were such a great thing in baseball—or had been. It was an ego thing. I thought I could bring something to the Yankees [that] I thought they needed to bring them back to a championship situation."[6] Green had signed a two-year contract at a salary of $700,000 a season.

To succeed Green, who left behind a sixth-place club with a record of 56–65, Steinbrenner summoned former Yankee shortstop Bucky Dent, who was managing the team's Triple-A farm club in Columbus. Dent said he was told Steinbrenner was sending his private plane to Columbus and he better "be on it." Asked how long he expected to manage the Yankees, Dent answered simply, "Who knows?"[7]

Green thought he knew. He was retained as a "consultant" to Steinbrenner and said he'd never consider managing the club again. He also predicted that Dent's tenure in the Yankee dugout would be brief, and he was right. The Yankees won 18 and lost 22 for Dent to come home fifth with a mark of 74–87. He would barely last beyond Memorial Day of 1990.

Cleveland Indians
"Doc" Edwards to John Hart

Some late-season managerial changes fall under the category of "why bother?" Not that Hank Peters didn't have a specific reason for dismissing Doc Edwards with

19 games left in the 1989 season. Edwards had replaced Pat Corrales after the Indians fell apart before the All-Star break in 1987 and was re-hired for 1988 after restoring some semblance of order to the free-falling team. Edwards's Indians caused some excitement by winning 16 of their first 20 games in '88, but seven of those victories came at the expense of the Baltimore Orioles, who opened the season by losing their first 21 games. Thoughts of contention soon vanished as the Tribe fell from first place on May 2 to fifth on May 9. Cleveland finished sixth with a record of 78–84, but Edwards was given a one-year contract extension because, according to the news release announcing the re-hiring, club officials "couldn't think of a good reason not to."

No one seemed to want to win the AL East early in 1989, and Edwards steered the Indians into first place with a 21–21 record on May 22. The Tribe was still at the .500 mark on August 4, when its 54–54 record left it just 1½ games out of first. Before pennant fever could grip Cleveland, however, the Indians lost 24 of their next 35 games. Peters had found a good reason not to bring Edwards back in 1990, and saw no reason to keep him around to fulfill the remaining weeks of his contract.

In Peters's opinion, Edwards had allowed the team to grow accustomed to losing, and that wasn't acceptable: "I think the ball club had reached the point where they were satisfied with the type of baseball they were playing. I wasn't."[8]

Edwards was replaced for the season's final 19 games by John Hart, a former minor league manager serving Cleveland as a special assignment scout. Hart took over a team with a 65–78 record, and the Indians won eight and lost 11 for Hart, who was interested in the full-time job. Peters had other plans for his protégé, however. Hart was being groomed to replace Peters as team president when he retired after the 1991 season.

The Indians finished sixth with a record of 73–89, 16 games behind the division-winning Blue Jays. Hart was kicked upstairs as expected and never managed in the big leagues again. Neither did Edwards, who fashioned a record of 173–207 in two years and two months at the Indians' helm.

1990

New York Mets
Davey Johnson to Bud Harrelson

The New York Mets averaged 96 victories a year since former major league infielder Davey Johnson was hired as their manager for the 1984 season. Johnson set the bar so high even his sterling record couldn't save his job when New York got off to a slow start in 1990.

Johnson's Mets won 100 or more games twice. In 1986, the Mets won 108 en route to a World Series championship, and the '88 Mets, winners an even 100 times, were National League East champions. The Mets dropped to second with 87 wins in 1989, their worst showing under Johnson, and when the 1990 team started slowly (by Johnson's standards), general manager Frank Cashen decided a change was in order. "I thought the club was underachieving and needed to go in a new direction," Cashen explained. "Part of the blame is certainly mine. Part of the blame has to be with the organization, and part of the blame has to be with the team. It's not all Davey's. I have very little experience in letting managers go. If I had to let Davey go, it's great to have somebody of Bud Harrelson's stripe in the organization."[1]

Harrelson spent 13 seasons playing shortstop for the Mets from 1965 through 1977 and was serving as their third base coach when Johnson was dismissed. He took over a team with a record of 20–22 and positioned in fourth place in the NL East, 5½ games out of first. Harrelson identified the Mets' problem as a lack of discipline.

"I just had a meeting with the players," said the new manager. "We discussed rules that have been in existence since 1984, which I think the players really didn't pay attention to this season. I think they agree they have been abusing the set-down rules for a while. I think they agree it was in the best interest of the club to start living up to those rules."[2]

Harrelson made Cashen's decision to dump a highly successful manager at the first sign of trouble look inspired, guiding the Mets to a 71–49 record. Their final mark of 91–71 wasn't good enough to overcome the division's new power, Pittsburgh, which captured the first of three consecutive championships, outdistancing the Mets by four games. Harrelson would be fired with eight games left in the 1991 season and New York floundering in third place with a 74–80 record. He didn't manage in the majors again and had a mark of 145–129 for his brief career.

Despite his outstanding record, Johnson was unemployed much longer than logic would have dictated. He wouldn't manage again until hired by Cincinnati in June of 1993.

New York Yankees
"Bucky" Dent to "Stump" Merrill

There were no miracles this time.

Bucky Dent will always be revered in New York and reviled in New England for dropping a 305-foot fly ball into the screen atop the Green Monster in Fenway Park on October 2, 1978, giving the Yankees the lead in a one-game, winner-take-all playoff for the Eastern Division championship that they'd eventually win on their way to a World Series title. He'll also be remembered as having one of the shortest careers of any Yankee manager, even during the George Steinbrenner era.

Dent's tour of duty ended after 89 games spread over the 1989 and '90 seasons. With the Yankees in seventh place in the AL East on June 6 with an 18–31 record, Dent was fired. General manager Harding (Pete) Peterson delivered the bad news.

"Mr. Steinbrenner anguished long and hard over this decision," said Peterson, before adding the obligatory, "We feel that the club is better than our won-loss record indicates."[3] Even though all managers, Steinbrenner's in particular, are hired to be fired, Dent's longevity was a matter of speculation from the moment he succeeded Dallas Green in August of 1989. He was rumored to be on the way out from the first game of the 1990 season. At age 38, he was the youngest manager in the major leagues. Coaches John (Champ) Summers, Joe Sparks and Gary Tuck were also fired.

"They said they thought the club hadn't shown any signs of turning around,"[4] said Dent when asked for the explanation given to him for his dismissal. He was replaced by Carl (Stump) Merrill, who had been a Philadelphia farmhand for six seasons and managed in the

Yankees organization from 1978–1985 before joining the big club as a coach. Merrill's teams won five league championships in the minors.

"I feel sad for Bucky, but I look at it in terms of what it means for Stump Merrill," he told reporters. "It's one of the happiest days of my life. From watching them, it looked like a listless ball club to me. I'm easy-going. Once they put that baseball hat on, it's business and business only. It took me 14 years to get to this point. I'm not saying we'll win the pennant, but we're going to put a product on that field that will perform. We'll play hard and we're going to have fun."[5]

Yankee fans didn't have much fun during Merrill's season and two-thirds in the New York dugout. The team didn't show much more life for him than it had for Dent, going 49–64 to wind up in last place at 67–95. Surprisingly, he was retained for 1991 and the Yankees came in fifth with a 71–91 record. Merrill never managed in the majors again, and his career record for 275 games in pinstripes was 120–155.

Dent didn't manage again, either. His brief tenure in New York produced 36 wins and 53 defeats.

Atlanta Braves
Russ Nixon to Bobby Cox

If you want a job done right, do it yourself.

That thought may have run through Bobby Cox's mind before he called Russ Nixon on the morning of June 22. "I called Russ this morning and told him it was not a good phone call," said Cox at the press conference announcing Nixon's firing and Cox's hiring as his replacement. "He knew what I meant. It's upsetting when somebody fails below you. It's the same as if you failed. He said he felt tremendous relief that it was all over. He had been under a lot of pressure the last few days."[6]

"I've been expecting it," Nixon admitted. "It's been evident the last two weeks, one of the bullets was going to get me. They've been shooting so many at me."[7] The bullets aimed at Nixon started flying when the Braves lost 13 of their first 15 games and were 10½ games out of first before April was over.

Cox had managed the Braves from 1978 through 1981, and the Blue Jays from 1982 through 1985. He returned to Atlanta to serve as general manager and was largely responsible for the club Nixon hadn't been able to win with. "I hope I can breathe a breath of fresh air into this club," said Cox. "I don't know if any major changes need to be made. Maybe some minor ones."[8] One change was the demotion of pitching coach Bruce Dal Canton to Atlanta's Triple-A affiliate in Richmond, Virginia, and the promotion of Richmond's pitching coach, Leo Mazzone, to the Braves. Together, starting in 1991, Cox and Mazzone would preside over one of baseball's all-time strongest pitching staffs.

Club president Stan Kasten said Cox would handle the dual roles of general manager and field manager for the rest of the season, then surrender one of the positions. Under its new manager, Atlanta would win 40 and lose 57 and stay anchored in last place with a final mark of 65–97. Cox would jettison the general manager's job at season's end.

Nixon's major league managerial career was over. He was among the sport's least successful field bosses. His Cincinnati and Atlanta clubs won just 40 percent of their games (231–347) and never finished above the cellar in the NL West.

St. Louis Cardinals
"Whitey" Herzog to Joe Torre

All good things must come to an end, and so it was with the Whitey Herzog era in St. Louis.

Herzog's Cardinals won three division titles, three pennants, and one World Series between 1982 and 1987. His defending NL champions dropped to fifth in 1988, rebounded to third in 1989, and were mired in last place when they were swept by the Giants in Candlestick Park on July 2, 3 and 4. A victory over the Padres on July 5 didn't lift Herzog's spirits, and he resigned on July 6.

"I was totally embarrassed by the way our team played [in San Francisco]. I just feel bad for the ball club, the organization, the fans," said Herzog. "I don't think I have done a good job as a manager this year. I just can't get the guys to play, and I think anybody could do a better job than me."[9]

Herzog had spoken of stepping down throughout the season, according to Cardinals president Fred Kuhlmann. "When Whitey brought up the subject of resigning several weeks ago, we said 'no!' But everybody feels it's in the best interests of the team to make a change now."[10]

Herzog handed a club with a 33–47 record to Red Schoendienst, the only manager to win more games for St. Louis than Herzog. While general manager Dal Maxvill interviewed potential replacements for Herzog, Schoendienst guided the Cardinals to a 13–11 record. On August 2, a press conference was held to introduce former Mets and Braves manager Joe Torre as the new head redbird.

"During the selection process, I interviewed a number of very good candidates," explained Maxvill. "But I kept coming back to Joe Torre. We couldn't find anyone better on Earth."[11] Torre, a former Cardinal who won the National League's MVP award while wearing a St. Louis uniform in 1971, had been a broadcaster for the California Angels since being fired by the Braves after the 1984 season. The highlight of his managerial career had been winning the 1982 NL West championship in Atlanta. The Braves were swept by Herzog's Cardinals in the League Championship Series.

Torre said he wouldn't try to replace Herzog: "I just look at this as coming back. When I moved into batting number four [for the Braves] it didn't mean I was better than Hank Aaron."[12]

It turned out Schoendienst was the most successful of St. Louis's three managers in 1990. The Cardinals won 24 and lost 34 for Torre and finished last with a 70–92 record.

Herzog's Hall of Fame managerial career was over. His Texas, Kansas City and St. Louis teams won 1,281 games and lost 1,125 with six division titles, three pennants and a World Series championship. Schoendienst was also finished managing. In 12 full seasons, and portions of two others, all with the Cardinals, his teams won 1,041 games and lost 955, capturing the 1967 and '68 pennants and the 1967 world's championship. Schoendienst is in the Hall of Fame both for his outstanding playing career and his success as a manager.

San Diego Padres
Jack McKeon to Greg Riddoch

When Jack McKeon took over the Padres as interim manager in 1988, he said he'd return to his front office job exclusively at the end of the season. The success of the Padres under his leadership dictated otherwise, however. McKeon stayed in the dugout in 1989 and guided San Diego to a second-place finish with 89 wins and 73 losses. By the All-Star break of 1990, however, being both field manager and vice president of baseball operations was taking its toll on the 59-year-old McKeon. Rather than waiting until the end of the season to step aside as manager, he resigned on July 11.

"I just felt two jobs was too much," said McKeon. "I was really getting burdened. I didn't have the time to devote to both jobs. I was cheating the organization and I was cheating myself. Now I can go out and try to get Greg some better players."[13] Greg Riddoch had been McKeon's bench coach and would take over as manager immediately.

"I still think we have the nucleus to have an outstanding ball club here and in the future," McKeon continued, "and we're going to work to try to fill the holes in the very near future. I know the club has been an underachieving club. We expected great things of the players, but it hasn't happened. I haven't gotten the job done. Maybe Greg can do it. I had hoped to bring some continuity to the club, but I did not intend to make a career out of managing."[14]

Riddoch, who took over a team with a 37–43 record, sounded like someone who did intend to make a career out of managing: "I have signed a contract through the end of this year. I am the manager, not the interim manager, and I am going to make it as hard on these people as it can conceivably be to get rid of me."[15] Riddoch immediately put his stamp on the team by firing batting coach Amos Otis. He said other changes to the coaching staff would be forthcoming.

The Padres, from whom McKeon had expected great things, didn't produce for Riddoch, either, winning 38 and losing 44 for a final mark of 75–87 and a fourth-place finish. Despite his determination not to give the Padres cause to fire him, Riddoch's career in the San Diego dugout would be brief. And despite his insistence that he didn't want to be a career manager, McKeon would return to manage again. And again.

1991

Philadelphia Phillies
Nick Leyva to Jim Fregosi

It was almost a record.

Differences between Philadelphia Phillies general manager Lee Thomas and field manager Nick Leyva emerged during spring training of 1991. Leyva managed the Phillies to a last-place finish in 1989, but improved the club by ten games in 1990, coming in fourth, although still with a losing record of 77–85. It became obvious in the spring of 1991 that the two men weren't on the same page philosophically, and it was only a matter of time before Leyva was out.

Thomas waited just 13 games before ending Leyva's employment. Philadelphia won three of its first five games, but lost seven of the next eight, and Thomas had seen enough. Leyva's firing was the third fastest in modern major league history, topped only by Cal Ripken, Sr.'s dismissal six games into the 1988 season by the Baltimore Orioles and Preston Gomez's firing by the San Diego Padres after just 11 games in 1972.

"I didn't like the way the club was going," explained Thomas. "It's best for the organization, before we get too far into the season."[1]

Leyva wasn't surprised by the firing. "The club is not playing good. When it doesn't, somebody takes the blame. I tried to do the best job I could, and it didn't work out."[2]

Thomas's choice to succeed Leyva, who had been a Phillies coach before becoming manager at the end of the 1988 season, was former Angels and White Sox skipper Jim Fregosi, who was serving the club as a minor league instructor. Thomas bypassed a pair of ex-managers, Hal Lanier and Larry Bowa, who were coaches on Leyva's staff.

"He can handle modern-day players," said Thomas of Fregosi. "He's a people person, he's a good strategist."[3] Fregosi took over a team with a 4–9 record and strategized it to 74 wins and 75 losses. The Phillies finished third with a mark of 78–84.

Leyva never managed in the major leagues again. His record in two and a fraction years in Philadelphia was 148–189.

Chicago Cubs
Don Zimmer to Jim Essian

Jim Frey knew exactly how Don Zimmer felt.

Frey and Zimmer were childhood friends, having grown up together in Cincinnati. Two years after leading the Cubs to the 1984 NL East championship, Frey was fired. Two years after leading the Cubs to the 1989 NL East championship, Zimmer was fired.

"No, I'm not bitter," said the 1989 NL Manager of the Year. "There's nothing to be bitter about. The only thing I'm really sorry about was that we didn't play better for the fans of Chicago."[4]

Frey had returned to the Cubs in 1988, taking over for general manager Dallas Green after Green made the ill-fated decision to accept George Steinbrenner's offer to manage the Yankees. Firing Zimmer wasn't Frey's idea.

"The club is not performing the way we expected it to," said the man whose idea it was, team president Don Grenesko, "especially in view of the talent that is on the team."[5] The Cubs had been expected to win the division after signing free agents George Bell, Danny Jackson and Dave Smith, to add to the talent still on hand from the 1989 title winners. Instead, Chicago was in fourth place with an 18–19 record, but only five games behind the division-leading Pirates.

A testy meeting between Zimmer and Grenesko earlier in May led to the change in managers. "He made some comments in the paper about evaluating me at the end of the year, and I told him to evaluate me by July 1," said Zimmer, who resented the thought of being evaluated at all. "They didn't feel that July 1 was enough time, and they felt they should do it now. I've been in the game 43 years. I've gotta be evaluated at the end of the season? I didn't like what he said, and evidently he didn't like what I said."[6]

Frey carried out Grenesko's order reluctantly. "The guy we fired today is the same guy who won the title in 1989. I still have the same respect for him, for his honesty, his character, and the way he went about doing things."[7]

Zimmer was replaced by former major league catcher Jim Essian, who played for the Phillies, Athletics, White Sox, Mariners and Indians from 1973 through 1984. Essian had been a minor league manager since 1985 and was in charge of Chicago's Triple-A affiliate in Des Moines when he got the call from Frey. He said Zimmer hadn't been to blame for the Cubs' sluggish start.

"The problem didn't lie with Don Zimmer. He's a great character. He's been a great manager through the years. He's very knowledgeable. I admire him very much. The problem is out on the field—pitching, hitting and catching."[8] The 40-year-old Essian became the youngest manager in the major leagues—briefly. He led the Cubs to a 59–63 record and a fourth-place finish at 77–83. Although he was signed through 1992, he was fired at the end of the season and didn't manage in the majors again.

Zimmer's career as a manager was over. His San Diego, Boston, Texas and Chicago teams won 885 and lost 858, with one division title.

Kansas City Royals
John Wathan to Hal McRae

The week before Memorial Day was a tough one for big league managers. Three managers were fired within a four-day span. John Wathan was the second.

"John Wathan probably does not deserve full blame for this," said Kansas City general manager "Herk" Robinson in announcing Wathan's firing on May 22. "I wish we had a more creative way to fix a situation like this. Had there been, we would have used it. It came down to the fact we were simply not winning enough games. Whether that was through strategy or motivation or intensity, or whatever, we simply weren't winning enough games. I don't know that it's the manager's fault, per se. We have 25 players, coaches, a manager, and me in the front office. I think it represents a degree of failure on everybody. But I think it was necessary that some change be made."[9]

Sounding a lot like Jim Frey, Royals third baseman George Brett noted, "He's the same guy who won 92 games for us two years ago. It's easier to get rid of one guy. I just feel for him."[10] Wathan and Brett had been teammates from 1976 through 1985.

Two years is an eternity in sports, and in the two years since Wathan's Royals won 92 games and finished second in the AL West, management spent $33 million acquiring free agents. With the added talent (and payroll), Kansas City came in sixth in 1990, and was in seventh place with a 15–22 record when Wathan was dismissed.

"I have always wanted what is best for the organization," said the former manager. "I hope whoever comes in to manage will be successful and turn it around. I think it is a good club and will grow in the future, and I hope everyone will be patient with the new manager."[11]

The new manager was Wathan's former teammate Hal McRae, who'd been offered the job and rejected it before Wathan took it in 1987. McRae was a coach with the Expos when Robinson offered him the Kansas City managing job a second time. "For a while I was kind of reluctant to do it, but I felt that this was the second time around, that I almost had to take the job. I don't see how I couldn't take it, if I wanted to manage ... if I felt I was capable of managing."[12] McRae's son, Brian, was the Royals' centerfielder.

McRae lifted Kansas City from seventh to sixth place, guiding the club to a 66–58 record for a final ledger of 82–80. He'd return for the 1992 season.

Wathan's career as a major league manager wasn't quite over. He'd win 39 games and lose 50 while filling in for an ailing Buck Rodgers with the Angels in 1992, giving him a record of 326–320.

Baltimore Orioles
Frank Robinson to Johnny Oates

Frank Robinson's removal from the Baltimore dugout was subject to interpretation. According to the press release announcing the change in managers from Robinson to Johnny Oates on May 23, Robinson had been "re-assigned" to a talent evaluation position in the Orioles' organization. The deposed manager saw it differently.

"I wasn't re-assigned," growled Robinson. "I was fired."[13]

"He has done a tremendous job for our ball club," said general manager Roland Hemond. "We will forever remember and enjoy and cherish the memories of the 1989 season—the 'why not' season."[14] Robinson had taken over for Cal Ripken Senior six games into the 1988 season, as the Orioles were in the midst of an historic 21-game losing streak to open the campaign. Baltimore was 0–6 under Ripken, and started 0–15 for Robinson, en route to a seventh-place finish and final record of 54–107. Robinson then engineered one of baseball's most remarkable one-season turnarounds as the '89 Orioles won 87 games, chased the division-winning Blue Jays down to the season's final weekend, and came in second.

Baltimore slid back to fifth place in 1990 and was in the cellar of the AL East with a record of 13–24 in 1991 when Hemond pulled the plug. "Things have not been going well, and all of us share some responsibility. We are hopeful a change of managers will lead to improvement in the way our team is performing."[15]

Oates spent the first two seasons of his 11-year major league career with Baltimore, and had been a coach on Robinson's staff since 1989. He managed three years in the minor leagues, winning the International League's "Manager of the Year" award at Rochester in 1988.

"We've got a lot of work to do. We cannot come back to being a .500 level team in one inning or one game. We're going to have to go one game at a time. I'm excited by the challenge. I look forward to it. I hope it can be a long tenure here in Baltimore," said the new Oriole boss.[16] Oates's Orioles struggled, going 54–71 and finishing sixth with a mark of 67–95.

It would be more than a decade before Robinson would manage again. He'd take the thankless job of managing the doomed Montreal Expos in 2002. Robinson's career record for 16 seasons as a manager would be 1,065–1,176 with no playoff appearances.

Montreal Expos
"Buck" Rodgers to Tom Runnells

How did Buck Rodgers receive the news that he was no longer the manager of the Expos? He hung up the phone, rolled over and went back to sleep.

"I don't have any sour grapes. We did a lot of good things. Six and a half years is a good ride, and I'm proud of what we did while I was here. I think the firing was inevitable. I'm not happy about it, but I'm not sad."[17] Rodgers said he planned to play some golf and sit around and do nothing while collecting paychecks from the Expos, who owed him the remainder of his $500,000 salary for the rest of the season.

Montreal had lost five in a row and fallen to sixth place in the NL East with a record of 20–29 when general manager Dave Dombrowski called Rodgers on the morning of June 3 to inform he was out of a job. Rodgers's dismissal ended a two-week period during which four managers were replaced. Rodgers's replacement was Expos third base coach Tom Runnells. At age 36, Runnells became major league baseball's youngest manager. He had been skipper of Montreal's Triple-A Indianapolis farm team the previous season.

"I want to get the focus back where it should be, winning ball games," said Dombrowski. As for Montreal's new manager, "I think he'll have a total commitment to building a championship team. I think you'll see a burning desire to succeed."[18]

Rodgers admitted that there'd been friction between himself and Dombrowski since the summer of 1989, when the general manager wanted to fire one of Rodgers's coaches in mid-season. The firing didn't come off, and the coach in question wasn't identified, but batting coach Joe Sparks was let go at season's end. Relations between manager and general manager were chilly after that.

Despite Dombrowski's high praise, Runnells proved to be a poor choice to take over in the Montreal dugout. The Expos won 51 and lost 61 the rest of the season to finish 71–90 and in last place. Runnells wouldn't be managing Montreal by Memorial Day of 1992.

Rodgers would enjoy a brief paid vacation and return to managing before the 1991 season was over.

Cleveland Indians
John McNamara to Mike Hargrove

John McNamara wanted one more chance.
Not a chance to tie Dick Williams's record of managing six different big league teams. McNamara was embarrassed by the circumstances under which he'd been dismissed by the Red Sox in 1988. Rumors made the rounds that McNamara had been drinking liberally during his last few months with Boston, and he yearned for the opportunity to prove the rumors unfounded. He termed the rumors "a vicious lie"[19] the day his old friend, Hank Peters, hired him to manage the Indians.

McNamara signed a two-year deal with the understanding that he'd retire after the 1991 season, no matter how well (or poorly) the Indians were doing. McNamara was to spend the 1990 and 1991 seasons showing newly hired first base coach Mike Hargrove the ropes. Hargrove had played with the Indians from 1979 through 1985 and managed for three seasons in their minor league system. He would take over when McNamara retired.

The Indians finished fourth in the AL East for McNamara in 1990, with a record of 77–85. The following season was not only to be McNamara's last as manager, but Peters's last as team president and general manager. Just as Hargrove was being groomed to take over in the Tribe's dugout, John Hart was being groomed to replace Peters in the front office.

Hart and McNamara differed over how committed to youth the Indians should be in 1991. Hart wanted to play the youngsters. McNamara, hoping to go out with the best record possible, favored playing a mix of kids and veterans to win a few more games. After a poor start, the Indians completely collapsed, winning just five of 30 games from June 3 until July 6, the day McNamara was fired. Cleveland's 25–52 record was the worst in the major leagues, and the team was 20 games out of first place.

"I want to make one thing clear," said Peters. "John McNamara was not let go because we needed a scapegoat. I thought John did a great job for us last year and started the development of our younger players. It's my belief that this type of club might not be the best for John to manage. I don't know if he's had to deal with this many young players at one time before. I think this will give John some peace of mind and give a younger manager a chance to grow with the team."[20] McNamara was 59, Hargrove 41. The Indians had already used 43 players by the time McNamara was dismissed. Seventeen were rookies.

"I feel I'm here because I paid my dues," said Hargrove. "I went down and saw the game from the other side of the fence. I'll do some things different, but that doesn't mean Johnny Mac was wrong and I'm right. I'm excited. But as far as being nervous or scared, no."[21] Having played six years for the Indians in huge, dark, dank Municipal Stadium, Hargrove knew better than most the depths to which the once-proud franchise had sunk. He wasn't intimidated by the massive rebuilding job he'd be undertaking. The Indians had some serious talent in the high minors, as well as some serious talent at the big league level, and the voters of Cuyahoga County had approved a tax levy to finance a shiny new baseball-only park that would open in the spring of 1994. Better days were ahead.

As for the rest of the 1991 season, the Indians set a club record with 105 defeats. They won 32 and lost 53 for Hargrove. And, as fate would have it, McNamara's managerial career wasn't quite complete after all.

California Angels
Doug Rader to "Buck" Rodgers

So, what was the big deal?

The Minnesota Twins and Atlanta Braves grabbed the headlines for meeting in the first-ever "worst to first" World Series in 1991. Both clubs had finished in last place in their divisions in 1990. The Twins vaulted over six teams to finish first in 1991, and the Braves had to hurdle over five. On the other end of the spectrum, the Angels went from first to worst in a month. And the plunge cost manager Doug Rader his job.

Rader was hired to pilot the Angels in 1989 and led the team to a third-place finish with a 91–71 record. California slipped to 80–82 and fourth place in 1990, and owner Gene Autry went on another spending spree, signing free agents Dave Winfield, Mark Langston and Gary Gaetti. The Angels were in first place, albeit for only one day, with a record of 44–33 on July 3 before sliding all the way to seventh on August 4. In the stacked AL West, California's .500 record was good for last place. When the skid continued, general manager Dan O'Brien decided to make a change. Rader was fired on August 26, with the Angels at 61–63, trailing the division leader by 13 games.

Buck Rodgers, an original Angel from the expansion season of 1961, ended his brief vacation, imposed on him when he was fired by the Expos in June, to take the reins from Rader. "This is kind of a dream come true," said the new boss of the Angels. "There's always a bittersweet to any managerial change. I got the bitter about three months ago. It's sweet for me today. I'm going to come in here and listen to my coaches, and keep a wide open mind. I think there are some outstanding players on this club. Why it's not a contender I don't know. I don't expect to be a quick fixer. I'm going to be around here for a while."[22] Rodgers had reason to be confident, having signed a three-year contract.

O'Brien said of his former manager, "I don't think he was surprised. At least, I didn't get that feeling. He reacted very well. He said he understood."[23] O'Brien's contract was extended through the 1994 season on the same day he fired Rader.

Rodgers managed the Angels to 20 wins and 18 losses for a final record of 81–81 and a last-place finish—the best record ever for a seventh-place club in the divisional era, whatever that distinction may have been worth. Rader's managerial career was over. His Texas and California clubs (and two games as interim manager of the White Sox) won 388 games and lost 417.

1992

Montreal Expos
Tom Runnells to Felipe Alou

Dave Dombrowski didn't make many mistakes as an executive with the Expos, Florida Marlins and Detroit Tigers. When he did, he corrected them quickly.

Despite what Dombrowski had termed a "burning desire to succeed," Tom Runnells, at age 36, wasn't ready to be a major league manager when he was promoted to succeed Buck Rodgers in June of 1991. Dombrowski recognized his new manager's shortcomings, and moved to rectify his error in May of 1992. Although the Expos record wasn't dreadful at 17–20, and they were only 5½ games out of first place, Dombrowski dismissed Runnells and replaced him with Montreal's bench coach, former major league outfielder Felipe Alou.

Alou had compiled a .286 batting average in a 17-year career spent with six teams. He joined the Expos organization in 1976 and worked his way up to the position of bench coach when he was tapped to replace Runnells. Little was said about the deposed manager at the press conference announcing Alou's hiring. Instead, the Expos showered themselves with credit for hiring baseball's first Hispanic manager. Alou also became the first manager in history to have his son (outfielder Moises Alou) and nephew (pitcher Mel Rojas) on his team.

The 57-year-old Alou proved to be an inspired choice. The Expos responded to him and went 70–55 the rest of the way, finishing second in the NL East with an 87–75 record, a distant nine games behind the Pirates. Montreal was loaded with young talent and Alou knew how to handle it. The Expos won 94 games in 1993, finishing second to the surprising Phillies, and had baseball's best record at 74–40 in mid–August of 1994 when the players' strike brought the season to a premature end. The agreement that ended the strike forced the Expos to begin dispersing that talent, knowing they lacked the money to keep the players once they became free agents. Montreal's record suffered, but Alou remained at the helm until 2001.

Runnells didn't manage in the major leagues again. His record in 149 games with the Expos was 68–81.

Texas Rangers
Bobby Valentine to Toby Harrah

The best the Rangers had done since Bobby Valentine became their manager in 1985 was a second-place finish in his first full season of 1986.

Valentine was in his eighth year at the Texas helm when the club's new ownership, headed by George W. Bush, decided a change was needed. Many observers thought he'd held onto the job as long as he had only due to his close friendship with general manager Tom Grieve.

Bush described Valentine as "a good man, a good manager, he's done a lot for the community. But having said that, we were concerned about the 1992 pennant race getting away from us."[1] Bush made the statement on July 9 as he announced his manager's firing. The Rangers held first place for three days in late May, but had faltered and fallen to third with a record of 45–41 when Bush ran out of patience.

"I think Bobby was surprised it happened," said Grieve, who was on the hot seat himself as the club continued to fail to live up to the expectations of its owners. "He took it like a true professional."[2]

Valentine's replacement, on an interim basis, was former Rangers infielder Toby Harrah, who was signed by the franchise when it was the Washington Senators and played for it through 1978. Harrah returned to the Rangers in 1985 and had been a coach with the team since 1989. He had some managing experience, piloting Texas's Triple-A farm club in Oklahoma City in 1987 and '88.

"I guess I'm kind of cautiously excited," he said. "I think I'm just really interim manager."[3] Texas won just 32 and lost 44 for Harrah, finishing fourth with a record of 77–85. He wasn't offered a contract for 1993 and didn't manage in the major leagues again. Valentine, on the other hand, did.

San Diego Padres
Greg Riddoch to Jim Riggleman

Greg Riddoch did his best to make the vow he made the day he was hired come true. Riddoch planned to manage the Padres for a long time and promised to do everything in his power not to give his bosses a reason to fire him. Nonetheless, rumors spread through the 1991 season that Riddoch's job was in jeopardy as he was leading San Diego to an 84–78 record and third place finish in the NL West. The Padres were again in third place, with a mark of 78–72, when, with just a dozen games left in the 1992 season, the club made a change.

"This is kind of a happy-sad day for the Padres," said general manager Joe McIlvane as he announced the switch. "Whenever you change a manager, it is a difficult task." McIlvane said the original plan had been to allow Riddoch to finish the season, but circumstances changed. "It seemed to me that the club was so down and out that I'd rather do it now and give Jim the advantage of managing the team for 12 games so he can answer some questions on his own before we go to spring training."[4] The Padres had been seven games out of first place over the Labor Day weekend, but had dropped to 12 games back when Riddoch was dismissed.

The tone of the press conference sounded as if McIlvane was more concerned with losing Riggleman than he was dissatisfied with Riddoch. Riggleman spent nine years in the Cardinals' organization, the last two as first base coach for Whitey Herzog, before joining the Padres. He managed San Diego's Triple-A affiliate in Las Vegas in 1991 and '92. Seattle interviewed Riggleman for its managerial vacancy after the 1991 season, and the Florida Marlins, who would open for business in 1993, had asked McIlvane for permission to talk to Riggleman.

"I think Jim Riggleman has the potential to be one of the finest managers in baseball. I think it will be a short time before others realize that," said McIlvane.[5] Despite his praise, he gave the Padres' new skipper a contract for only one year.

The Padres went 4–8 for the man McIlvane thought would become one of the best managers in baseball. San Diego finished third with a record of 82–80, 16 games behind the division-winning Braves.

Riddoch's short career as a big league manager was finished. His Padres won 200 and lost 194. Coincidentally, in baseball reference books, the name Riddoch is immediately followed by the name Riggleman in the alphabetical manager register.

1993

New York Mets
Jeff Torborg to Dallas Green

Jeff Torborg arrived in New York amid the kind of fanfare that usually accompanied the hiring of a new manager by the Yankees.

Torborg had just managed the White Sox to consecutive second-place finishes in the AL West in 1990 and '91, winning 94 and 87 games. It took a four-year contract to lure him away from Chicago, and he wouldn't even make it halfway through before suffering the type of fate more commonly reserved for the men who prowled the dugout at Yankee Stadium.

Torborg's first Mets team finished a disappointing fifth in the NL East with a 72–90 record. His second team was floundering in last place with a 13–25 mark when he was fired on May 19, with two and three-quarters seasons remaining on his contract. "I saw no indication that things were turning around," said general manager Al Harazin. "We all share the blame for the start the ball club has had. We have all let Jeff down."[1]

Torborg, who had coached for the Yankees for several seasons and somehow managed to avoid incurring George Steinbrenner's wrath, took the dismissal in stride and accepted responsibility for the Mets' poor performance on his watch. "I'm sorry I couldn't get them to play. We didn't play well. We earned where we are…. I thought about it tonight during the game. I thought that maybe some new face would turn it around."[2]

Torborg had been criticized almost from the opening pitch of the 1992 season for being too passive and too accommodating of his players. His replacement, former Phillies and Yankees manager Dallas Green, didn't have those faults. Green was scouting for the Mets when he was promoted by Harazin, but New York needed more than a new face to turn things around. Actually, the club got three new faces. In addition to Torborg, first base coach Barry Foote and bullpen coach Dave LaRoche were also let go.

Green and a revamped coaching staff couldn't make a respectable team out of the Mets. It was noted that the club's record when it changed managers was just one game better than the 1962 Mets had compiled after 38 games. Those Mets lost 120 games. Their 1993 counterparts lost only 103. They were 46–78 under Green's leadership.

Torborg and New York City simply weren't a good mix. But he would manage in the major leagues again.

Cincinnati Reds
Tony Perez to Davey Johnson

It had worked for the Reds once before, so why not try it again?

Three seasons working for owner Marge Schott, including the world's championship year of 1990, had been quite enough for Lou Piniella, who departed for Seattle's Kingdome after the 1992 season. General manager Jim Bowden interviewed several candidates, including Davey Johnson, before announcing a surprise choice to manage the Reds in 1993: former star first baseman Tony Perez. Perez was a key member of the "Big Red Machine" of 1970–1976, but had no managerial experience. Neither had Pete Rose when he was hired to manage the Reds in August of 1984, and Rose guided the team to second-place finishes his first three years on the job.

Bowden showed little confidence in Perez, however, signing him to a one-year contract. The Reds had invested $43 million in the team they put on the field in 1993, and Perez was expected to win big and win immediately. When he didn't, Bowden wasted no time cutting his losses. Perez was fired on May 24, with the Reds in fifth place (20–24) and losers of six of their last seven games.

"It's something we've been studying for a period of time, trying to diagnose why the team is playing so poorly,"[3] said Bowden of the switch in managers from Perez to former Mets manager Johnson. Johnson had been out of baseball since being fired by the Mets in 1990. After passing him over in favor of Perez, Bowden hired Johnson as a "consultant," so he was available when the Reds sputtered early.

"I don't think it's fair," said Perez of Bowden's quick hook. "Was I cheated? I don't know. But I don't think it's fair. I think I did a good job."[4] Bowden fired pitching coach Larry Rothschild and third base coach Dave Bristol along with Perez. First base coach and former Reds player Ron Oester, a close friend of Perez, quit in protest.

Johnson couldn't get the Reds out of their rut in 1993, winning 53 and losing 65 for a final record of 73–89 and a fifth-place finish.

Perez would get a second chance at managing. He'd take charge of the Florida Marlins in 2001.

1994

California Angels
"Buck" Rodgers to Marcel Lachemann

Buck Rodgers's return to Los Angeles wasn't the happy homecoming he'd expected.

Rodgers had been selected by the original Angels in the expansion draft of 1961 and played for the club until 1969. His return as manager was marred by a serious accident on the team bus in May of 1992 that sidelined him for more than half a season. Rodgers and several players were hurt when the bus was involved in a crash en route from New York to Baltimore. Rodgers sustained the most serious injuries and had to turn the club over to coach John Wathan for 89 games. The Angels won only 33 of the 73 games Rodgers managed, finishing fifth, and the 1993 edition was a lackluster 71–91, as they came in fifth again.

The American League West was easily the weakest division in baseball in 1994. Both leagues had split into three divisions, and the worst-case scenario, that a team could win its division with a losing record, appeared to be inevitable right off the bat. Rodgers's Angels moved into first place in the west on May 11 by sweeping a double-header from the Rangers and improving their record to 15–20. California won the next day, then lost three straight. Although the Angels were just two games out of first place on May 17, Rodgers was shown the door.

"I surprised him, I think. I don't think he was expecting it right now," said general manager Bill Bavasi, who added that Rodgers "was very professional"[1] in handling his dismissal. Bavasi said the idea of changing managers was entirely his, although club owners Gene and Jackie Autry and club president Richard Brown signed off on it.

Bavasi's choice to replace Rodgers was former Angels pitching coach Marcel Lachemann, who was then performing the same job for his brother, Rene, the manager of the second-year expansion team in Miami. "It's an opportunity that might not come again," said Marcel of the chance to manage the team he'd served as pitching coach for nine years, through the 1992 season. "I hate to leave Rene, especially with what is starting to become a very promising situation."[2] It was the first time brothers had managed major league clubs at the same time in modern baseball history.

Marcel Lachemann didn't fare any better than Rodgers had. He took over an Angels team with a 16–23 record and won 30 while losing 44, before the players' strike put an end to the 1994 season. California was in second place with a mark of 46–67 when the work stoppage occurred.

Anaheim was Rodgers's last stop as a big league manager. His Milwaukee, Montreal and California clubs won 784 and lost 773. His Brewers won the "second half" title in the AL East in the strike-shortened 1981 season.

1995

Chicago White Sox
Gene Lamont to Terry Bevington

Gene Lamont's White Sox had battled the rejuvenated Indians tooth-and-nail in 1994. When the players' strike ended the season, Chicago held first place in the newly created AL Central Division at 67–46. The Indians were a game behind.

The battle was expected to resume in 1995, but the White Sox started slowly. A four-game pasting at the hands of the Indians in late May left Lamont's team with an 11–20 record and 11 games out of first place. It also left Lamont without a job.

Lamont's playing career encompassed 87 games with Detroit spread over five seasons between 1970 and 1975. He had been plucked from former Chicago coach Jim Leyland's Pittsburgh staff to run the White Sox in 1992 and piloted the club to a third-place finish with 86 victories. His 1993 White Sox won 94 games and the AL West before losing to Toronto in the League Championship Series, and Lamont was named "Manager of the Year."

None of that mattered to general manager Ron Schueler, who fired Lamont on June 3. Schueler cited lackluster play as his reason for dismissing Lamont, who said he was "surprised and hurt."[1] He was replaced by third base coach Terry Bevington.

The White Sox played .500 ball for their new manager, winning 57 and losing 56. They finished third with 68 victories and 76 losses in the abbreviated 1995 campaign, 32 games behind the Indians. Bevington stayed at the helm through 1997, finishing second both seasons. He never managed in the majors again, and his record in almost three full seasons with the White Sox was 222–214.

Lamont would be hired to manage the Pirates in 1997, succeeding his mentor, Leyland.

St. Louis Cardinals
Joe Torre to Mike Jorgensen

It's a general manager's prerogative to change his mind.

"Ten days ago, I was hoping that we would have a 10-game winning streak or whatever to try to turn this thing around," St. Louis general manager Walt Jocketty said when reminded on June 16, the day he fired manager Joe Torre, that earlier in the month he had absolved Torre of all blame for the Cardinals' sluggish performance. "I think Joe did as good a job as he could with all the problems we have with injuries, but I just felt after looking at it again for another 10 days or two weeks that a change was needed."

Jocketty continued, "We're not satisfied that we're 10 games out. We're not satisfied with the team chemistry, and we're not satisfied with the focus and the direction of the ball club. We will not stand pat."[2]

Team president Mark Lamping backed his general manager, saying, "I don't think we want to become an organization that sits back and hopes things will change."[3]

It was the third time Torre had been fired, so he was getting accustomed to the routine.

"St. Louis and the many great Cardinal fans will always hold a special place in my heart," he said in his farewell address. "My only regret is that we were never able to deliver a winning team while I was here."[4] Actually, Torre had delivered three winning teams to the fans of St. Louis. The Cardinals won 84, 83 and 87 games in Torre's first three years as manager. But a division title had eluded him. The Cardinals were fourth in the NL Central with a 20–27 record when he was dismissed.

Torre's replacement was former major league infielder Mike Jorgensen, who had played for five clubs during a career that stretched from 1968 through 1985. Jorgensen wrapped up his playing days with the Cardinals in 1984 and '85 and was the team's director of player personnel, a position he'd held since 1992, when Jocketty chose him to succeed Torre.

The change in managers resulted in no appreciable improvement on the field. Jorgensen's Cardinals won 42 and lost 54, staying in fourth place with a final record of 62–81 for the strike-shortened season. It was Jorgensen's only whirl at managing in the major leagues.

Torre's best days as a manager were still ahead of him, beginning in 1996 with the Yankees.

1996

Florida Marlins
Rene Lachemann to John Boles

Florida wasn't just for spring training anymore.

Florida was the most heavily populated state in the nation without a major league baseball franchise until 1993, when the National League put an expansion team in Miami. Owner Wayne Huizenga christened the club the "Florida" Marlins so as to appeal to baseball fans throughout the state, and then set about spending a portion of his vast fortune to make the team a winner as quickly as possible.

Former Seattle and Milwaukee manager Rene Lachemann was chosen to guide the Marlins, bringing with him a career record of 207–274. The Marlins performed like a typical expansion team, finishing last in the NL East with a mark of 64–98. But the Marlins enjoyed three advantages previous expansion teams hadn't: Huizenga's money (and his willingness to spend it), no state income tax, and the Florida sunshine, important selling points for free agents. By their second season, the Marlins were respectable, with a record of 51–54 (better than every team in the AL West) when the players' strike shut down the season in mid–August.

Florida finished fourth with a 67–76 record in the abbreviated 1995 campaign, and was in fourth place again with a disappointing 39–47 ledger on July 7, 1996, when Lachemann was fired. He accepted his firing philosophically. "When you don't win and you don't execute, the manager goes. It's as simple as that."[1] Batting coach Jose Morales went, too.

Marlins general manager Dave Dombrowski turned the Marlins over to the man who knew their personnel better than anyone else: director of player personnel John Boles, who'd been acquiring and developing players since November of 1991, a full year and a half before the team played its first exhibition game. Boles had managerial experience, fashioning a 349–271 record in 5½ seasons in the minor leagues.

The Marlins showed some spark for their new manager, winning 40 and losing 35. Florida finished third with a record of 80–82, and stood ready to make a run at the pennant in just its fifth season of existence in 1997. Boles returned to the club's front office, but would be summoned back to the dugout to manage again in 1999.

Lachemann's career as a major league manager was finished. His teams won 428 and lost 549.

California Angels
Marcel Lachemann to John McNamara

It wasn't a good year for the Lachemann brothers.

First, Rene was fired as manager of the Florida Marlins. Roughly a month later, Marcel resigned as manager of the California Angels. The Lachemanns had been the first brothers to manage in the major leagues at the same time since baseball pioneers George and Harry Wright in 1879.

Marcel Lachemann likened losing to "water torture." His Angels had blown a 10½ game lead in the AL West on August 15, 1995, and lost a one-game playoff for the division title to Seattle. The Angels continued to flounder in 1996 and were in last place with a 52–60 record when Lachemann submitted his resignation on August 7. "I'm 55 years old, and my goal never really was to manage," he said. "When I started out, and when this job came up, what I wanted to do was try to put together a solid organization and a foundation that could be built on for many years. I didn't have long-range goals of being a manager, and I don't now."[2]

"Marcel took the bullet for the entire organization," said team president Tony Tavares. "I've often discussed the club's effort more than his effort."[3] To replace Lachemann while the club conducted a "very patient" search for its next full-time manager, Tavares turned to an old warhorse: John McNamara. McNamara hadn't managed since being fired in Cleveland in July of 1991, and was asked only to mind the store for the rest of the season.

There is a discrepancy between baseball reference books and websites and the newspapers used by this author to research this book. The reference material has Lachemann resigning on August 11 with a record of 53–64. The newspaper story of Lachemann's resignation ran on August 7, complete with a picture of McNamara at a news conference introducing him as the Angels' interim manager. An Associated Press game story about California's 18–3 loss to Kansas City on August 10 specifically stated that it dropped the team's record to "0–4 under interim manager John McNamara."

The Angels' confusing managerial saga doesn't end there. On August 21, McNamara was hospitalized with a blood clot in his leg. The Angels had won three and lost five since he'd succeeded Lachemann (or 3–9 if he took over on August 7, as newspaper accounts indicate he did). While he recovered, bench coach Joe Maddon was placed in charge of the club. California won eight and lost 14 for its "interim interim" manager, and McNamara returned to the Angels' dugout on September 13, leading the team to five wins and nine losses in its 14 remaining games. For the record, *Total Baseball Sixth Edition* does not show Maddon in its manager register for the 1996 season, and credits McNamara with having managed the Angels for their final 44 games. However, the websites baseball-library.com and baseball-reference.com both show Maddon as having been California's manager from August 21 through September 12.

Neither McNamara nor Lachemann ever managed in the major leagues again. Lachemann's 336 games as California manager produced 161 wins and 175 losses. McNamara's "official" managerial record for 19 seasons with Oakland, San Diego, Cincinnati, California (twice), Boston and Cleveland was 1,167 wins and 1,242 defeats. If the five games he managed from August 7 through August 11, 1996, for which he doesn't receive credit in reference material but which newspaper accounts indicate he was responsible for, are included, the record changes slightly to 1,168 wins and 1,246 defeats. McNamara's teams won two division titles and one pennant.

New York Mets
Dallas Green to Bobby Valentine

The Mets, in the words of general manager Joe McIlvane, hadn't done as well as anticipated since spring training. In fact, they hadn't done as well as anticipated since Dallas Green had replaced Jeff Torborg as manager in 1993.

Green's Mets finished third and second in 1994 and '95, losing more games than they won both seasons. The Mets had just returned from a western road trip, with a record of 59–72, when McIlvane decided to make a change on August 26. "Our hope is that with this change, our young players can begin to blossom more," the general manager said.

Green greased the skids for his departure with critical comments made about two of the team's prized pitching prospects, 23-year-olds Jason Isringhausen and Paul Wilson. Between them, they'd won just nine games while losing 23, and Green questioned what they were doing on his roster. "These guys really don't belong in the big leagues," said the 62-year-old manager. "It sounds very harsh and very negative, but what have they done to get here?"[4]

McIlvane said Green's bluntness played a part in his decision to fire his manager: "It was a factor. I wasn't happy with that comment. I was expecting in the second half that our younger players would come to the forefront. That didn't happen. I was concerned we were beginning to lose some of our younger players."[5] Under terms of Green's contract, the Mets had to inform him by September 15 whether he'd be returning in 1997. McIlvane made the decision early. He also fired pitching coach Greg Pavlick and bench coach Bobby Wine.

To succeed Green, the Mets promoted former coach and Texas manager Bobby Valentine, who was calling the shots for the club's Triple-A affiliate in Norfolk, Virginia. Valentine was 16 years younger than Green, and it was hoped he'd relate better to the club's young talent. He led the team to 12 wins and 19 losses in the season's final weeks. The Mets finished last with 71 wins and 91 defeats.

Valentine settled in for an extended stay in the Mets' dugout. Green was through as a major league manager. His Phillies, Yankees and Mets were 454–478 with one pennant and one World Series championship.

1997

Kansas City Royals
Bob Boone to Tony Muser

The Royals kept on spending money, and kept on losing, as the decade of the '90s progressed.

For the 1997 season, Kansas City added first baseman Jeff King, shortstop Jay Bell, and designated hitter Chili Davis. The cost in salaries for the trio was $9.3 million. And while all three players produced as expected, the Royals were still in last place at the All-Star break with a record of 36–46 and in the midst of a losing streak that would stretch to 12 straight games. Bob Boone managed the first eight of those games before being fired by general manager "Herk" Robinson on July 9.

Boone, who held the major league record for most games caught in a career (2,264) that spanned 19 seasons and concluded in Kansas City in 1990, was hired to manage the Royals after the dismissal of Hal McRae in 1994. Boone's Royals finished second in the AL Central in 1995, an astonishing 30 games behind the division-winning Indians, and sank to fifth in 1996. Nonetheless, Robinson gave his manager a strong vote of confidence in the form of a two-year contract extension. A year and a half was left on that extension when Boone was fired. Batting coach Greg Luzinski and first base coach Mitchell Page were given the boot with him.

Kansas City's new manager was Chicago Cubs batting instructor Tony Muser. Muser spent most of his nine-year career with the Red Sox, White Sox, Orioles and Brewers playing first base. He spent seven years managing in the minor leagues in preparation for the opportunity the Royals gave him.

Muser fared worse than Boone had, despite Kansas City's infusion of expensive talent. The Royals were 31–48 under their new manager, finishing last with a record of 67–94. He'd return in 1998.

Boone's managing career wasn't over. He'd be hired by the Reds for the 2001 season.

Cincinnati Reds
Ray Knight to Jack McKeon

Ray Knight managed the way he played. That probably explained why his career as a manager was much shorter than his career as a player.

Knight backed down from no one during his 13 seasons with the Reds, Astros, Mets, Orioles and Tigers. But his always-ready-for-a-confrontation style didn't play nearly as well in a dugout as it did on a diamond.

"I hate to go out like this, but that's just the way life is," said Knight after being fired as manager of the Reds on July 25. "You can't choose your spots. It boils down to being able to get your players to play. If mine were resentful for any reason, I treated them like men. Nobody in that clubhouse wanted to win more than I did, and maybe my intensity rubbed some people the wrong way."[1]

Knight was in the second year of a two-year contract. His first Cincinnati club finished third in the NL Central with an 81–81 record. His second was fourth with a mark of 43–56 when Knight was fired. As he departed, he suggested that a clubhouse insurrection may have been responsible for his dismissal, led by shortstop and team captain Barry Larkin. Knight heard rumors that Larkin, and other players, asked general manager Jim Bowden to fire him. "I heard a lot of stuff," said the ex-manager on his way out. "I hope it's not them, but now it looks like maybe it was."[2]

Larkin fired back, "I didn't make this happen. No player on this team made this happen. When a team doesn't do well, you either change the people on the team or change the person running the team. So, a change was going to happen. A change needed to be made. They chose to change the manager."[3] Bowden denied that Larkin, or any other player, talked to him about Knight.

The new boss in Cincinnati was veteran manager Jack McKeon, who'd been an "advisor" for the Reds for the past five seasons. He was expected to bring a calming presence to an explosive dugout. "I'm a very patient guy," said McKeon. "I'm a low-key guy. I'm not going to throw any water coolers or kick any dugouts. I don't think I will—occasionally I've done it."[4]

The Reds calmed down and played better for McKeon than they had for Knight, going 33–30 the rest of the way to finish fourth at 76–86. McKeon was asked to return for the 1998 season.

Knight would return to Cincinnati as a coach, but save for one game as interim manager of the Reds in 2003, his managerial career was over. His teams won 125 and lost 137.

1998

Los Angeles Dodgers
Bill Russell to Glenn Hoffmann

It is said that there's a first time for everything. And so it was that on June 22, 1998, for the first time in the modern history of major league baseball, the franchise known at various times as the Superbas, the Trolley Dodgers, the Robins, and the Dodgers fired its manager during a season.

The Dodgers had changed managers in-season only twice before: in 1948, Leo Durocher resigned to accept the same position with the arch-rival New York Giants. In 1996, longtime field boss Tommy Lasorda stepped aside for health reasons and was succeeded on an interim basis by his chief lieutenant, Bill Russell. When Lasorda was forced by those health problems to retire at age 68, the "interim" tag was removed from Russell's title.

In baseball's so-called modern era, dating from the 1901 season, the Dodgers, in Brooklyn and Los Angeles, simply didn't fire a manager during the season. No matter how badly the team performed, and some Dodger teams had performed exceedingly poorly, the front office stayed with its field manager until the end of the year.

But the times were changing by the end of the 20th century. In March of 1998, the O'Malley family, which had owned the Dodgers since 1950, sold them to the Fox Sports

Division of media mogul Rupert Murdoch's News Corporation. Peter O'Malley stayed on as chairman of the board, but it wouldn't be business as usual at Dodger Stadium. The first piece of evidence that News Corporation did things differently was provided in late June. With the Dodgers in third place in the NL West, hovering around the .500 mark, and trailing the first-place Padres by 12½ lengths, field manager Russell and general manager Fred Claire were both fired. Russell had succeeded Lasorda as manager 86 games into the 1996 season, after Lasorda underwent heart surgery and was forced eventually to retire. Claire, with 13 years in charge of the Dodgers' front office, was the longest-tenured GM in the major leagues. He was replaced by Lasorda.

The firings, ironically, were recommended not by Fox Sports executives, but by O'Malley and team president Bob Graziano. Graziano had been with the club as long as Claire, and assumed the role of team president when O'Malley became board chairman. O'Malley stated, "I've been asked probably 100 times the hypothetical question, 'Peter, if your family still owned the club, would you have done the same thing?' And the honest answer is yes. I've been disappointed in the team's performance, felt we were flat and have been for some time. I think it's time for a change."[1]

Said Graziano, "over the course of the last several weeks, I have spent many, many hours thinking about how to get this team back on track. The last couple of weeks, I have spent countless hours with Peter O'Malley, getting his advice on the best way to right this team. Once I made that decision [to fire Russell and Claire], it made no sense to wait until the end of the season, or three days, four days."[2]

To replace Russell, Graziano promoted former major league shortstop Glenn Hoffman, who spent all but 40 games of his nine-year career in the American League. Those 40 games were played with the Dodgers in 1987. Hoffmann was managing the Dodgers' Triple-A farm club in Albuquerque when he was promoted.

Hoffmann took over a club with a 36–38 record and went 47–41 the rest of the way, but couldn't lift Los Angeles out of third place. The Dodgers finished with a mark of 83–79.

Hoffman didn't manage in the majors again, and neither did Russell. Russell's record in one full season with the Dodgers and parts of two others was 173–149, with a second-place finish.

Detroit Tigers
"Buddy" Bell to Larry Parrish

Mike Ilitch had made a lot of money selling pizzas, but he wasn't spending much of it on his baseball team.

The Tigers' $28 million payroll was among the lowest in the major leagues in 1998, and the results on the field were predictable. When former major league infielder David (Buddy) Bell was plucked from the Cleveland Indians' coaching staff after the Tribe's 1995 pennant-winning season, he knew he faced a lengthy rebuilding process and was assured his new employers would be patient. The Tigers lost 109 games in 1996, but rebounded to a 79–83 record the next year. Nineteen teams in modern baseball history had lost 109 or more games in a season, and none had ever posted a 27-game improvement the following year.

The turnaround earned for Bell a two-year contract extension from Detroit general manager Randy Smith.

Unfortunately for Bell, the Tigers staggered out of the gate in 1998, losing 17 of their first 21 games, and spent the rest of the season vainly trying to catch up to the rest of the AL Central. Detroit was in fifth place with a record of 53–85, 23½ games behind the pace-setting Indians, when a frustrated Bell confronted Smith on September 1. The Tigers were in the midst of a 5–22 tailspin, and Bell wanted to know just how committed the team was to winning, and, ignoring the fact he was under contract through the 2000 season, how committed it was to him as its manager. Smith answered the latter question by firing Bell on the spot.

"Working with a small payroll, it is difficult to compete at the major league level, and the losses have taken their toll," said Bell afterward. "Along the way, relationships have become strained, and I regret they deteriorated to the point where they decided I could no longer continue to manage the team."[3]

"He's had a very difficult job in terms of mixing very young players with veterans and being able to deal with it when it's not going well,"[4] said Ilitch of his manager's performance. And things hadn't gone well for Detroit all season.

Smith said he had no intention of firing Bell, at least not until season's end, before his manager forced the issue. "Buddy wanted a definitive answer [September 1]. He wanted a clarification. We looked at it and decided things just weren't going as smoothly as they should be." Smith admitted that he had given some thought to changing managers prior to his confrontation with Bell. "Obviously, if you arrive at this decision, it's been in the back of your mind. This is where it ended up."[5]

Bell was replaced by his bench coach, Larry Parrish, who played nearly 1,900 games for Montreal, Texas and Boston from 1974 through 1988. Parrish had managed in the minor leagues and won the 1996 Southern League championship after taking over the Jacksonville club for the second half of the season.

"This is probably not ideal,"[6] said Parrish of his ascension to manager. The Tigers won 12 and lost 12 for their new boss, and he was invited to return in 1999. Bell would be hired to manage the Colorado Rockies in 2000.

1999

Milwaukee Brewers
Phil Garner to Jim Lefebvre

Phil Garner's managerial career started so promisingly.

Garner and his former Oakland teammate, Sal Bando, learned how to win during their days with the dynastic Athletics of the 1970s. Bando signed with Milwaukee as a free agent after the 1976 season, and was named the team's general manager in October of 1991. He selected Garner to manage the Brewers and was rewarded with a 92–70 record and second-place finish in the AL East in 1992. Garner finished second in the league's Manager of the Year balloting. It turned out to be the only winning season Garner would enjoy in Milwaukee.

The Brewers sank to the basement in 1993 and then finished fifth, fourth, third, third and fifth through 1998. The patience of the fans with the tandem of Bando and Garner was wearing thin by the summer of 1999. The patience of club owner Wendy Selig-Prieb was growing thinner. No one, however, expected Bando to approach Selig-Prieb and suggest massive changes in the Milwaukee organization, starting in the dugout and including the general manager's office. On August 12, Garner was fired and Bando was demoted from GM to special assistant to the owner.

"I'm a Brewer, and I've been a Brewer since 1977," said Bando. "We needed to make a change for the sake of the organization, and that's always my first priority."[1]

Garner couldn't argue with his dismissal, since the Brewers were headed for their seventh straight losing season on his watch. Only Connie Mack had managed one team to more consecutive losing seasons, and that was only because Mack owned the team. "We didn't play up to my expectations, or their expectations," said the former Brewers boss. "In this situation, I think it's deserved."[2]

"This is a results business, make no mistake about it," said Selig-Prieb. "This is not a complacent organization. We will not accept mediocrity."[3]

Garner left Milwaukee as the team's winningest and losingest manager in its 29-year history. The team he handed over to interim manager Jim Lefebvre, the Brewers' batting coach, was in fifth place with a record of 52–60. Lefebvre, a former major league infielder, had the distinction of being the first manager to lead the Seattle Mariners to a winning season. Under Lefebvre, Seattle was 83–79 in 1991, and he was rewarded by being fired. Hired by the Cubs in 1992, Lefebvre's teams posted records of 78–84 and 84–78. As the Mariners had, the Cubs thanked Lefebvre for winning more games than he lost by firing him.

Milwaukee won 22 and lost 27 for Lefebvre for a fifth-place finish and a record of 74–87. He wasn't asked back for 2000, and never managed in the majors again. Lefebvre's Seattle, Chicago and Milwaukee clubs won 417 and lost 442.

Garner was back in the majors the next year, hired by the Tigers.

Anaheim Angels
Terry Collins to Joe Maddon

The fact that he never played in the major leagues may have given Terry Collins an appreciation for "the show" that most of his players lacked.

Collins brought a reputation for being blunt and demanding to his first big league managing job in Houston in 1994. He produced three winning seasons, and three second-place finishes, before moving on to the Anaheim Angels for the 1997 season. Collins's first two Angels squads came home second in the AL West, but his 1999 team imploded. Although Anaheim struggled from the first pitch of the season, management showed its commitment to its manager by signing him to a two-year contract extension. Less than three months later, Collins resigned. The Angels were in last place in their division and had baseball's worst record at 51–82.

General manager Bill Bavasi said both he and Collins agreed it was best for the manager to step down. "I know he's not bitter, but I'm bitter," said Bavasi on September 3. "This club had every reason to respond but didn't. This is just bad chemistry in the clubhouse."[4]

"The bottom line is, the team's got to perform," said Collins. "When you don't perform, the manager's accountable. I had a feeling today that this is the time."[5]

Collins was replaced on an interim basis by his bench coach, Joe Maddon, who was the antithesis of the intense, heavy-handed Collins. It was the second time Maddon had been given control of the club following the departure of the previous manager, and the Angels perked up considerably, going 19–10 for a final record of 70–92. Anaheim stayed in last place.

Despite the improvement, Maddon would return to his job as bench coach in 2000. Twelve years would pass before Collins would manage in the major leagues again. He'd be hired to take over the Mets after the 2010 season.

2001

Tampa Bay Devil Rays
Larry Rothschild to Hal McRae

For the first time in 46 years, since 1953 to be exact, no managerial changes were made during the 2000 season.

It was open season on managers once again in 2001, however, and Tampa Bay Devil Rays general manager Chuck Lamar wasted no time disposing of the first manager in the franchise's brief history. Larry Rothschild was fired just 14 games into the season, with the team sitting in last place in the AL East with a 4–10 record. Hal McRae, the Devil Rays' bench coach, had been tipped off about the firing and feared the worst when his phone rang at 7:00 a.m. on April 18.

"I didn't know what to think," McRae confessed. "I was shocked when Chuck asked me to manage the ball club and to come over as soon as possible to discuss the situation. I thought the worst. I thought, 'What, me too? What did I do?' The only reason you take a job is because you think you can do the job."[1] McRae thought he could do the Tampa Bay job and took it.

The expansion Devil Rays had won 63, 69 and 69 games in their first three seasons. Although McRae had posted winning seasons in three of his four years in charge of the Kansas City Royals from 1991 through 1994, Tampa Bay regressed under his leadership. The Devil Rays won 58 and lost 90 under McRae in 2001, for another last-place finish and a record of 62–100. Tampa Bay sank to its worst record ever, 55–106, in 2002. McRae wasn't asked to return in 2003.

Neither Rothschild nor McRae ever managed in the major leagues after departing Tampa-St. Petersburg. Rothschild's record in the thankless job of piloting an expansion team was 205–294. McRae's record with the Royals and Devil Rays was 399–473.

Texas Rangers
Johnny Oates to Jerry Narron

Johnny Oates made like a real Texas Ranger and beat his opponent to the draw. Rangers owner Tom Hicks had stunned his colleagues by signing free agent shortstop

Alex Rodriguez to a 10-year, $250 million contract after the 2000 season. For that kind of money, Hicks wanted a fast return on his investment, and he wasn't getting it in early May. Oates managed the Rangers to three AL West titles between 1996 and 1999, but the team fell to the western division's cellar in 2000 and was struggling in 2001. Texas's 11–17 record represented its worst start since 1985, and Oates knew Hicks and team president Doug Melvin were thinking about replacing him. So he beat them to the punch and resigned on May 4.

"It will be a lot easier to get a new voice in the clubhouse than new players,"[2] said Oates, who insisted he was satisfied that he'd done all he could through 28 games to get the Rangers moving in the right direction. Although 134 games remained, Hicks and Melvin were content to finish the season with bench coach Jerry Narron calling the shots. Texas was 62–72 for Narron and finished last for the second straight season, despite the presence of Rodriguez, with a record of 73–89. Nonetheless, Narron was retained for 2002.

Oates didn't manage in the big leagues after 2001. His career record with Baltimore and Texas was 797–746 with three Western Division titles.

Florida Marlins
John Boles to Tony Perez

John Boles didn't give his boss much of a choice.

"Bolesy felt he had lost the clubhouse," explained Dave Dombrowski as he announced the Marlins' change of managers. "That happens sometimes. If the manager has that feeling, that he doesn't have the answer, you make a decision and it's a hard decision."[3] Dombrowski's manager had that feeling, so Dombrowski made him the ex-manager.

Boles had been summoned from the front office to manage the Marlins for 75 games in 1996, and was called upon again after Jim Leyland left south Florida to manage the Colorado Rockies after the 1998 season. Boles never played in the major leagues, and some of his players apparently held that against him. He managed the rebuilding Marlins to a last-place finish in the NL East with a 64–98 record in 1999, but the team improved to 79–82 the following season. Florida had a record of 22–26 when relief pitcher Dan Miceli unloaded on Boles and his staff after a frustrating one-run loss to the Mets on May 27. Miceli took the loss, his fourth without a victory, giving up three runs in a third of an inning.

"It's the talk of the locker room," fumed Miceli. "They don't make the right moves in the right situations … there are grown men in this locker room who have worked their whole lives to get to the big leagues, and they're not getting the right type of instruction from the staff. Stupid moves."[4]

Miceli's outburst convinced Boles he'd lost the respect of his players, and he was fired the next day. His replacement was former Reds and Expos first baseman Tony Perez, who was serving as a special assistant to Dombrowski. Perez's only managerial experience at the big league level consisted of 44 games with Cincinnati in 1993. Perez agreed to take the job, but only to give Dombrowski time to find a permanent replacement.

"I have a lot of commitments," said Perez. "If you are going to be the manager, you have to be able to do that full time."[5] Dombrowski asked Perez to reconsider taking the job for the rest of the season. Perez thought it over and, perhaps motivated by a desire to show the Reds they'd made a mistake by firing him so hastily, agreed.

The Marlins won 54 and lost 60 under Perez, finishing third with a record of 76–86. Neither Perez nor Boles ever managed again. Boles's Florida clubs won 205 and lost 241. Perez's Reds and Marlins, in four games short of a full season, were 74–84.

Montreal Expos
Felipe Alou to Jeff Torborg

The beginning of the end was at hand for the Montreal Expos.

With no plan in place for a new facility to replace the crumbling, inadequate and partially domed Olympic Stadium, owner Jeffrey Loria was looking to divest himself of the Expos. First, however, he divested himself of his manager, Felipe Alou. Montreal had managed just one winning season for Alou since the 1994 strike. When the 2001 Expos started slowly, Loria decided to make a change.

"Our team has been underperforming for some time," he said. "For some time before the season started, and many times since, I have reiterated the fact that we expect to win and that excuses of the past years will not be tolerated."[6]

Alou was glad to be fired. "I almost feel relieved. I could feel it coming," he said.[7]

One player came to his former manager's defense. "I don't think it's Felipe's fault," said second baseman Jose Vidro. "We didn't play the way we could. It's our fault."[8] Regardless of whose fault the Expos' 21–32 record was, the responsibility for correcting the problems belonged to former Indians, White Sox and Mets manager Jeff Torborg, a close friend of Loria's. Torborg signed a three-year contract but couldn't coax an improved performance from the club. Montreal was 47–62 under Torborg and finished last with a 68–94 record.

Torborg would manage in 2002, but not in Montreal. Loria sold the Expos to his 29 fellow owners and purchased the Florida Marlins. He took Torborg with him as his manager. Alou wasn't absent from a major league dugout for long. He was hired to manage the San Francisco Giants in 2003.

Boston Red Sox
Jimy Williams to Joe Kerrigan

When Jimy Williams was fired as manager of the Toronto Blue Jays in 1989, his team was 12 games below .500 with a record of 12–24. When Williams was fired by the Red Sox on August 16, 2001, his team was 12 games above .500 with a record of 65–53.

It seemed that Williams was doing a stellar job with the Red Sox. Eight of his players were on the disabled list, including ace pitcher Pedro Martinez, who hadn't seen action since June 26. Boston's star shortstop, Nomar Garciaparra, had undergone surgery on his wrist on opening day and missed 103 games. But the Red Sox were scuffling in mid–August, having lost six of seven games, and that gave general manager Dan Duquette the opening he needed to dismiss a manager he wasn't enamored of.

"I am really surprised," said pitching coach Joe Kerrigan of being told to meet Duquette for lunch. "I figured he was going to talk to me about Pedro."[9] Instead, Duquette offered Kerrigan a two-year contract to manage the Red Sox. Kerrigan accepted.

Kerrigan wasn't Duquette's first choice to replace Williams. He offered the job to Felipe Alou, the recently deposed manager of the Expos. Duquette warned Alou, however, that the Red Sox were being sold, and there was no guarantee the new ownership would retain the manager it inherited ... or the general manager, for that matter. Alou thanked Duquette for his candor and declined the offer.

The Red Sox didn't respond to Kerrigan, winning 17 and losing 26. When he took over the club was in second place, five games behind the Yankees. When the season ended, the Red Sox were still second, but their record was 82–79, and they were 13½ games behind the division-winning Yankees. New owners assumed control of the Red Sox after the season, and despite Kerrigan's multi-year contract, he was among those dismissed by the incoming regime. He never managed in the major leagues again.

Williams would be back in a big league dugout. He was hired to manage the Astros in 2002.

2002

Milwaukee Brewers
Davey Lopes to Jerry Royster

Take two!

If only it was as easy to wipe the slate clean as Milwaukee general manager Dean Taylor tried to make it on April 18, the day he fired manager Davey Lopes. Taylor declared, "You can take your batting average, your earned run average, whatever it is prior to today, it's gone, it's history, it's done. Today is Opening Day II. We're turning a new page and starting a new chapter in the book. And I believe that's the message we send to the fans, as well. We are committed to winning regardless of the economic circumstance that's out there."[1] The era had arrived when franchises were not only classified by the divisions and leagues they played in, but by the size of their market and of their payrolls. Milwaukee was a small market which suffered even further from its location just 90 miles north of Chicago and its two clubs. The Brewers started the season with the 21st highest payroll (or the ninth lowest, depending on the vantage point) in the major leagues. Taylor, however, felt he'd built a team capable of playing .500 ball.

Lopes hadn't experienced much success since being hired to manage the Brewers for the 2000 season. Milwaukee finished third with a record of 73–89, and followed that with a fourth-place finish and a 68–94 record in 2001. Both teams finished more than 20 games out of first place. The Brewers were off to their worst start ever at 3–12 when Taylor pulled the plug.

Lopes was replaced by his bench coach, Jerry Royster. Like Lopes, Royster was a former major league infielder. He and Lopes had been teammates with the Dodgers from 1973 through 1975. Royster was at first dubbed an interim manager while Taylor searched for a permanent replacement for Lopes. The "interim" tag was removed from Royster's title on April 30 when he was given the job for the rest of the year.

"Jerry is well-prepared for this opportunity and is very excited," said Taylor. "He has confidence in his abilities to lead this club, and we strongly share that belief."[2]

Taylor's "Opening Day II" was a rousing success as the Brewers topped the Cardinals, 7–5, at Miller Park. Milwaukee won its first four games for its new manager, then reverted to form and dropped six in a row. The Brewers weren't a .500 club and played just as badly for Royster as they had for Lopes. Milwaukee was 53–94 under Royster and finished last in the NL Central with a mark of 56–106. Royster wasn't invited to return in 2003 and never managed in the majors again. Neither did Lopes, whose two and a fraction seasons in Milwaukee produced 144 wins and 195 losses.

Colorado Rockies
"Buddy" Bell to Clint Hurdle

The Brewers weren't the only team to get off to their worst start ever in 2002.

The Colorado Rockies were 6–16 when general manager Dan O'Dowd decided things weren't working out with Buddy Bell in the dugout. Bell and O'Dowd had worked together with the Indians in the mid–1990s and hoped to duplicate that success in Denver. O'Dowd hired Bell after Jim Leyland, deciding he'd had his fill of managing, jumped ship after the 1999 season. Bell's Rockies finished fourth in 2000 with an 82–80 mark, Bell's only winning season as a manager, and then fell to fifth with just 73 victories in 2001. When the Rockies stumbled from the gate in '02, O'Dowd made a change.

"I am disappointed that this has not worked out the way I wanted it to," said Bell. "I wanted to see this thing through."[3] O'Dowd said the firing wasn't about assigning blame for the Rockies' miserable start, but about turning the team around. He assigned that duty to batting coach Clint Hurdle, a former major league outfielder who spent 10 seasons with the Royals, Reds, Mets and Cardinals. Hurdle had been instructing the Rockies' batters for six seasons.

Colorado didn't get things turned around. The Rockies were 67–73 under Hurdle to come home fourth at 73–89. Hurdle would return to manage the club in 2003.

Bell would find himself back in the American League in 2005 when Kansas City needed a new manager.

Kansas City Royals
Tony Muser to Tony Pena

Tony Muser had managed the Royals since the All-Star break of 1997 with disappointing results. Kansas City's best record for Muser was 77–85 in 2000, and the Royals had dropped to a basement finish in the AL Central with 97 losses in 2001. He was in the final year of his contract in 2002 and needed to produce a winner to earn an extension.

Instead, the Royals won just eight of their first 23 games and general manager Allard Baird released Muser with five months to go in the season. Muser wasn't surprised.

"Everybody understands the circumstances, the mood of our fans," said the former Royals boss. "They need a change. It's just a part of the business. Managers are hired to be fired. I understand it, and life goes on. The most important thing is the success of the organization."[4] Muser departed his only major league managing job with a record of 317–431.

Muser's interim replacement was bullpen coach John Mizerock, who guided the team to five wins and eight losses while Baird searched for a permanent replacement. The job of getting the Royals moving in the right direction went to Houston coach, and former major league catcher, Tony Pena.

"I believe you go out and play hard baseball," said Pena at his introductory press conference. "I believe in that. There will be rules, and we're going to have to follow the rules." Asked what he planned to say at his first team meeting, Pena said he'd tell his players, "I am the new DJ. I play the music. You are to dance. If you don't know how to dance, get off the dance floor."[5]

The disk jockey may have changed, but the tune stayed the same. Kansas City won 49 and lost 77 for Pena, coming home last with a record of 62–100.

Toronto Blue Jays
"Buck" Martinez to Carlos Tosca

It would be hard to blame former major league catcher John (Buck) Martinez if he was confused by his firing.

Martinez spent 17 years behind the plate for Kansas City, Milwaukee and Toronto. He was working as a broadcaster for the Blue Jays when he was hired to manage the club in 2001. The fledgling Arizona Diamondbacks did the same thing, hiring former catcher Bob Brenly from the announcer's booth to manage their club, and were rewarded with a World Series championship. The 2001 World Series was not a battle of former broadcasters turned managers, however, as Martinez's Blue Jays finished third in the AL East with an 80–82 record, 16 games behind the division-winning Yankees. Not a great season, but hardly a disaster.

Nonetheless, 53 games into the 2002 season, Blue Jays general manager J.P. Ricciardi decided the manager hired away from the press box with no managerial experience had to go ... because he had no managerial experience. "I don't know if Buck even knows what his philosophy or style is because he hasn't had a lot of time to manage," said Ricciardi in announcing Martinez's firing. "It's not so much the wins, the losses at this point, it's the leadership."[6] Or the lack of it, as Ricciardi cited Toronto's need for leadership as another reason for changing managers.

Martinez and first base coach Garth Iorg, who was also fired, were deemed responsible for the Blue Jays' 20–33 start, the team's worst break from the gate in two decades. Martinez was replaced by coach Carlos Tosca, who got a better performance out of the team than Martinez had. Toronto was 58–51 under Tosca, finishing third with a 78–84 record. Tosca returned for the 2003 season.

Martinez didn't manage in the major leagues again. Under his direction, Toronto won 100 and lost 115.

Chicago Cubs
Don Baylor to Bruce Kimm

After winning 88 games and finishing third, five games behind the division-winning Astros, in 2001, big things were expected from Don Baylor's Cubs. The 88 victories represented a 23-game improvement over Baylor's first season in charge of the club. Baylor's six seasons with the expansion Colorado Rockies produced three winning years and a wild-card playoff berth, and the Cubs expected similar results when they hired him for the 2000 season.

Baylor's 2002 season got off to a bad start in 2001. At the end of an otherwise upbeat campaign, Baylor had demanded the resignation of Chicago's popular pitching coach, Oscar Acosta. Acosta stepped aside, but no one in the club house or the front office backed Baylor in his disagreement with Acosta, and that would prove to be a preview of coming attractions.

Several highly paid players failed to perform up to expectations in 2002, and the Cubs wheezed toward the All-Star break with a 34–49 record. Team president and general manager Andy MacPhail didn't wait until the mid–July three-day break to end Baylor's days as Chicago's manager. "When the talent on the field doesn't equal the amount of victories in the standings, that is the criteria for making a change," explained MacPhail. "It's not always a fair one, but that's the way we see it."[7] Bruce Kimm, the manager of the Cubs' Triple-A farm club in Des Moines, would take over for the rest of the season.

Baylor himself admitted to having no relationships with any of his players. Bench coach Rene Lachemann, a former manager twice fired himself, pointed the finger for the Cubs' poor season at those players. "He didn't spend all winter taking dumb pills," said Lachemann of Chicago's deposed skipper. "He won 88 games last year. What happens in this game, if the players don't produce, it's find somebody else to blame."[8]

Lachemann managed the Cubs to one loss while waiting for Kimm to arrive, and Kimm won 33 and lost 45 in his stint as interim manager. Those 78 games constituted Kimm's entire big league managerial career. Baylor was through as a manager and looked back on a career with the Rockies and Cubs that produced 552 wins and 689 losses, with one playoff appearance.

Cleveland Indians
Charlie Manuel to Joel Skinner

The Indians were rebuilding in 2002. The players who'd helped the club win six AL Central Division titles and two pennants, and come within two outs of winning the 1997 World Series, between 1994 and 2001 had either grown old or, more likely, departed as free agents. Charlie Manuel, who'd been promoted by former general manager John Hart from batting coach to manager after the 1999 season, declared himself the right man to oversee the influx of youth. Hart's successor, Mark Shapiro, wasn't so sure.

After a blazing 11–1 start, the Indians collapsed. They entered the All-Star break with a 39–47 record. Shapiro had begun the rebuilding process in earnest in late June by trading Manuel's best pitcher, 10-game winner Bartolo Colon, to Montreal for three prospects. More deals were anticipated. Shapiro and Manuel were scheduled to meet the day before the season resumed to discuss their plans for the rest of the year. "The meeting didn't last long," Manuel remembered. "Mark started to talk about our young players. I asked where I fit in their plans. He said this was not the time to talk about it. He seemed surprised that I wanted to talk about it."[9]

"I told Charlie I wanted him to manage the team in the second half, and that I would consider him to be our long-term manager at the end of the season," said Shapiro. "He told me now is the time, that he wasn't going to wait. I asked him to go home and think about it overnight."[10]

Manuel did what Shapiro asked. "I was either going to get a contract or get fired,"[11] he said of his attitude entering a second meeting the following morning. He got fired. Actually, he was offered a four-year contract as a scout, to take effect in 2003, if Shapiro decided not to re-hire him as manager at season's end. Manuel wasn't interested.

Third base coach Joel Skinner took over for Manuel and led the Indians to a 35–41 record the rest of the way. Cleveland finished third with 74 wins and 88 losses. Although Skinner was regarded as a sure-fire future manager, the call never came.

Manuel was hired to manage an up-and-coming Philadelphia team in 2005.

2003

Florida Marlins
Jeff Torborg to Jack McKeon

Friend of the owner or no, Jeff Torborg had to go.

When Jeffrey Loria bought the Florida Marlins after the 2001 season, he released Jeff Torborg from his contract with Montreal, the club Loria palmed off on the other 29 major league baseball owners, and brought him to sunny south Florida with him. Torborg's Marlins finished fourth in the NL East in 2002 with a record of 79–83, but started slowly in 2003. Too slowly, in the opinion of general manager Larry Beinfest. Despite Loria's personal friendship with Torborg, he gave Beinfest the okay to change managers.

Beinfest gave the usual reasons for dismissing Torborg: "This is a better team than the way we've played. The fans here in south Florida deserve to have hope this summer. There is enough time to turn it around and get back into it."[1] In this case, Beinfest wasn't spouting the usual blather general managers spout when firing their managers. The Marlins had a good team and should have been contenders. They would become contenders under Beinfest's choice to succeed Torborg.

The snickers could be heard from Boston to San Diego when Beinfest introduced 73-year-old veteran manager and front office executive Jack McKeon as Florida's new manager. Many observers assumed Beinfest had taken leave of his senses. McKeon became the third oldest manager in modern baseball history, surpassed only by Connie Mack and Casey Stengel.

Torborg left Miami with a smile and a hug for his friend Loria. Pitching coach Brad Arnsberg was also fired.

Beinfest knew exactly what he was doing by hiring McKeon. Taking over a team with a 16–22 record, McKeon led the team to seven losses in his first 10 games to drop its record to 19–29 on May 22. The Marlins were in last place, 13½ games behind the division leader. The snickers grew louder, but Beinfest and McKeon enjoyed the last laugh. From May 23 through the end of the season, Florida won 72 and lost 42. The Marlins finished second with a record of 91–71 and captured the National League's wild card playoff spot. Florida defeated Western champion San Francisco in the Division Series, and overcame a 3–1 deficit to oust the Central champion Cubs in the League Championship Series, winning games six and seven in the unfriendly confines of Wrigley Field. For icing on the cake, the Marlins took out the Yankees in six games in the World Series, winning the deciding game in Yankee Stadium.

McKeon joined Bob Lemon as the only managers appointed in mid-season to lead their clubs to a world's championship. He stayed with the Marlins through 2005, finishing third twice with records of 83–79, and then retired at age 76. He wasn't through managing, however.

Torborg was through managing. In 11 seasons with the Indians, White Sox, Mets, Expos and Marlins, his teams won 634 games and lost 718. He posted two second-place finishes in Chicago and was the 1990 American League "Manager of the Year."

Cincinnati Reds
Bob Boone to Dave Miley

This one wasn't your standard managerial firing.

When the Reds released Bob Boone on July 28, general manager Jim Bowden didn't stand before the media making the usual statement that the team was underperforming and change at the top was needed. The Reds did need a change at the top, and they made it. In addition to firing Boone, they also fired Bowden.

Boone was in his third season with the Reds. His 2001 club finished in the NL Central basement with a record of 66–96. The Reds improved to third at 78–84 in Boone's second season, but in 2003 they'd moved into sparkling new (and taxpayer financed) Great American Ballpark. Bowden had promised the people of Cincinnati, "If you build it, we will win." They built it, but the Reds weren't living up to their part of the bargain. Although Cincinnati had won three straight, July 25–27, all the short streak did was bring the club's record to 47–58. The Reds were in last place, 10 games out of first, when owner Carl Linder decided to cut ties with both his manager and general manager. Bowden had been running the Reds' front office since 1992, making him the second-longest tenured GM in the game.

Boone was replaced by Dave Miley, who'd been the club's Triple-A manager since 1996. Third base coach Tim Foli and batting coach Tom Robson were also dismissed. Miley was promoted to be Cincinnati's interim manager, but was retained for 2004 despite a record of 22–35 the rest of the way. The Reds finished last with a 69–93 mark.

Boone's career as a big league manager was over. His Kansas City and Cincinnati clubs won 371 and lost 444, with one second-place finish.

2004

Arizona Diamondbacks
Bob Brenly to Al Pedrique

What does one do for an encore when one wins the World Series in one's first season as a major league manager?

It's a nice problem to have, and former broadcaster and major league catcher Bob Brenly had it. Brenly made the switch from the broadcast booth to the dugout in 2001 and rewarded the Diamondbacks with the NL West championship, the pennant, and a dramatic World Series triumph over the Yankees. The D-Backs repeated as western champions in 2002 with 98 victories but slipped to third in 2003 with a mark of 84–78. There was further slippage, all the way to the cellar of the West in 2004, and Brenly was pink-slipped with the team showing a 29–50 record.

Brenly was replaced by third base coach Al Pedrique on an interim basis. Pedrique was a former major league infielder who spent eight seasons managing in the minor leagues, including the 2002 and '03 campaigns at Arizona's Triple-A affiliate in nearby Tucson. The Diamondbacks mailed in the rest of the season under Pedrique, winning just 22 and losing 61 to finish with an unsightly 51–111 record ... just three seasons removed from a world's championship, and a mere two seasons removed from 98 wins and a division title. Pedrique wasn't invited back for 2005.

Brenly returned to the broadcast booth and has remained there. His record as a major league manager was 303–262, with a pair of division titles, a pennant and a world's championship.

Houston Astros
Jimy Williams to Phil Garner

Jimy Williams was getting accustomed to this.

The Astros were the third team Williams had managed, and on July 14, they became the third team to fire him. Houston started well, holding first place in the NL Central in early May with a record of 21–11, but a slow decline set in shortly afterward. The Astros entered the All-Star break with a record of 44–44, and general manager Gerry Hunsicker decided to make a change while the season was still salvageable.

"We needed to make a move quickly," said Hunsicker. "We needed to jump start this club right now. We didn't have time to fool around here."[1] Hunsicker's curious choice to succeed Williams was former Astro player Phil Garner, who decided to make Houston his home after his playing career ended. Garner had only one winning season (his first) on a 10-year managerial resume, and had been fired by the Tigers in 2002. He was dismissed after just six games by Detroit, tying the record for the earliest managerial firing in modern history.

"I'm excited," Garner enthused. "I'm a Houston guy and I'm looking forward to it. We got some boys on the team that I think can do something really special. This is an opportunity that I've been waiting for."[2]

Williams's pitching coach, Burt Hooton, and batting coach Harry Spilman were fired along with him. Houston marked the end of his managerial career. His Toronto, Boston and Houston clubs were 910–790 with two wild-card playoff berths, both with the Red Sox.

Garner lit a fire under the Astros, winning 48 and losing 26. Houston finished second in the NL Central at 92–70 and grabbed the wild-card playoff spot. Houston eliminated Eastern champion Atlanta in the Division Series, but lost a seven-game League Championship Series to the Cardinals.

Toronto Blue Jays
Carlos Tosca to John Gibbons

It wasn't easy for the Blue Jays to compete with Boston and New York in the AL East, but they held their own for a bit more than a season and a half under the leadership of Carlos Tosca.

Tosca picked up the pieces after replacing the overmatched Buck Martinez in June of 2002 and brought the Jays in third. They finished third again for Tosca in 2003, with a respectable record of 86–76. But Toronto never got going in 2004. The club's closest flirtation with the .500 mark was its 1–3 record in early April. The Jays were wallowing in last place in the East with a 47–64 record on August 9, after losing their fifth straight game, 8–2, to the Yankees. Tosca was relieved of his duties an hour after the game and replaced by first base coach John Gibbons.

The Blue Jays couldn't pick up the pace for Gibbons, winning 20 and losing 30 the rest of the season. They finished last with a record of 67–94, their worst finish since 1997, but Gibbons was re-hired for the 2005 season.

Tosca never managed in the major leagues again. He was as good a manager as he was bad, as his teams won 191 games and lost 191.

2005

Kansas City Royals
Tony Pena to "Buddy" Bell

Timing is everything.

Events taking place at the beginning of a baseball season become magnified. If the Kansas City Royals had won 17 of 21 games in June or July or August, when the club was already out of the race for the AL Central title, little attention would have been paid to the spurt. It would have been dismissed as what it was: the type of hot streak every team, no matter how weak, has during the course of a 162-game season.

The 2003 Royals, however, had their hot streak in April, and their 17–4 start made them, and manager Tony Pena, the talk of baseball. Reality set in slowly, and the Royals remained at or near the top of the division through late August. When all was said and done, Kansas City finished third with a record of 83–79, and Pena was the American League's "Manager of the Year." But happier days weren't ahead in the heartland.

Crunching the numbers shows the Royals were 66–75 after their blazing start, and in 2004 they crashed and burned, losing a franchise-record 104 games. Kansas City limped to an 8–25 start in 2005, and Pena resigned on May 11, with the club in last place. The Associated Press story announcing Pena's resignation made the point that finding a replacement may not have been a matter of finding the "right man" for the job. It may have been a matter of finding someone willing to take on the challenge. Kansas City's payroll of $37 million was the second-lowest in baseball, and voters had rejected a tax levy the previous November that would have paid for a much-needed renovation of Kauffman Stadium. Managing the Royals wasn't exactly a plum job.

Into the breach stepped Buddy Bell, the former manager of the Tigers and Rockies, who was eager for another chance at calling the shots. After coach Bob Schaefer led Kansas City to a 5–12 record while the search for Pena's replacement was conducted, Bell was hired and soon found out why his predecessor had jumped from a sinking ship. The Royals lacked just about everything and finished a dismal fifth in the Central with a 56–106 record. They won 43 and lost 69 for Bell.

Bell was retained for 2006 and Kansas City's record was virtually unchanged. The Royals finished last again with a mark of 62–100 and improved only marginally to 69–93 in 2007. Bell was dismissed at season's end and hasn't managed in the major leagues since. His record for six full seasons and parts of three others with Detroit, Colorado and Kansas City was 519–724. Bell's clubs finished last five times and never higher than third.

Pena hasn't managed since resigning in Kansas City. His record with the Royals was 198–285 with one third-place finish.

Cincinnati Reds
Dave Miley to Jerry Narron

It's difficult to see why the Reds retained interim manager Dave Miley after the 2003 season. Miley took over a team that was floundering under Bob Boone and lost 13 more games than he won the rest of the season. But Cincinnati kept him on in 2004, and the team finished fourth in the six-team NL Central with 76 wins and 86 losses. Miley's 2005 Reds broke from the gate slowly, and were in last place with a 27–43 record, 18½ games behind St. Louis, when the front office decided to make a change on June 21. He was replaced by his bench coach, Jerry Narron. Narron was familiar with the drill. He'd been bench coach in Texas under Johnny Oates and took over the Rangers when Oates resigned.

"We had huge expectations coming into the season and we did not live up to them,"[1] said Narron upon assuming command in Cincinnati. The Reds' problem was an inability to win away from home. The Reds were a respectable 21–19 at Great American Ballpark and a dismal 6–24 on the road.

Pitching coach Don Gullett was fired along with Miley. With a new manager and new leader of the pitching staff, the Reds improved to 46–46 the rest of the season. Cincinnati finished fifth with a record of 73–89, and Narron returned to manage the club in 2006.

Baltimore Orioles
Lee Mazilli to Sam Perlozzo

The once-proud Orioles had fallen on hard times. Lee Mazilli's job was to restore them to their former glory.

Baltimore hadn't posted a winning record since 1997. Under Davey Johnson, the Orioles won 98 games and the AL East, but lost the League Championship Series in six games to Cleveland. Johnson left, and the Birds began a run of six consecutive fourth-place finishes.

Mazilli, a former major league outfielder/first baseman for the Mets, Rangers, Yankees, Pirates and Blue Jays from 1976 through 1989, lifted Baltimore to third place in his first year as manager, although the club still lost more games than it won. The Orioles got off to a quick start in 2005 and were looking down at the rest of the division with a 42–28 record on June 21. But Baltimore would win only nine more games for Mazilli, and the 9–28 tailspin cost the manager his job.

In the throes of an eight-game losing streak and 14 defeats in 15 games, Mazilli was fired on August 4 and replaced by coach Sam Perlozzo. The Orioles had fallen from first place to fourth, 10½ games behind Boston. Mazilli was told of his firing two hours before a game against the Angels in Anaheim.

The Orioles didn't fare much better for Perlozzo than they had in late June and through July for Mazilli, winning 23 and losing 32. Baltimore finished fourth with a ledger of 74–88, but Perlozzo was retained for 2006.

Pittsburgh Pirates
Lloyd McClendon to Pete Mackanin

Lloyd McClendon was the first manager in Pittsburgh history to be retained after leading the club to four straight losing seasons. He almost got the chance to make it six.

The Pirates hadn't enjoyed a winning season since 1992, when they won the third of three consecutive NL East championships. McClendon, an outfielder/first baseman and occasional catcher during his playing career with Cincinnati and Pittsburgh, finished last in the NL Central in 2001, his first year at the Pirate helm, guiding the club to 100 defeats. Pittsburgh improved to fourth in 2002 and '03, and slipped back to fifth in 2004. The Pirates didn't win more than 75 games in any season during that span, but McClendon was retained for 2005 and appeared to have the team moving in the right direction. The Pirates held a contract option on McClendon for 2006, and general manager Dave Littlefield considered exercising it on June 11, when Pittsburgh's record was 30–30. He backed off, however, and was glad he did.

After breathing the heady air of the .500 mark, the Pirates promptly took a nose-dive. They lost 51 of their next 76 games, and McClendon was dismissed on September 6, with the team in last place, 31½ games behind the Cardinals. Pittsburgh had lost four straight, nine of 10, and 14 of its last 18 games.

"The way we've played the last three months hasn't been up to our capabilities," said Littlefield. "We have higher expectations with the players we have. We should be performing better."[2] Littlefield elevated coach Pete Mackanin to interim manager to complete the season. Mackanin took over a club with a 55–81 record and won 12 of the 26 games he managed. The Pirates finished last with 67 wins and 95 losses. Mackanin wasn't invited back for 2006.

McClendon's Pittsburgh teams were 336–446 with two fourth-place finishes. He was hired to manage the Mariners in 2014.

2007

Baltimore Orioles
Sam Perlozzo to Dave Trembley

Sam Perlozzo had given it his best shot.

It wasn't through lack of effort that Perlozzo joined the list of Baltimore managers who'd followed Davey Johnson and been unable to produce a winning season. In his only full year as Orioles manager, Perlozzo brought the Birds home fourth in the AL East with a record of 70–92 in 2006. Even the presence of Leo Mazzone, universally acclaimed as baseball's best pitching coach, hadn't helped. Perlozzo and Mazzone were lifelong friends, and Mazzone deserted Bobby Cox and the Braves to join Perlozzo as Baltimore's pitching instructor. Unfortunately for Mazzone, he also left behind the likes of Tom Glavine, Greg Maddux, and John Smoltz, to name just a few, when he departed Atlanta. He didn't find pitchers of similar ability on the Baltimore staff.

The Orioles started well in 2007, holding second place in the east on May 31 with a 27–27 record before their rapid descent began. Baltimore's record in June was a wretched 2–13, and the team had lost eight straight games, when executive vice president, and former Orioles pitcher, Mike Flanagan announced a change in managers on June 18.

"We felt Sam was prepared," admitted Flanagan. "We felt the club was prepared to do battle every night. For whatever reason, it just wasn't working."[1] Bullpen coach Dave Trembley was promoted to interim manager while Flanagan searched for a replacement for Perlozzo. Although several names were bandied about, including 2006 National League Manager of the Year Joe Girardi, who was fired after one season with the Florida Marlins due to differences with management, Flanagan eventually settled on Trembley to lead the Birds for the rest of the season. He took over a team with a 29–40 record that trailed first-place Boston by 15 games and lifted it from fifth place to fourth despite winning only 40 games and losing 53. Baltimore finished the year with a 69–93 record, but Trembley was retained for 2008.

Perlozzo hasn't managed since being fired by the Orioles. His career mark for one full season and portions of two others is 122–164.

Seattle Mariners
Mike Hargrove to John McLaren

Mike Hargrove was no hypocrite.

In 15 seasons as a manager with Cleveland, Baltimore and Seattle, Hargrove had demanded absolute commitment to winning from his players. In his 16th season, Hargrove felt he could no longer give his players the commitment he demanded of them, and resigned with his Mariners in the thick of the playoff chase.

"There are no dark, sinister reasons for this decision," said Hargrove on July 1. "This has been my decision. I have no reason to lie. I don't expect people to understand it, I really don't, because at times I don't understand it myself." Hargrove said his "passion had begun to fade,"[2] and he wasn't going to hang around simply to collect a paycheck.

"We're not happy about this, not one bit," moaned general manager Bill Bavasi. "This is an important, hurtful move for us. Now we've got guys who can recover."[3] Hargrove left a team on an eight-game winning streak. The Mariners extended the streak to nine games by beating Toronto, 2–1, after an emotional Hargrove announced his decision to step down. He became the first manager of the modern era to leave a club in the midst of such a streak.

The stunned Bavasi had little choice but to turn the team over to bench coach John McLaren. "I tried to talk [Hargrove] out of it," the new Seattle manager admitted. "He just shook his head and smiled and said, 'You're not going to do it. I've been thinking about this for a couple of weeks and it's not going to happen.' It's been a whirlwind. It was a roller coaster emotionally."[4]

McLaren was appointed manager for the rest of the season. He took command of a team with a 45–33 record. The Mariners were second in the AL West, trailing the Angels by four games. They won 43 and lost 41 under McLaren and failed to make the playoffs, finishing second with a record of 88–74. He would return in 2008.

Hargrove hasn't managed since his resignation in Seattle. His career mark with the Indians, Orioles and Mariners is 1,188–1,173. He won five division titles and two pennants with the Indians. His 1997 Cleveland team came within two outs of winning the World Series.

Cincinnati Reds
Jerry Narron to Pete Mackanin

On the same day Mike Hargrove resigned as manager of the Mariners, the Reds said goodbye to Jerry Narron.

The Reds had scuffled since moving into Great American Ballpark in 2003, and the fans were getting restless. Narron led the Reds to a third-place finish with 80 victories in 2006, and management had spent money to add talent during the off-season, leading to high expectations for 2007. Instead, Narron produced the worst record in the major leagues through the first half of the season, and the Reds were on a pace to lose 100 games for the first time in a quarter of a century. Those are the kind of results that get a manager fired, and Narron was dismissed on July 1.

Cincinnati's advance scout, Pete Mackanin, fresh off a stint as Pittsburgh's interim manager in 2005, became the Reds' interim pilot. Mackanin took a club with a 31–51 record and breathed some life into it. Cincinnati was 41–39 for the temporary manager, avoiding 100 defeats but still finishing last with a record of 72–90. Mackanin's record for two interim managing assignments was 53–53.

Narron hasn't resurfaced as a big league manager since being fired by Cincinnati. His record in two full seasons and parts of three others with Texas and the Reds is 291–341, with a third-place finish.

Houston Astros
Phil Garner to Cecil Cooper

It took Phil Garner only two years to go from being the toast of Houston to being unemployed.

Garner had been just the tonic the Astros needed when he was hired in mid-season of 2004 to replace Jimy Williams. He led Houston to the National League's wild card playoff spot and a five-game victory over Atlanta in the Division Series before losing in seven games to St. Louis in the League Championship Series. Houston's 89–73 record in 2005 was for good for another wild card berth, and the Astros ended their 42-year pennant drought by again defeating Atlanta in the Division Series and eliminating the Cardinals in six games in the LCS. Houston proved to be no match for the Chicago White Sox in the World Series, losing in four straight games.

It was all downhill for the Astros from there. Houston slipped to 82–80 in 2006, and had a 58–73 record on August 27, 2007, when owner Drayton McLane dismissed both Garner and general manager Tim Purpura. "I felt for a number of reasons we needed new direction, invigoration, to play with more enthusiasm and play more like a champion,"[5] McLane said of the decision to fire the only Houston manager to win a pennant.

Garner admitted things hadn't gone well in 2007. "We had really fallen into a pattern of so-so ball. We were never able to put together the run, like we made the previous two seasons. I think there were a number of reasons for that."[6]

As for his decision to fire Purpura, McLane said only, "There are some issues. It has been a series of things and observations."[7]

Garner was replaced by bench coach Cecil Cooper for the rest of the year. McLane admitted he was auditioning Cooper for the full-time job: "This is an opportunity for Cecil to show us his leadership. It wouldn't be bad if we won all 31 [remaining games.]"[8]

Cooper, a five-time All-Star first baseman during his 17-year career with Boston and Milwaukee, said he was eager for the challenge. "I've been to the World Series as a player and a coach," Cooper said. "Now, I want to try it as a manager. I know how to win. I really do believe I know what it takes to get the Houston Astros over the hump and back to the World Series."[9] Cooper took over a club in last place in the NL Central. Although the Astros showed some improvement for their new manager, winning 15 and losing 16, the best they could do was vacate the division basement and finish fourth with a record of 73–89. It was, however, good enough to earn Cooper a contract for 2008.

Garner's managerial career ended with his stop in Houston. In 11 full seasons and parts of four others, his teams won 985 and lost 1,054. He led the Astros to a pair of wild-card playoff berths and one pennant.

2008

New York Mets
Willie Randolph to Jerry Manuel

Willie Randolph couldn't escape the stigma of September 2007.

Randolph's Mets had the NL Eastern Division title all but sewn up. Their record of 83–62 led the second-place Phillies by seven games with only 17 to play. No major league club had ever blown such a sizable lead in such a short time. But, in a scenario reminiscent of 1964, when the Phillies coughed up a 6½-game advantage with 12 games left, Philadelphia got hot and the Mets hit the skids. New York lost 12 of its last 17 and surrendered the division lead to the Phillies on the season's final day, which is the only time leading the division truly matters. The Mets didn't even qualify for the wild card.

General manager Omar Minaya, stunned by the historic collapse, was given permission by the Mets' owners to fire Randolph if he chose. He instead chose not to. The Mets were expected to contend in 2008 but spent the first two months of the campaign hanging around the .500 mark, never more than three games above or three games below. The pressure was mounting on Minaya to fire his manager and on Randolph to get the Mets out of their rut. After splitting a double-header with Texas at Shea Stadium on June 15, Randolph had a conversation with his boss before the team got on a plane to Los Angeles to begin a western road swing.

Randolph relates, "I actually asked him. I said, 'Omar, do this now. If you're going to do this, do this now. I know you've got a lot of pressure on you, but if I'm not the guy to lead this team, don't let me get on this plane.' I did say that to him."[1] Minaya let Randolph get on the plane, and Randolph assumed his job was safe. He was mistaken. Minaya got on a plane to Los Angeles the next day and dismissed Randolph after the Mets' victory over the Angels. Thus Randolph's reaction: "I'm really stunned by it. I was surprised by it."[2] Pitching coach Rick Peterson and first base coach Tom Nieto were also released.

The speculation about Randolph's future went on "far too long," said Minaya. "It was not fair to the team, it was not fair to Willie Randolph, it was not fair to the organization."[3] Randolph was replaced by his bench coach, Jerry Manuel, the former manager of the White Sox. Manuel had won "Manager of the Year" honors in the American League in 2000 when Chicago broke Cleveland's stranglehold on the Central Division with 95 victories. He joined the Mets' coaching staff in 2006.

"Right now, I think we are somewhat underperforming," said the new head Met. "I think we need to freshen up our players."[4] Manuel's players had fashioned a 34–35 record for Randolph. They played like the contenders they were expected to be for Manuel, winning 55 and losing 38 and causing New Yorkers to wonder what might have happened had Minaya pulled the trigger sooner. The Mets' 89–73 record left them second to Philadelphia in the East and on the outside looking in as far as the playoffs were concerned. Manuel was invited back for the 2009 season.

Randolph hasn't managed since being fired by the Mets. His record in three full seasons and part of a fourth was 302–253 with one division title.

Seattle Mariners
John McLaren to Jim Riggleman

Was John McLaren just too nice of a guy to be a major league manager?

That question was asked frequently in Seattle after the Mariners fired McLaren on June 19. McLaren had taken over a club with a 45–33 record in early July of 2007 and failed to steer it into the playoffs, but the Mariners had spent $100 million on the players they put on the field in 2008, and much more was expected of them than the worst record in the major leagues at 25–47 in late June. General manager Bill Bavasi was the first to feel ownership's wrath, and Bavasi's interim replacement, Lee Pelekoudas, wasted no time putting his imprint on the club by changing managers.

"We hadn't shown any real improvement for the last couple of months," said Pelekoudas of his decision to replace McLaren. "In fact, we were probably regressing. To give the players a chance to improve ... we thought a new voice was needed."[5] The new voice belonged to bench coach Jim Riggleman, the former manager of the Padres and Cubs. Riggleman's managerial career was essentially undistinguished, save for guiding the Cubs to the NL wild card in 1998, achieved by defeating the San Francisco Giants in a one-game playoff at Wrigley Field. It was the Cubs' 90th win of the season.

"Jim's a serious guy," said Pelekoudas. "He's not a guy looking to have fun."[6] Just the antidote to the easygoing McLaren.

The Mariners hadn't had much fun through the first 72 games of the season, and they didn't have much under Riggleman. In addition to dismissing Bavasi and McLaren, the Mariners also fired batting coach Jeff Pentland and replaced him with 70-year-old former major league manager Lee Elia. Elia was promoted to bench coach after Riggleman was named manager. The shake-up didn't achieve the desired results as Seattle became the first team with a $100 million payroll to fail to make the playoffs. The Mariners were 36–54 under Riggleman to come home fourth in the AL West with a 61–101 record. Such a debacle called for a thorough housecleaning, and Riggleman was dismissed at season's end.

Riggleman had another managing job ahead of him, and he took McLaren with him as his bench coach. When Riggleman abruptly resigned as manager of the Washington Nationals in June of 2011, McLaren served as interim manager for three games. The Nationals won two of them, giving McLaren a career record of 70–89.

Toronto Blue Jays
John Gibbons to "Cito" Gaston

One of the drawbacks to being a major league club executive is they sometimes have to fire their friends.

Toronto general manager J.P. Ricciardi and manager John Gibbons had been roommates in the minor leagues and friends ever since. But Ricciardi couldn't, and didn't, let his friendship with Gibbons keep him from doing his duty when the Blue Jays failed to live up to lofty expectations in 2008. The Jays were in last place in the AL East with a 35–39 record, trailing the Red Sox by 10 games, and had lost 13 of their last 17 when Ricciardi fired his manager. Even Gibbons admitted it may have been the right thing to do.

"The team just wasn't doing what was expected of it," said the ex–Blue Jay boss. "Maybe changes were needed. There was a lot expected this year. We came in riding high and speaking high and that is not the results we're getting now."[7]

"From our standpoint, we know we've underachieved," said Ricciardi. "We know we have a better team than this. Right now, we want to see if we can spark this team, and we think Cito is the guy to do it."[8] Former Toronto manager Cito Gaston, who stepped down following the 1997 season, was serving as special assistant to the team's president and CEO when he answered Ricciardi's call to return to the dugout. Gaston's Blue Jays were world's champions in 1992 and '93 and hadn't made it back to the post-season since. He had a 681–635 record in his first go-around as Toronto's manager.

Gibbons had guided the Blue Jays since 2004 and had one second-place finish to show for his effort. The 2006 Jays were 87–75, but the season had been marred by a pair of confrontations between Gibbons and his players. He'd challenged infielder Shea Hillenbrand after Hillenbrand had written the words "the ship is sinking" on a blackboard in the clubhouse, and met pitcher Ted Lilly in a runway after Lilly had complained about being removed from a game.

In addition to firing Gibbons, Ricciardi also dismissed coaches Ernie Whitt, Marty Pevey and Gary Denbo. The Blue Jays showed some fight under Gaston, winning 51 and losing 37. They finished fourth with a record of 86–76, and Gaston returned to the Toronto dugout in 2009.

Gibbons would be re-hired by Toronto after Gaston's successor, former major league pitcher and Red Sox pitching coach John Farrell, defected to Boston following the 2012 season.

Milwaukee Brewers
Ned Yost to Dale Sveum

The collapse of the New York Mets the previous September was all too fresh in Doug Melvin's mind.

Melvin remembered how the Mets blew a seven-game lead with 17 to play, and was determined not to allow the same thing to happen to his Brewers. Milwaukee hadn't made the playoffs since its pennant-winning season of 1982, when it was in the American League, and Melvin wanted the drought of 26 seasons to end. He'd swung a huge trade with Cleveland to obtain CC Sabathia, the 2007 AL Cy Young Award winner, to bolster Milwaukee's pitching staff for the final 2½ months of the season. Sabathia would be a free agent at season's end, and there was no way the Indians could have met his salary demands. The Brewers couldn't, either, but if Sabathia could pitch them into the playoffs, the end of more than 25 years of futility would be worth the exorbitant price Melvin paid to obtain the ace left-hander. It was playoffs or bust for the Brewers, and when what appeared to be a sure-fire post-season berth began slipping away, Melvin took drastic action.

The Brewers entered September with a five-game lead over Philadelphia in the NL wild-card chase, but by mid-month the club had lost 11 of its last 14 games, including four straight to the onrushing Phillies. Suddenly, Milwaukee and Philadelphia were tied for the wild card, and Melvin decided to shock his team by the only means available to him: he fired manager Ned Yost, despite Milwaukee's 83–67 record.

"No, I didn't see it coming. The timing of it caught me off guard. I didn't see it coming,"[9] said a startled Yost, a former Brewers catcher who also played for Texas and Montreal in a six-year career. He was hired by Milwaukee off Bobby Cox's Atlanta coaching staff. He'd been part of 12 playoff teams with the Braves.

Melvin put the Brewers in the hands of coach Dale Sveum for the season's final 12 games. "Yost didn't have all the answers for what is going on the last two weeks, and I'm not sure I have all the answers," admitted Melvin. "I'm not sure this is the right one, either. We just felt a managerial change at least gives us a chance to see if we can turn it around." Melvin said the switch from Yost to Sveum "shows we're serious about winning."[10]

"I'm going to do this thing right," said Yost of his surprising dismissal. "I have nothing to be ashamed about. I'm walking out with my head held high."[11]

The Brewers didn't close with a rush, but their 7–5 record for their interim manager was good enough to finish second in the NL Central with a 90–72 mark. Milwaukee had to win the final game of the season to clinch the wild-card spot, and Sabathia's complete-game, four-hit, 3–1 victory over the Cubs at Miller Park got the job done. It was Sabathia's 11th win in 13 decisions since joining the Brewers, and the last game he'd win for them.

Milwaukee lost to Philadelphia, which wound up winning the NL East, in four games in the Division Series. Sveum didn't return to manage the Brewers in 2009.

Yost's record in almost six full seasons managing in Milwaukee was 457–502. He'd take over the Kansas City Royals 35 games into the 2010 season. Sveum would be hired to manage the Cubs in 2012 and fired after two seasons, with a career record of 134–202.

2009

Arizona Diamondbacks
Bob Melvin to A.J. Hinch

The 2009 season wasn't a good one for the two men who'd earned Manager of the Year Honors in 2007.

Arizona manager Bob Melvin was named the National League's Manager of the Year after leading the Diamondbacks to a 90–72 record and the Western Division title. Melvin's career as a manager began in Seattle, where he replaced Lou Piniella, the most successful manager in the franchise's history, after the 2002 season. Melvin's first Seattle team finished second in the AL West with 93 wins. His second finished last with 99 losses. Exit Melvin.

Melvin didn't have to wait long for his second managing job. He signed with Arizona for 2005 and finished second and fourth in his first two seasons. After winning the division title in 2007, the Diamondbacks slipped to second the next year, and were in fourth place with a record of 12–17 when general manager Josh Byrnes made what he admitted was an "unorthodox" move on May 8. Byrnes fired Melvin and replaced him with 34-year-old A.J. Hinch, the Diamondbacks' vice president for player development. Hinch had seen action, mostly as a catcher, in 350 games for Oakland, Kansas City, Detroit and Philadelphia in a seven-year playing career that ended in 2004. He had no experience as a manager at any level.

"This is a difficult decision, but I feel our organization needs to move forward with a new voice,"[1] said Byrnes of his decision to dismiss Melvin and replace him with the youngest manager in the major leagues.

Hinch took over a Diamondbacks team that trailed the front-running Dodgers by 8½ games. Arizona went 58–75 for Hinch and finished in the West's basement with a mark of 70–92. Melvin's career as a manager wasn't yet over. Hinch's soon would be.

The American League's 2007 Manager of the Year, Cleveland's Eric Wedge, and his entire staff were fired with a week to go in the 2009 season but stuck around to finish the campaign at management's request.

Colorado Rockies
Clint Hurdle to Jim Tracy

Clint Hurdle spent six relatively undistinguished seasons managing the Rockies. But his 2007 club put on the greatest finishing kick in baseball history to make the playoffs and capture the franchise's first and, to date, only National League pennant.

No one thought much of Colorado's 13–0 thrashing of the Florida Marlins on September 16. It improved the Rockies' record to 77–72 and snapped a three-game losing streak, but the Rockies were an afterthought in the NL wild card race. Twelve victories in 13 games later, the Rockies had finished in a tie for the wild card with San Diego, then defeated the Padres in a one-game playoff, 9–8.

Colorado suddenly couldn't lose. The Rockies flattened Eastern champion Philadelphia in three straight games in the Division Series, then swept Western champ Arizona in the League Championship Series to win the pennant. The Rockies had won 21 of their last 22 games.

Then, just as quickly, Colorado couldn't win. The Rockies were swept by Boston in the World Series and finished third in 2008 with a mark of 74–88. Colorado was stumbling along with a record of 18–28 on May 30 when Hurdle was fired.

"It was a tremendous ride. It was life lesson after life lesson," said Hurdle following his dismissal. "And I will tell you this: the last seven weeks, I have said the serenity prayer more times than I did in the last seven years. I'll be pulling for them from afar."[2]

First baseman Todd Helton said the players had to shoulder the blame for the popular Hurdle's firing. "Obviously, he takes the sword for us. He didn't have any bad at-bats. He didn't throw any bad pitches. He's the same manager he was two years ago. So, we realize that ultimately, we're the reason he got fired."[3] Hurdle had been with the Colorado organization for 16 years.

"We're an organization that values stability more than it values change," said general manager Dan O'Dowd. "Clint is someone who's been a part of everything we've done here. He deserved the benefit of the doubt until it got to the point where we realized we needed to do something." Of Hurdle's successor, bench coach Jim Tracy, O'Dowd said, "I'm not unrealistic. I don't expect miracles here."[4]

Tracy had been added to Hurdle's staff at O'Dowd's urging after the 2008 season. He'd formerly managed the Dodgers and Pirates, winning the 2004 NL West championship with Los Angeles. He had praise for the man whose place in the Colorado dugout he was taking:

"I want all of you to realize and understand that in no way, shape or form will I try to undo anything this man has done for this organization. Sixteen years to this organization is an eternity in the business today. He's done some wonderful things."[5]

O'Dowd may not have expected a miracle from Tracy, but he got a reasonable facsimile. The Rockies didn't duplicate their 21–1 streak of 2007, but they won 74 and lost 42 to finish second in the west at 92–70. It was good enough to earn Tracy the "Manager of the Year" award for his 116 games at the helm, but it didn't get Colorado into the playoffs. He returned in 2010.

Hurdle took a year off and then accepted the monumental task of turning the Pittsburgh Pirates into winners in 2011. His record with the Rockies was 534–625 with one pennant, thanks to one amazing hot streak.

Washington Nationals
Manny Acta to Jim Riggleman

The team nobody wanted finally found a home in 2005, when the Montreal Expos were transferred to Washington, D.C. An expensive new ballpark was on the drawing board, stable ownership had been acquired, and a new manager was hired for a new era of baseball in the nation's capital.

Manny Acta was hired off the staff of the Mets in 2007 to guide the Nationals through the growing pains of a club that was little better off than an expansion team when it was transferred south of the border. Acta's Nationals finished fourth in the NL East with a 73–89 record in 2007, and fell to the cellar in 2008. Despite the club's 59–102 record, the first of two club options years on his contract was picked up for 2009, with the understanding that drastic changes were to be made to his coaching staff. Acta was ordered to fire all of his assistants with the exception of pitching coach Randy St. Claire. Among those he was told to add was former Padres, Cubs, and Mariners manager Jim Riggleman as his bench coach.

In June of 2009, with the Nationals struggling again in last place, St. Claire was fired. There was no one left to take the blame for Washington's miserable 26–61 record but the manager, and Acta was dismissed on July 12. "It was a great learning experience," he said on departing. "I have no regrets."[6]

"I'm not satisfied with the way we play the game at times," said acting general manager Mike Rizzo of the decision to replace Acta with Riggleman. "We don't execute nearly as often as I expect them to. But the effort as far as the hustle and preparation is there; the consistency of the effort and the hustle needs work. The way we fundamentally play the game needs work."[7]

Riggleman brought a career managing record of 522–652 to Washington. The man whom Padres general manager Joe McIlvane had praised so highly when giving him his first managerial job in 1992 had logged just two winning seasons in six full years and parts of three others. The Nationals lacked the talent to compete with the rest of the NL, but they did show some improvement under Riggleman, winning 33 and losing 42. Washington stayed in the cellar with a mark of 59–103. Riggleman was retained for 2010.

Houston Astros
Cecil Cooper to Dave Clark

When Cecil Cooper was hired in 2007, he claimed to know how to get the Astros back to the World Series. He managed just a .500 record in two years on the job before getting his walking papers.

Houston's payroll was $107 million heading into the 2009 season, and the 70–79 record Cooper produced wasn't the return on his investment owner Drayton McLane wanted. "This is the most expensive baseball team the Houston Astros have ever had," said McLane in explaining why he gave general manager Ed Wade the go-ahead to fire Cooper. "We've made a huge investment of over $100 million. We invested in players we thought could be championship players. You could go back and look at players that were here or someplace else."[8]

Wade explained why he didn't wait until season's end to terminate Cooper's employment: "I thought it was going to be awkward to go all the way to the end of the season ... and make a move. I think the practicality of it didn't make sense to me, and the fact we can put Dave in place, we can have a different set of circumstances working for two weeks. Albeit a short period of time, but we may find some things out, and hopefully this creates a spark and gets us on a run so we can finish on a high note."[9]

Third base coach Dave Clark would manage the Astros for the rest of the season. Clark was a former top draft pick of the Indians who played 13 years in the major leagues, compiling a .264 lifetime average. "This is really bittersweet for me," Clark said. "I enjoyed my time with Coop, and you hate to see anybody lose his job. He brought me along to be his third base coach, and here I am replacing him. It's not a real good day for me in that perspective. But the opportunity and chance I'm getting to manage the next two weeks is outstanding."[10] Clark brought four years of minor league managing experience to his interim position.

The high note Wade hoped Clark would finish on didn't materialize. Houston won four and lost nine for its interim manager and came in last with a record of 74–88. Cooper's record for just over two full seasons in Houston was 171–170.

2010

Kansas City Royals
Trey Hillman to Ned Yost

In their quest to put an end to years of losing, the Royals looked overseas for a manager.

Actually, Trey Hillman had spent a dozen years in the Yankees organization and racked up several "Manager of the Year" awards in the minor leagues before spending five seasons managing in Japan. His record there earned him a shot with the Royals in 2008.

Hillman's first Kansas City team finished fourth in the AL Central with a record of 75–87. His second team was also fourth, despite winning 10 fewer games. When the Royals started the 2010 season with a miserable 12–23 record and dropped into the division cellar,

Hillman met the same fate as every Kansas City manager since Dick Howser was forced to resign due to a fatal illness in 1987. Hillman was fired by a club executive claiming a new manager was needed for the good of the organization. In Hillman's case, it was general manager Dayton Moore.

"Obviously, it's a very difficult decision. The process is very difficult, relationships that are formed are strong, but at the end of the day, we've got to make decisions that are best for the baseball team, and our organization long-term, and that's the conclusion we made,"[1] said Moore, who fought back tears as he announced Hillman's dismissal.

Hillman took the firing in stride: "There won't be any second guessing. I have the ultimate respect for the people I work for; but to put it into perspective, sometimes things work in this business, and sometimes they don't."[2]

Hillman was replaced by former Milwaukee manager Ned Yost, who had been hired by the Royals during the off-season as a special adviser for baseball operations. That led to immediate speculation that he was also Kansas City's manager-in-waiting, in the event the team got off to a slow start. The Royals had lost seven straight when Yost assumed command. He didn't have the cure for what ailed the club, and it won 55 and lost 72 for him. Kansas City finished last with 67 wins and 95 losses, but Yost returned as manager in 2011.

Hillman's record in two and a fraction years with the Royals was 152–207.

Baltimore Orioles
Dave Trembley to Juan Samuel to "Buck" Showalter

By 2010, a fan needed a long memory to recall when Kansas City had perennially been one of the American League's strongest teams. The same fan may have been hard-pressed to recall when the Baltimore Orioles were one of the league's elite teams as well.

No one was talking about a "curse of Davey Johnson," but the bottom line was the Orioles hadn't even sniffed contention in the AL East since Johnson left town after managing the club to the 1997 division title. The latest manager to fail to revive the Birds was Dave Trembley, the former bullpen coach who'd been elevated to manager when Sam Perlozzo was fired in 2007. Trembley became the seventh manager in major league history to never have played the game professionally. He wasn't given much to work with, and he didn't do a lot with what he had. Trembley's 2010 team stirred up unpleasant recollections of the 1988 Orioles (who lost their first 21 games) by getting off to the second-worst start in franchise history at a gruesome 2–16. The Orioles were staggering along in last place with baseball's worst record (15–39) when Trembley was relieved of his duties on June 3.

"What you're hoping to accomplish when you make a change like this," explained president of baseball operations Andy MacPhail, "is you're hoping to ignite a spark, give everyone a clean slate. Sort of get out of that drum beat of what's going to happen day-to-day."[3]

"The results on the field are not what any of us would have hoped for, and I understand that the organization felt the time was right to move in a different direction," said Trembley. "While I am disappointed at the outcome, I feel it was a privilege to wear the Orioles uniform each day."[4]

MacPhail was willing to shoulder some of the blame for what would become Baltimore's 13th straight losing season: "This is a negative reflection on the entire baseball operations department, starting with me. Nobody believes the reason we have the record we have is somehow Dave Trembley's fault, or that making this change is somehow going to magically solve all the issues and problems we have. But we did reach a point where we thought it was the appropriate thing to do."[5]

Trembley was replaced by Baltimore's third base coach, former major league shortstop Juan Samuel, who played for seven teams in his 16-season career. Samuel had 11 years of big league coaching experience, but just one season of minor league managing experience, in Double-A ball. Samuel served as Baltimore's interim manager until July 29, when he was succeeded by former Yankees, Diamondbacks and Rangers skipper Buck Showalter. Samuel's Birds won 17 games and lost 34. He hasn't managed in the major leagues since.

"It's been a good experience," Samuel said of his 51 games at the helm. "The guys played hard for me. I know the record doesn't reflect that, but I thank them for that."[6] Samuel returned to the third base coaching box for the rest of the season.

"Buck Showalter's proven track record makes him the right choice for manager of the Orioles," said MacPhail. "We believe Buck's extensive experience and expertise will be a major benefit to us as we look towards a more successful future."[7]

Said Baltimore's new manager, "Although the current record may seem to indicate otherwise, I see enormous potential with this club."[8] Baltimore's current record was 32–73 when Showalter arrived, and the Birds snapped to attention for their new manager, going 34–23 the rest of the way for a final mark of 66–96. They still finished last in the AL East.

Trembley's ledger for two full seasons and parts of two others was 187–283.

Florida Marlins
Fredi Gonzalez to Edwin Rodriguez

The Marlins wanted to put the pedal to the metal.

That was why manager Fredi Gonzalez was fired on June 24, with the Marlins treading water in the NL East. Florida was in fourth place, 6½ games out of first, with a 34–36 record. Gonzalez, who never played in the major leagues, had prepared for his shot at managing by coaching for Bobby Cox in Atlanta.

"This team seems to be stuck in neutral, and our competitors are on the accelerator," said president of baseball operations Larry Beinfest. "We were looking for a leadership change to hopefully get us on the accelerator. That's a big part of what we did today."[9]

Owner Jeffrey Loria added succinctly, "We can do better and be better."[10]

"It doesn't surprise me," said Gonzalez of his dismissal. "These things are normal in this job."[11] He insisted that his numerous differences with star shortstop Hanley Ramirez had nothing to do with his firing. Gonzalez had one year remaining on his contract and left south Florida with a record of 276–279 for almost 3½ seasons on the job. Bench coach Carlos Tosca and batting coach Jim Presley were also given the axe.

Beinfest selected Florida's Triple-A manager, Edwin Rodriguez, to succeed Gonzalez. Rodriguez had spent the past year and a half calling the shots for New Orleans. His major league playing career consisted of three games with the Yankees and eight games with the Padres. He led Florida to a 46–46 record for the rest of the season. The Marlins finished third with a record of 80–82.

Rodriguez would return as Florida's manager in 2011, but wouldn't last through the season. When Cox announced the 2010 season would be his final one as Braves manager, Gonzalez was hired to succeed him.

Arizona Diamondbacks
A.J. Hinch to Kirk Gibson

The Diamondbacks decided to get back to basics.

Josh Byrnes was one of the new breed of baseball front office executives, part of the "Moneyball" school. Byrnes was only 35 years old when he was hired away from the world champion Red Sox to take the general manager's job in Arizona in 2005. When the Diamondbacks won the 2007 Western Division title, Byrnes became a hot commodity and was rumored to be in line for several higher profile GM jobs with older, more established teams. To keep him, the Diamondbacks extended his contract through the 2017 season. No sooner had they done so than the walls began crashing down around them.

The 2008 D-Backs coughed up the division lead late in the season and finished out of the playoffs. Byrnes fired manager Bob Melvin in 2009 and replaced him with the team's player personnel director, 34-year-old A.J. Hinch, who had no previous managerial or coaching experience. Byrnes admitted it was an unorthodox move but explained it by saying he liked Hinch's "organizational advocacy."

Hinch said of his 2010 Diamondbacks at the conclusion of spring training, "I like this team."[12] But the Snakes slithered slowly from the starting gate. At one point, Arizona lost 10 straight games, nine of them during a winless road trip, the franchise's worst ever. Hinch confessed after the debacle, "This group hasn't responded that well to me."[13]

Ownership didn't like what was transpiring on the field and initiated a 30-day review of the franchise's entire operation from top to bottom. It led to the firings of both Byrnes and Hinch on July 2, despite the seven seasons left on the general manager's contract. "The evaluation basically drew us to a conclusion that a change was necessary, hopefully to bring a new energy to the club and to the organization,"[14] said managing partner Ken Kendrick.

Added team president Derrick Hall, "The players are underperforming. I think we all know that. I think the players would be the first to tell you that they've underperformed."[15]

Former major league pitcher Jerry DiPoto, Arizona's player personnel director, replaced Byrnes on an interim basis. The Diamondbacks' new manager, also on an interim basis, was former major league outfielder Kirk Gibson. Gibson was Hinch's bench coach, and had served Melvin in the same capacity during Arizona's 2007 division title-winning season. He'd also been bench coach in Detroit, where he spent much of his playing career, from 2003 through 2005.

"He has a great resume," said Kendrick of Gibson. "He has a passion for the game that was demonstrated in the way he played it, and we expect it will come through now that he has the position of leadership the manager's title carries."[16] In other words, Gibson was "old school."

The D-Backs were 31–48 for Hinch, giving him a record of 89–123 for slightly more than a full season's worth of games as manager. They were 34–49 under Gibson and finished last in the west with a record of 65–97. Nonetheless, the Diamondbacks removed the "interim" from Gibson's title and retained him for 2011. They were rewarded with 94 victories and a Western Division championship. Gibson was named NL "Manager of the Year."

Seattle Mariners
Don Wakamatsu to Daren Brown

It deteriorated in a hurry for Don Wakamatsu.

Wakamatsu, whose playing career comprised 18 games with the White Sox in 1991, was named baseball's first Asian-American manager after the 2008 season and led the Mariners to an 85–77 record and third-place finish in the AL West. Improvement was anticipated in 2010, but instead the team collapsed, despite the addition of 2008 Cy Young Award winner Cliff Lee.

Wakamatsu benched Seattle icon Ken Griffey, Junior, who'd returned in 2009 to end his Hall of Fame career in the city in which it had begun. The 40-year-old Griffey's talent had clearly eroded, but the benching was handled so poorly, Griffey angrily announced his retirement after seeing action in 33 games and batting .198 with no homers and seven RBI. By August, Lee had been traded to Texas for prospects and the Mariners owned the second-worst record in the major leagues at 42–70. General manager Jack Zduriencik admitted his first crack at hiring a manager had been a failure. He fired Wakamatsu, bench coach Ty Van Burkleo, and pitching coach Rick Adair.

Zduriencik minced no words about his decision: "The truth of the matter is, I lost confidence in Don, Ty and Rick. New leadership is needed, and it is needed now. To look around and see so many players having sub-par seasons is very disturbing."[17]

"My single biggest disappointment is that we were not able to finish what we wanted to finish here, bringing a championship club to the fans," said Wakamatsu.[18] His record for a season and two-thirds at the Mariner helm was 127–147. Daren Brown, Seattle's Triple-A manager at Tacoma, occupied the dugout at Safeco Field for the rest of the year. The Mariners were 19–31 for Brown and finished last in their division with a record of 61–101.

Brown wasn't invited back for the 2011 season.

Chicago Cubs
Lou Piniella to Mike Quade

Baseball managers have resigned for a myriad of reasons over the 111-year period covered by this book. Lou Piniella was the first to forsake the dugout to care for an ailing relative.

The 66-year-old Piniella, whose resume included six division titles, one pennant and one World Series championship, announced his retirement on July 20, but planned to stick it out for the rest of the season. He was going to return home to Tampa to care for his 90-year-old mother, Margaret. "Mom needs me, and that's where I'm going," he explained simply.[19]

Piniella's plans changed on August 21. He resigned, calling Wrigley Field "probably the most fun place in baseball."[20] It wasn't much fun for Piniella on his final day as Cubs manager. Atlanta blasted Chicago, 16–5. It was Piniella's 1,713th loss, as compared to 1,835 victories.

Of those victories, 116 had been earned with the 2001 Mariners, tying the major league record for most wins in a season.

Piniella turned the Cubs, their 51–74 record, and their fifth-place standing in the NL Central, over to third base coach Mike Quade. Quade couldn't lift the Cubs out of fifth place, but they won 24 and lost 13 and earned him a full season at the helm in 2011. Quade's Cubs finished last again, with a record of 75–87, and he was dismissed when Theo Epstein left the Red Sox to take over the Cubs' front office in 2012. His major league managerial ledger reads 95 wins and 104 defeats.

2011

Oakland Athletics
Bob Geren to Bob Melvin

Bill Virdon had joked after being dismissed as Pirates manager at the height of the frantic race for the 1973 NL Eastern Division title, "They say you aren't a real manager until you get fired." Using that logic, Oakland's Billy Beane didn't become a real general manager until he had to fire a manager during the season for the first time.

The first Oakland manager to feel the sting of Beane's axe during the season was Bob Geren, who spent five seasons in the major leagues as a catcher and designated hitter with the Yankees and Padres. He was in his fifth year as manager of the Athletics in 2011 and had yet to post a winning record. Geren's best season had been 2010, when Oakland finished second in the AL West with an 81–81 record.

The Athletics pitching staff was decimated by injuries early in 2011. Four of Geren's starting pitchers were on the disabled list, and the club was averaging an anemic 3.5 runs per game, on June 9. Oakland's ninth straight loss dropped its record to 27–36, eight games behind the front-running Rangers. Speculation about Geren's status had been running rampant, and Beane decided to put an end to it.

"I felt at this point, a change was necessary," said the general manager. "It got to the point where the emphasis was on the status of the manager on a daily basis, and no longer on the field. When that starts to happen, you need to shift the focus to what's really important, which is performance. That's how we came to this decision."[1]

Geren was replaced by Bob Melvin, the former manager of the Mariners and Diamondbacks. Melvin was born in Palo Alto, California, and played collegiate baseball at the University of California at Berkeley. Beane gave him a chance to come home.

"It's a dream come true," said Oakland's new manager. "This doesn't happen very often in baseball, where you literally get to come home in the capacity that I do."[2] In his capacity as manager, Melvin led the Athletics to 47 wins and 52 losses. Oakland finished third with a record of 74–88.

Geren's record in four full seasons and part of a fifth with the Athletics was 334–376. "Whenever you replace your manager, it's a drastic move," said Beane, the creator of the "Moneyball" school of baseball front office operation. "I've never had to do it in my tenure as general manager. This is a new script for myself. I don't know if you ever know what the right time is."[3]

Florida Marlins
Edwin Rodriguez to Jack McKeon

Jack was back in Miami.

Five days after naming Edwin Rodriguez their interim manager following the dismissal of Fredi Gonzalez in June of 2010, the Marlins announced that Rodriguez would manage the team for the rest of the season. The 46–46 record he compiled earned him a contract for 2011, and the Marlins opened the season strongly. Florida had a record of 31–22 on May 31 before embarking on a tailspin of historic proportions.

Following a 5–2 victory over Arizona on the last day of May, the Marlins lost eight straight games, won one, and then dropped nine in a row. The 17 losses in 18 games were more than Rodriguez could tolerate, and he stunned his bosses and his players by resigning on June 19.

"I can't say enough about the effort that this staff and these players have put into this season," Rodriguez said in announcing his decision to step down. "I could tell that they continued to give 100 percent effort each and every day on the field."[4] That may have been true of Rodriguez's staff, but some observers felt his players had quit on him, leading to his resignation.

"It's been extremely frustrating for everyone," said president of baseball operations Larry Beinfest of the Marlins' plunge off a cliff. "I think everyone here knows what is going on—the way we've played, the way we've performed. It's tough on everyone, especially [Rodriguez]. This is an extremely frustrated, proud man."[5] Beinfest said the Marlins had no intention of firing Rodriguez despite what was shaping up to be a historically bad month.

As he had done in 2003 when he fired Jeff Torborg, Beinfest once again turned to the venerable Jack McKeon to manage the team. McKeon was 80 years old and couldn't duplicate the miracle he had performed eight seasons earlier, when he took over a slumbering ball club and led it to a World Series victory. He couldn't even get the Marlins back to the .500 mark. The team may have been performing above its head for the first third of the campaign. McKeon inherited a team with a 32–40 record that had lost 18 of its last 19 games and managed it to a record of 40–50. The Marlins finished fifth in the NL East with 72 wins and 90 defeats.

Rodriguez, the first Puerto Rican–born manager in major league history, managed the Marlins for the equivalent of one full season, winning 78 and losing 85. McKeon stepped down at the end of the season. His record with the Royals, Athletics, Padres, Reds and Marlins was 1,051 wins against 990 losses. McKeon's teams claimed one wild card playoff spot, won one pennant and one World Series.

Washington Nationals
Jim Riggleman to Davey Johnson

Ultimatum or no, Jim Riggleman was finished as manager of the Nationals.

Riggleman had been promoted from bench coach to manager following the dismissal of Manny Acta in July of 2009. He was offered a one-year contract for 2010, and led the Nationals to a last-place finish in the NL East with a record of 69–93. Riggleman was invited to return in 2011, on another one-year deal ... with a club option for a second season.

On June 23, the Nationals had won 11 of their last 12 games. Their 38–37 record put them above .500 so late in the season for the first time since moving to Washington in 2005. The club was about to begin a road trip to Chicago when Riggleman decided the time had come to solidify his contract status for 2012.

"It's been brewing for a while," said Riggleman. "I know I'm not Casey Stengel, but I feel like I know what I'm doing. It's not a situation where I felt I should continue on such a short leash."[6] He wanted his contract extended immediately.

"Jim told me pre-game today that if we wouldn't pick up his option, he wouldn't get on the team bus," explained general manager Mike Rizzo, who'd recently signed a five-year deal with the Nationals. "I felt that the time wasn't right for me to pick up the option, and certainly today's conversation, put to me in the way it was put to me, you certainly can't make that decision in a knee-jerk reaction. It's too big of a decision."[7]

"I just felt that if there's not going to be some type of commitment, then there obviously never will be. I'm just not the guy they thought they could move forward with,"[8] said Riggleman, who denied presenting Rizzo with an ultimatum. According to Riggleman, he said he wanted to meet with Rizzo to discuss his contract situation when the team arrived in Chicago. However, he confessed that had such a meeting taken place, he would've demanded that Rizzo pick up his contract option or look for a new manager immediately. Rizzo rejected the idea of meeting with Riggleman in Chicago, and Riggleman quit.

The ex-manager of the Nationals admitted he may have ruined his chance of ever piloting a club again by resigning over a contract issue. He said if he was ever offered another managing job, he'd demand a multi-year contract.

Rizzo promoted special assistant Davey Johnson to replace Riggleman. Johnson hadn't managed since leaving the Dodgers after the 2000 season. Rizzo said of the 68-year-old veteran, "We could have no better choice to lead the Nationals at this time than Davey Johnson. He knows the game, he knows our players, he knows our fans, he knows the Washington, D.C., area, and he knows what we need to be doing to build the Nationals into a contender."[9]

Johnson took over a third-place team and kept it there, winning 40 and losing 43. The Nationals were 2–1 for interim manager John McLaren, and barely missed posting their first winning season at 80–81. Riggleman left Washington with a lifetime managerial record of 662–824, with one wild card playoff berth.

2012

Houston Astros
Brad Mills to Tony DeFrancesco

Brad Mills had the credentials.

Mills spent six years as Terry Francona's bench coach in Boston from 2003 through 2009. He was Francona's chief assistant when the Red Sox broke the "Curse of the Bambino" by winning the 2004 World Series, and added another world title in 2007. But that didn't prepare him for the mess he'd face in Houston.

Mills's first Houston team finished fourth in the NL Central with a record of 76–86. The Astros were being sold by Drayton McLane to businessman Jim Crane while they plunged into the basement in 2011 with a mark of 56–106. As most new owners do, Crane hired his own people to run the front office. General manager Ed Wade was replaced by Jeff Luhnow, and the Astros began preparing for their move into the American League in 2013. When the team started slowly in 2012, Crane made the decision to gut the franchise and essentially begin from scratch. Luhnow started trading Mills's best players, reducing the payroll by some $40 million. By August, the Astros had the youngest roster in the National League, a scant $21 million payroll, and very few victories. The fewest in the major leagues, to be exact.

At one point in the 2012 season, the Astros lost 34 of 38 games ... a pace even the 1962 Mets would have been embarrassed by. Crane admitted of the opening stages of what figured to be a long and painful rebuilding process, "We knew we might slide back a bit, but we didn't think it would be this bad."[1]

When Houston's record hit 39–82 on August 18, the worst in the big leagues, Mills was fired. The announcement was made via e-mail. Batting coach Mike Barnett and first base coach Bobby Meacham were also fired. "I tried to do the best job I could," said Mills. "It's hard not to let it get to you. You don't want to expect to lose."[2]

Luhnow named Tony DeFrancesco, the manager of Houston's Triple-A affiliate in Oklahoma City, the Astros' interim manager for the rest of the year. The team had dropped a club-record 12 straight games. Houston was a lost cause by that point in the campaign, and the best DeFrancesco could do was 16 wins and 25 losses. The Astros finished in the division cellar with 55 wins and 107 defeats, the worst record in franchise history. DeFrancesco wouldn't return in 2013.

Mills found conditions in Houston much different from what he'd grown accustomed to in Boston. His record with the Astros was 171–274.

2013

Philadelphia Phillies
Charlie Manuel to Ryne Sandberg

Charlie Manuel belongs to an exclusive club. Only two managers have guided the Phillies to a World Series championship. Dallas Green did it in 1980. Manuel did it in 2008, then became the only manager in Phillies history to win back-to-back pennants in 2009. The Phillies came up short against the Yankees in their bid to capture consecutive world championships.

Manuel led the star-studded Phillies to East Division titles in 2010 and 2011, but the team began to show signs of age in 2012, declining from 102 victories to 81. The decline continued in 2013, and general manager Ruben Amaro, Junior made the decision not to offer the 69-year-old Manuel a new contract at season's end. With the Phillies in a tailspin in mid–August, having won just five games while losing 19 since the All-Star break, and with the decision to hire a new manager for 2014 having been made, Amaro saw no sense in leaving Manuel dangling for the final six weeks of the campaign. He fired his manager on August 16. The Phillies record was 53–67.

Amaro was a utility player on the 1995 American League pennant-winning Cleveland Indians, where his batting coach had been Manuel. He had tears in his eyes as he discussed his special relationship with Manuel at the news conference announcing the manager's firing. Amaro insisted Manuel wasn't taking the fall for the Phillies' failure to contend for the past two seasons despite the club's sizable payroll. "This isn't a blame game," said Amaro, who took over from Ed Wade as general manager following the 2008 world's championship. Wade had taken considerable flak when he hired Manuel after the 2004 season. Amaro took as much, if not more, flak for firing him.

"I'm not here to blame Charlie for our issues. We all have a part in it,"[1] said Amaro, who expressed the hope Manuel would accept another job in the organization. Manuel said he'd have to think about it, and made it clear he wanted to manage for several more seasons, despite being the second-oldest manager in the major leagues.

"I never quit nothing and I didn't resign,"[2] said Manuel, who may have had a sense of déjà vu during the 2013 season. He was in the final season of his contract, as had been the case in Cleveland in 2002. Speculation swirled through April, May and June as to whether he'd be offered a contract for 2003, and when Manuel demanded at the All-Star break that general manager Mark Shapiro make a decision immediately, Shapiro fired him. Manuel didn't issue a similar ultimatum to Amaro, but undoubtedly had grown weary of media speculation about his status as the season continued and may have read the handwriting on the wall when no extension was offered.

Manuel was replaced on an interim basis by the Phillies' third base coach, former Hall of Fame second baseman Ryne Sandberg. Sandberg had paid his dues managing in the minor leagues and was thought to be the heir apparent to the Cubs' managing job. But he was passed over twice by the team he played for and was eager for the opportunity Amaro presented.

"I've always had the attitude that things happen for a reason," said Sandberg. "But also, I put in the work, put in the time to give myself a chance to be [at] this point now. I didn't want to have the opportunity I have now and not be prepared."[3] The Phillies removed the "interim" tag from Sandberg's title on September 22, signing him through the 2016 season. The Phillies were 20–22 after Sandberg succeeded Manuel, losing five of the seven games they played after Sandberg was named the club's "permanent" manager.

Manuel left Philadelphia having won more games (780) and more pennants (2) than any manager in Phillies history. His career record showed an even 1,000 victories against 826 defeats.

Afterword

One hundred twelve seasons from 1901 through 2013 saw a total of 287 changes of managers. Some were initiated by the manager who grew weary of his inability to motivate his players and resigned, although many of those resignations were unquestionably the result of pressure from owners who wanted to make a change but didn't want to pay the deposed manager what remained on his contract. Most were firings instigated by owners or, by the 1940s, general managers convinced the team they'd put together wasn't playing as well as it should be and deciding the manager (and, sometimes, a coach or two) was at the root of the problem ... or looking to deflect the blame from themselves.

All of the changes were made "for the good of the organization," even when the executive making the change acknowledged a new manager probably wouldn't do any better than the previous boss. Detroit Tigers owner Spike Briggs made that rare confession when he fired manager Red Rolfe in 1952. Briggs admitted that a change in managers most likely wouldn't lift his team out of the American League's basement, and he was right. The Tigers were in last place when Rolfe was fired, and they stayed in last place under Fred Hutchinson. But a change had to be made.

Some changes were based on nothing more than hope, such as when the Cleveland Indians dismissed Alvin Dark in 1971. "We hope this helps us start winning," was the only explanation team president Gabe Paul could offer for making the switch from Dark to the Indians' third base coach, Johnny Lipon. It didn't. Lipon owns the lowest winning percentage of any Indians manager for his 59 games at the helm.

Still, firing the manager isn't always a cop-out. The 1932 Cubs floundered under Rogers Hornsby, but kicked it into high gear for Charlie Grimm and won the National League pennant. The 1982 Brewers were in the same boat playing for Buck Rodgers, then won the division title and pennant for Harvey Kuenn. Ditto the 2003 Marlins, who started the season listlessly under Jeff Torborg and finished it, after being 10 games below the .500 mark at one point, as world's champions for Jack McKeon. Those are extreme cases, but of the 287 changes of managers chronicled in this book, 109 (37.7 percent) resulted in the team's playing significantly better for its new manager for the rest of the season. A change in managers isn't always slapping a Band-Aid on a sick elephant.

The majority of the time, however (178 of the cases studied here, or 62.3 percent), changing managers made little or no difference in a club's performance. Occasionally, such as the 1971 Indians, the 1908 New York Highlanders or the 2004 Arizona Diamondbacks, the club nosedived after replacing its manager. Allowing for the fact that a new manager can bring a positive change of atmosphere to a team's clubhouse while not improving its record, the wins and losses remain the bottom line and were the only measurement used in this book to determine whether a managerial change had an impact or not.

Managerial changes increased drastically following the advent of free agency in 1976. Impatient owners who spent huge amounts of money to import talent put pressure on their managers to win games with that talent, and weren't shy about making a change if the results on the field were unsatisfactory. The pace slowed somewhat in the mid–1990s, then picked up again early in the 21st century and shows little sign of abating.

After all, as so many executives admitted, it's easier to fire one manager (and possibly a couple of coaches) than to fire 25 players.

NOTES

1908
1. *Cleveland Plain Dealer*, June 25.
2. *Plain Dealer*, August 29.

1909
1. *Cleveland Plain Dealer*, August 18.
2. Ibid.
3. *Plain Dealer*, August 22.
4. Ibid.

1910
1. *Cleveland Plain Dealer*, September 21.
2. *Plain Dealer*, September 22.
3. Ibid.
4. *Plain Dealer*, September 24.

1912
1. *Cleveland Plain Dealer*, October 29, 1911.
2. *Plain Dealer*, September 3, 1912.
3. Norman L. Macht, *Connie Mack and the Early Years of Baseball*, p. 381.
4. *Plain Dealer*, September 3, 1912.
5. Ibid.
6. Ibid.
7. Ibid.

1913
1. *Cleveland Plain Dealer*, July 17.
2. Ibid.
3. Ibid.

1915
1. *Cleveland Plain Dealer*, May 22, 1915.
2. Ibid.
3. Ibid.

1918
1. *Cleveland Plain Dealer*, June 18.

1921
1. *Cleveland Plain Dealer*, August 3.
2. Ibid.

1922
1. *Cleveland Plain Dealer*, July 1.

1923
1. *Cleveland Plain Dealer*, August 7.

1925
1. *Cleveland Plain Dealer*, September 4.

1928
1. *Cleveland Plain Dealer*, May 24.

1929
1. *Cleveland Plain Dealer*, August 29.
2. Ibid.

1932
1. *Cleveland Plain Dealer*, June 4.
2. Ibid.
3. Ibid.
4. Ibid.
5. Ibid.
6. *Plain Dealer*, June 19.
7. Ibid.
8. Ibid.
9. *Plain Dealer*, August 3.
10. Ibid.
11. Ibid.
12. *Plain Dealer*, August 4.
13. *Plain Dealer*, August 5.
14. *Plain Dealer*, August 3.

1933
1. *Cleveland Plain Dealer*, June 10.
2. Ibid.
3. *Plain Dealer*, July 26.
4. Ibid.

1934
1. *Cleveland Plain Dealer*, May 8.
2. *Plain Dealer*, June 19.

1935
1. Franklin Lewis, *The Cleveland Indians*, p. 182.
2. Lewis, p. 182.
3. *Cleveland Plain Dealer*, August 5.
4. Ibid.
5. Ibid.

1937
1. *Cleveland Plain Dealer*, July 21.
2. *Plain Dealer*, September 13.

1938
1. *Cleveland Plain Dealer*, July 21.
2. Ibid.
3. Ibid.

4. *Plain Dealer*, August 6.
5. Ibid.
6. Ibid.
7. Ibid.
8. *Plain Dealer*, September 13.
9. Ibid.

1940
1. *Cleveland Plain Dealer*, June 7.

1941
1. *Cleveland Plain Dealer*, June 4.
2. Ibid.
3. Ibid.
4. Ibid.
5. Ibid.

1943
1. *Cleveland Plain Dealer*, July 27.
2. Ibid.

1944
1. *Cleveland Plain Dealer*, May 1.
2. Ibid.

1945
1. *Cleveland Plain Dealer*, June 30.

1946
1. *Cleveland Plain Dealer*, May 25.
2. Ibid.
3. Ibid.
4. Ibid.
5. Ibid.
6. *Plain Dealer*, September 1.
7. Ibid.
8. *Plain Dealer*, September 13.

1948
1. *Cleveland Plain Dealer*, July 16.
2. Ibid.
3. Ibid.
4. *Plain Dealer*, July 17.
5. Ibid.
6. Donald Honig, *The Cincinnati Reds: An Illustrated History*, p. 143.

1950
1. *Cleveland Plain Dealer*, May 27.
2. *Plain Dealer*, May 23.

3. *Plain Dealer*, May 24.
4. Ibid.

1951
1. *Cleveland Plain Dealer*, June 20.
2. Ibid.
3. Ibid.

1952
1. *Cleveland Plain Dealer*, June 1.
2. Ibid.
3. *Plain Dealer*, June 11.
4. Ibid.
5. Ibid.
6. Ibid.
7. Ibid.
8. Ibid.
9. Ibid.
10. *Plain Dealer*, June 29.
11. *Plain Dealer*, July 6.
12. *Plain Dealer*, July 29.
13. Ibid.
14. *Plain Dealer*, August 4.

1954
1. *Cleveland Plain Dealer*, July 16.
2. Ibid.

1955
1. *Cleveland Plain Dealer*, May 29.
2. Ibid.
3. Ibid.

1956
1. *Cleveland Plain Dealer*, June 18.
2. Ibid.
3. Ibid.

1957
1. *Cleveland Plain Dealer*, May 7.
2. *Plain Dealer*, August 4.
3. Ibid.
4. *Plain Dealer*, August 6.
5. Ibid.
6. Lou Boudreau, *Covering All the Bases*, p. 169.
7. *Plain Dealer*, August 6.

1958
1. *Cleveland Plain Dealer*, June 11.

2. Ibid.
3. Ibid.
4. Ibid.
5. *Plain Dealer*, June 27.
6. Ibid.
7. Ibid.
8. Ibid.
9. Ibid.
10. Ibid.
11. *Plain Dealer*, July 23.
12. Ibid.
13. Ibid.
14. *Plain Dealer*, August 15.
15. Ibid.
16. *Plain Dealer*, September 18.

1959
1. *Cleveland Plain Dealer*, May 3.
2. Ibid.
3. Ibid.
4. Ibid.
5. *Plain Dealer*, July 4.

1960
1. *Cleveland Plain Dealer*, May 5.
2. Ibid.
3. Ibid.
4. *Plain Dealer*, June 13.
5. *Plain Dealer*, June 19.
6. Ibid.
7. *Plain Dealer*, August 4.
8. Ibid.
9. Ibid.

1961
1. *Cleveland Plain Dealer*, June 8.
2. *Plain Dealer*, June 24.
3. *Plain Dealer*, June 20.
4. Ibid.
5. Ibid.
6. *Plain Dealer*, July 7.
7. *Plain Dealer*, September 3.
8. Ibid.
9. Ibid.

1963
1. *Cleveland Plain Dealer*, May 23.
2. Ibid.
3. Ibid.
4. Ibid.

1964
1. *Cleveland Plain Dealer*, June 12.

Notes—1965–1977

2. Ibid.
3. Ibid.
4. Ibid.

1965
1. *Cleveland Plain Dealer*, August 31.

1966
1. *Cleveland Plain Dealer*, May 8.
2. Ibid.
3. Ibid.
4. Ibid.
5. *Plain Dealer*, July 15.
6. *Plain Dealer*, August 10.
7. Ibid.
8. Ibid.
9. Ibid.
10. Ibid.
11. *Plain Dealer*, August 20.
12. Ibid.
13. Russell Schneider, *The Cleveland Indians Encyclopedia*, p. 324.
14. *Cleveland Press*, August 20.
15. *Plain Dealer*, September 10.
16. Ibid.

1967
1. *Cleveland Plain Dealer*, June 10.
2. Ibid.
3. Ibid.
4. *Plain Dealer*, July 19.
5. Ibid.
6. *Plain Dealer*, August 20.
7. Ibid.
8. *Plain Dealer*, August 21.
9. Ibid.
10. Ibid.
11. Ibid.
12. *Plain Dealer*, August 22.
13. *Plain Dealer*, September 22.
14. Ibid.

1968
1. *Cleveland Plain Dealer*, June 19.
2. Ibid.
3. *Plain Dealer*, July 11.
4. Ibid.
5. Ibid.
6. Ibid.
7. *Plain Dealer*, July 13.
8. Ibid.

1969
1. *Cleveland Plain Dealer*, May 3.
2. *Plain Dealer*, May 28.
3. Ibid.
4. Ibid.
5. Ibid.
6. *Plain Dealer*, August 8.
7. Ibid.

1970
1. *Cleveland Plain Dealer*, May 24.
2. Ibid.
3. *Plain Dealer*, June 4.
4. Ibid.
5. *Plain Dealer*, September 4.
6. *Plain Dealer*, July 23.

1971
1. *Cleveland Press*, July 31, 1971.
2. Ibid.
3. Ibid.
4. Ibid.

1972
1. *Cleveland Plain Dealer*, April 28.
2. *Plain Dealer*, May 29.
3. Ibid.
4. Ibid.
5. *Plain Dealer*, July 7.
6. Ibid.
7. Ibid.
8. Ibid.
9. *Plain Dealer*, July 11.
10. Ibid.
11. *Plain Dealer*, July 26.
12. Ibid.
13. *Plain Dealer*, August 8.
14. *Plain Dealer*, August 27.

1973
1. *Cleveland Plain Dealer*, September 3.
2. Ibid.
3. Ibid.
4. *Plain Dealer*, September 7.
5. Ibid.
6. Ibid.
7. *Plain Dealer*, September 8.
8. Ibid.
9. Ibid.
10. Ibid.

1974
1. *Cleveland Plain Dealer*, June 28.
2. Ibid.
3. Ibid.
4. Ibid.
5. Ibid.
6. Ibid.
7. Ibid.
8. *Plain Dealer*, June 29.
9. Ibid.
10. *Plain Dealer*, July 22.
11. Ibid.
12. Ibid.
13. Ibid.
14. Ibid.

1975
1. *Cleveland Plain Dealer*, July 23.
2. Ibid.
3. Ibid.
4. Ibid.
5. *Plain Dealer*, July 25.
6. Ibid.
7. Ibid.
8. Ibid.
9. *Plain Dealer*, August 3.
10. Ibid.
11. Ibid.
12. *Plain Dealer*, August 7.
13. Ibid.
14. *Plain Dealer*, August 19.
15. *Plain Dealer*, August 31.
16. Ibid.

1976
1. *Cleveland Plain Dealer*, July 20.
2. Ibid.
3. Ibid.
4. *Plain Dealer*, July 24.
5. Ibid.
6. Ibid.

1977
1. *Cleveland Plain Dealer*, May 29.
2. Ibid.
3. *Plain Dealer*, June 1.
4. Ibid.
5. *Plain Dealer*, June 11.
6. Ibid.
7. *Plain Dealer*, June 20.
8. Ibid.
9. Ibid.
10. Ibid.
11. Schneider, p. 331.
12. *Plain Dealer*, June 22.
13. Ibid.
14. Ibid.
15. *Plain Dealer*, June 24.
16. *Plain Dealer*, June 29.
17. *Plain Dealer*, July 12.

1978
1. *New York Times*, April 26.
2. Ibid.
3. *Cleveland Plain Dealer*, May 24.
4. *Plain Dealer*, June 2.
5. Ibid.
6. *Plain Dealer*, July 1.
7. *Plain Dealer*, July 25.
8. *Hartford Courant*, July 25.
9. *Plain Dealer*, July 26.

1979
1. *Cleveland Plain Dealer*, June 13.
2. Ibid.
3. *Plain Dealer*, June 19.
4. Ibid.
5. Ibid.
6. *Plain Dealer*, August 3.
7. Ibid.
8. *Plain Dealer*, September 1.
9. Ibid.

1980
1. *Cleveland Plain Dealer*, June 9.
2. *Plain Dealer*, August 25.

1981
1. *Cleveland Plain Dealer*, May 8.
2. Ibid.
3. Ibid.
4. *Plain Dealer*, May 26.
5. *Plain Dealer*, May 30.
6. Ibid.
7. *Plain Dealer*, August 30.
8. Ibid.
9. *Plain Dealer*, September 7.
10. Ibid.
11. Ibid.
12. *Plain Dealer*, September 8.
13. Ibid.
14. Ibid.

1982
1. *Cleveland Plain Dealer*, April 27.
2. Ibid.
3. Ibid.
4. *Plain Dealer*, June 3.
5. Ibid.
6. *Plain Dealer*, June 22.
7. Ibid.
8. *Plain Dealer*, June 29.
9. Ibid.
10. *Plain Dealer*, August 5.
11. Ibid.
12. Ibid.
13. *Plain Dealer*, August 11.
14. Ibid.
15. Ibid.
16. Ibid.

1983
1. *Cleveland Plain Dealer*, June 4.
2. Ibid.
3. *Plain Dealer*, June 27.
4. *Plain Dealer*, July 19.
5. *Plain Dealer*, July 31.
6. Ibid.
7. Ibid.
8. Ibid.
9. *Plain Dealer*, August 23.
10. Ibid.
11. Ibid.
12. Ibid.

1984
1. *Cleveland Plain Dealer*, May 25.
2. Ibid.
3. Ibid.
4. *Plain Dealer*, August 5.
5. Ibid.
6. Ibid.
7. Ibid.
8. Ibid.
9. *Plain Dealer*, August 17.
10. Ibid.
11. *Plain Dealer*, August 31.
12. Ibid.
13. Ibid.

1985
1. *Cleveland Plain Dealer*, April 29.
2. Ibid.
3. Ibid.
4. Ibid.
5. *Plain Dealer*, May 18.
6. Ibid.
7. *Plain Dealer*, June 14.
8. Ibid.
9. *Plain Dealer*, June 22.
10. Ibid.
11. *Plain Dealer*, August 27.
12. Ibid.

1986
1. *Cleveland Plain Dealer*, May 9.
2. Ibid.
3. Ibid.
4. Ibid.
5. *Plain Dealer*, June 13.
6. Ibid.
7. Ibid.
8. Ibid.
9. *Plain Dealer*, June 21.
10. Ibid.
11. *Plain Dealer*, September 13.
12. Ibid.
13. Ibid.

1987
1. *Cleveland Plain Dealer*, June 19.
2. Ibid.
3. Ibid.
4. Ibid.
5. *Plain Dealer*, July 16.
6. Ibid.
7. *Plain Dealer*, August 26.
8. Ibid.
9. *Plain Dealer*, September 9.
10. Ibid.
11. Ibid.
12. Ibid.

1988
1. *Cleveland Plain Dealer*, May 24.
2. *Plain Dealer*, May 29.
3. Ibid.
4. Ibid.
5. Ibid.
6. *Plain Dealer*, June 7.
7. Ibid.
8. *Plain Dealer*, June 24.
9. Ibid.
10. *Plain Dealer*, July 15.
11. Ibid.

1989
1. *Cleveland Plain Dealer*, May 16.
2. Ibid.
3. *Plain Dealer*, August 19.
4. Ibid.
5. Ibid.
6. Ibid.
7. Ibid.
8. *Plain Dealer*, September 12.

1990
1. *Cleveland Plain Dealer*, May 30.
2. Ibid.
3. *Plain Dealer*, June 7.
4. Ibid.

5. Ibid.
6. *Plain Dealer*, June 23.
7. Ibid.
8. Ibid.
9. *Plain Dealer*, July 7.
10. Ibid.
11. *Plain Dealer*, August 3.
12. Ibid.
13. *Plain Dealer*, July 12.
14. Ibid.
15. Ibid.

1991

1. *Cleveland Plain Dealer*, April 24.
2. Ibid.
3. Ibid.
4. *Plain Dealer*, May 22.
5. Ibid.
6. Ibid.
7. Ibid.
8. Ibid.
9. *Plain Dealer*, May 23.
10. Ibid.
11. Ibid.
12. Ibid.
13. *Plain Dealer*, May 24.
14. Ibid.
15. Ibid.
16. Ibid.
17. *Plain Dealer*, June 4.
18. Ibid.
19. *Plain Dealer*, November 4, 1989.
20. *Plain Dealer*, July 7.
21. Ibid.
22. *Plain Dealer*, August 27.
23. Ibid.

1992

1. *Cleveland Plain Dealer*, July 10.
2. Ibid.
3. Ibid.
4. *Plain Dealer*, September 24.
5. Ibid.

1993

1. *Cleveland Plain Dealer*, May 20.
2. Ibid.
3. *Plain Dealer*, May 24.
4. Ibid.

1994

1. *Cleveland Plain Dealer*, May 18.
2. Ibid.

1995

1. *Cleveland Plain Dealer*, June 4.
2. *Plain Dealer*, June 17.
3. Ibid.
4. Ibid.

1996

1. *Cleveland Plain Dealer*, July 8.
2. *Plain Dealer*, August 8.
3. Ibid.
4. *Plain Dealer*, August 27.
5. Ibid.

1997

1. *Cleveland Plain Dealer*, July 26.
2. Ibid.
3. Ibid.
4. Ibid.

1998

1. *Cleveland Plain Dealer*, June 23.
2. Ibid.
3. *Plain Dealer*, September 2.
4. Ibid.
5. Ibid.
6. Ibid.

1999

1. *Cleveland Plain Dealer*, August 13.
2. Ibid.
3. Ibid.
4. *Plain Dealer*, September 5.
5. Ibid.

2001

1. *Cleveland Plain Dealer*, April 19.
2. *Plain Dealer*, May 5.
3. *Plain Dealer*, May 29.
4. Ibid.
5. Ibid.
6. *Plain Dealer*, June 1.
7. Ibid.
8. Ibid.
9. *Plain Dealer*, August 17.

2002

1. *Cleveland Plain Dealer*, April 19.
2. *Plain Dealer*, May 1.
3. *Plain Dealer*, April 27.
4. *Plain Dealer*, May 15.
5. Ibid.
6. *Plain Dealer*, June 4.
7. Ibid.
8. Ibid.
9. *Plain Dealer*, July 11.
10. Ibid.
11. Ibid.

2003

1. *Cleveland Plain Dealer*, May 12.

2004

1. *Cleveland Plain Dealer*, July 15.
2. Ibid.

2005

1. *Cleveland Plain Dealer*, July 22.
2. *Plain Dealer*, September 7.

2007

1. *Cleveland Plain Dealer*, June 19.
2. *Plain Dealer*, July 2.
3. Ibid.
4. *Plain Dealer*, July 3.
5. *Plain Dealer*, August 28.
6. Ibid.
7. Ibid.
8. Ibid.
9. *Plain Dealer*, August 29.

2008

1. ESPN.com, June 18.
2. Ibid.
3. Ibid.
4. Ibid.
5. ESPN.com, June 20.
6. Ibid.
7. ESPN.com, June 21.
8. Ibid.
9. ESPN.com, September 16.
10. Ibid.
11. Ibid.

2009

1. ESPN.com, May 8.
2. ESPN.com, May 30.
3. Ibid.
4. Ibid.
5. Ibid.
6. ESPN.com, June 13.
7. Ibid.
8. Astros.com, August 21.

9. Ibid.
10. Ibid.

2010

1. ESPN.com, May 13.
2. Ibid.
3. ESPN.com, June 5.
4. Ibid.
5. Ibid.
6. ESPN.com, July 30.
7. Ibid.
8. Ibid.
9. ESPN.com, June 24.
10. Ibid.
11. Ibid.
12. ESPN.com, July 2.
13. Ibid.
14. Ibid.
15. Ibid.
16. Ibid.
17. ESPN.com, August 10.
18. Ibid.
19. AOL news, August 22.
20. *Chicago Tribune,* August 22.

2011

1. ESPN.com, June 10.
2. Ibid.
3. Ibid.
4. ESPN.com, June 19.
5. Ibid.
6. ESPN.com, June 24.
7. Ibid.
8. Ibid.
9. Ibid.

2012

1. ESPN.com, August 18.
2. Ibid.

2013

1. ESPN.com, August 16.
2. Ibid.
3. *USA Today,* September 22.

Bibliography

Books

Appel, Marty. *Pinstripe Empire*. New York: Bloomsbury, 2012.

Deford, Frank. *The Old Ball Game*. New York: Atlantic Monthly Press, 2005.

Honig, Donald. *The Chicago Cubs: An Illustrated History*. New York: Prentice Hall, 1991.

_____. *The Cincinnati Reds: An Illustrated History*. New York: Simon & Shuster, 1992.

James, Bill. *The Bill James Guide to Baseball Managers, 1870 to Today*. New York: Scribner, 1997.

Lewis, Franklin. *The Cleveland Indians*. New York: Putnam's, 1949.

Macht, Norman L. *Connie Mack and the Early Years of Baseball*. Lincoln: University of Nebraska Press, 2007.

Schneider, Russell. *The Cleveland Indians Encyclopedia*. Norwalk, CT: Easton Press, 2001.

Newspapers

Chicago Tribune
Cleveland Plain Dealer
Cleveland Press
New York Times

Internet

ESPN.com
AOL

INDEX

Aaron, Hank 137
Aaron, Tommie 144
Acta, Manny 245
Adair, Bill 132–133
Adair, Rick 250
Adcock, Joe 133
Aker, Jack 123, 192
Alderson, Sandy 179
Alexander, Grover Cleveland 45
Allen, Johnny 73
Allen, Richie 125, 129
Allyn, Arthur 127
Allyn, John 132
Alou, Felipe 210, 226
Alou, Moises 210
Alston, Walter 94
Altobelli, Joe 164, 184–185
Amalfitano, Joe 165, 173
Amaro, Ruben 129
Amaro, Ruben, Jr. 254–255
American Association (1882–1891) 6, 10
American Association (minor league) 39
American League 1, 5, 7, 9, 10–12, 14–17, 19, 23, 25–27, 29–32, 34, 50, 52, 57–58, 61–63, 65, 73–74, 79, 84, 90, 106, 111, 119–121, 128, 130–131, 135, 138–140, 145–146, 149–150, 153–155, 157–158, 160, 166, 168–169, 172, 178, 180, 183–184, 187, 190, 192–193, 198, 200–201, 206, 208, 212, 214–215, 217, 219, 222–225, 228–230, 234–235, 237, 241–242, 246–248, 250
Anaheim Angels 223, 224, 236
Anaheim Stadium 150
Anderson, George (Sparky) 138, 160–161, 173, 197
Andrews, Paul 68
Appalachian League 155
Appling, Luke 84, 124
Argyros, George 176, 182, 187
Armstrong, Chuck 182, 187, 196
Arizona Diamondbacks 229, 233, 243–244, 248–249, 251
Arizona State University 141
Armour, Bill 21
Astrodome 113
Atlanta Braves 15, 118, 135, 137–138, 143–144, 149, 164, 180, 186, 194–195, 198, 202, 209, 233, 237, 243, 248, 251
Austin, Jimmy 33, 41, 49
Autry, Gene 128–129, 150, 155, 158, 168, 173, 209, 214
Autry, Jackie 214

Baird, Allard 228
Baker, Del 70–71, 105
Baker, William F. 41, 43–44, 74
Ball, Phil 40, 49, 61
Baltimore Orioles: (1901–02) 5–7, 56–57; (1954–present) 100, 108–110, 114, 116, 119, 126–127, 137, 140, 161, 164, 168, 175, 177, 191, 205, 207, 219, 235, 237–238, 247, 248
Bamberger, George 2, 175, 176
Bancroft, Dave (Beauty) 2, 51, 52, 56
Bancroft, Frank 6
Bando, Sal 222
Barfield, Jesse 198
Barnes, Donald 68, 73
Barrow, Ed 12
Bartell, Dick 90
Bartirome, Tony 194
Bassler, Johnny 74
Bauer, Hank 108–109, 112, 114, 126–127, 130
Bavasi, Bill 214, 223, 238, 241
Bavasi, Buzzie 134, 151, 158, 168
Baylor, Don 155, 229–230
Beane, Billy 251
Beaumont, Ginger 21
Becker, Beals 21
Beinfest, Larry 231, 248, 252
Bell, David (Buddy) 221–222, 228, 235
Bell, George 198, 205
Bell, Jay 219
Bengough, Benny 89
Benson, Vern 109, 117
Benswanger, Bill 65
Berra, Dale 183
Berra, Lawrence (Yogi) 116, 147–148, 183–184
Bevens, Floyd (Bill) 94
Bevington, Terry 215

Bezdek, Hugo 39, 47
Birmingham, Joe 28–29, 35, 36
Bissonnette, Del 77
Blackburne, Russell (Lena) 54
Blades, Ray 72
Blanding, Fred 35
Boddicker, Mike 185
Boles, John 216–217, 225–226
Bonda, Ted 153–154
Boone, Bob 219, 232, 235
Boros, Steve 179
Borton, Babe 34
Bosman, Dick 189
Boston Beaneaters 6, 10, 13–14
Boston Braves 2, 14, 24, 51–52, 55–56, 62, 77, 83, 85–86, 92, 116, 141, 149
Boston College 52, 141
Boston Doves 20–21
Boston Pilgrims 10–12, 16
Boston Red Sox 13, 16–17, 19–20, 22, 29–31, 35, 43, 50, 57–58, 63, 71, 73–74, 77, 84–85, 89, 96–97, 101, 104–105, 120–121, 134, 147, 149–150, 160, 168, 171, 173–174, 188, 196–198, 206, 208, 218–219, 222, 226–227, 233, 236–237, 239, 241–242, 251, 254
Bottomley, Jim 68
Boudreau, Lou 85, 95–96, 102, 104
Bowa, Larry 195, 205
Bowden, Jim 213, 220, 232
Bowerman, Frank 20–21
Bowman, Bob 72
Boyer, Clete 196
Boyer, Ken 156, 164
Bradley, Alva 59, 61, 66–67, 73
Bragan, Bobby 95, 97–98, 118–119
Brandt, Ed 53
Braves Field 87
Breadon, Sam 50–51, 54, 62, 71–72
Brenly, Bob 229, 233
Brett, George 206
Briggs, Walter 70–71
Briggs, Walter (Spike) 90, 256
Bristol, Dave 15, 118, 134–135, 164, 180, 213
Brooklyn Dodgers 7, 33, 42, 45, 51, 58, 69, 73, 74
Brouthers, Dan 57

267

Index

Brown, Chris 195
Brown, Daren 250
Brown, Joe L. 95, 122, 139–140
Brown, Mace 70
Brown, Mordecai (Three-Finger) 37
Brown, Richard 214
Brucker, Earle 91
Brush, John 5, 8
Buckner, Bill 197
Burke, Jimmy 13–15, 41, 49
Burke, Joe 146, 169
Burleson, Rick 150
Busch, August A. 92, 116, 156
Bush, George W. 211
Bush, Owen (Donie) 55, 63
Byrnes, Josh 243–244, 249

Cady, Forrest (Hick) 43
California Angels 1, 122, 128, 141–142, 146, 150, 154, 157–158, 168, 172, 183–184, 196, 209–210, 214, 217, 218
Callahan, Jimmy (Nixey) 11–12, 38–39
Campanella, Roy 94
Campbell, Jim 112, 139, 159
Carpenter, Robert 76, 82, 89, 129, 136
Carpenter, Ruly 163
Carrigan, Bill 29, 31
Carroll, Parke 96
Cashen, Frank 175–176, 195, 200
Caster, George 73
Cavarretta, Phil 86, 112
Chance, Frank 14, 33–35, 46
Chandler, Albert (Happy) 81, 86
Chandler, Spurgeon (Spud) 96
Chapman, Ben 77, 82
Chappas, Harry 163
Chase, Hal 23–24, 33
Chicago Colts 10, 12
Chicago Cubs 2–3, 12, 14, 18, 40, 44–45, 51, 54, 58–59, 61–62, 64, 69–70, 72, 83, 86, 92, 102–104, 109, 114–115, 124, 132, 136–137, 143–144, 152, 163–164, 169, 172, 178–179, 185, 188, 191, 193–194, 205, 219, 223, 229–230, 241, 243, 245, 250–251, 255
Chicago White Sox 2, 15–16, 21, 34, 39–40, 52, 54–55, 57, 62–63, 73, 77, 79, 84, 90, 108, 110, 114, 116, 119, 121, 127–128, 132, 149, 158–159, 162–163, 184, 189–190, 192, 194, 206, 210, 214, 219, 226, 232, 239, 240, 250
Chiles, Eddie 173–174, 184
Cincinnati Reds 3, 5–6, 36–38, 55, 64–65, 68, 72, 75–76, 80, 82, 90–92, 100, 102, 108, 110, 117–120, 131, 134, 137–139, 143, 148–149, 159–160, 163, 172–173, 181–182, 195, 201, 213, 218–219, 225, 228, 232, 235, 238, 252
Claiborne, John 164
Claire, Fred 221
Clark, Dave 246

Cleveland Indians 1, 2, 31, 35, 43, 49, 57, 59–61, 66, 68, 71, 73–74, 77, 84–85, 97–98, 102, 106, 108, 119–120, 124, 128, 131–133, 139, 146, 153–154, 156, 158–159, 162, 164–165, 172–173, 178, 180, 185, 189, 192, 200, 206, 208–209, 214, 218, 221, 226, 228, 230, 232, 235, 237–238, 240, 242, 246, 255, 256
Cleveland Naps 21–22, 25–29, 35
Cleveland Rams 39
Cleveland Spiders 68
Cobb, Ty 25, 181
Cochrane, Gordon (Mickey) 2, 70
Coffey, Jack 21
Coffman, Dick 68
Coleman, Bob 77
College of Coaches 3, 115
Collins, Dave 173
Collins, Eddie 53
Collins, Jimmy 11, 15
Collins, John (Shano) 57–58
Collins, Terry 223–224
Colon, Bartolo 230
Colorado Rockies 222, 228, 230, 235
Colt Stadium (Houston) 113
Comiskey, Charles 12, 54
Comiskey, Grace 64, 79
Comiskey, Lou 64
Comiskey Park 57
Cooke, Allen (Dusty) 82, 89
Coombs, Jack 42–43
Cooney, Johnny 86
Cooper, Cecil 239
Cooper, Wilbur 47
Corbett, Brad 145, 147
Corrales, Pat 177–178, 192, 199
Corriden, John (Red) 84
Coryell, Don 141
Cottier, Chuck 183, 187–188
Coumbe, Fred (Fritz) 44
County Stadium (Milwaukee) 172
Cox, Bobby 194, 198, 202, 237, 243, 248–249
Cox, William 74–75
Craft, Harry 96, 113–114
Craig, Roger 187
Crandall, Del 135, 176–177, 182–183
Crane, Jim 254
Cravath, Clifford (Gavvy) 43–44
Cronin, Joe 84, 89, 102, 139
Crosley, Powel 91
Cruz, Todd 177
Cuellar, Mike 175
Cuyler, Hazen (Kiki) 55

Dahlen, Bill 21
Dal Canton, Bruce 202
Dalton, Harry 127, 142, 150, 155, 172
Danforth, Dave 49
Dark, Alvin 1, 115, 123–124, 133, 135, 151–152, 187, 256
Davenport, Jim 186–187
Davis, Chili 219
Davis, Curt 72
Davis, George 5

Davis, Harry 25–29, 35
Davis, Willie 145
D.C. Stadium 111
DeFrancesco, Tony 254
Delaney, Art 53
Denbo, Gary 242
Dent, Bucky 199, 201–202
Detroit Tigers 2, 10, 12, 21, 23, 25, 44, 66–67, 70, 74–76, 84–85, 90, 96–97, 101, 103, 106–108, 110–112, 121–122, 126, 131–132, 138–140, 160–161, 166, 172, 180, 187, 197, 210, 219, 221–223, 243, 249, 256
Devery, Bill 33–34
Devine, Bing 109, 116
DeWitt, Bill 107, 117–118
Dickey, Bill 78, 80, 82
DiPoto, Jerry 249
Doby, Larry 151, 158
Dodger Stadium 165, 221
Dombrowski, Dave 208, 210, 216, 225
Donovan, "Wild Bill" 44
Doyle, Larry 39
Dressen, Chuck 2, 65, 68–69, 94, 110–112
Dreyfuss, Barney 39, 47, 55
Duncan, Dave 189
Dunn, Jim 43
DuPont Chemical Company 76
Duquette, Dan 226–227
Durocher, Leo 81–82, 105, 124, 136–138, 220
Dwyer, Frank 12
Dykes, Jimmy 63, 79, 100–102, 106–107, 133

Eastern League 77
Ebbets Field 51, 58
Edwards, Henry 49
Edwards, Howard (Doc) 192, 199–200
Eisenhardt, Roy 179
Elberfeld, Norman (Kid) 18–19
Elia, Lee 179, 191–192, 199, 241
Ens, Jewel 55, 64
Epstein, Theo 251
Ermer, Cal 121–122
Essian, Jim 206
Etchebarren, Andy 155
Evans, Billy 59
Evans, Darrell 143
Evers, Johnny 2, 45–47, 53
Exhibition Stadium 169

Faber, Urban (Red) 79
Fadden, Jack 104
Falkenberg, Cy 35
Fanning, Jim 171, 182
Farrell, Frank 18, 23–24, 33–34
Farrell, John 242
Farrell, Kerby 98
Federal League 33, 35, 40
Feeney, Charles (Chub) 195
Felske, John 191–192
Fenway Park 29, 84, 87, 97, 134, 159, 197, 201

Index

Ferguson, George 21
Ferraro, Mike 177–178, 193
Ferrell, Rick 73, 101–102
Ferrick, Tom 112
Finley, Charles O. 108, 112, 114–115, 123–124, 130, 133, 144, 146, 153, 157, 183
Fisk, Carlton 149
Fitzsimmons, Fred 75–77
Flanagan, Mike 185, 237
Florida Marlins 2, 210, 212–213, 216, 225–226, 231, 237, 244, 248, 252, 256
Fogel, Horace 5–6
Fohl, Lee 35, 43–44, 49–50
Foli, Tim 232
Fonseca, Lew 63–64
Foote, Barry 165, 213
Forbes Field 39, 47, 54–55
Foster, George 173
Fowler, Art 145, 196
Fox, Charlie 130, 143, 151, 179, 199
Fox, Howard 185, 190–191
Francona, Terry 254
Franks, Herman 165
Frazee, Harry 50
Frazier, Joe 152
Freedman, Andrew 5–7
Freese, Gene 109
Fregosi, Jim 129, 158, 168, 189–190, 205
Frey, Jim 169, 188, 205–206
Frick, Ford 81
Friday, Pat 113
Frisch, Frank 51, 62, 71–72, 83, 86–87, 164
Fuchs, Emil (Judge) 14, 52, 55
Furillo, Carl 94

Gaetti, Gary 209
Galehouse, Denny 73, 84
Gallagher, Jimmy 76
Garcia, Dave 155–157, 162, 177
Garciaparra, Nomar 226
Gardner, Billy 167–168, 185–186, 193
Gardner, Larry 31
Garner, Phil 222, 233, 239
Garver, Ned 88
"Gas House Gang" 63, 71, 83, 87
Gaston, Clarence (Cito) 198, 242
George, Tom (Lefty) 26–27
Geren, Bob 251
Gibbons, John 234, 241
Gibson, George 47, 52, 64
Gibson, Kirk 249–250
Giles, Bill 177, 191
Giles, Warren 68
Gillick, Pat 198
Girardi, Joe 237
Glavine, Tom 237
Gleason, William (Kid) 53
Gomez, Preston 134, 148, 165, 205
Gonzalez, Fredi 248
Gonzalez, Mike 72
Gordon, Joe 98, 106–108
Gorman, Lou 197
Goryl, Johnny 166–168

Grant, M. Donald 125, 147–148
Graziano, Bob 221
Great American Ballpark (Cincinnati) 232, 235
Green, Dallas 163, 179, 188, 191, 193–194, 199, 201, 212–213, 218, 254
Green Monster 201
Greenberg, Hank 97–98
Grenesko, Don 205
Grich, Bobby 155, 157
Grieve, Tom 184, 211
Griffey, Ken 173
Griffey, Ken, Jr. 250
Griffith, Calvin 94, 107, 111, 121, 135–136, 139, 166, 168
Griffith, Clark 12, 17–18, 38
Griffith Stadium 64
Grimm, Charlie 59, 69–71, 76, 83, 86–87, 93–94, 103–104, 115, 256
Groh, Heinie 38
Gullett, Don 235
Gutteridge, Don 128, 132–133
Gwynn, Tony 195

Haas, Eddie 186
Haas, Mule 64
Hack, Stan 87, 101
Hall, Derrick 249
Hamey, Roy 91, 99
Haney, Fred 73–74, 93–94, 110, 116
Harazin, Al 212
Harder, Mel 132
Hargrove, Mike 208–209, 237–238
Harrah, Toby 178, 211
Harrelson, Bud 200
Harrelson, Ken (Hawk) 189–190
Harridge, Will 61
Harris, Luman 110, 114, 137–138
Harris, Stanley (Bucky) 74, 80, 104–105
Hart, John 200, 208, 230
Hartnett, Leo (Gabby) 69–70
Harvard College 52
Hatton, Grady 125–126
Hedges, Bob 32
Heffner, Don 117–118
Helton, Todd 244
Hemond, Roland 207
Hemsley, Rollie 68
Hemus, Solly 109
Hendricks, Jack 39
Henrich, Tommy 101
Herzog, Buck 36
Herzog, Dorrell (Whitey) 140–141, 146, 164–165, 203, 212
Hicks, Tom 224–225
Higgins, Mike (Pinky) 102, 105
Hillenbrand, Shea 242
Hillman, Trey 246
Hilltop Park 18
Hinch, A.J. 243–244, 249
Hitchcock, Billy 101, 118–119
Hodges, Gil 94, 111–112
Hoffman, Glenn 221
Hogan, Shanty 52
Holcomb, Stu 132
Holland, John 104

Hollingsworth, Al 101
Holmes, Tommy 86–87
Hooton, Burt 233
Hornsby, Rogers 50–53, 56, 58, 59, 61–62, 64, 67–70, 88–91, 100, 103, 141, 256
Houk, Ralph 117, 160
Houston Astros 125–126, 134, 138, 148, 151, 165, 173, 175, 182, 184, 187, 219, 223, 227, 229, 233, 239, 246, 253, 254
Houston Colt .45s 110, 113–114
Howard, Elston 117
Howard, Frank 176, 199
Howser, Dick 169–170, 193, 247
Hudlin, Willis 101
Huff, George 17
Huggins, Miller 3
Huizenga, Wayne 216
Hunsicker, Gerry 233
Hunter, Billy 126, 155
Huntington Avenue Grounds (Boston) 19
Hurdle, Clint 228, 244
Huston, Tillinghast 44
Hutchinson, Fred 3, 90, 100, 103

Ilitch, Mike 221–222
International League 82, 88
Isringhausen, Jason 218

Jackson, Danny 205
Jackson, Joe 36
Jackson, Reggie 141, 159
Jennings, Hughie 56
Jocketty, Walt 215
Johnson, Arnold 95–96
Johnson, Byron Bancroft (Ban) 6, 8, 9, 11–12, 24, 26, 30–31, 35
Johnson, Darrell 109, 149–150, 166, 173–174
Johnson, Davey 143, 200–201, 213, 235, 237, 247, 253
Johnson, Roy 76
Johnson, Walter 59–60, 66–67, 79
Jones, Fielder 12, 40–41
Jorgensen, Mike 216
Jurges, Billy 102, 104–105

Kamm, Willie 66
Kansas City Athletics 95–96, 107–109, 111–115, 120, 123–124, 130–131, 140, 163, 167, 189, 192
Kansas City Royals 3, 131–132, 141, 146, 155, 158, 162, 166, 169, 178, 180, 185, 189, 193, 197, 203, 206–207, 217, 219, 224, 228–229, 232, 234–235, 243, 246, 252
Kauffman, Ewing 146
Keane, Johnny 109, 116–117
Keeley, Bob 93
Keller, Hal 182
Kelley, Joe 6, 8
Kelly, George 68
Kelly, Tom 190–91
Kendrick, Ken 249
Kennedy, Bob 3, 115, 165
Kerrigan, Joe 226–227

Index

Kessinger, Don 162–163
Kilfoyl, John 22
Killebrew, Harmon 146
Killefer, Bill 45, 51, 61
Killefer, Wade 37
Killilea, Henry 11
Kimm, Bruce 230
King, Clyde 130, 144, 149, 174–175
King, Jeff 218
Kingdome (Seattle) 213
Kingman, Dave 165
Kittridge, Malachi 9, 10, 12
Klein, Joe 192
Klein, Lou 115
Knight, Ray 173, 219–220
Konetchy, Ed 45
Koufax, Sandy 122
Krausse, Lew 123
Krol, Jack 164
Kruk, John 195
Kuehl, Karl 151
Kuenn, Harvey 1, 101, 172, 256

Lachemann, Marcel 214, 217–218
Lachemann, Rene 167, 176, 188, 216–217, 230
Lajoie, Napoleon (Larry) 2, 21, 25, 35
Lake, Fred 19–21
Lamar, Chuck 224
Lamont, Gene 215
Lamping, Mark 215
Landis, Kenesaw Mountain 75–76
Lane, Frank 84, 97–98, 106–110
Langston, Mark 209
Lanier, Hal 205
Larkin, Barry 220
LaRoche, Dave 213
LaRussa, Tony 162–163, 184, 189–190
Lary, Lyn 68
Lasorda, Tommy 220–221
Lau, Charlie 146
Lavagetto, Harry (Cookie) 94, 107, 108
League Park (Cleveland) 21, 24, 44, 60–61, 66
Lebovitz, Hal 127
Lee, Cliff 250
Lefebvre, Jim 223
Lemon, Bob 131–132, 158–159, 160–162, 170–172, 174, 232
Lemon, Jerry 161
Lemon, Jim 121
Lewis, Duffy 31
Leyland, Jim 215, 225, 228
Leyva, Nick 204
Lillis, Bob 175
Lilly, Ted 242
Linder, Carl 232
Lipon, Johnny 1, 133, 135, 256
Littlefield, Dave 236
Lockman, Carroll (Whitey) 137, 144–145
Loftus, Tom 10
Lopat, Ed 113–114, 123, 126
Lopes, Davey 227–228
Lopez, Al 120, 127, 132

Loria, Jeffrey 226, 248
Los Angeles Angels 106, 111, 132
Los Angeles Angels of Anaheim 240
Los Angeles Dodgers 103, 112, 118, 122, 125, 134–135, 150, 154, 159, 166, 176–177, 180, 184, 220–221, 227, 244, 253
Lowe, Bobby 13
Lucchesi, Frank 136, 145, 154, 177, 194
Luhnow, Jeff 254
Lurie, Bob 164, 180–181, 187
Luzinski, Greg 219
Lynn, Fred 150
Lyons, Ted 78, 84, 90

Macht, Norman L. 27
Mack, Connie 2, 10–12, 26, 27, 39, 35–36, 42, 57, 62–63, 95, 102, 110, 112, 223, 231
Mack, Earle 95
Mackanin, Pete 236, 238
MacPhail, Andy 230, 247
MacPhail, Larry 65, 78, 80
Maddon, Joe 217, 224
Maddux, Greg 237
Manning, Jimmy 10
Mantle, Mickey 117
Manuel, Charlie 230–231, 254–255
Manuel, Jerry 240
Maranville, Rabbit 51
Marion, Marty 88–89
Maris, Roger 109, 117
Martin, Billy 121–122, 135, 138–139, 141, 145–147, 159, 161, 170, 174, 179, 183, 187, 196
Martin, John (Pepper) 62
Martinez, John (Buck) 229, 234
Martinez, Pedro 226
Mathews, Eddie 137, 143–144, 149
Mathewson, Christy 5, 7, 36–38
Mattern, Al 21
Mauch, Gene 125, 129, 134, 166, 168, 172–173
Maxville, Dal 203
Mazzilli, Lee 235–236
Mazzone, Leo 202, 237
McAleer, Jimmy 26, 29–31
McCarthy, Joe 58–59, 62, 70, 73, 78–80, 84–85, 102
McCarthy, Ralph 104
McClendon, Lloyd 236
McCloskey, John 15
McDonald, Joe 152
McGaha, Mel 113–114, 133
McGann, Dan 8
McGinnity, Joe 7–8
McGraw, John 2, 5–8, 14, 30, 34, 36, 47, 51, 56
McGregor, Scott 185
McGuire, Jim (Deacon) 16, 19, 21–22, 24–25, 27
McHale, John 97, 110, 118, 170–171, 182
McIlvane, Joe 211–212, 218, 245
McKechnie, Bill (Deacon) 37, 47, 54–55, 71, 75, 82

McKeon, Jack 2, 146, 153, 157, 195, 204, 220, 231, 252, 256
McLane, Drayton 239, 246
McLaren, John 238, 241, 253
McManus, Marty 58
McMillan, Roy 135, 147–148
McMullen, John 175, 184
McNally, Dave 175
McNamara, John 130, 151, 172–173, 197–198, 208–209, 217–218
McPhee, John (Bid) 5
McRae, Brian 207
McRae, Hal 193, 206, 219, 224
Mele, Sam 108, 121
Melton, Bill 150
Melvin, Bob 243–244, 249, 251
Melvin, Doug 225, 242
Merrill, Carl (Stump) 201–202
Metro, Charlie 115, 131–132
Metropolitan Stadium (Minnesota) 108, 136, 166
Mexican League 166–167
Miceli, Dan 225
Michael, Gene 170, 172, 174, 188–189, 193–194
Miley, Dave 232, 235
Miller, Ray 185, 190–191
Miller Park (Milwaukee) 228, 243
Mills, Brad 253–254
Milwaukee Braves 93–94, 100, 110, 112, 120, 132
Milwaukee Brewers 1–2, 134–135, 147–148, 157, 168, 170, 172–173, 175–176, 178, 183, 214, 216, 219, 222–223, 227, 228–229, 239, 242, 247, 256
Milwaukee Brewers (American Association) 76
Minaya, Omar 240
Minnesota Twins 94, 107–108, 116, 121, 130, 135–136, 139, 154, 164, 166–168, 173, 185–186, 190–191, 193, 197, 209
Mitterwald, George 196
Mizerock, John 229
Monchak, Al 194
"Moneyball" 249
Montgomery, Monty 123
Montreal Expos 125, 143, 148, 150–152, 156, 159, 164, 170–172, 175, 179, 182, 186, 196, 206–207, 210, 214, 222, 225–227, 230, 232, 243, 245
Moore, Dayton 247
Moore, Jackie 180, 190
Moore, Terry 92, 101
Morales, Jose 216
Moran, Pat 38, 41, 45
Morgan, Joe 197–198
Moseby, Lloyd 198
Moss, Les 127, 160–161
Muckerman, Richard 80
Muffett, Billy 155
Mullen, John 186
Municipal Stadium (Cleveland) 60–61, 119, 192, 209
Municipal Stadium (Kansas City) 112

Murdoch, Rupert 221
Murphy, Charles 34, 46
Murtaugh, Danny 95, 100, 122, 139–140
Muser, Tony 219, 228–229
Myatt, George 112, 125, 129
Myatt, Glenn 66

Naragon, Hal 121
Narron, Jerry 225, 235, 238
National League 5–6, 8, 10, 12–14, 17, 21, 26, 33, 35–36, 38, 40, 44, 46–47, 51–55, 57–58, 61, 63, 65, 68, 72–73, 75–76, 81, 86–87, 99, 102, 104, 110, 112, 115, 118, 129, 134, 137–139, 143–144, 148, 151–152, 156, 163–164, 166, 170, 173, 175–176, 179–180, 184, 187, 193–195, 200–203, 205, 208, 210–211, 216, 220–221, 225, 228, 231–233, 235–236, 239–240, 243–245, 248, 250–254
Navin, Frank 13, 70
Navin Field (Detroit) 70
Neun, Johnny 80, 82–83
New England League 19
New York Giants 2, 5, 14, 33, 36, 47, 52, 56, 62–64, 68–69, 71, 75, 89, 92, 102, 105, 110, 137, 149, 168, 220
New York Highlanders 10–12, 17, 23, 256
New York Mets 113, 115–117, 124–125, 134, 137, 147–148, 150, 152, 163, 175–176, 184, 195, 197, 200, 203, 212, 218–219, 226, 228, 232, 236, 240, 245, 254
New York Yankees 3, 33, 44, 49–51, 54–55, 57–58, 66, 68–70, 73, 75, 77–78, 82, 85, 90, 94, 96, 108–109, 113, 116, 120, 122, 126, 146–149, 152, 159–162, 169, 171–172, 174, 182–183, 187, 192, 196–197, 201–202, 212–213, 218, 227, 232–235, 246–247
Newman, Jeff 190
News Corporation 221
Nichols, Charles (Kid) 13–15, 41
Nieto, Tom 240
Nixon, Richard 136
Nixon, Russ 173, 194–195, 202
Norman, Bill 97, 101
Nugent, Gerry 74

Oakland Alameda County Coliseum 112, 157
Oakland Athletics 135, 142, 144, 146, 150–151, 153, 157, 163, 167, 169–170, 174, 179–180, 186, 190, 194, 197–198, 206, 218, 222, 243, 251–252
Oates, Johnny 207, 224–225
O'Brien, Dan 166–167, 209–210
O'Connell, Dick 120, 149
O'Connor, Jack 26
O'Dowd, Dan 228, 244
Oester, Ron 213
O'Farrell, Bob 54, 65

O'Hare Airport 159
O'Leary, Charlie 68
Oliver, Bob 141–142
Olympic Stadium 164, 226
O'Malley, Peter 221
O'Neill, Steve 66–67, 85, 89, 91
Onslow, Jack 84
Ostermuller, Fritz 73
Ott, Mel 81
Owens, Jesse 64
Owens, Paul 136, 163, 177
Ozark, Danny 163, 180–181

Pacific Coast League 87, 98, 100, 102, 109
Packard, Gene 43
Page, Mitchell 219
Palmer, Jim 175, 185
Parker, Francis (Salty) 125, 138
Parrish, Larry 222
Patterson, Red 150
Paul, Gabe 1, 90–91, 100, 102, 119–120, 123, 133, 135, 147, 162, 178, 256
Pavlick, Greg 218
Peckinpaugh, Roger 34–35, 59, 66
Pedrique, Al 233
Pelekoudas, Lee 241
Pena, Tony 229, 234–235
Pennock, Herb 76–77
Pentland, Jeff 241
Perez, Tony 213, 225, 226
Perini, Lou 77, 86–87, 93, 110
Perkins, Cy 89
Perlozzo, Sam 236–237
Perry, Gaylord 139, 177
Peters, Hank 185, 199–200, 208–209
Peterson, Harding 201
Peterson, Rick 240
Pevey, Marty 242
Philadelphia Athletics 2, 10, 12, 21, 23, 25–26, 28–29, 35, 42, 62–63, 67–68, 70
Philadelphia Phillies 5, 12, 14, 41, 44–45, 52, 55, 74–76, 82, 89, 91–92, 99, 102, 109, 113, 116, 125, 136, 145, 149, 152, 154, 163, 171–172, 175, 177, 179–181, 185–186, 188, 191–192, 194, 201, 204–206, 210, 212–213, 218, 240, 242–244, 254
Phillips, Harold (Lefty) 128–129
Piche, Ron 151
Piedmont League 77
Piniella, Lou 196–197, 213, 250–251
Piniella, Margaret 250
Pinson, Vada 165
Pittsburgh Pirates 5, 7, 10, 18, 21, 38–39, 46, 50, 52, 54, 58, 64–65, 70–71, 74, 83, 94–95, 100, 120, 122, 126, 137–139, 143, 148, 158, 164, 171, 182, 189, 194, 198, 201, 210, 215, 236, 244–245, 251
Polo Grounds 18, 56
Popowski, Eddie 150
Presley, Jim 248

Providence Grays 6
Purpura, Tim 239

Quade, Mike 251
Quilici, Frank 135–136
Quinn, Bob 57, 84
Quinn, John 87, 129

Rader, Doug 184, 209–210
Ramsay, Jack 141
Randolph, Willie 240
Rapp, Vern 156, 181
Reese, Harold (Pee-Wee) 94
RFK Stadium (Washington) 111, 140
Ricciardi, J.P. 229, 241
Rice, Del 141
Rice, Grantland 57
Richards, Paul 84, 109–110, 113
Richardson, Spec 138, 148
Riddoch, Greg 204, 211–212
Rigney, Bill 105–106, 111, 128–129, 136, 164
Ring, Jimmy 45, 51
Ripken, Cal, Sr. 205, 207
Rixey, Eppa 45
Rizzo, Mike 245, 253
Robinson, Eddie 143–144, 149, 154
Robinson, Frank 141–142, 146, 153–154, 156, 159, 180–181, 207
Robinson, Herk 206, 219
Robinson, Jackie 94
Robinson, Wilbert 7, 8, 42
Robison, Frank 13, 15
Robison, M. Stanley 13–15, 41
Robison Field (St. Louis) 15
Robson, Tom 232
Rodgers, Bob (Buck) 1–2, 172, 207–209, 210, 214, 256
Rodriguez, Alex 225
Rodriguez, Edwin 248, 252
Rojas, Cookie 149, 155
Rojas, Mel 210
Rolfe, Red 90, 256
Root, Charley 93
Rose, Pete 163, 181
Rosen, Al 159
Rothschild, Larry 213, 224
Royals Stadium 146, 170
Royster, Jerry 227–228
Rudi, Joe 155, 157
Ruffing, Charlie (Red) 78
Runnells, Tom 208, 210–211
Ruppert, Jacob 44
Rusie, Amos 57
Russell, Bill 220–221
Ryan, Connie 149, 155

Sabathia, CC 242
Safeco Field (Seattle) 250
Sain, Johnny 121, 132
St. Claire, Randy 245
St. Louis Browns 10, 14, 20–21, 32, 36, 41, 49–50, 59, 61–62, 67–68, 73, 78–80, 83, 88–90, 92, 97, 100, 110
St. Louis Cardinals 1, 10–11, 13, 26, 41, 47, 54–55, 61, 63, 68, 70–71,

Index

75, 78, 82, 86, 88, 92, 94, 100, 103, 109, 116, 137–138, 145, 152, 156, 164–165, 172, 175, 203, 212, 215–216, 228, 233, 236, 239
St. Louis Terriers 40
Samuel, Juan 248
San Diego Padres 134, 143, 150–151, 158, 176, 180, 184, 187–188, 195–196, 198, 204–206, 211, 218, 241, 244–245
San Diego Padres (PCL) 118, 125
San Francisco Giants 2, 105–106, 131, 143–144, 151–153, 164, 172, 179–181, 185–186, 195, 226, 232
San Francisco Seals 98
Sandberg, Ryne 255
Santurce Crabbers 142
Sawyer, Eddie 77, 82, 89, 91, 99
Schaefer, Bob 235
Schalk, Ray 53–54
Scheffing, Bob 103, 112
Schmidt, Mike 191
Schoendienst, Albert (Red) 109, 153, 156–157, 165, 203
Schott, Marge 213
Schueler, Ron 215
Schuerholz, John 193, 206, 214
Schultz, Joe 139
Seattle Mariners 150, 153, 165–167, 174, 176–178, 182–184, 187–189, 196, 206, 216, 223, 236–238, 241, 243, 250–251
Seattle Pilots 139, 151
Seattle Rainiers 132
Seaver, Tom 173
Seghi, Phil 153, 162
Seitz, Peter 155
Selee, Frank 12, 14
Selig, Allan (Bud) 134
Selig-Prieb, Wendy 223
Selkirk, George 111
Sewell, Luke 73, 79, 83, 90–91
Seys, John 51
Shakespeare, William 114
Shapiro, Mark 230–231, 254
Shea Stadium 152, 240
Sheehan, Tom 68, 105–106
Sherdel, Bill 47
Sherry, Norm 150, 155
Shibe Park (Philadelphia) 77, 89–90
Shocker, Urban 49
Short, Bob 140–141, 145
Shotton, Burt 65, 73, 81–82
Shoun, Clyde 72–73
Showalter, Buck 248
Silvera, Charlie 145
Simmons, Al 64
Simmons, Ted 156
Sisler, George 49, 53
Skinner, Bob 125, 129, 194
Skinner, Joel 231
Slapnicka, Cy 74
Slattery, Jack 52–53, 141
Smith, Bob 53
Smith, Dave 205
Smith, George 45
Smith, Harry 20–21

Smith, Heinie 5
Smith, Mayo 99, 102
Smith, Randy 222
Smith, Tal 148
Smoltz, John 237
Snider, Duke 94
Snyder, Jim 196
Solters, Julius (Moose) 68
Somers, Charley 21–22, 26, 35
Sorenson, Lary 178
Sothoron, Allen 61
Southern Association 65
Southern League 222
Southworth, Billy 54–55, 72, 85–86
Sparks, Joe 201, 208
Speaker, Tris 43
Spilman, Harry 233
Sports Illustrated 192
Sportsman's Park 54, 68
Stagg, Amos Alonzo 39
Stahl, Charles (Chick) 16
Stahl, Jake 29, 149
Stallings, George 12, 23–24, 33
Stange, Lee 157
Stanky, Eddie 92–93, 127, 154
Stapleton, Dave 197
Stargell, Willie 194
Steinbrenner, George 147, 149, 159, 161–162, 169–170, 172, 174–175, 183, 189, 194, 196–197, 199, 201, 212
Stengel, Casey 77, 84–85, 115–116, 122, 124–125, 128, 231, 253
Stone, Mike 184
Stone, Steve 185
Stoneham, Horace 81, 105, 131, 143
Stouffer, Vernon 1, 133
Stovall, George 25–26, 28, 32
Street, Gabby 54, 58, 62, 68
Strickland, George 119–120
Sukeforth, Clyde 95
Sullivan, Denny 17
Sullivan, Haywood 114
Summers, John (Champ) 201
Sutcliffe, Rick 178
Sveum, Dale 243
Swanson, Evar 64
Sweeney, Bill 21
Swift, Bob 96

Tampa Bay Devil Rays 224
Tanner, Chuck 132, 194–195
Tavares, Tony 217
Taylor, Dean 227–228
Taylor, Jack 13
Taylor, Jim (Zack) 14, 80
Taylor, John I. 15, 17, 19, 24
Tebbetts, George (Birdie) 2, 100, 102, 110–111, 119, 133
Terry, Bill 56–57, 59, 64, 72
Texas League 88
Texas Rangers 136, 140–141, 145–147, 149, 154–155, 158, 173–174, 176–177, 184, 194, 197, 203, 206, 210–211, 222, 224–225, 235–236, 238, 243, 248, 250–251
Thomas, Lee 204

Tighe, Jack 96–97
Topping, Dan 115, 117
Torborg, Jeff 154, 158, 162, 212–213, 218, 226, 231–232, 252, 256
Toronto Blue Jays 184, 197–198, 200, 226, 229, 233–234, 236, 241–242
Torre, Joe 152, 186, 203, 215
Tosca, Carlos 229, 234, 248
Tracy, Jim 244–245
Traynor, Harold (Pie) 65
Trembley, Dave 237, 247–248
Tuck, Gary 201
Tufts College 52
Turner, Terry 36
Turnpike Stadium (Arlington) 140

Unglaub, Bob 16
Union Association (1884) 10
Union Park (Baltimore) 7
University of California–Berkeley 251
University of Michigan 179
University of South Alabama 154–155

Valentine, Bobby 184, 211, 218
Van Burkleo, Ty 250
Veeck, Bill 14, 87, 90, 110, 158, 162–163
Veeck, William 45, 51–52, 58–59, 87
Vernon, Mickey 111–113
Virdon, Bill 139–141, 147–148, 175, 182, 251
Virgil, Ozzie 195
Vukovich, John 194

Wade, Ed 246, 254
Wagner, Dick 160, 173
Wagner, Heinie 31
Wagner, Honus 39
Wakamatsu, Don 250
Walker, Dixie 93
Walker, Harry 92, 122, 126, 138–139
Wallace, Roderick (Bobby) 26, 68–69
Walsh, Dick 128
Walters, Bucky 83
Washington (1892–1899) 17, 44
Washington Nationals 241, 245, 252–253
Washington Senators (1901–1960) 9, 12–13, 18, 48, 51–52, 57, 59–60, 64, 66, 74, 77, 94, 107–108
Washington Senators (1961–1971) 111–112, 140, 163, 168, 176, 189, 211
Weaver, Earl 1, 126–127, 175, 185
Webb, Del 115
Welsh, Jimmy 52
Westrum, Wes 115–116, 124–125, 143
White House 136
Whitt, Ernie 242
Wilhelm, Irvin (Kaiser) 45
Williams, Dick 133, 142, 150–151, 155, 170, 187–188, 196, 208

Williams, Edward Bennett 185
Williams, Jimy 198, 199, 226, 233, 238
Williams, Ken 49
Williams, Stan 159
Williams, Ted 140
Wills, Maury 166–167
Wilson, Jimmie 75–76
Wilson, Mookie 197
Wilson, Paul 218
Wine, Bobby 186, 218
Winfield, Dave 209
Winkles, Bobby 141–142, 153, 157
Wolverton, Harry 24, 33–34, 39
Wood, Joe 29
World Series 1–2, 14–15, 24, 26, 29, 31, 38, 40, 42, 48, 51, 54, 57, 63, 69–71, 73, 75–76, 85–87, 91–92, 103, 116, 122, 126, 136, 138, 139–140, 152, 160–161, 163, 169–171, 184, 187–188, 191, 196–197, 209, 218, 229, 232–233, 244, 246, 251–252
Wright, George 217
Wright, Harry 217
Wright, Richard 104
Wrigley, P.K. 3, 59, 69–70, 76, 86–87, 93–94, 103–104, 115
Wrigley Field 69, 114, 148, 188, 232, 251

Yankee Stadium 51, 56, 78, 84, 161, 170, 212, 232
Yawkey, Jean 197
Yawkey, Tom 84, 102
Yerkes, Steve 31
Yost, Eddie 112
Yost, Ned 242, 247
Young, Cy 17

Zduriencik, Jack 250
Zeider, Rollie 34
Zimmer, Don 134, 149, 173–174, 205–206

www.ingramcontent.com/pod-product-compliance
Lightning Source LLC
Chambersburg PA
CBHW081546300426
44116CB00015B/2769